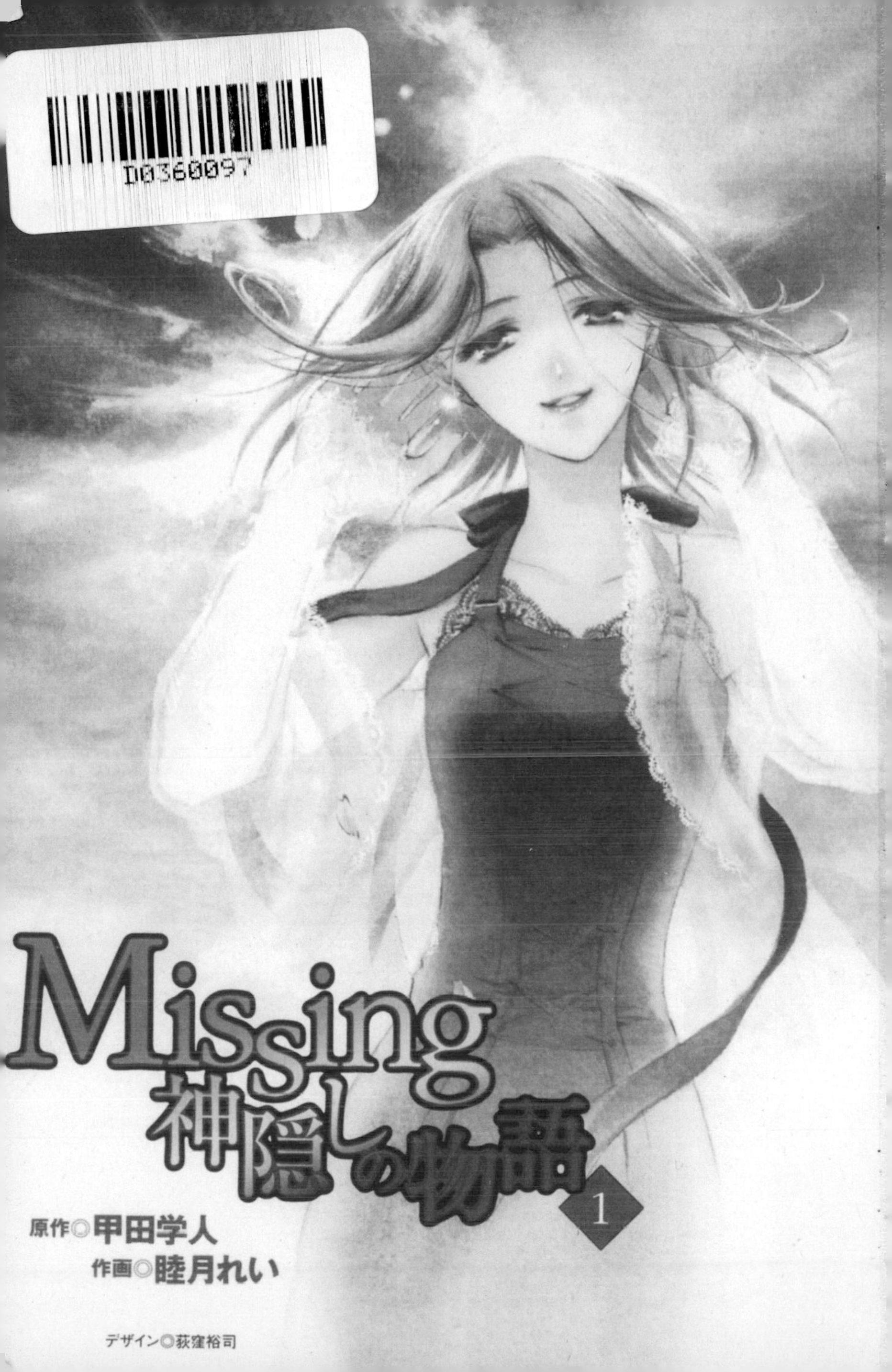

Missing 神隠しの物語

1

原作◎甲田学人

作画◎睦月れい

デザイン◎荻窪裕司

Missing -Kamikakushi no Monogatari- Volume 1
Story By Gakuto Coda
Art By Rei Mutsuki

Translation - Nan Rymer
English Adaptation - Jason Deitrich
Retouch and Lettering - Star Print Brokers
Production Artist - Vicente Rivera, Jr. and Bowen Park
Cover Designer - Louis Csontos

Editor - Hope Donovan
Digital Imaging Manager - Chris Buford
Pre-Production Supervisor - Erika Terriquez
Art Director - Anne Marie Horne
Production Manager - Elisabeth Brizzi
Managing Editor - Vy Nguyen
VP of Production - Ron Klamert
Editor-in-Chief - Rob Tokar
Publisher - Mike Kiley
President and C.O.O. - John Parker
C.E.O. and Chief Creative Officer - Stuart Levy

A **TOKYOPOP** Manga

TOKYOPOP and 👁 are trademarks or registered trademarks of TOKYOPOP Inc.

TOKYOPOP Inc.
5900 Wilshire Blvd. Suite 2000
Los Angeles, CA 90036

E-mail: info@TOKYOPOP.com
Come visit us online at www.TOKYOPOP.com

ISBN: 978-1-4278-0066-4

First TOKYOPOP printing: August 2007

10 9 8 7 6 5 4 3 2 1

Printed in the USA

MISSING
KAMIKAKUSHI NO MONOGATARI

Story by Gakuto Coda
Art by Rei Mutsuki

HAMBURG // LONDON // LOS ANGELES // TOKYO

Table of Contents

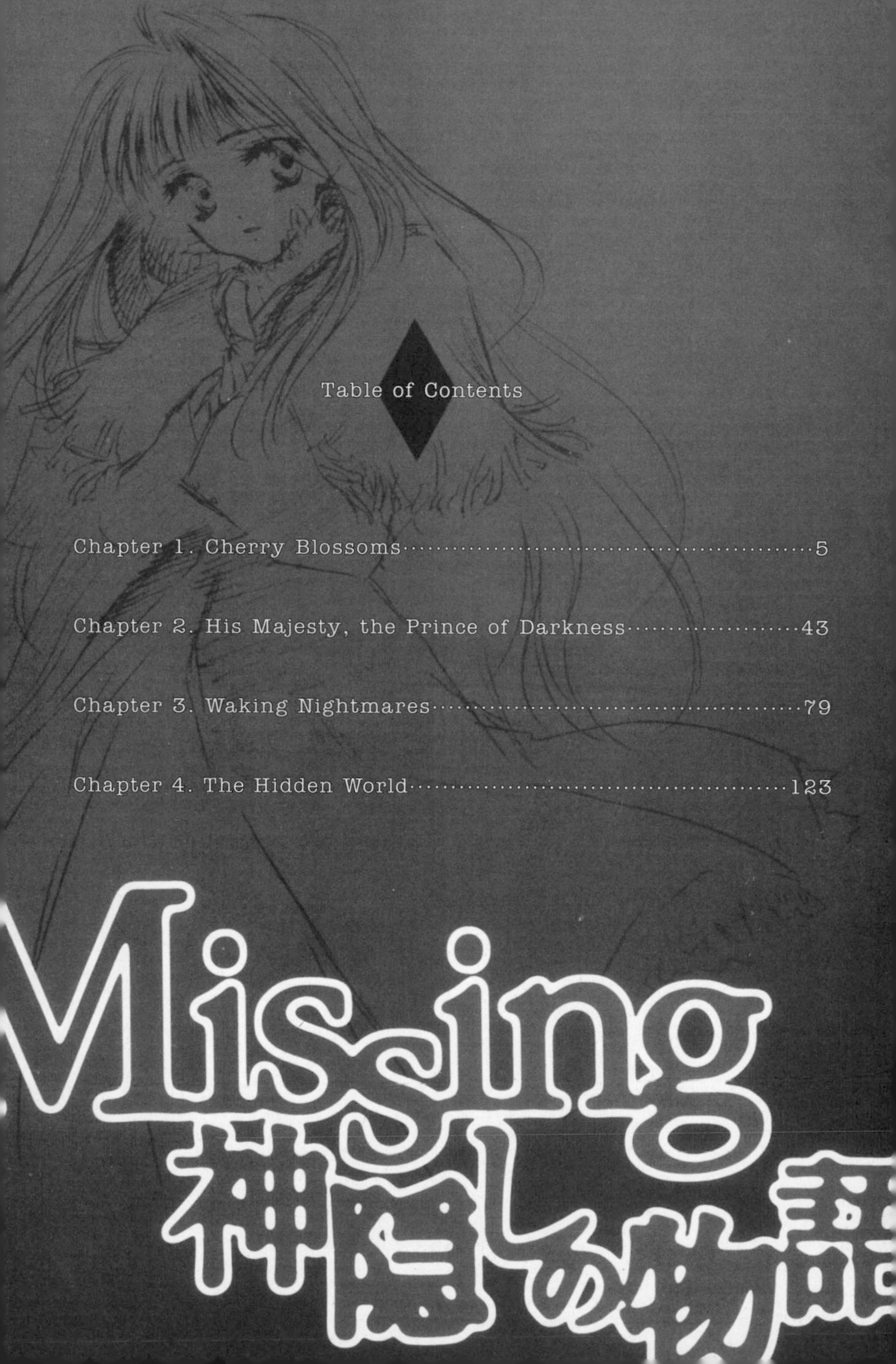

Missing
神隠しの物語

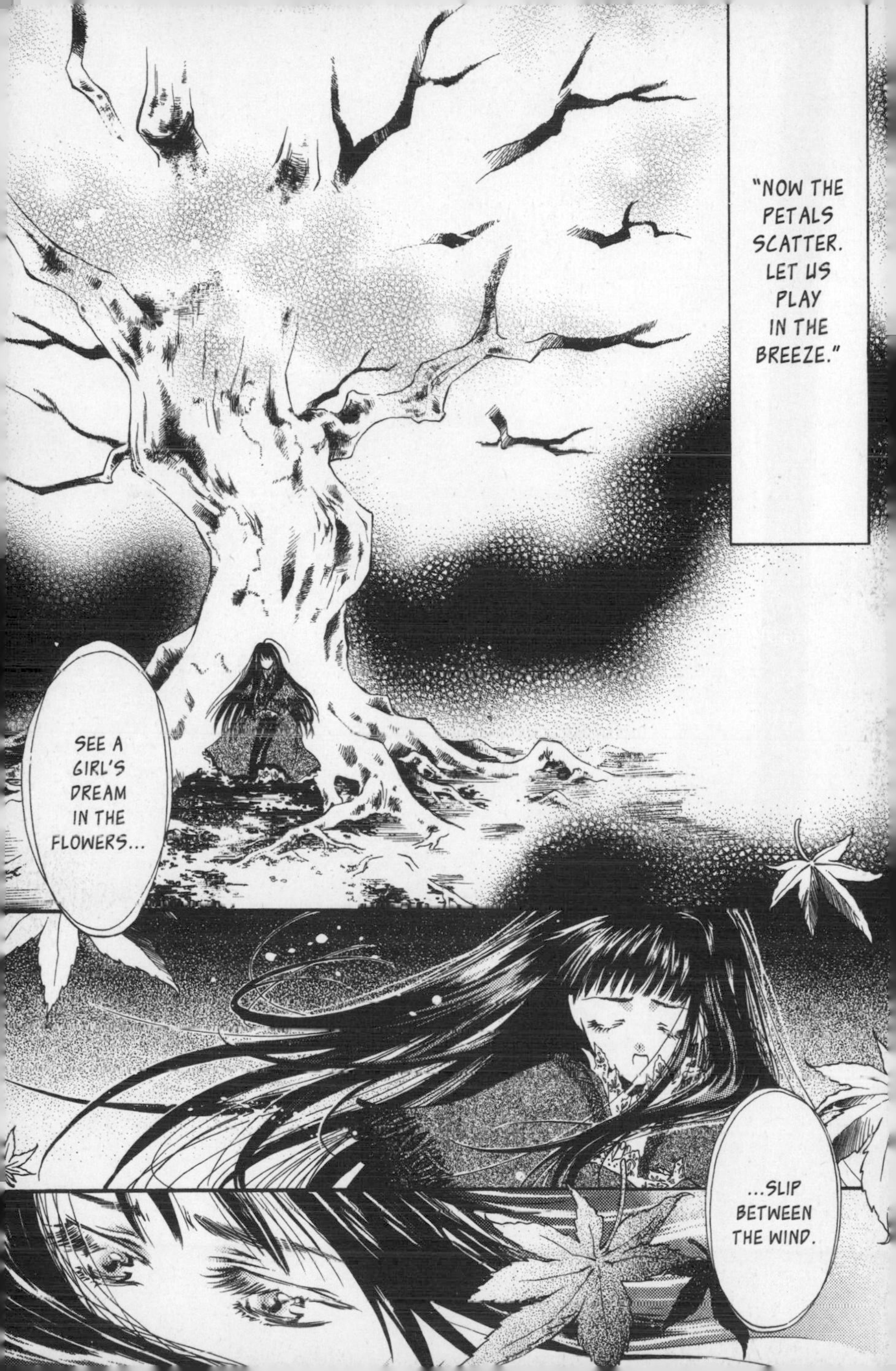
"NOW THE PETALS SCATTER. LET US PLAY IN THE BREEZE."
SEE A GIRL'S DREAM IN THE FLOWERS...
...SLIP BETWEEN THE WIND.

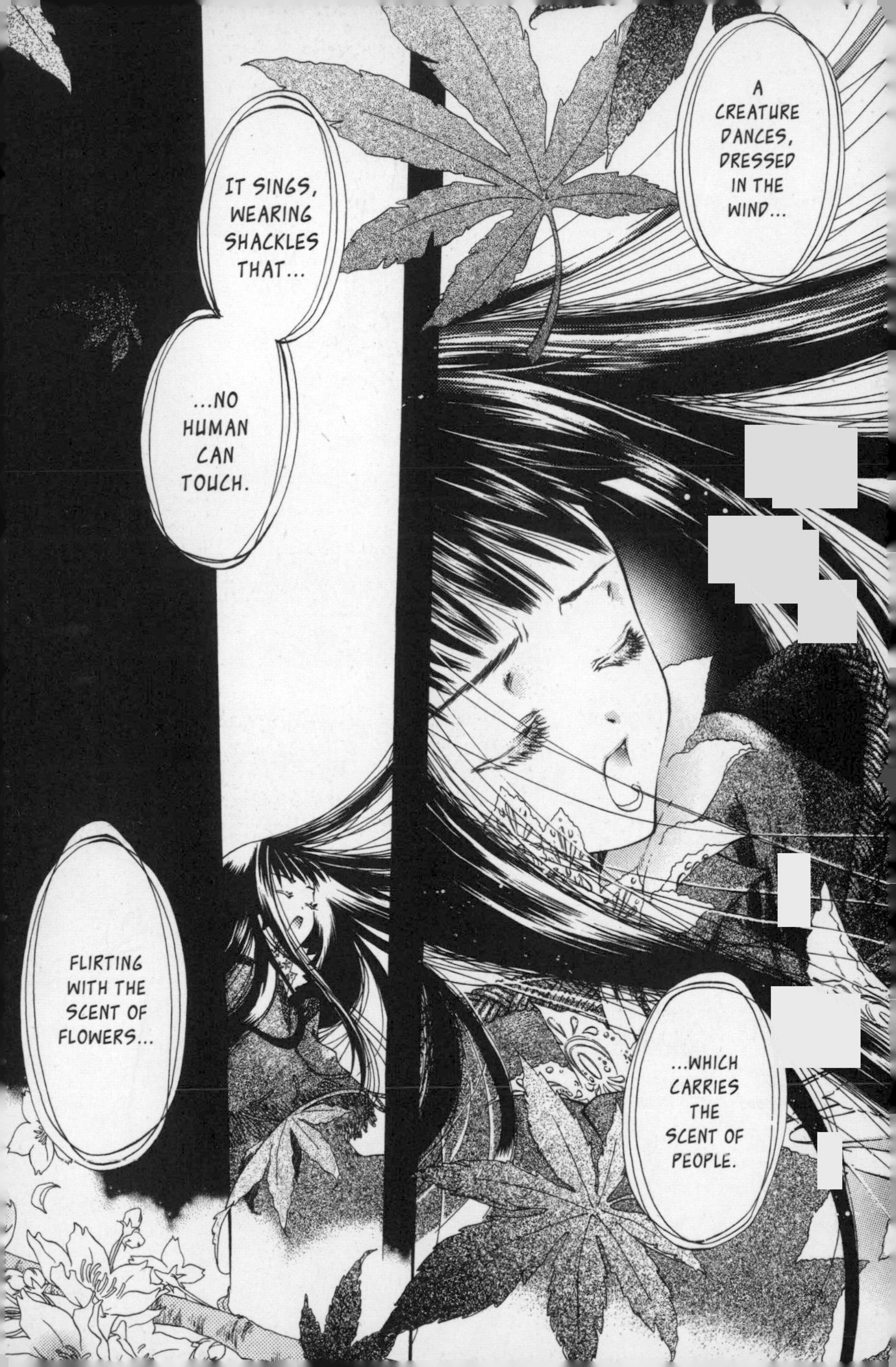
A CREATURE DANCES, DRESSED IN THE WIND...
...WHICH CARRIES THE SCENT OF PEOPLE.
IT SINGS, WEARING SHACKLES THAT...
...NO HUMAN CAN TOUCH.
FLIRTING WITH THE SCENT OF FLOWERS...

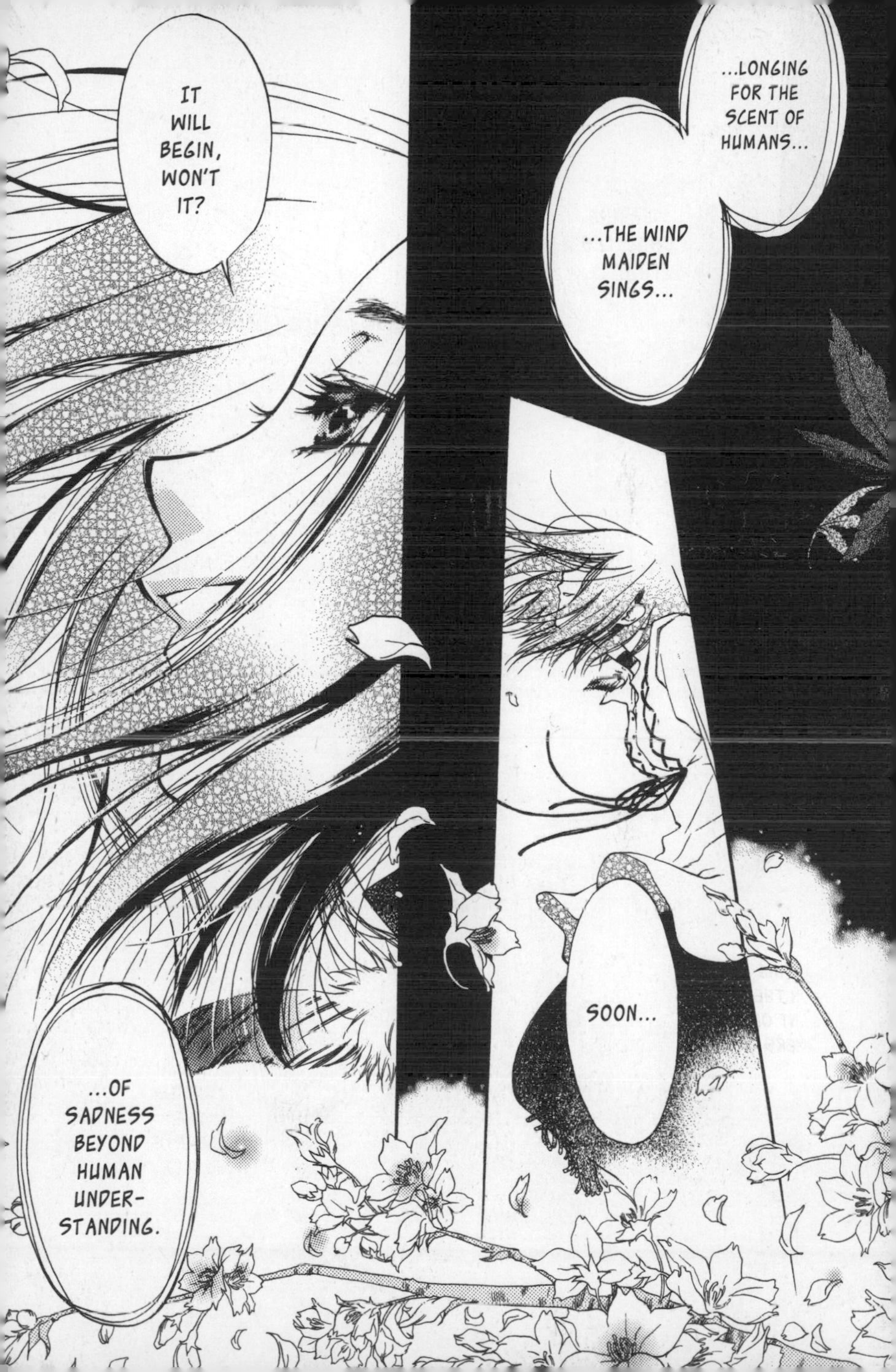
...LONGING FOR THE SCENT OF HUMANS...
...THE WIND MAIDEN SINGS...
SOON...
IT WILL BEGIN, WON'T IT?
...OF SADNESS BEYOND HUMAN UNDER-STANDING.

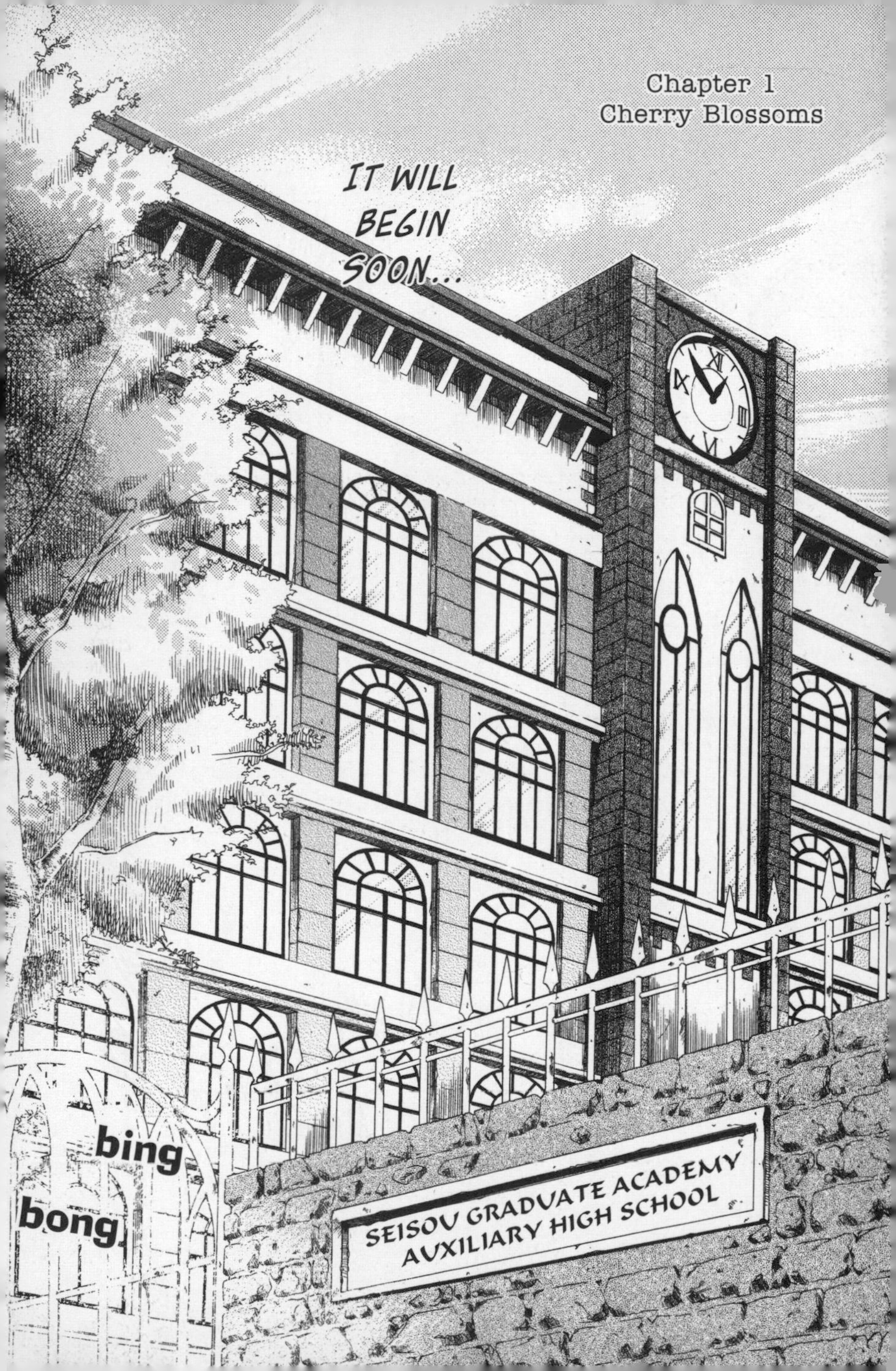
Chapter 1
Cherry Blossoms
IT WILL BEGIN SOON...
SEISOU GRADUATE ACADEMY
AUXILIARY HIGH SCHOOL
bing
bong

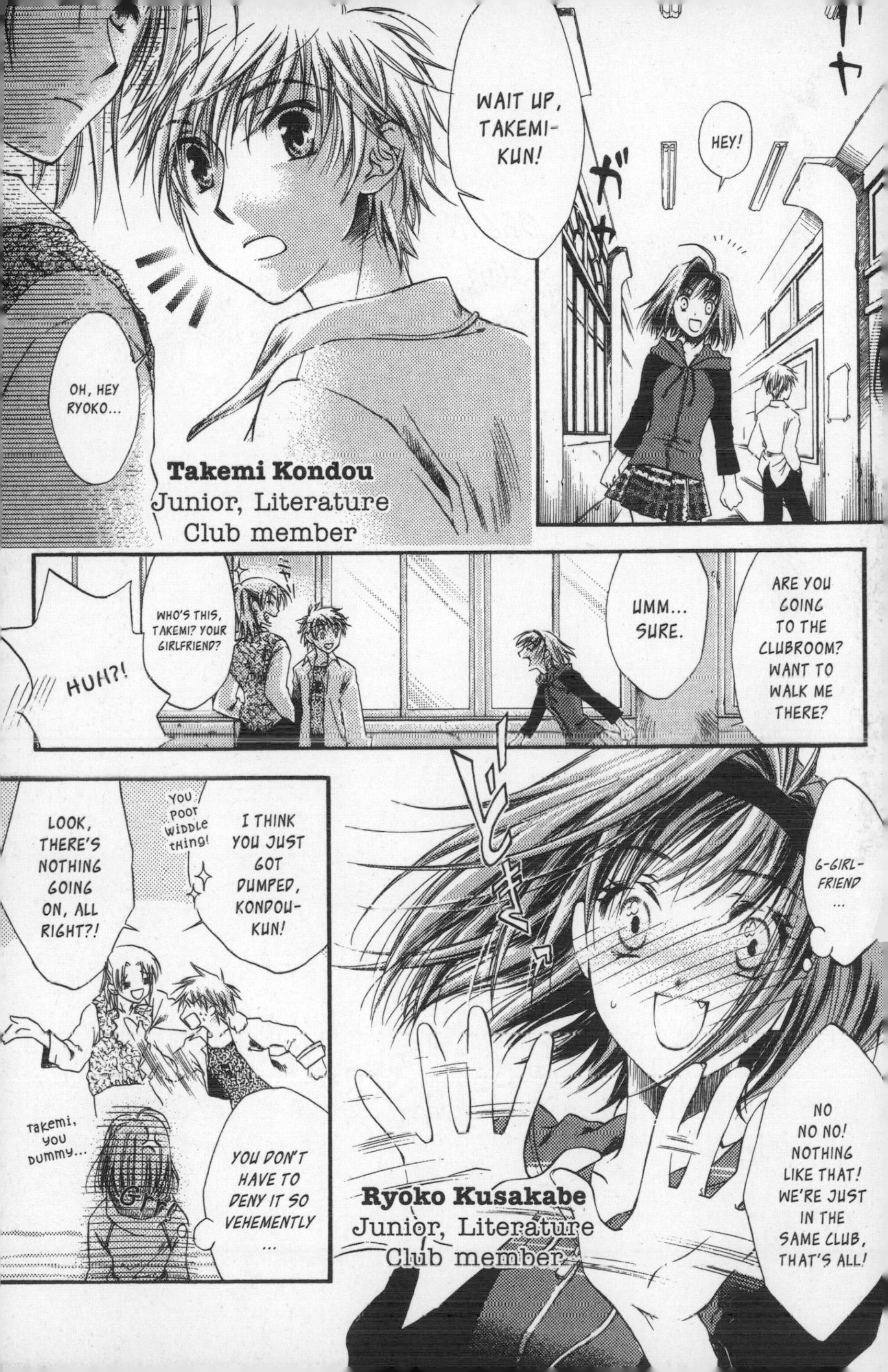
HEY!
WAIT UP, TAKEMI-KUN!
OH, HEY RYOKO...
Takemi Kondou
Junior, Literature Club member
ARE YOU GOING TO THE CLUBROOM? WANT TO WALK ME THERE?
UMM... SURE.
WHO'S THIS, TAKEMI? YOUR GIRLFRIEND?
HUH?!
G-GIRLFRIEND...
NO NO NO! NOTHING LIKE THAT! WE'RE JUST IN THE SAME CLUB, THAT'S ALL!
Ryoko Kusakabe
Junior, Literature Club member
I THINK YOU JUST GOT DUMPED, KONDOU-KUN!
You poor widdle thing!
LOOK, THERE'S NOTHING GOING ON, ALL RIGHT?!
YOU DON'T HAVE TO DENY IT SO VEHEMENTLY ...
Takemi, you dummy...
Grr!

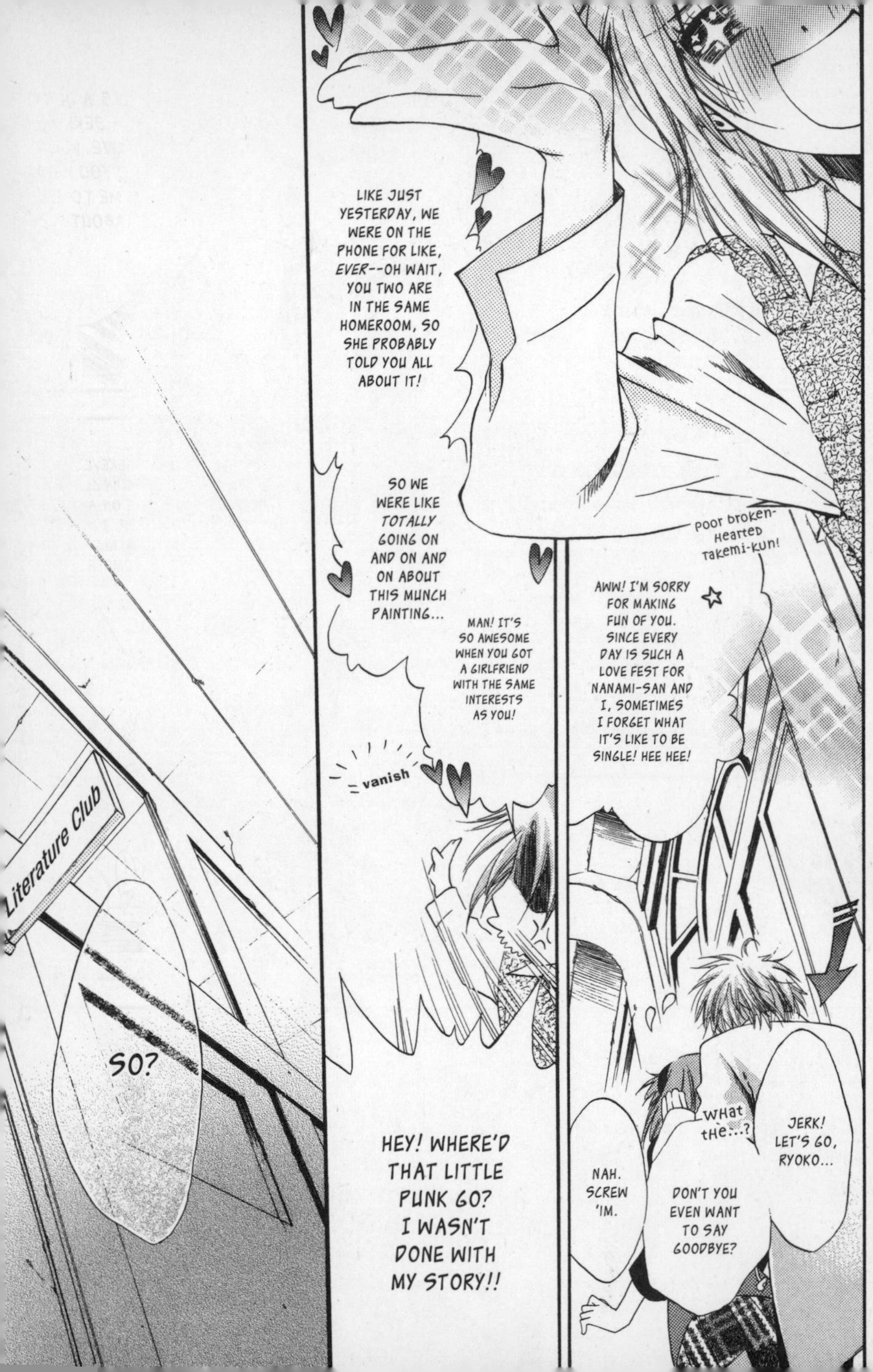
LIKE JUST YESTERDAY, WE WERE ON THE PHONE FOR LIKE, EVER--OH WAIT, YOU TWO ARE IN THE SAME HOMEROOM, SO SHE PROBABLY TOLD YOU ALL ABOUT IT!
SO WE WERE LIKE TOTALLY GOING ON AND ON AND ON ABOUT THIS MUNCH PAINTING...
Poor broken-hearted Takemi-kun!
AWW! I'M SORRY FOR MAKING FUN OF YOU. SINCE EVERY DAY IS SUCH A LOVE FEST FOR NANAMI-SAN AND I, SOMETIMES I FORGET WHAT IT'S LIKE TO BE SINGLE! HEE HEE!
What the...?
JERK! LET'S GO, RYOKO...
DON'T YOU EVEN WANT TO SAY GOODBYE?
NAH. SCREW 'IM.
MAN! IT'S SO AWESOME WHEN YOU GOT A GIRLFRIEND WITH THE SAME INTERESTS AS YOU!
vanish
HEY! WHERE'D THAT LITTLE PUNK GO? I WASN'T DONE WITH MY STORY!!
Literature Club
SO?

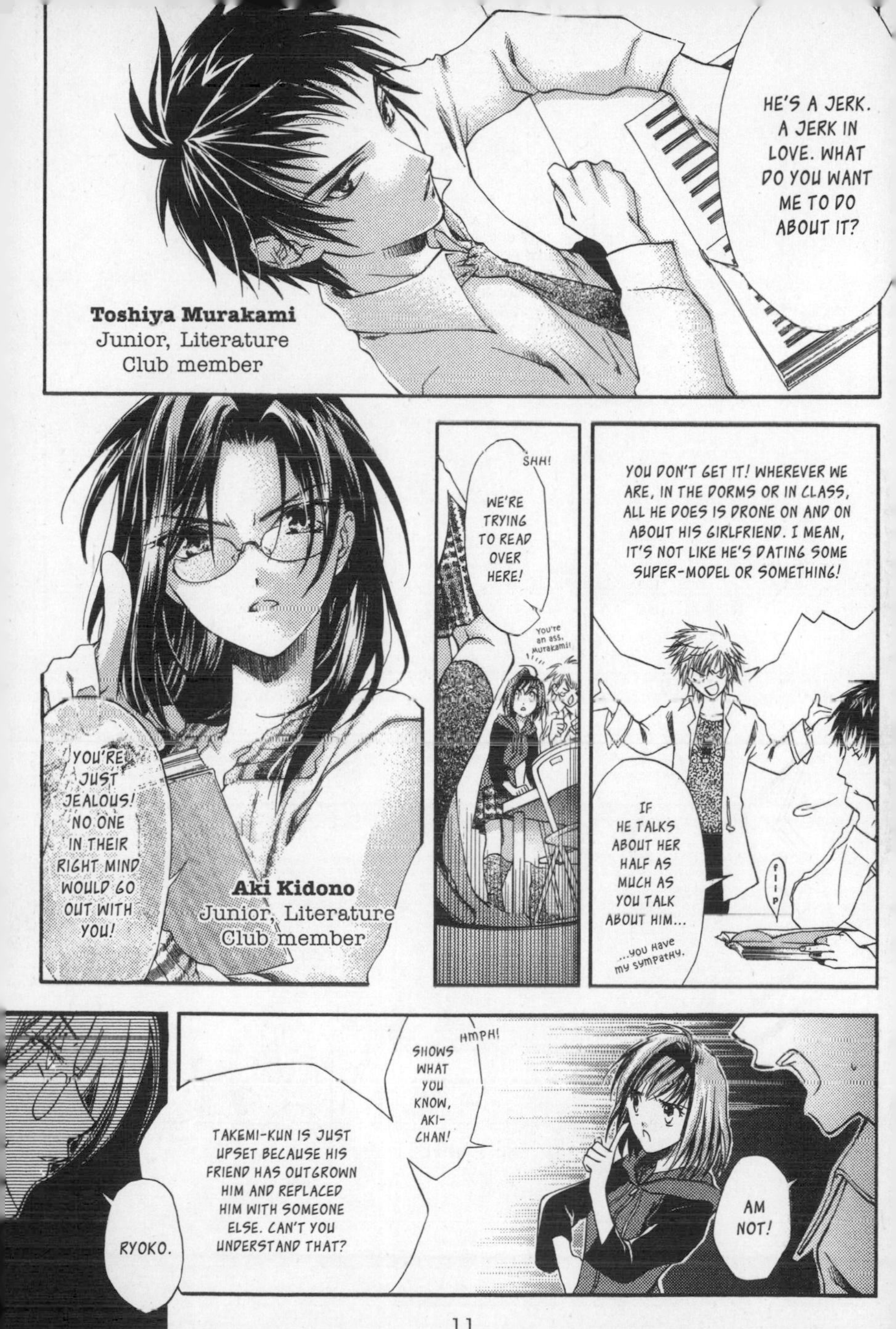
HE'S A JERK. A JERK IN LOVE. WHAT DO YOU WANT ME TO DO ABOUT IT?
Toshiya Murakami
Junior, Literature Club member
YOU DON'T GET IT! WHEREVER WE ARE, IN THE DORMS OR IN CLASS, ALL HE DOES IS DRONE ON AND ON ABOUT HIS GIRLFRIEND. I MEAN, IT'S NOT LIKE HE'S DATING SOME SUPER-MODEL OR SOMETHING!
IF HE TALKS ABOUT HER HALF AS MUCH AS YOU TALK ABOUT HIM...
flip
...you have my sympathy.
SHH!
WE'RE TRYING TO READ OVER HERE!
You're an ass, Murakami!
YOU'RE JUST JEALOUS! NO ONE IN THEIR RIGHT MIND WOULD GO OUT WITH YOU!
Aki Kidono
Junior, Literature Club member
HMPH!
SHOWS WHAT YOU KNOW, AKI-CHAN!
AM NOT!
TAKEMI-KUN IS JUST UPSET BECAUSE HIS FRIEND HAS OUTGROWN HIM AND REPLACED HIM WITH SOMEONE ELSE. CAN'T YOU UNDERSTAND THAT?
RYOKO.

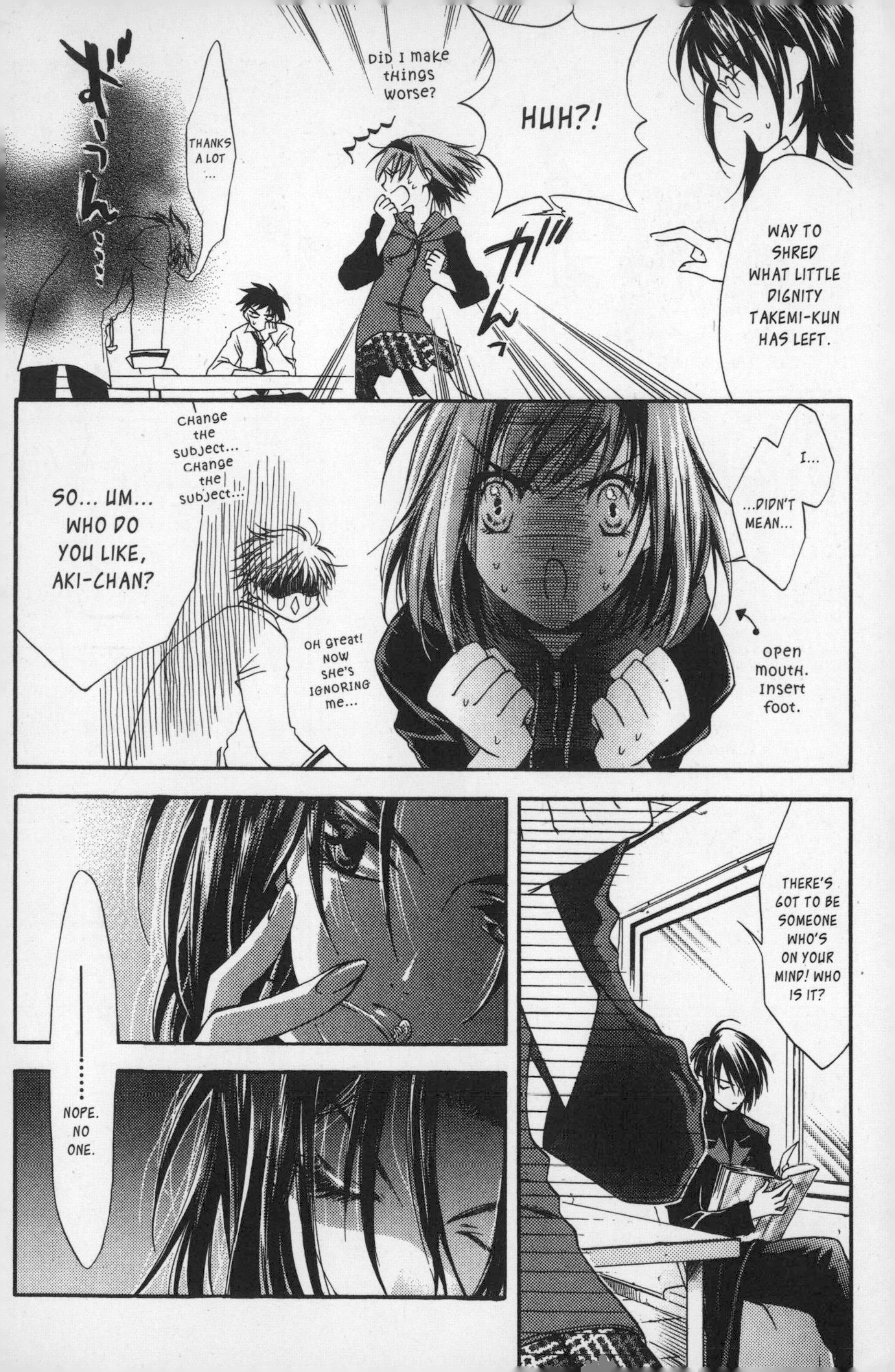
HUH?!
WAY TO SHRED WHAT LITTLE DIGNITY TAKEMI-KUN HAS LEFT.
DID I make things worse?
THANKS A LOT ...
I...
...DIDN'T MEAN...
open mouth. Insert foot.
Change the subject... Change the subject...
SO... UM... WHO DO YOU LIKE, AKI-CHAN?
OH great! NOW SHE'S IGNORING me...
THERE'S GOT TO BE SOMEONE WHO'S ON YOUR MIND! WHO IS IT?
NOPE. NO ONE.

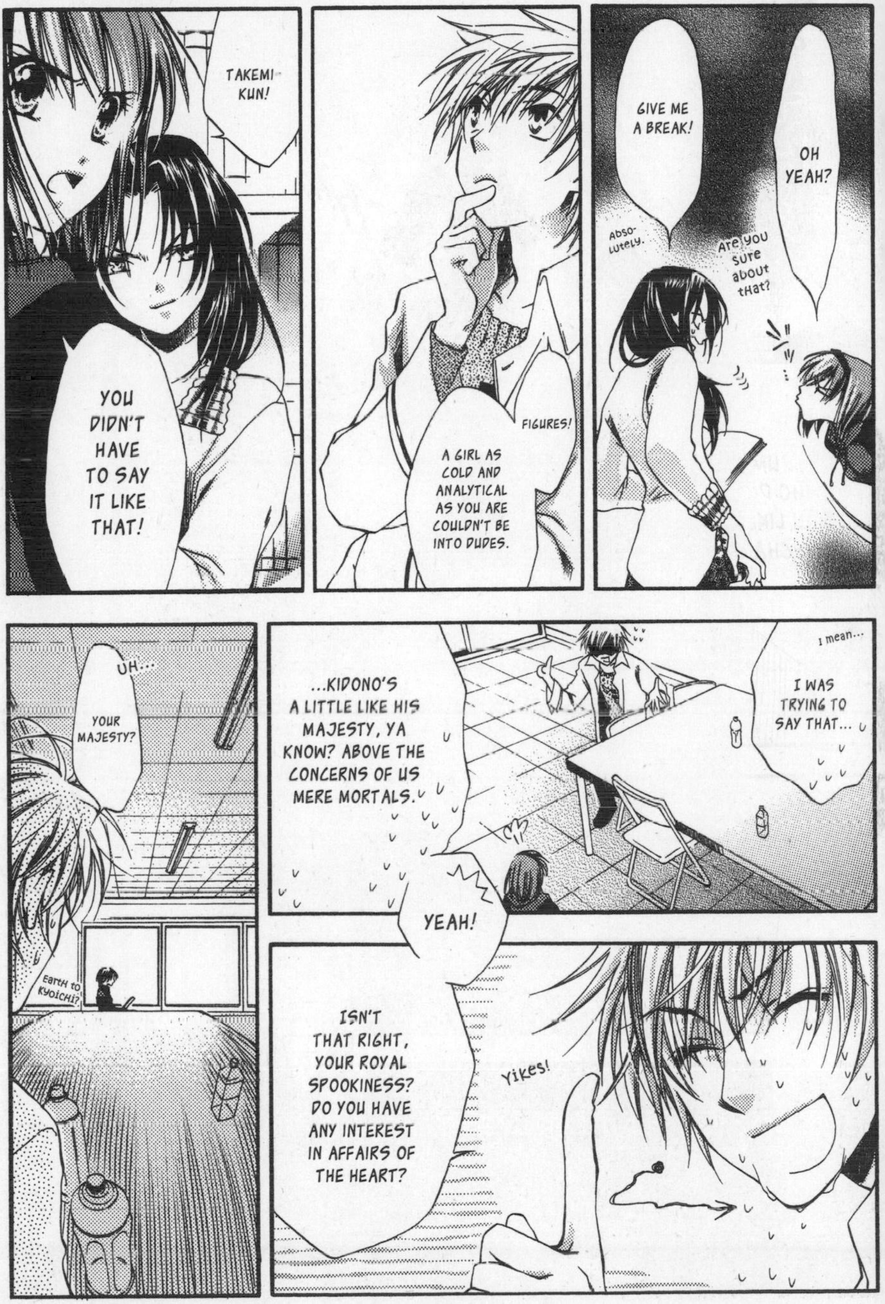
OH YEAH?
GIVE ME A BREAK!
Are YOU Sure about tHat?
Abso-lutely.
FIGURES!
A GIRL AS COLD AND ANALYTICAL AS YOU ARE COULDN'T BE INTO DUDES.
TAKEMI-KUN!
YOU DIDN'T HAVE TO SAY IT LIKE THAT!
I mean...
I WAS TRYING TO SAY THAT...
...KIDONO'S A LITTLE LIKE HIS MAJESTY, YA KNOW? ABOVE THE CONCERNS OF US MERE MORTALS.
YEAH!
Yikes!
ISN'T THAT RIGHT, YOUR ROYAL SPOOKINESS? DO YOU HAVE ANY INTEREST IN AFFAIRS OF THE HEART?
UH...
YOUR MAJESTY?
EartH to KYOICHI?

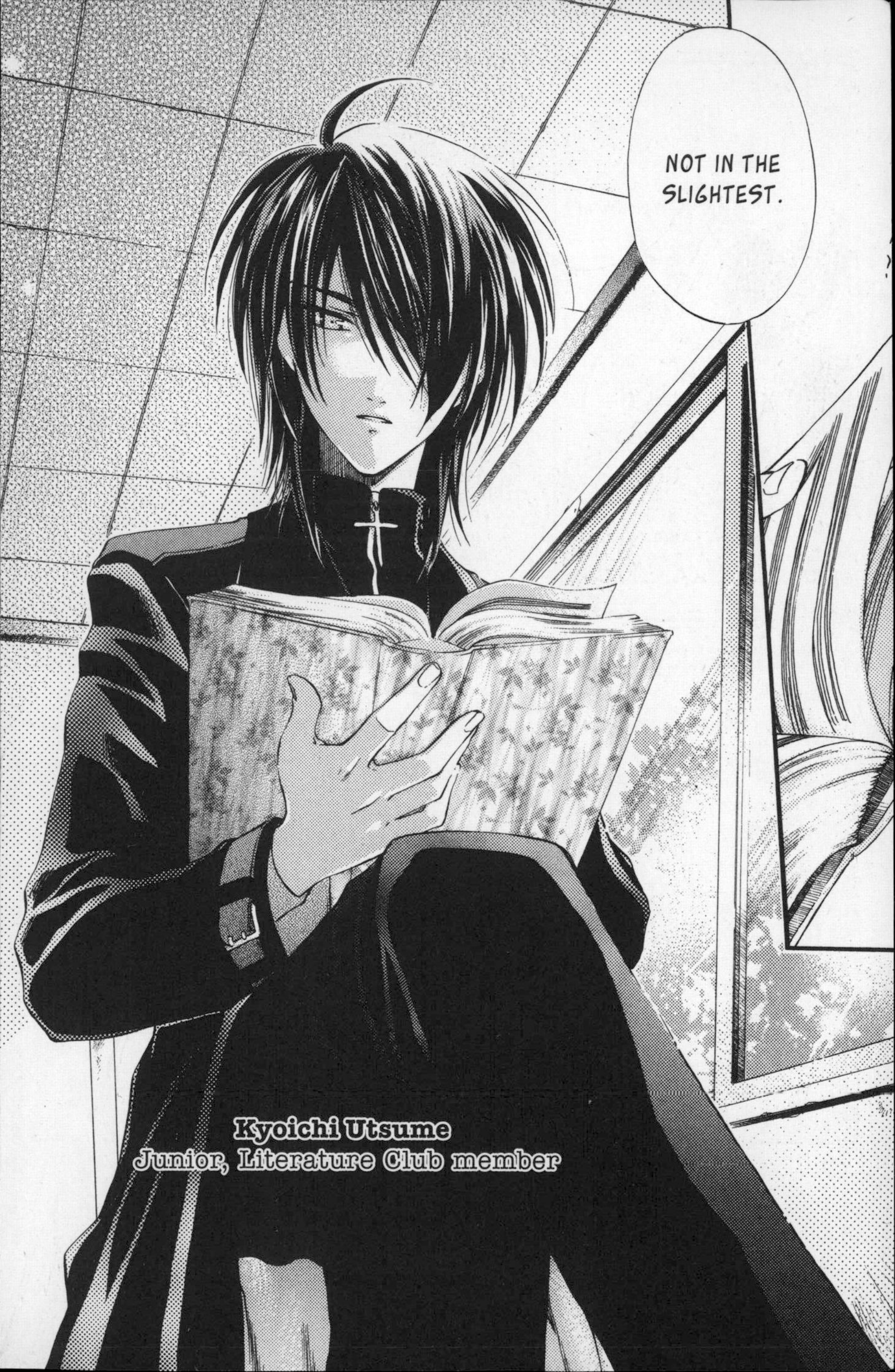
NOT IN THE SLIGHTEST.
Kyoichi Utsume
Junior, Literature Club member

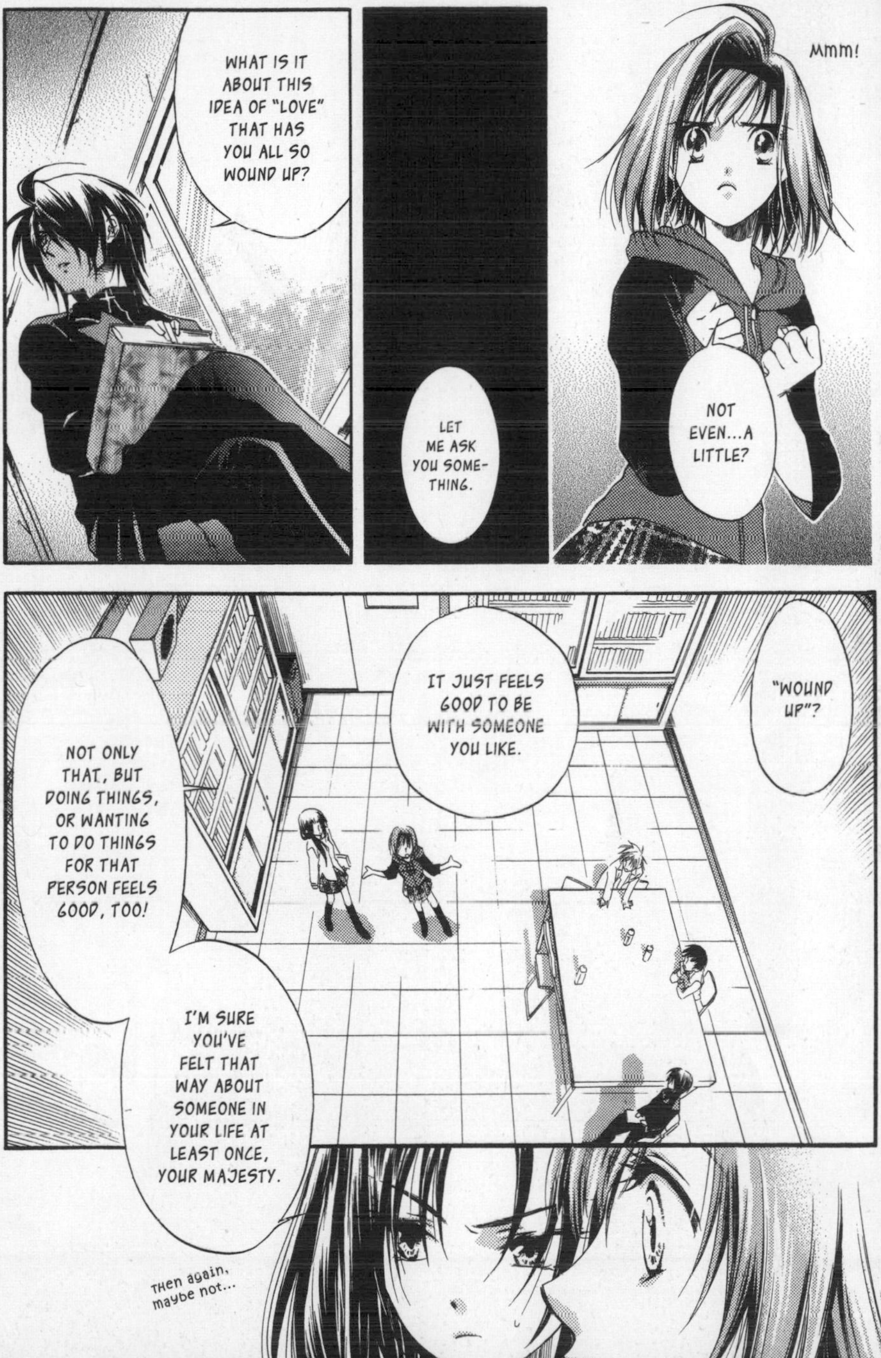
Mmm!
Not even...a little?
Let me ask you some-thing.
What is it about this idea of "love" that has you all so wound up?
"Wound up"?
It just feels good to be with someone you like.
Not only that, but doing things, or wanting to do things for that person feels good, too!
I'm sure you've felt that way about someone in your life at least once, your majesty.
Then again, maybe not...

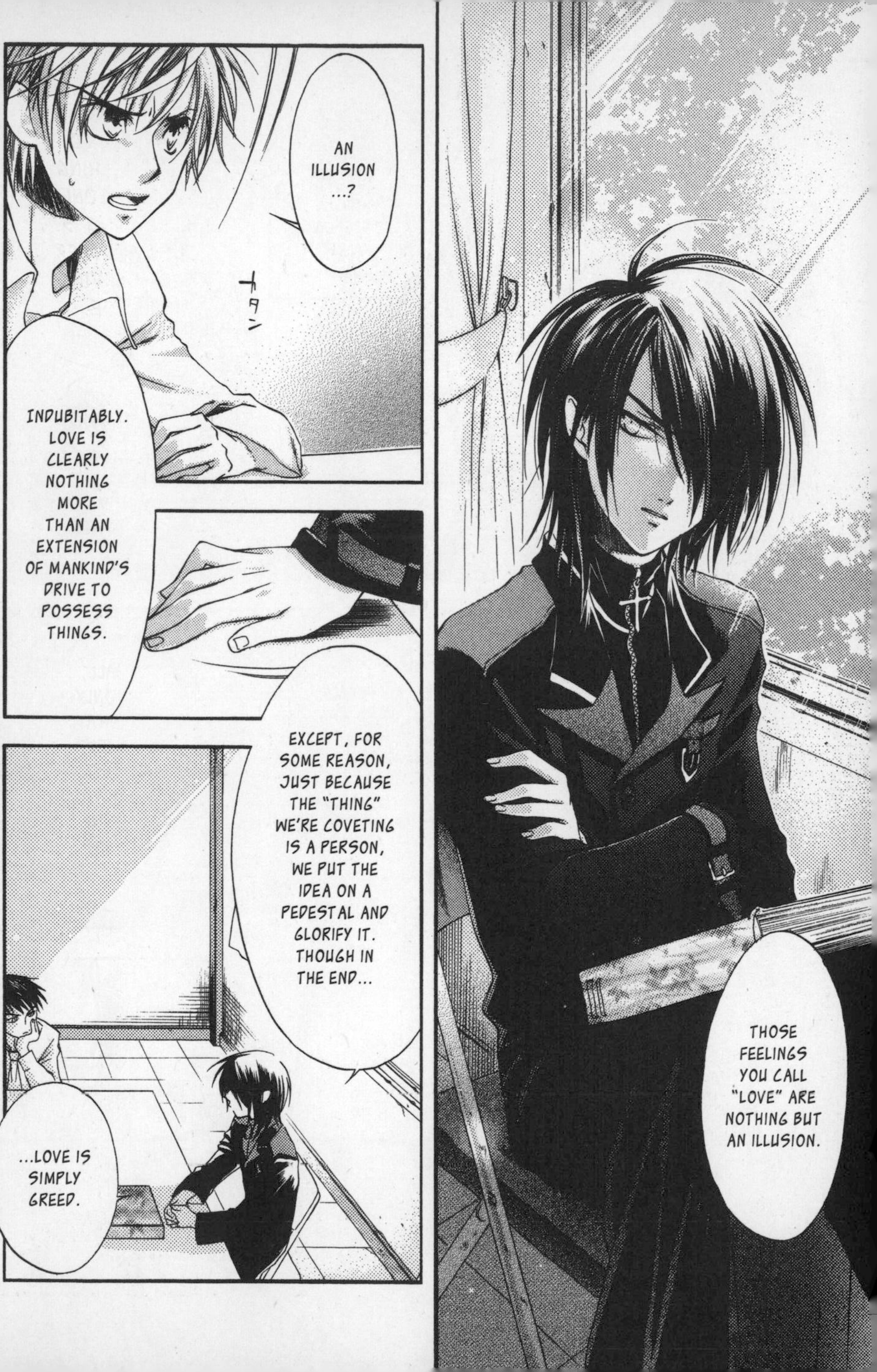
THOSE FEELINGS YOU CALL "LOVE" ARE NOTHING BUT AN ILLUSION.
AN ILLUSION ...?
INDUBITABLY. LOVE IS CLEARLY NOTHING MORE THAN AN EXTENSION OF MANKIND'S DRIVE TO POSSESS THINGS.
EXCEPT, FOR SOME REASON, JUST BECAUSE THE "THING" WE'RE COVETING IS A PERSON, WE PUT THE IDEA ON A PEDESTAL AND GLORIFY IT. THOUGH IN THE END...
...LOVE IS SIMPLY GREED.

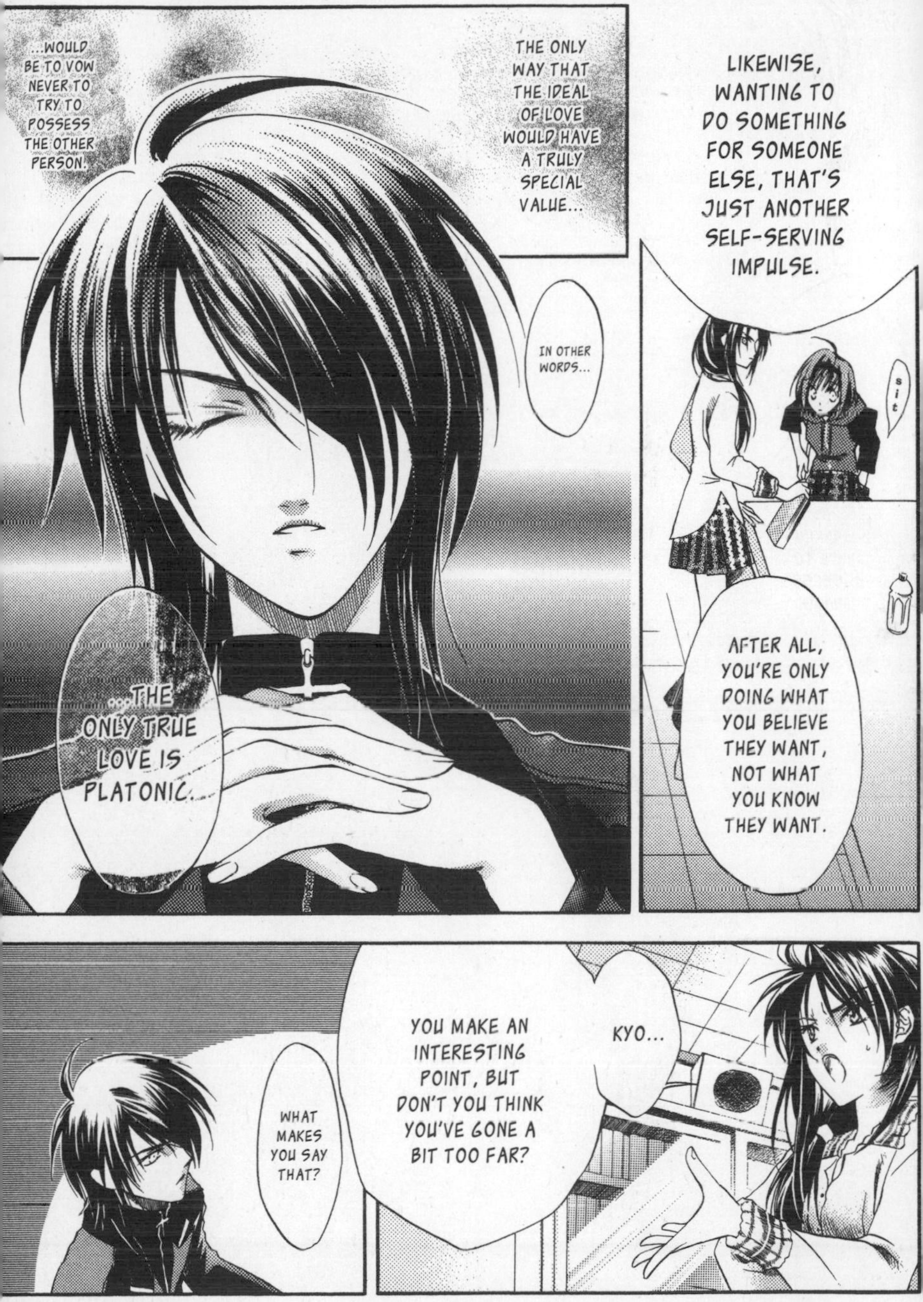
LIKEWISE, WANTING TO DO SOMETHING FOR SOMEONE ELSE, THAT'S JUST ANOTHER SELF-SERVING IMPULSE.
sit
AFTER ALL, YOU'RE ONLY DOING WHAT YOU BELIEVE THEY WANT, NOT WHAT YOU KNOW THEY WANT.
THE ONLY WAY THAT THE IDEAL OF LOVE WOULD HAVE A TRULY SPECIAL VALUE...
...WOULD BE TO VOW NEVER TO TRY TO POSSESS THE OTHER PERSON.
IN OTHER WORDS...
...THE ONLY TRUE LOVE IS PLATONIC.
KYO...
YOU MAKE AN INTERESTING POINT, BUT DON'T YOU THINK YOU'VE GONE A BIT TOO FAR?
WHAT MAKES YOU SAY THAT?

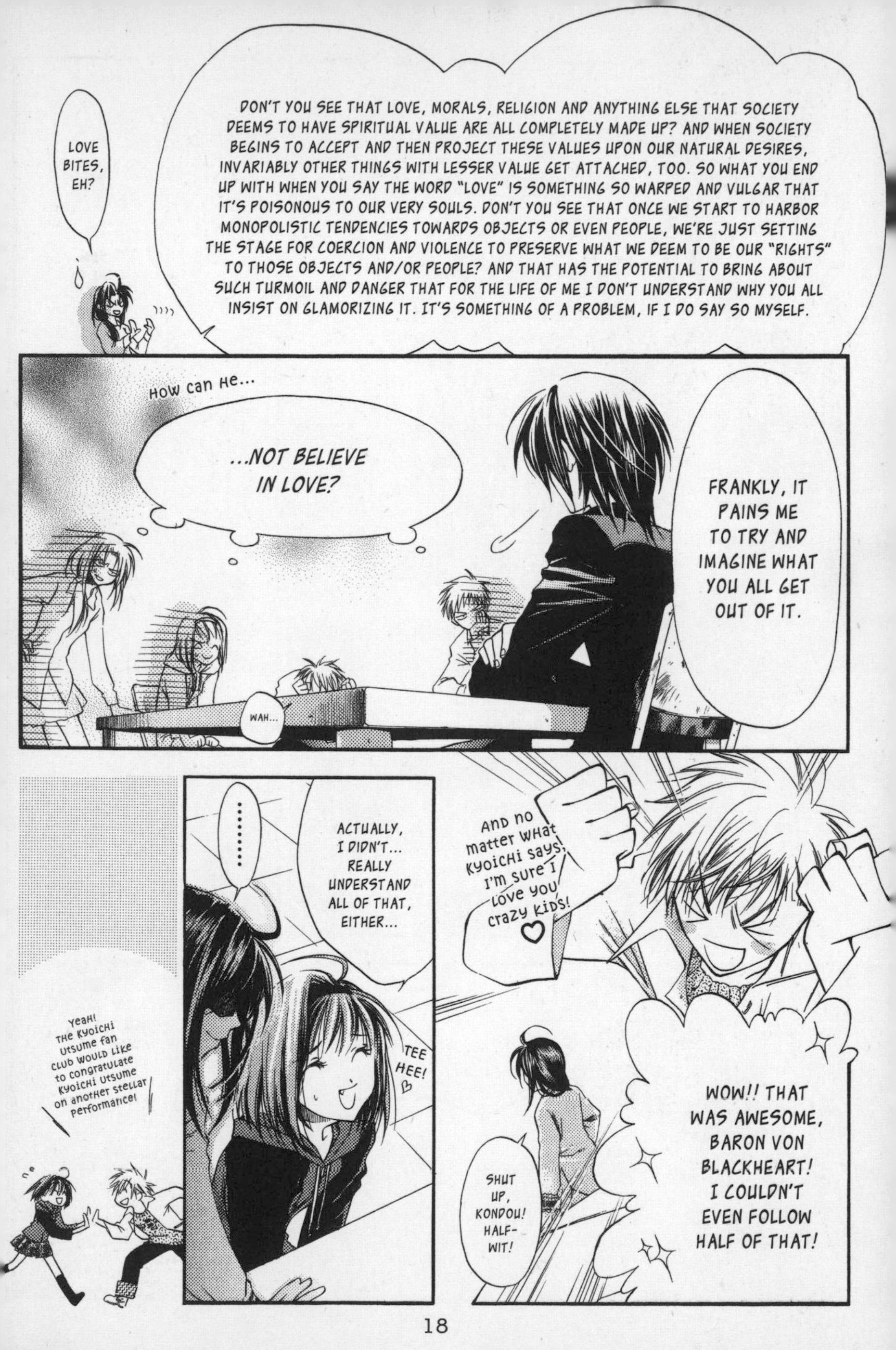
DON'T YOU SEE THAT LOVE, MORALS, RELIGION AND ANYTHING ELSE THAT SOCIETY DEEMS TO HAVE SPIRITUAL VALUE ARE ALL COMPLETELY MADE UP? AND WHEN SOCIETY BEGINS TO ACCEPT AND THEN PROJECT THESE VALUES UPON OUR NATURAL DESIRES, INVARIABLY OTHER THINGS WITH LESSER VALUE GET ATTACHED, TOO. SO WHAT YOU END UP WITH WHEN YOU SAY THE WORD "LOVE" IS SOMETHING SO WARPED AND VULGAR THAT IT'S POISONOUS TO OUR VERY SOULS. DON'T YOU SEE THAT ONCE WE START TO HARBOR MONOPOLISTIC TENDENCIES TOWARDS OBJECTS OR EVEN PEOPLE, WE'RE JUST SETTING THE STAGE FOR COERCION AND VIOLENCE TO PRESERVE WHAT WE DEEM TO BE OUR "RIGHTS" TO THOSE OBJECTS AND/OR PEOPLE? AND THAT HAS THE POTENTIAL TO BRING ABOUT SUCH TURMOIL AND DANGER THAT FOR THE LIFE OF ME I DON'T UNDERSTAND WHY YOU ALL INSIST ON GLAMORIZING IT. IT'S SOMETHING OF A PROBLEM, IF I DO SAY SO MYSELF.
LOVE BITES, EH?
FRANKLY, IT PAINS ME TO TRY AND IMAGINE WHAT YOU ALL GET OUT OF IT.
How can he...
...NOT BELIEVE IN LOVE?
WAH...
WOW!! THAT WAS AWESOME, BARON VON BLACKHEART! I COULDN'T EVEN FOLLOW HALF OF THAT!
SHUT UP, KONDOU! HALF-WIT!
And no matter what Kyoichi says, I'm sure I love you crazy kids! ♡
....
ACTUALLY, I DIDN'T... REALLY UNDERSTAND ALL OF THAT, EITHER...
TEE HEE! ♡
Yeah! The Kyoichi Utsume fan club would like to congratulate Kyoichi Utsume on another stellar performance!

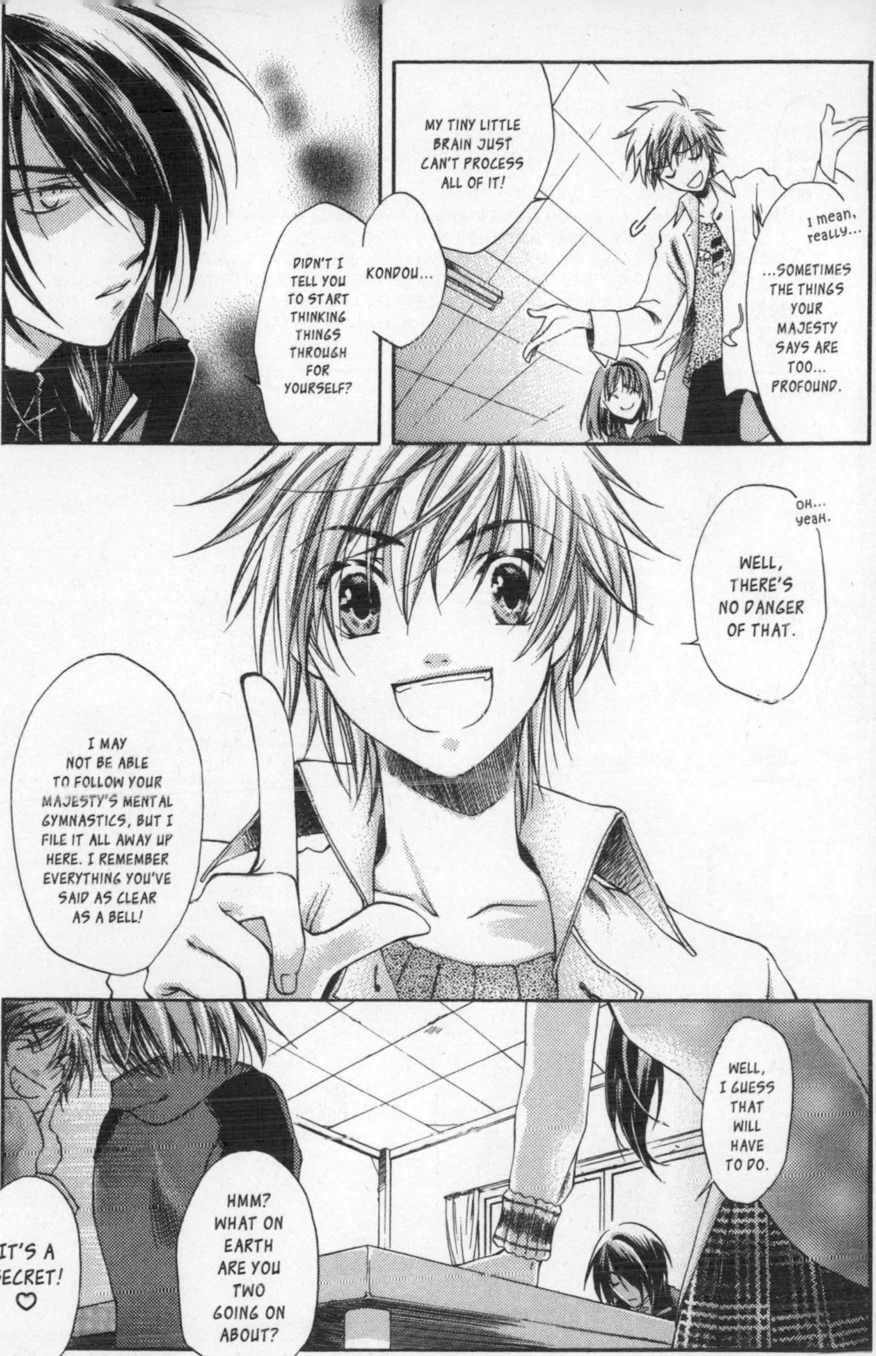
I mean, really...
...SOMETIMES THE THINGS YOUR MAJESTY SAYS ARE TOO... PROFOUND.
MY TINY LITTLE BRAIN JUST CAN'T PROCESS ALL OF IT!
KONDOU...
DIDN'T I TELL YOU TO START THINKING THINGS THROUGH FOR YOURSELF?
OH... YEAH.
WELL, THERE'S NO DANGER OF THAT.
I MAY NOT BE ABLE TO FOLLOW YOUR MAJESTY'S MENTAL GYMNASTICS, BUT I FILE IT ALL AWAY UP HERE. I REMEMBER EVERYTHING YOU'VE SAID AS CLEAR AS A BELL!
WELL, I GUESS THAT WILL HAVE TO DO.
HMM? WHAT ON EARTH ARE YOU TWO GOING ON ABOUT?
IT'S A SECRET! ♡

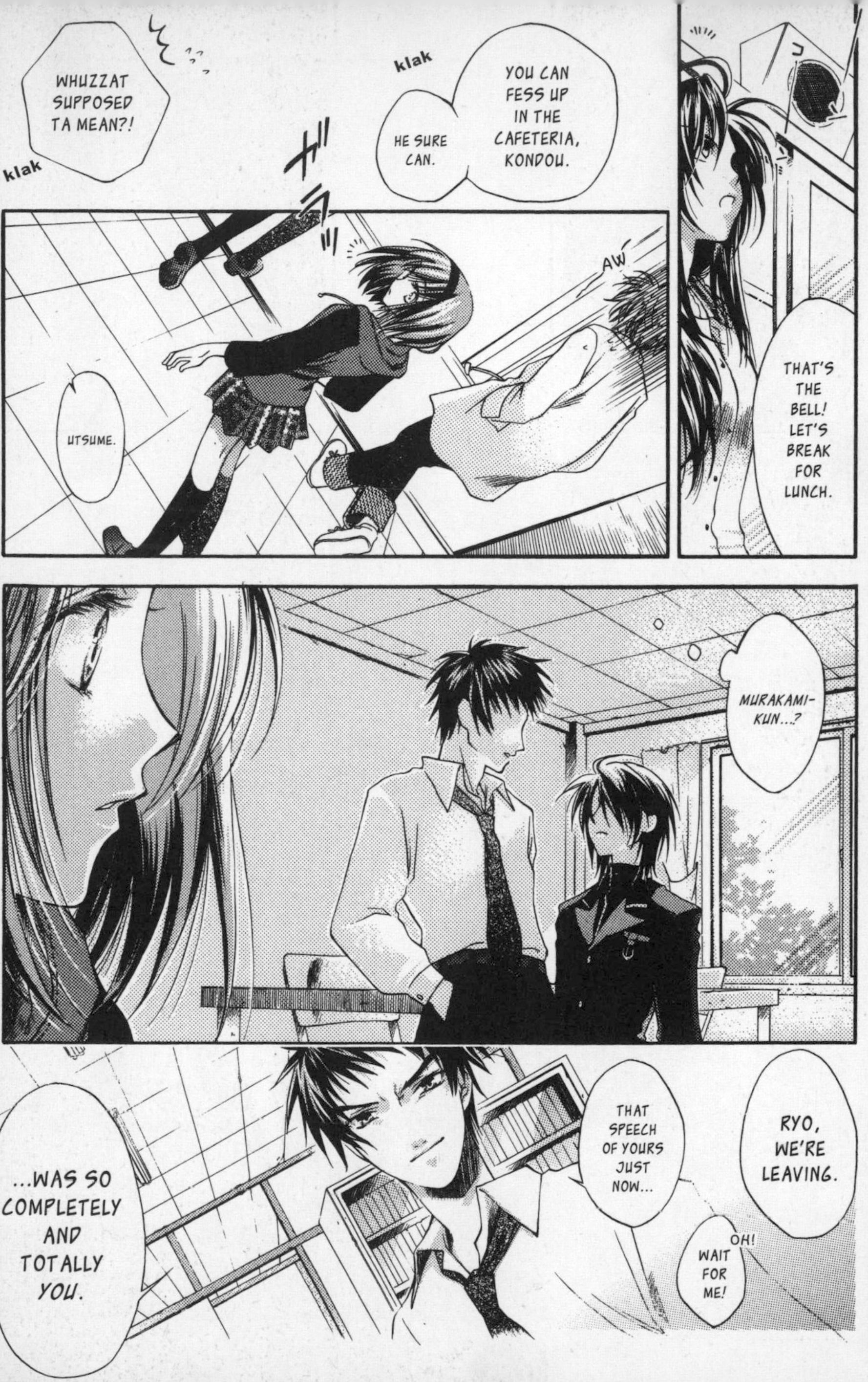
THAT'S THE BELL! LET'S BREAK FOR LUNCH.
YOU CAN FESS UP IN THE CAFETERIA, KONDOU.
HE SURE CAN.
klak
WHUZZAT SUPPOSED TA MEAN?!
klak
AW
UTSUME.
MURAKAMI-KUN...?
RYO, WE'RE LEAVING.
OH! WAIT FOR ME!
THAT SPEECH OF YOURS JUST NOW...
...WAS SO COMPLETELY AND TOTALLY YOU.

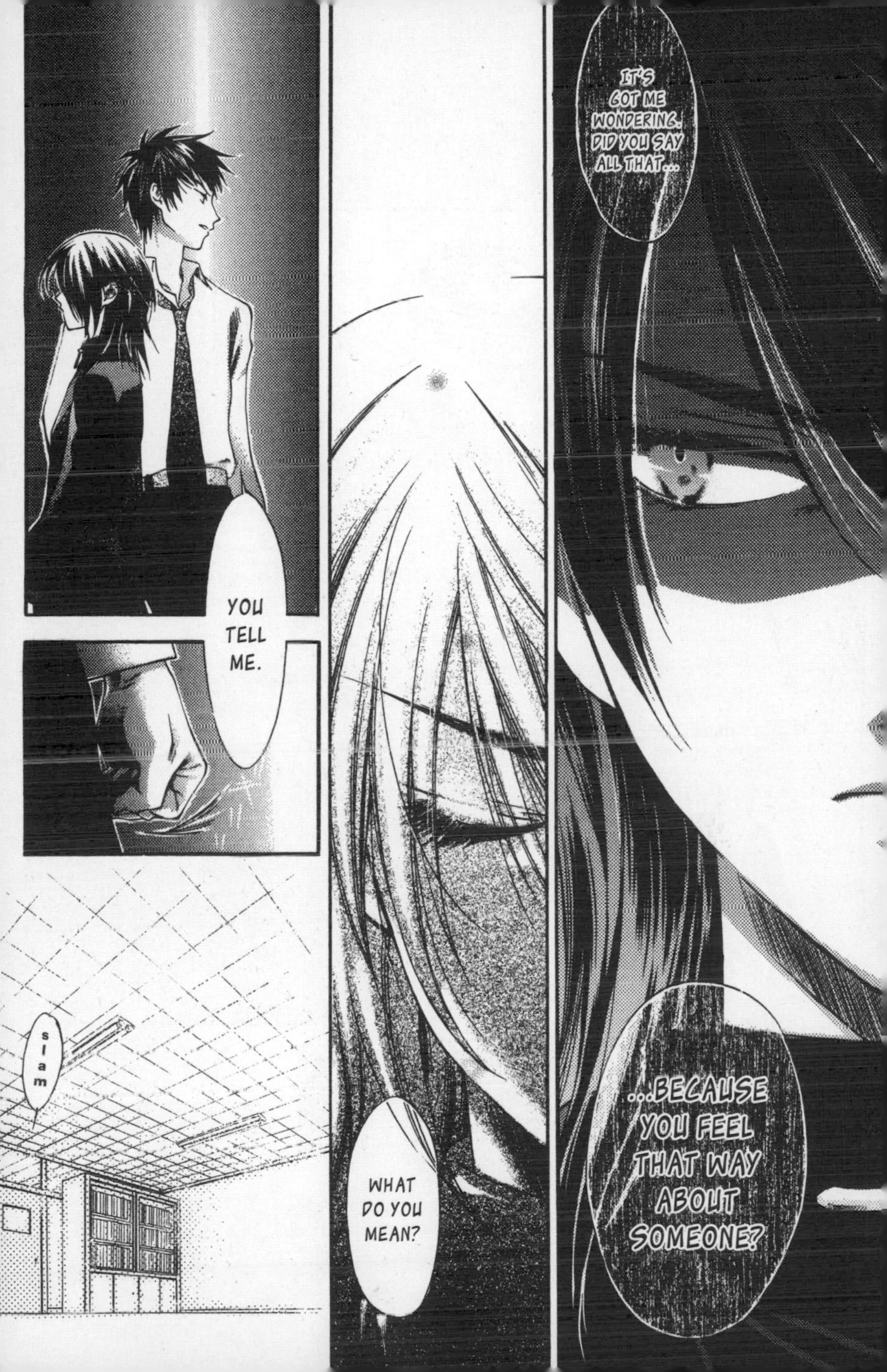
IT'S GOT ME WONDERING. DID YOU SAY ALL THAT...
...BECAUSE YOU FEEL THAT WAY ABOUT SOMEONE?
WHAT DO YOU MEAN?
YOU TELL ME.
slam

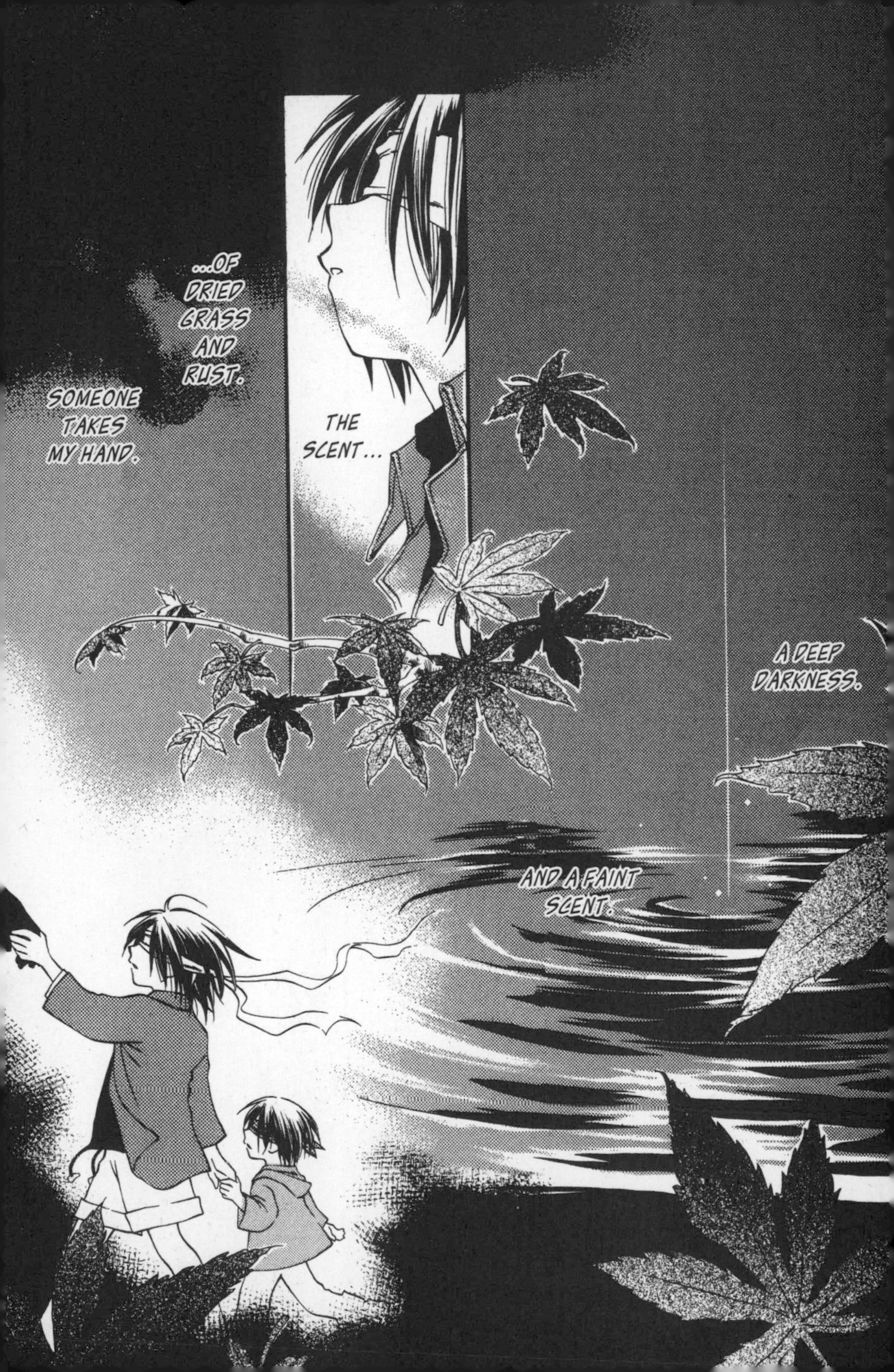
A DEEP DARKNESS.
AND A FAINT SCENT.
THE SCENT...
...OF DRIED GRASS AND RUST.
SOMEONE TAKES MY HAND.

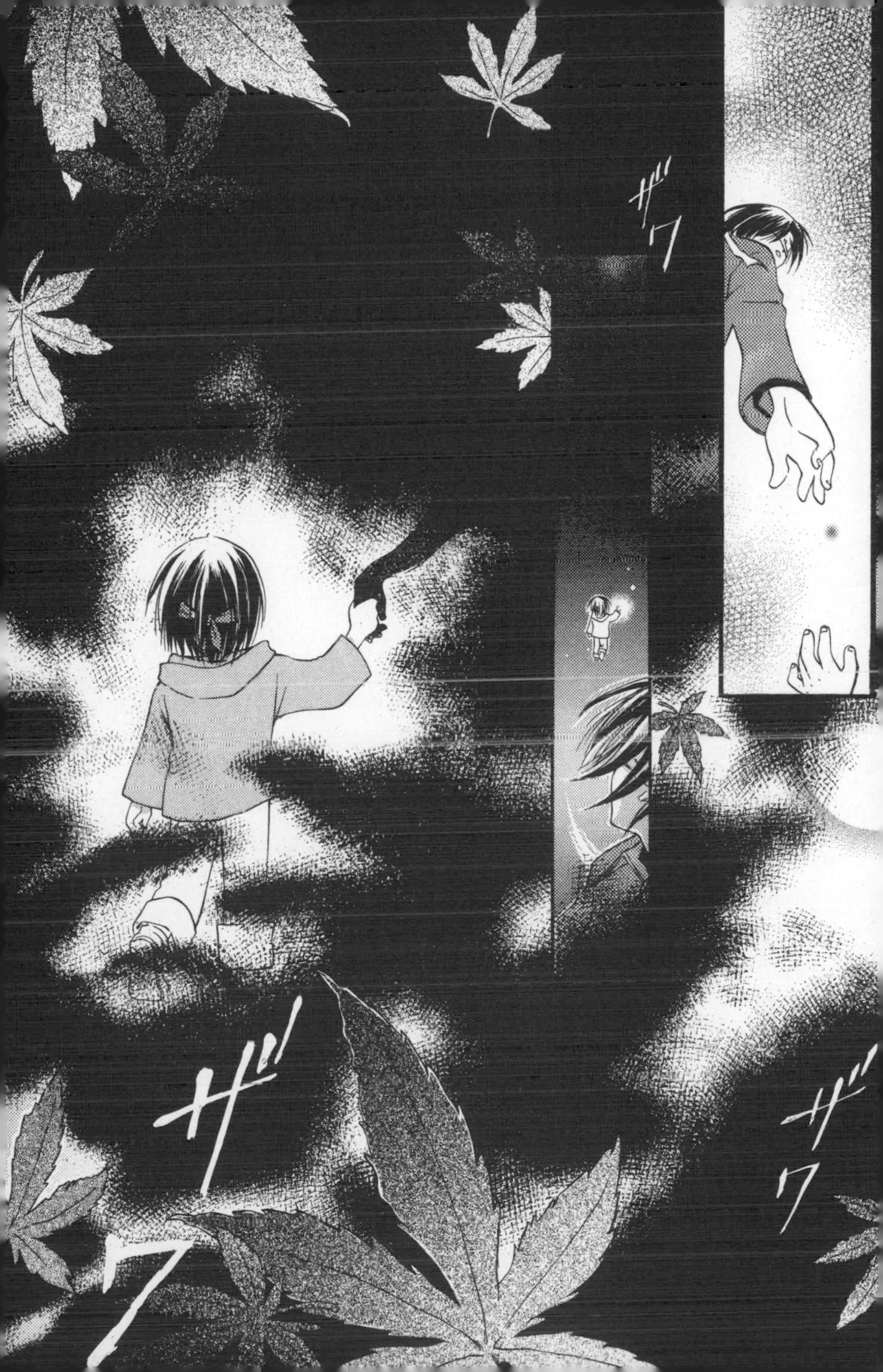
ザワ
ザワ
ザワ

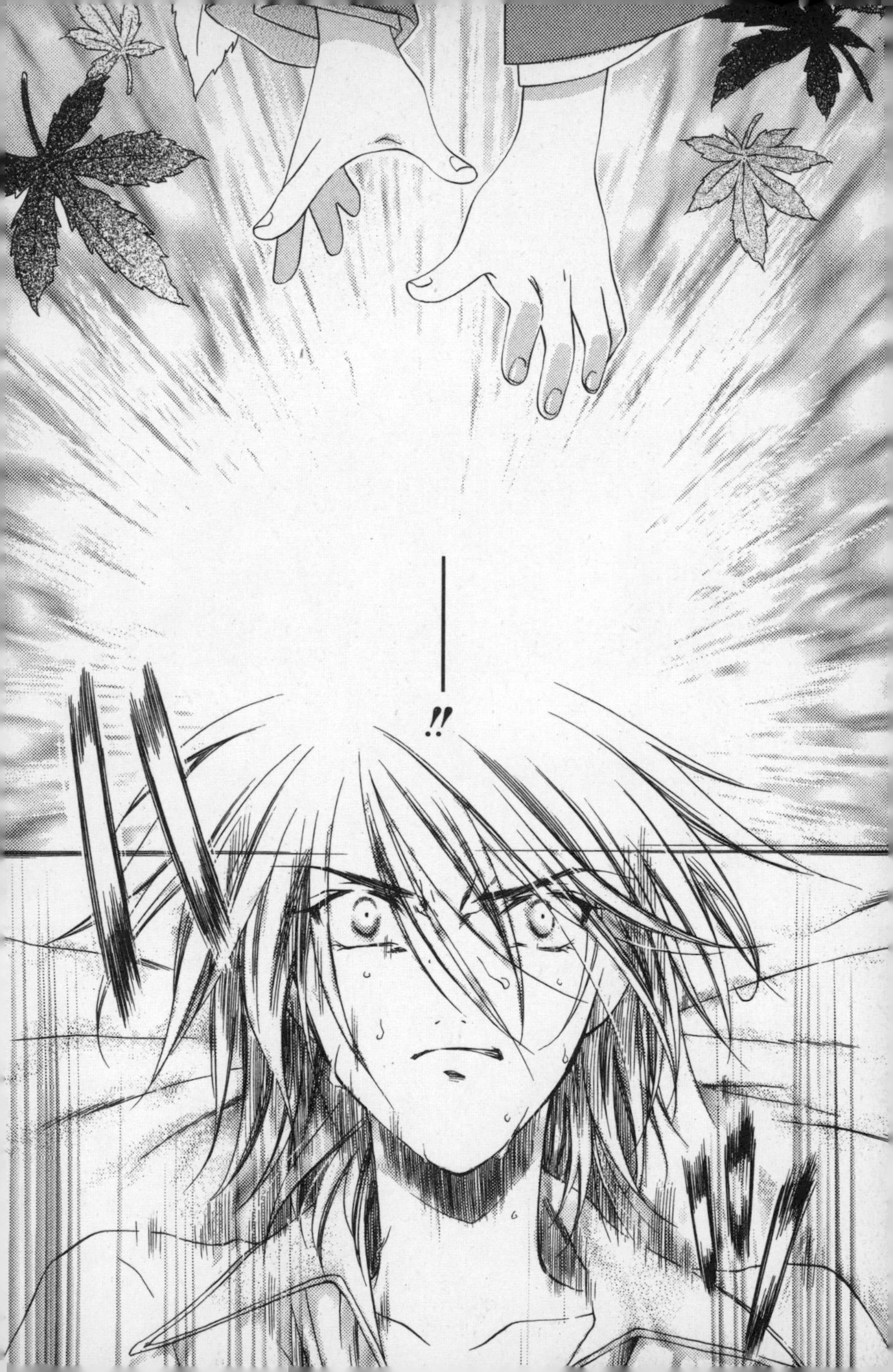
—!!

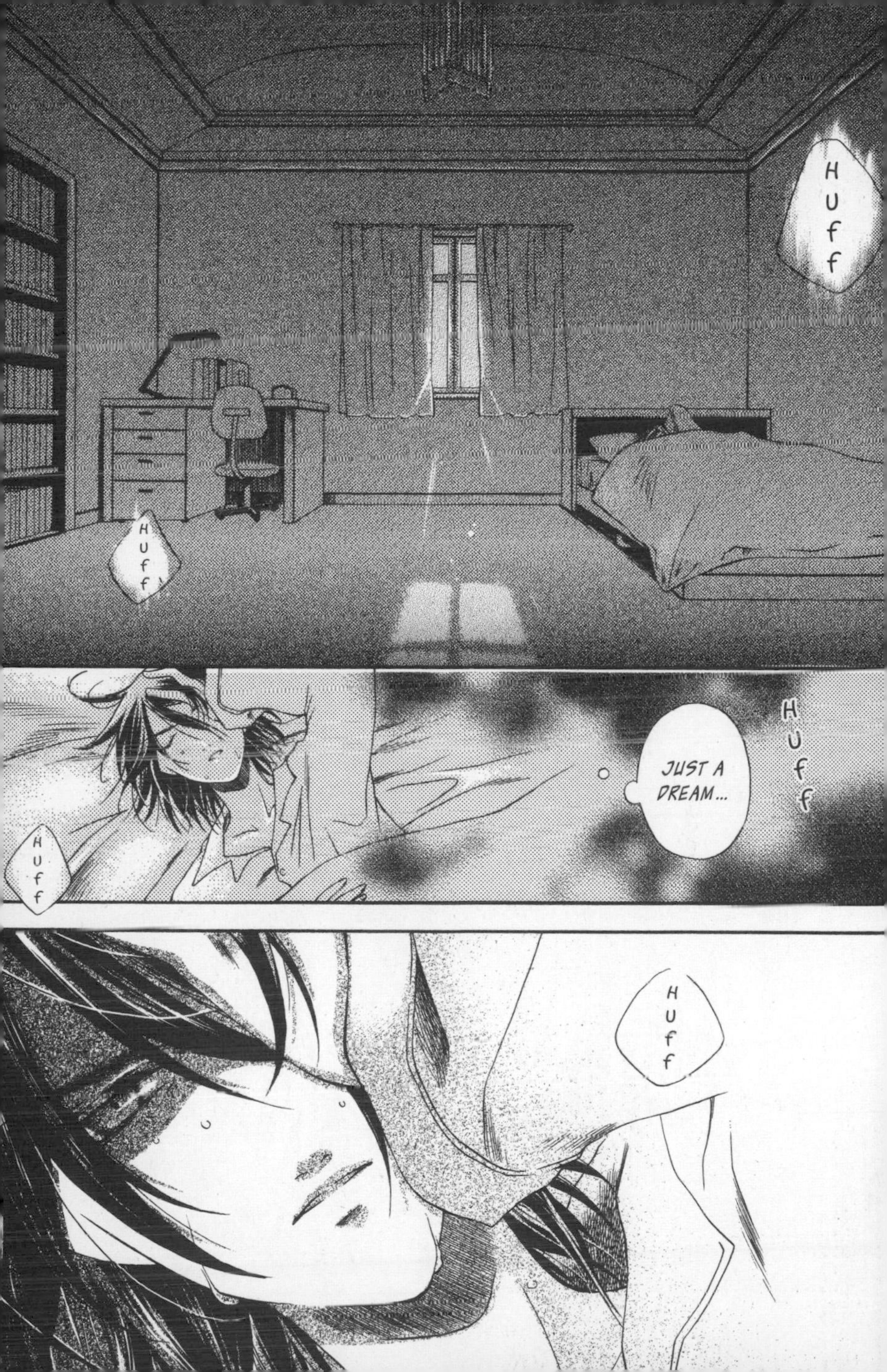
HUFF
HUFF
HUFF
JUST A DREAM...
HUFF
HUFF

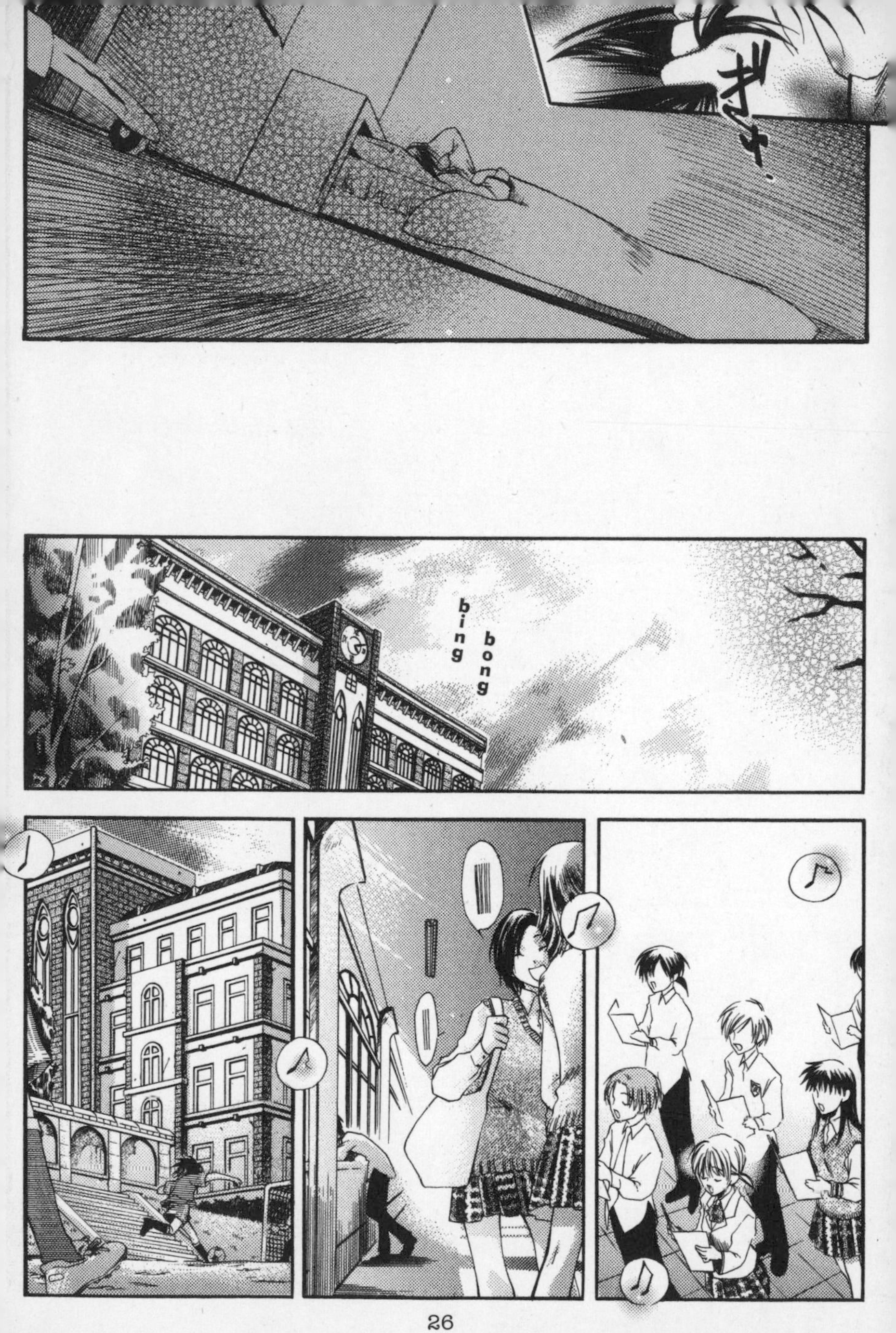
ぎゅ
bing bong

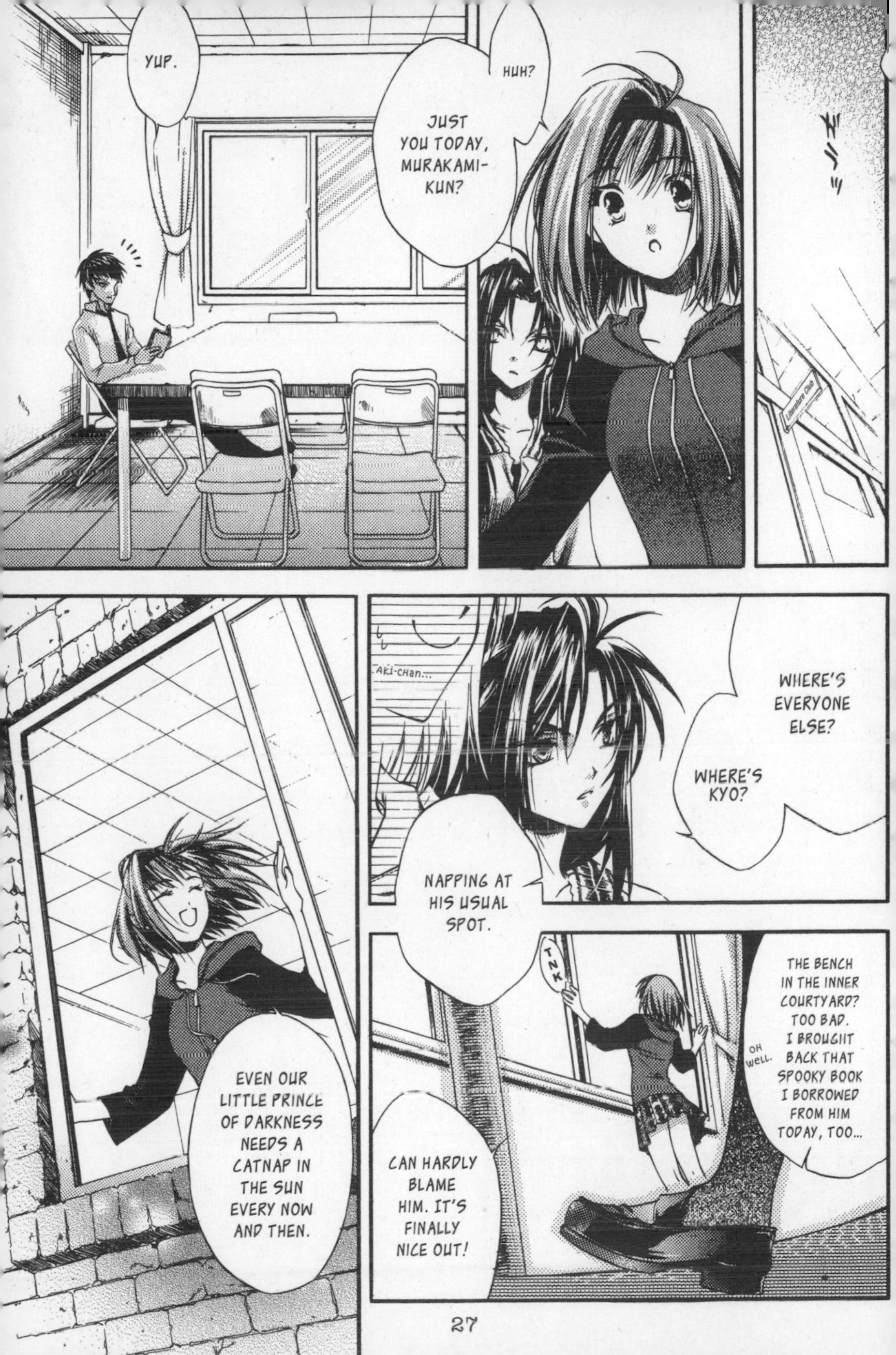
Literature Club
HUH?
JUST YOU TODAY, MURAKAMI-KUN?
YUP.
WHERE'S EVERYONE ELSE?
WHERE'S KYO?
AKI-CHAN...
NAPPING AT HIS USUAL SPOT.
TNK
THE BENCH IN THE INNER COURTYARD? TOO BAD. I BROUGIIT BACK THAT SPOOKY BOOK I BORROWED FROM HIM TODAY, TOO...
OH WELL.
CAN HARDLY BLAME HIM. IT'S FINALLY NICE OUT!
EVEN OUR LITTLE PRINCE OF DARKNESS NEEDS A CATNAP IN THE SUN EVERY NOW AND THEN.

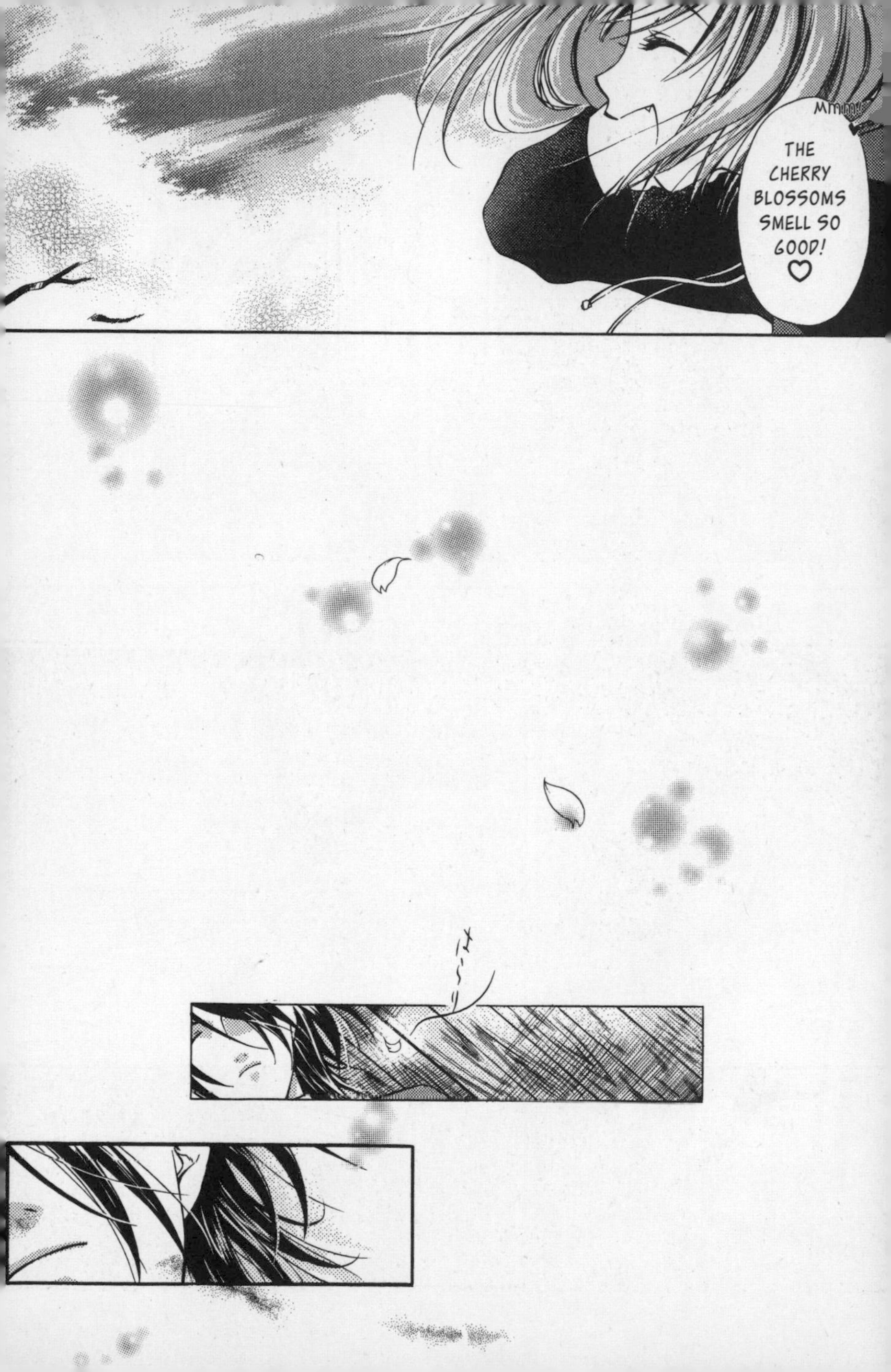
MMMM!
THE CHERRY BLOSSOMS SMELL SO GOOD! ♡

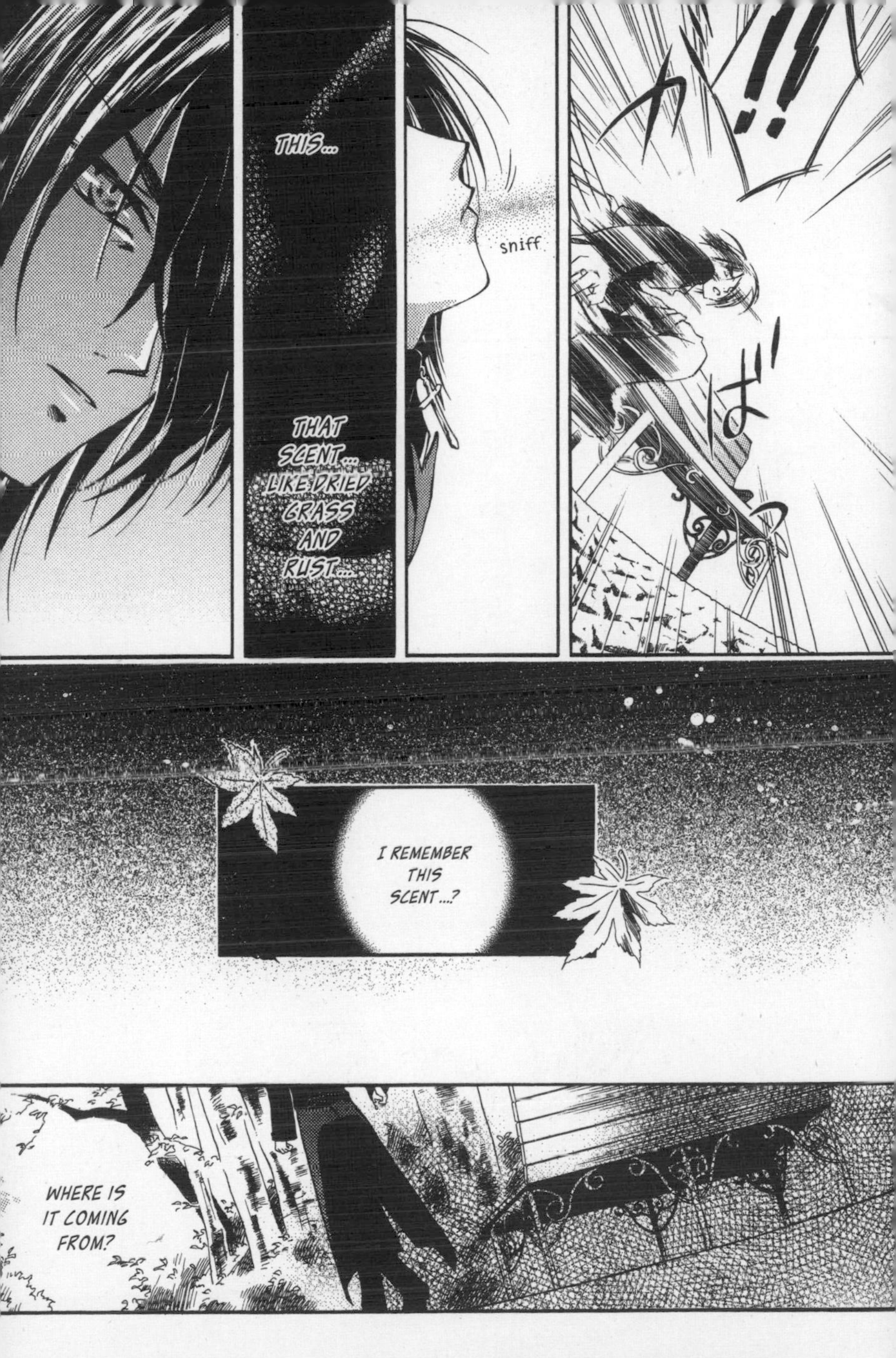
カッ!!
ばっ
sniff
THIS...
THAT SCENT... LIKE DRIED GRASS AND RUST...
I REMEMBER THIS SCENT...?
WHERE IS IT COMING FROM?

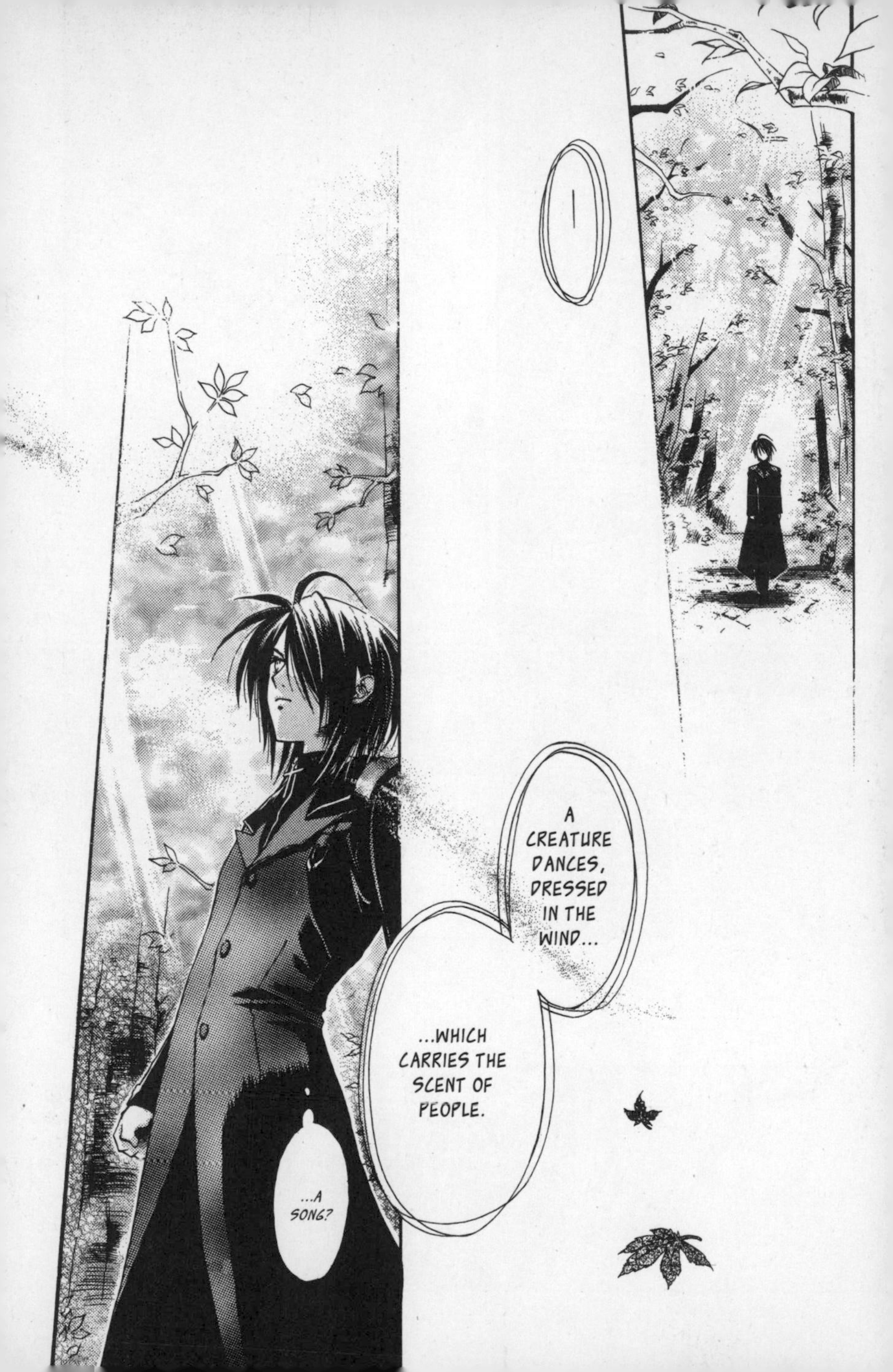
A CREATURE DANCES, DRESSED IN THE WIND...
...WHICH CARRIES THE SCENT OF PEOPLE.
...A SONG?

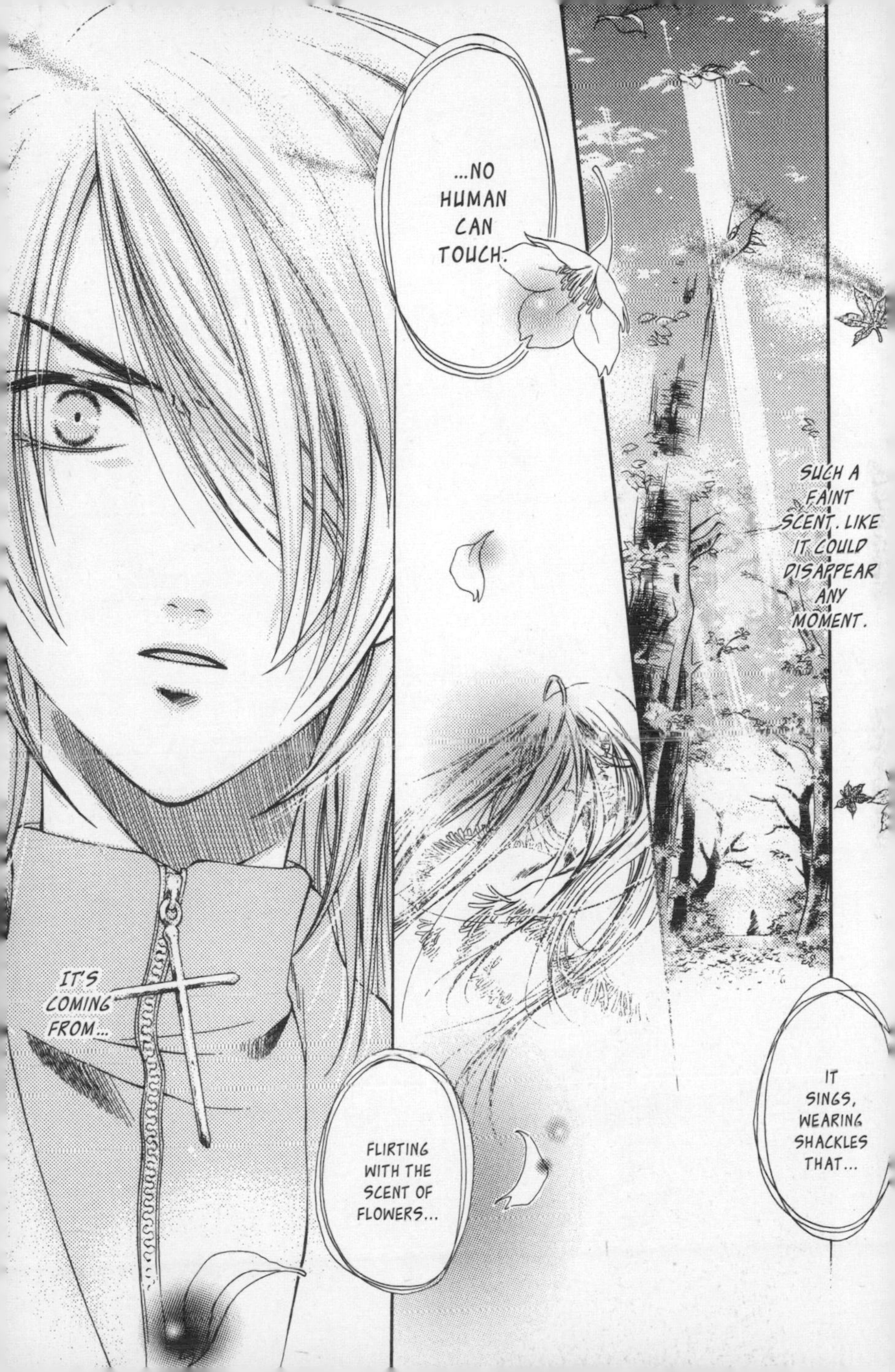
SUCH A FAINT SCENT. LIKE IT COULD DISAPPEAR ANY MOMENT.
IT SINGS, WEARING SHACKLES THAT...
...NO HUMAN CAN TOUCH.
FLIRTING WITH THE SCENT OF FLOWERS...
IT'S COMING FROM...

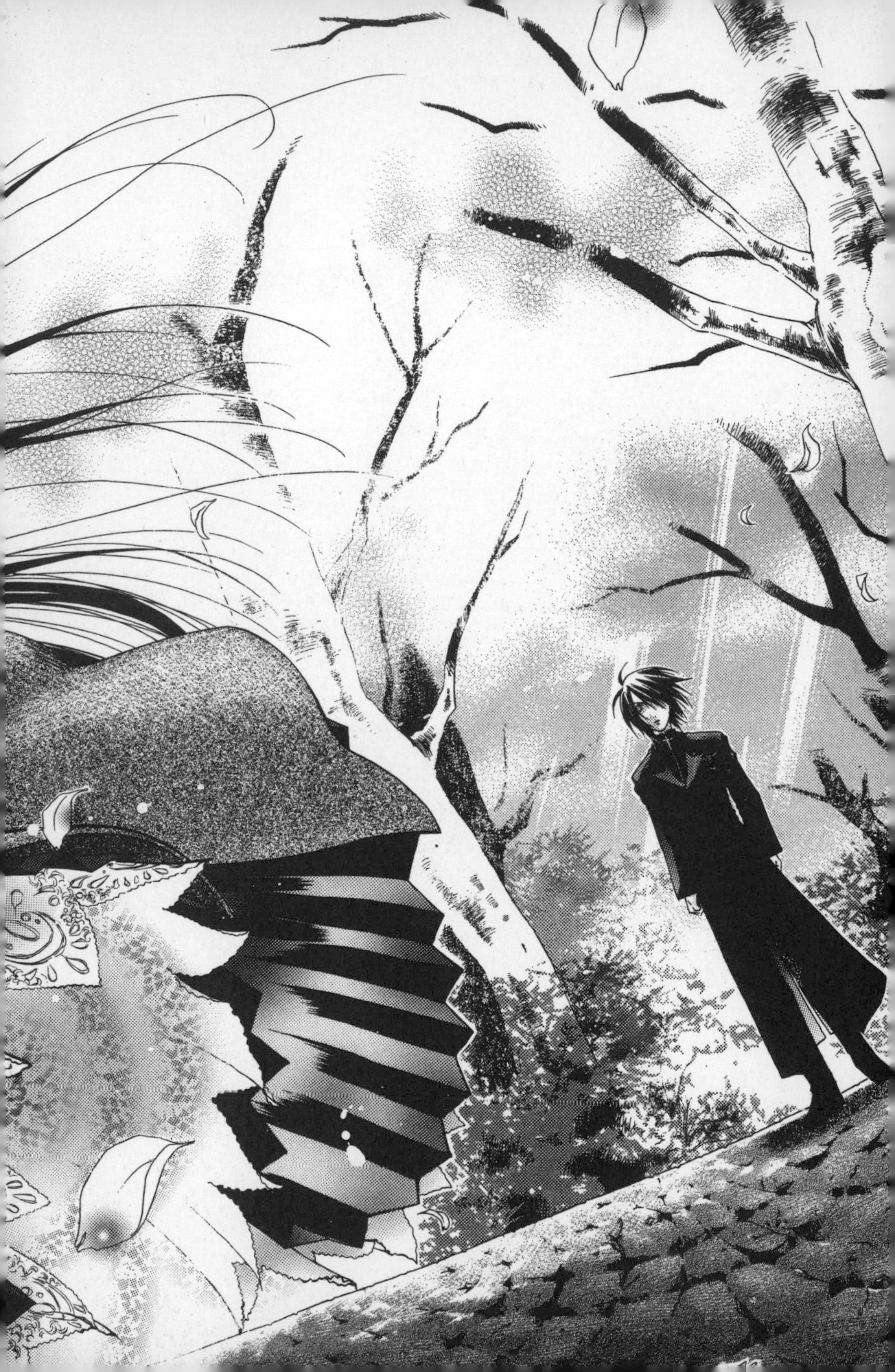

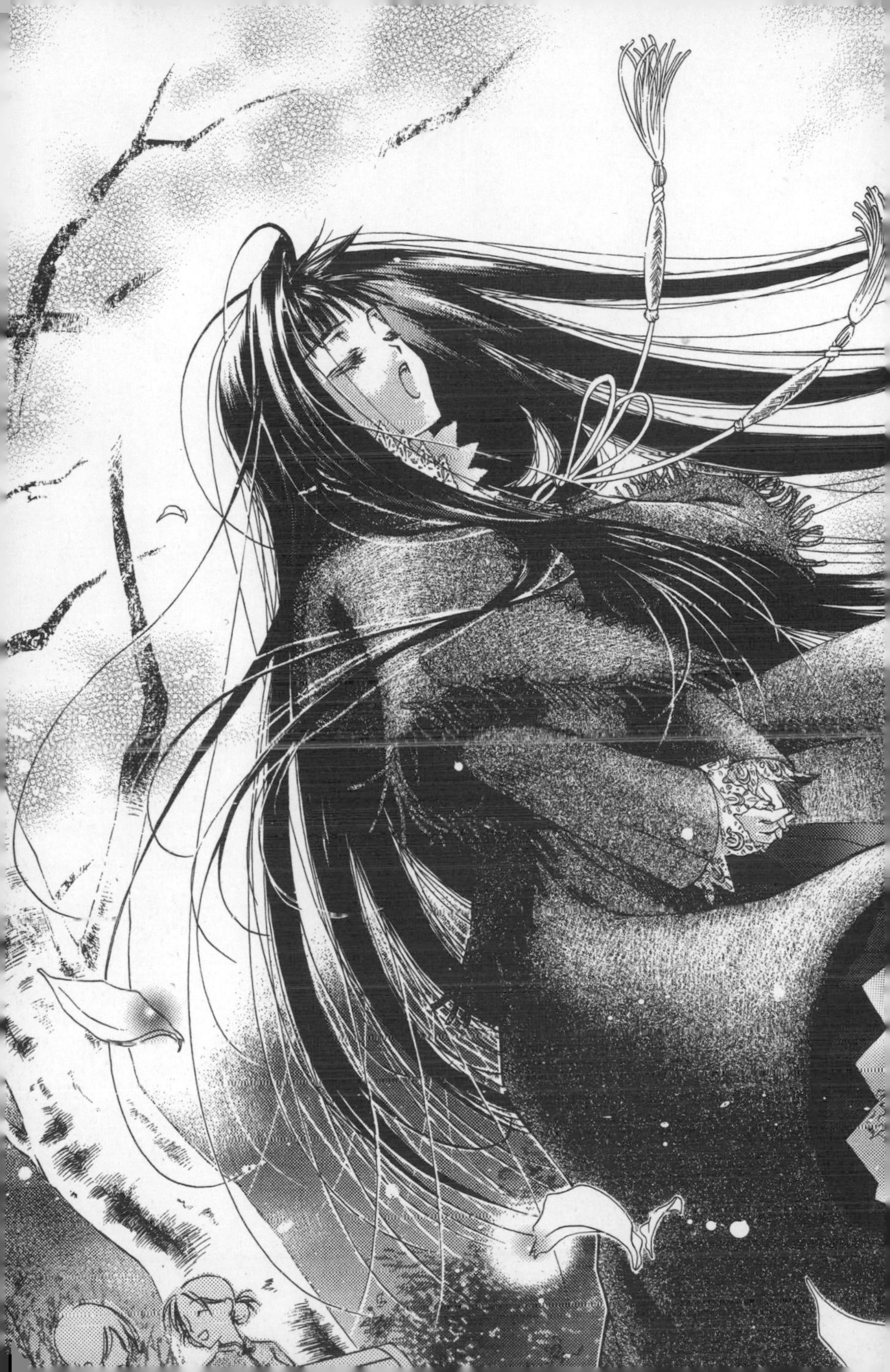

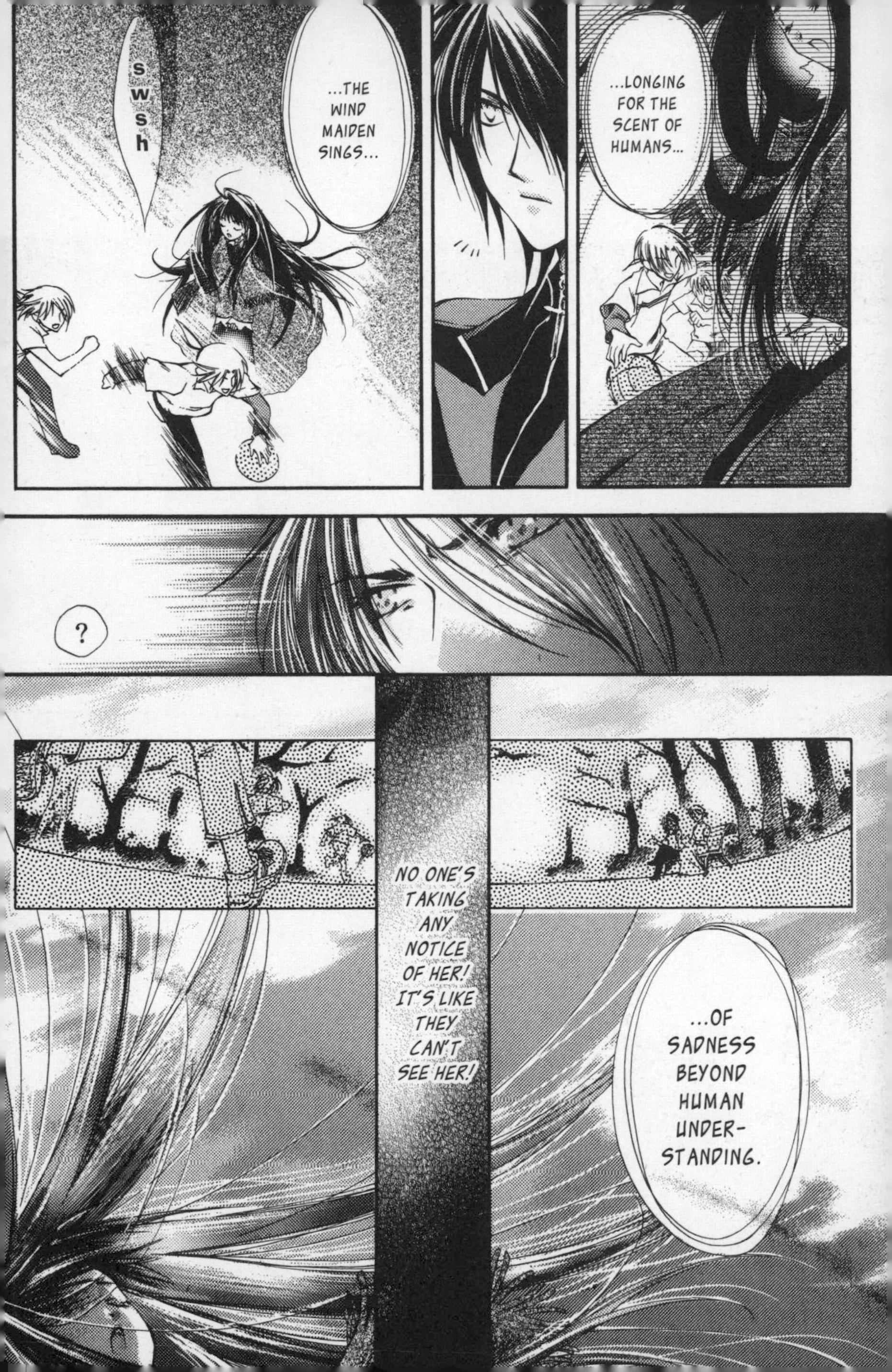
...LONGING FOR THE SCENT OF HUMANS...
...THE WIND MAIDEN SINGS...
swsh
?
NO ONE'S TAKING ANY NOTICE OF HER! IT'S LIKE THEY CAN'T SEE HER!
...OF SADNESS BEYOND HUMAN UNDER-STANDING.

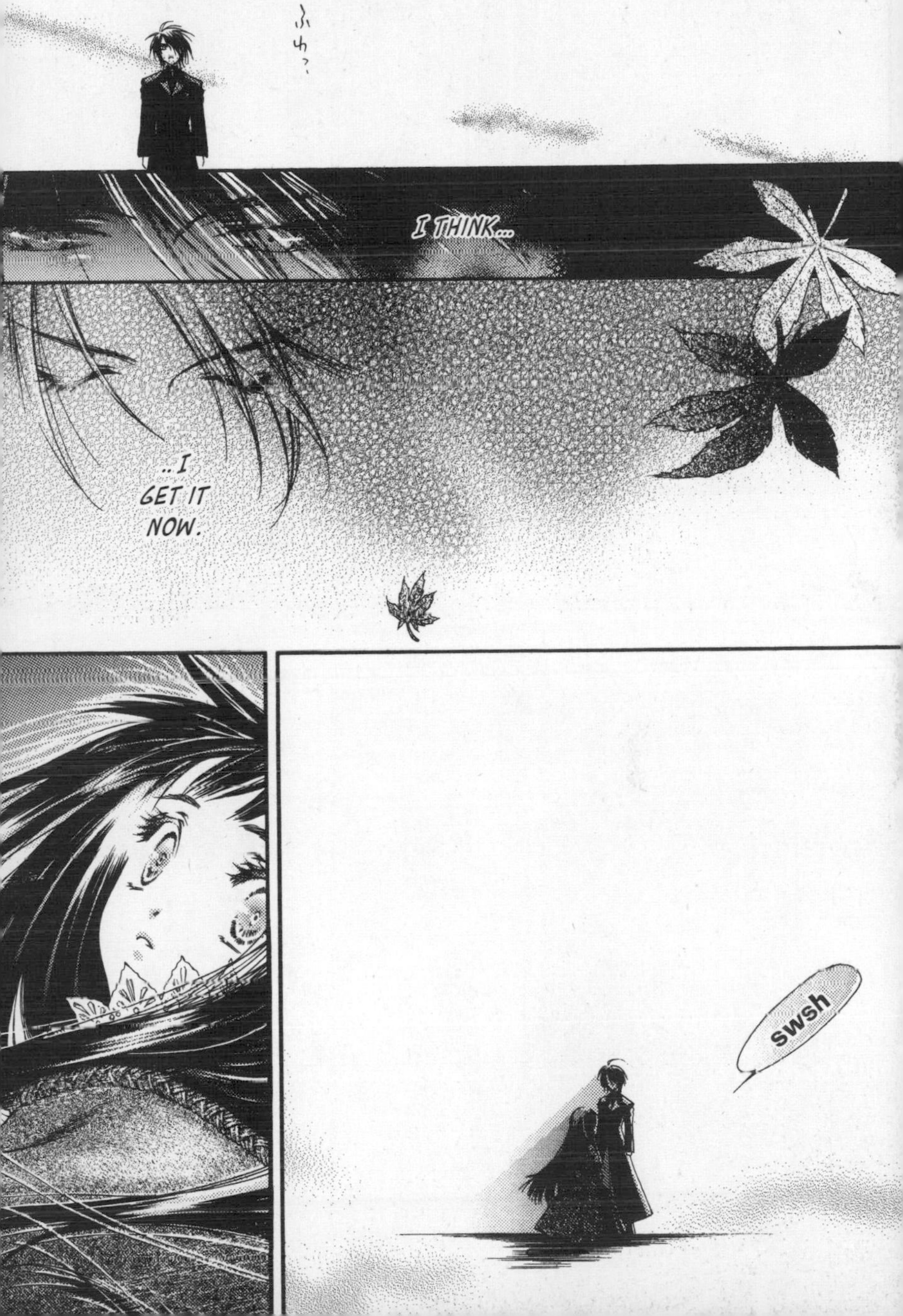
ふわっ
I THINK...
..I GET IT NOW.
swsh

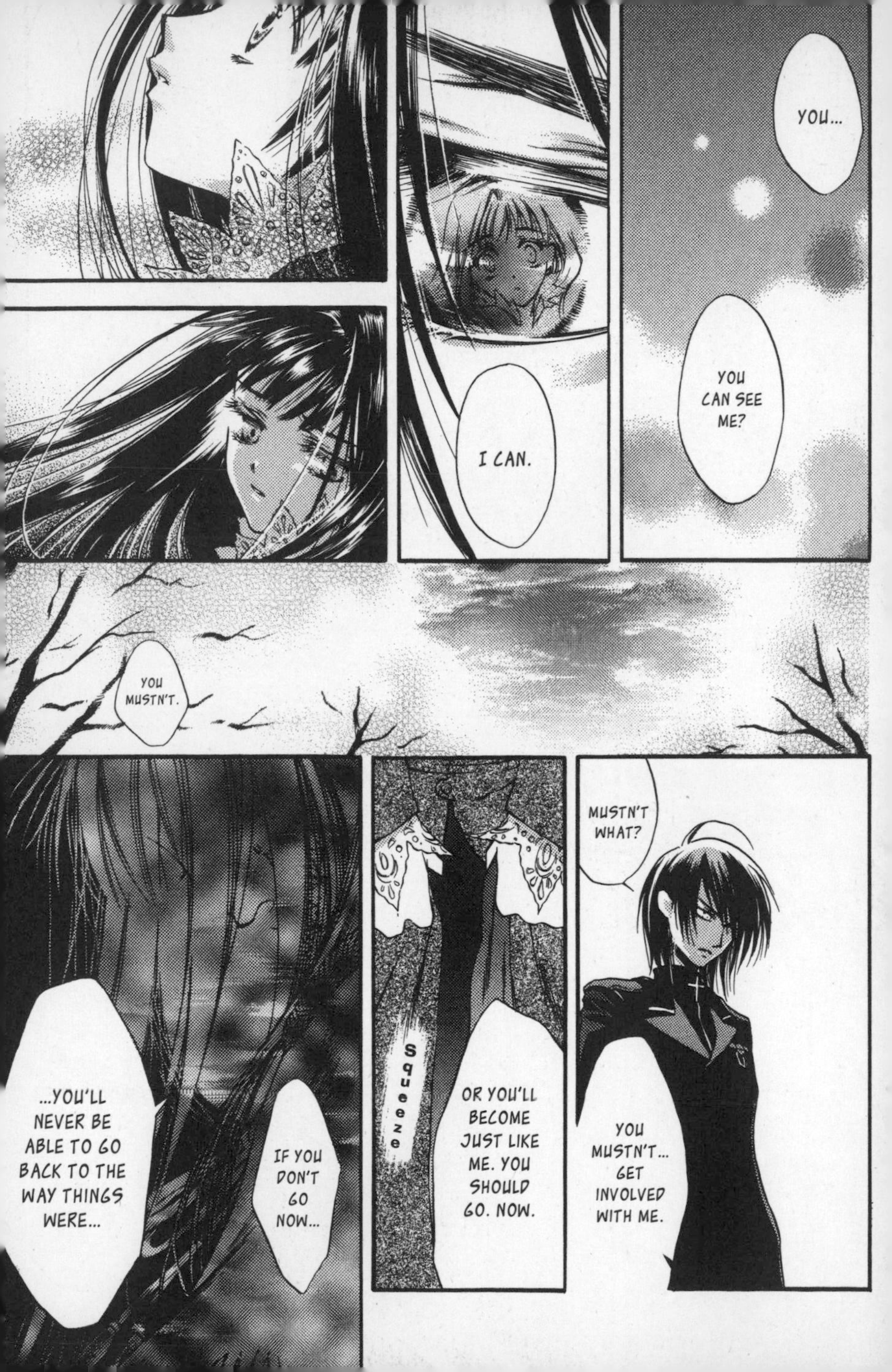
YOU...
YOU CAN SEE ME?
I CAN.
YOU MUSTN'T.
MUSTN'T WHAT?
YOU MUSTN'T... GET INVOLVED WITH ME.
Squeeze
OR YOU'LL BECOME JUST LIKE ME. YOU SHOULD GO. NOW.
IF YOU DON'T GO NOW...
...YOU'LL NEVER BE ABLE TO GO BACK TO THE WAY THINGS WERE...

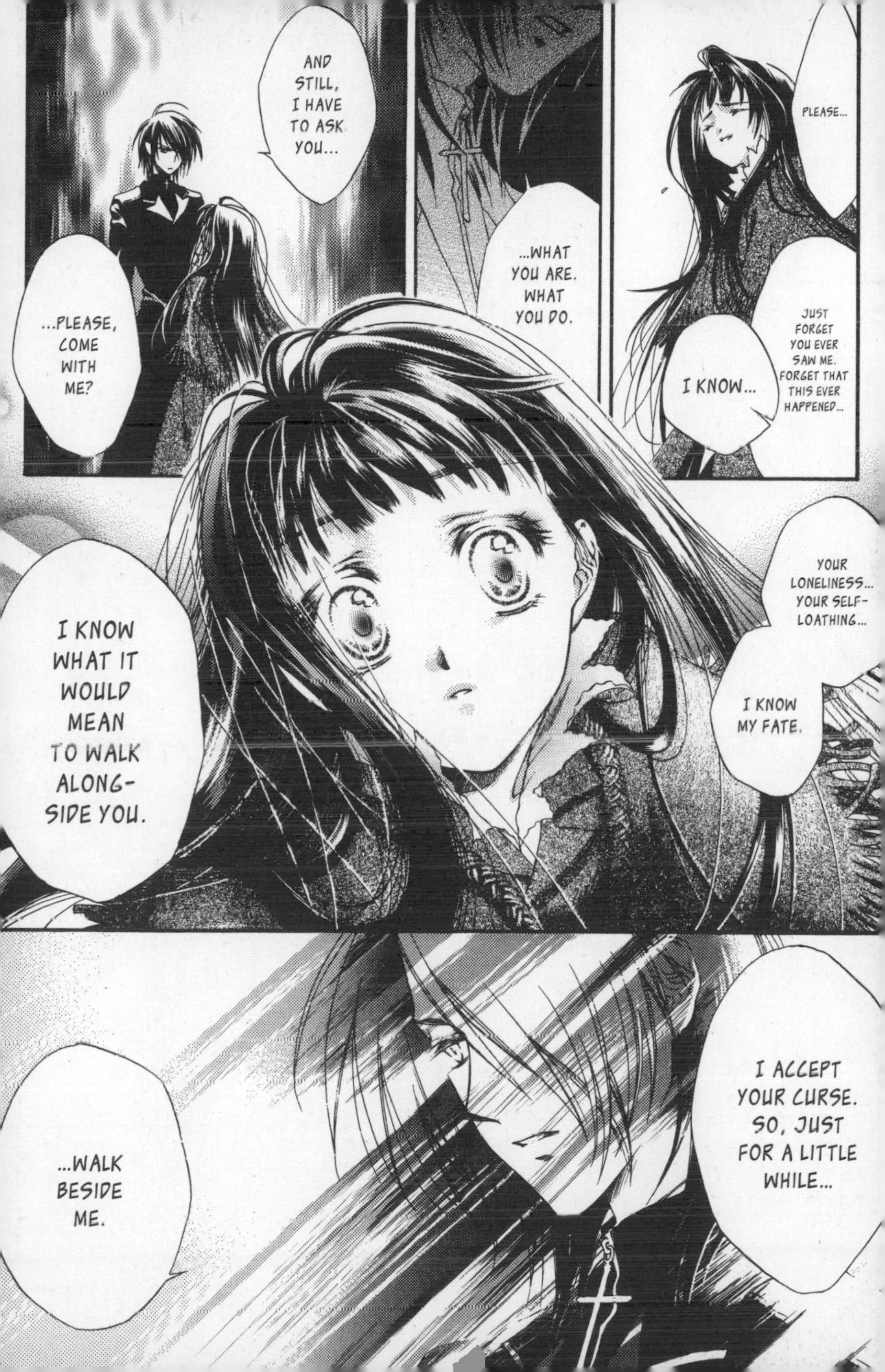
PLEASE...
JUST FORGET YOU EVER SAW ME. FORGET THAT THIS EVER HAPPENED...
I KNOW...
...WHAT YOU ARE. WHAT YOU DO.
AND STILL, I HAVE TO ASK YOU...
...PLEASE, COME WITH ME?
YOUR LONELINESS... YOUR SELF-LOATHING...
I KNOW MY FATE.
I KNOW WHAT IT WOULD MEAN TO WALK ALONG-SIDE YOU.
I ACCEPT YOUR CURSE. SO, JUST FOR A LITTLE WHILE...
...WALK BESIDE ME.

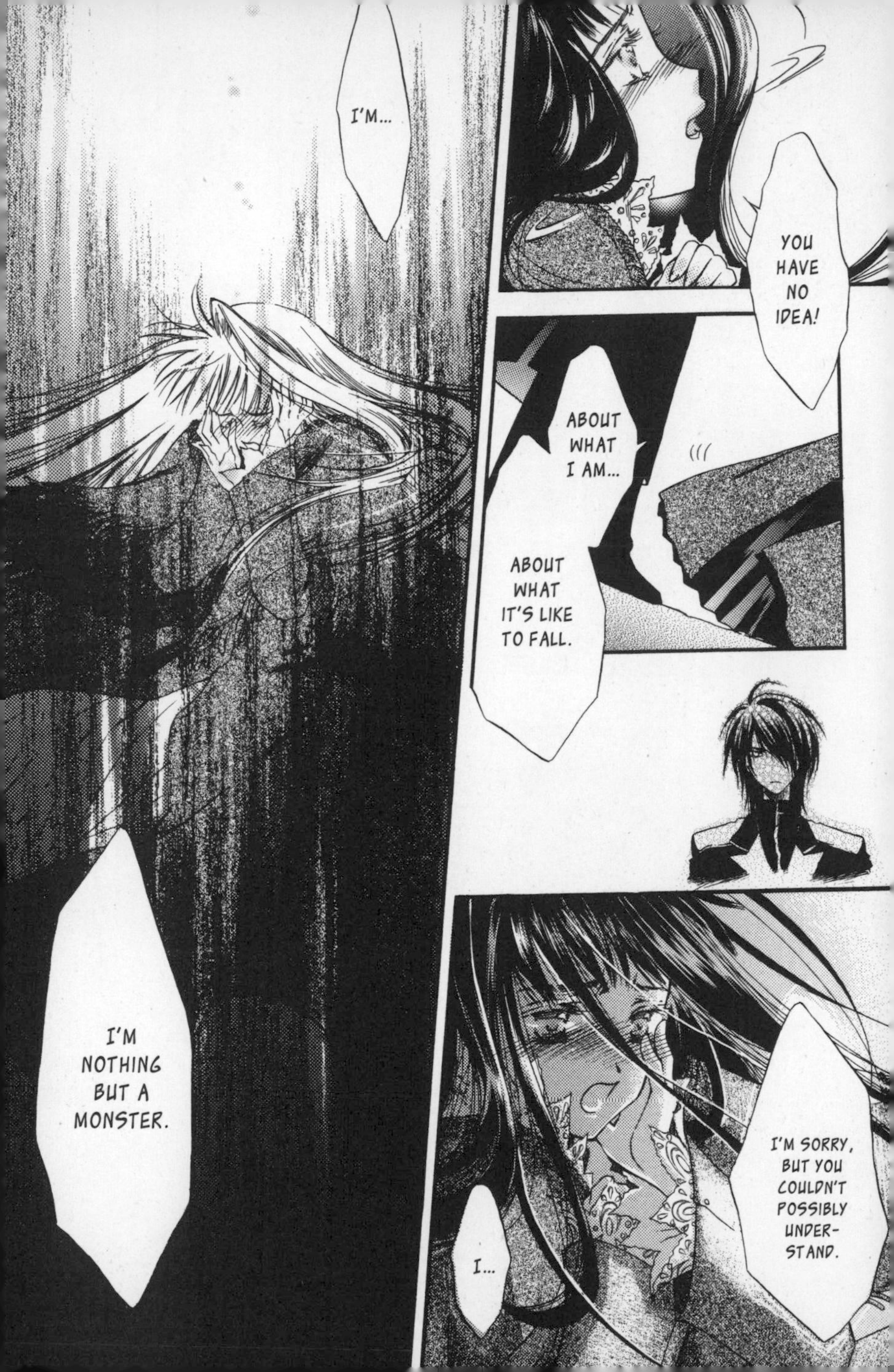
YOU HAVE NO IDEA!
ABOUT WHAT I AM...
ABOUT WHAT IT'S LIKE TO FALL.
I'M SORRY, BUT YOU COULDN'T POSSIBLY UNDER-STAND.
I...
I'M...
I'M NOTHING BUT A MONSTER.

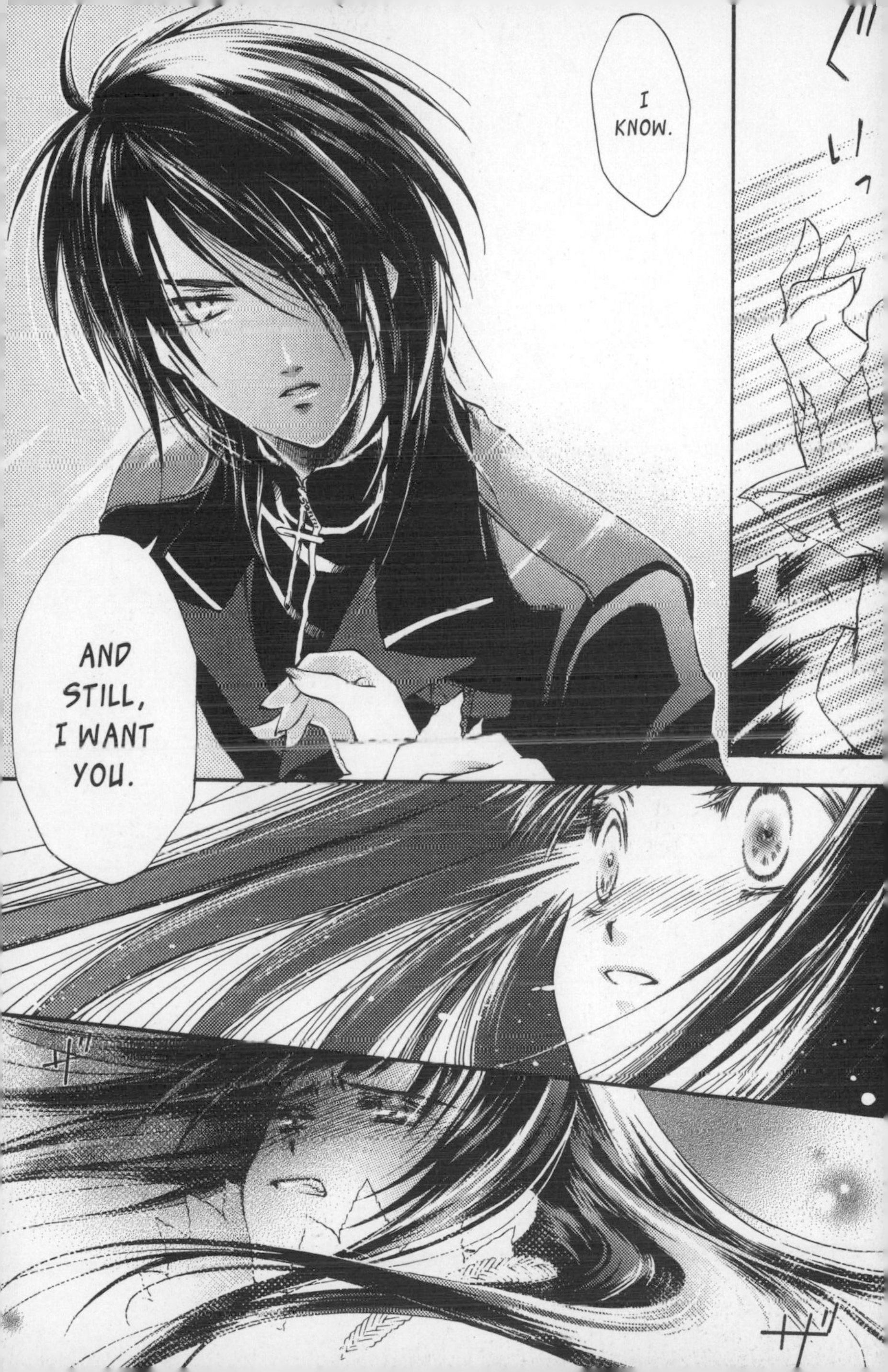
I KNOW.
AND STILL, I WANT YOU.

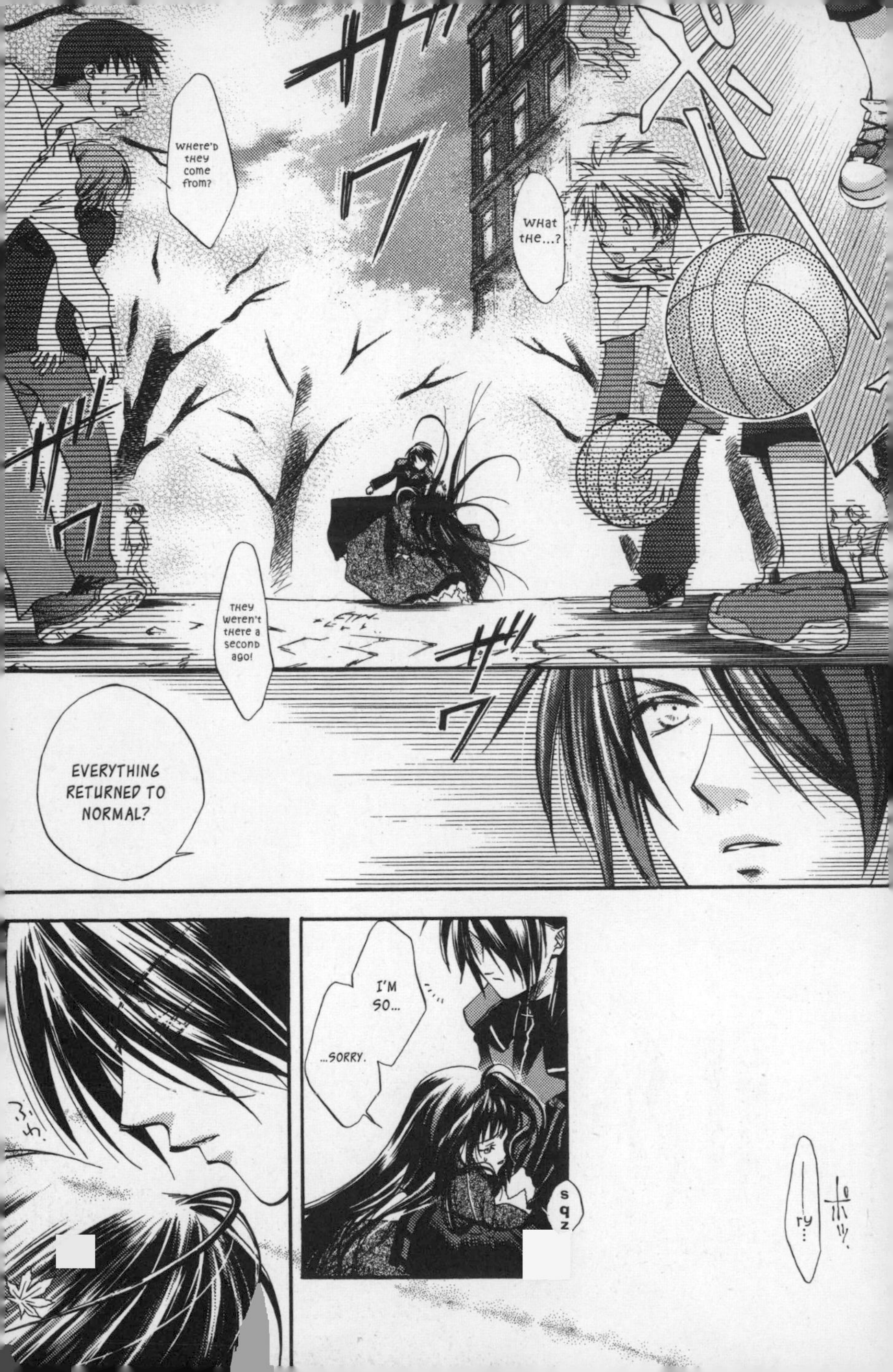

WHAT THE...?
WHERE'D THEY COME FROM?
THEY WEREN'T THERE A SECOND AGO!
EVERYTHING RETURNED TO NORMAL?
ホッ
...RY...
I'M SO...
...SORRY.
S Q Z
ふわ

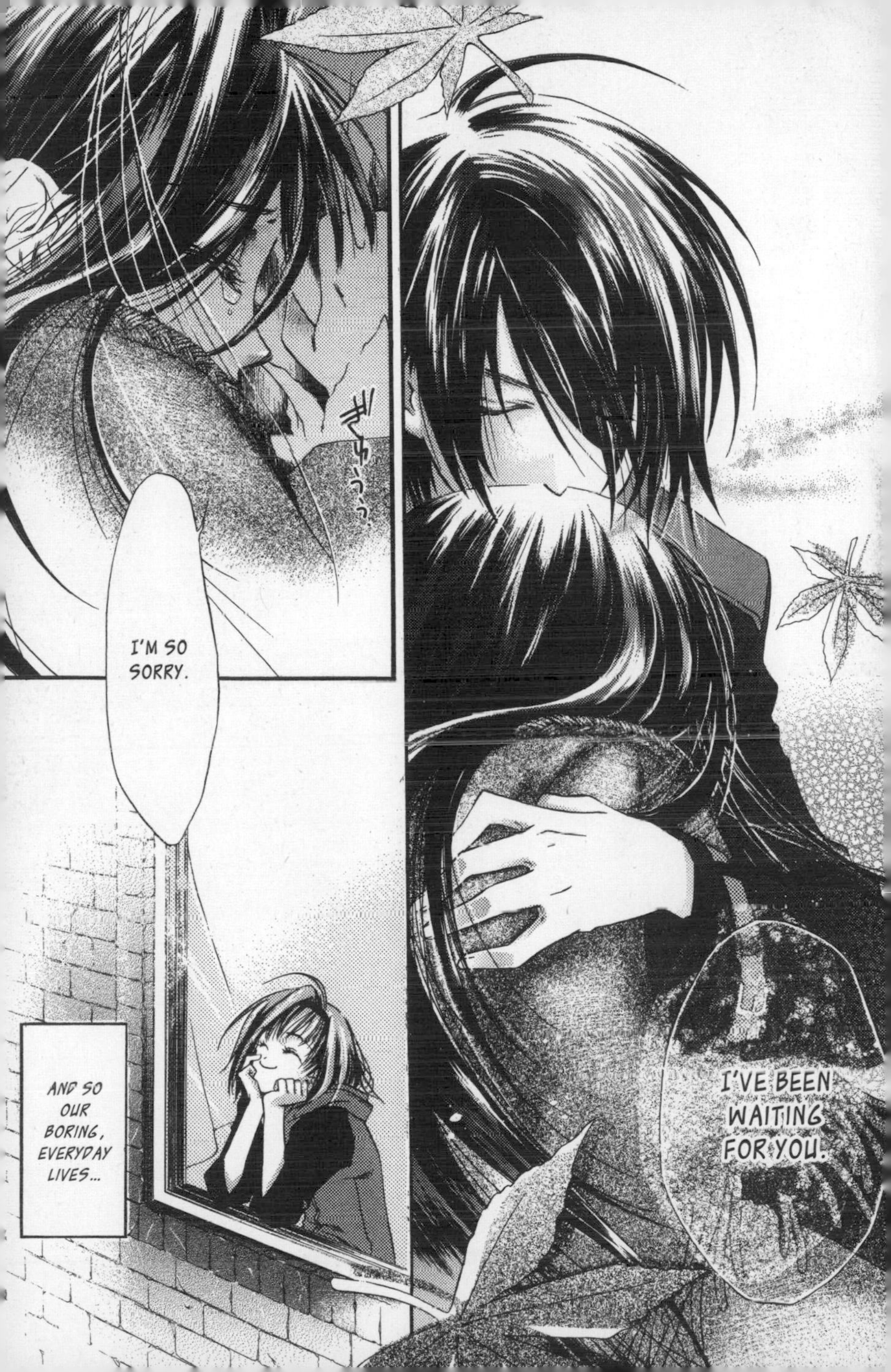
I'VE BEEN WAITING FOR YOU.
I'M SO SORRY.
AND SO OUR BORING, EVERYDAY LIVES...

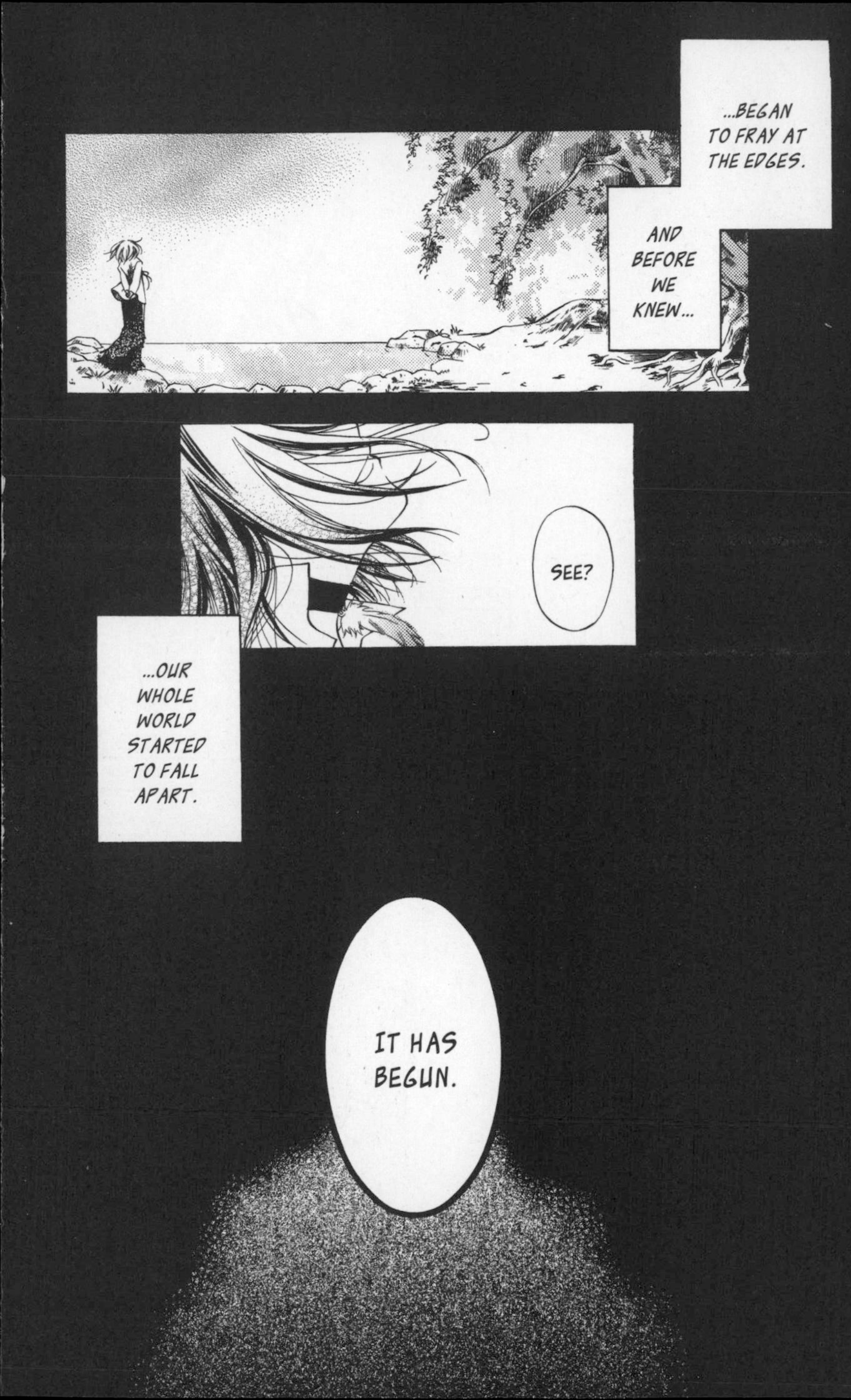
...BEGAN TO FRAY AT THE EDGES.
AND BEFORE WE KNEW...
SEE?
...OUR WHOLE WORLD STARTED TO FALL APART.
IT HAS BEGUN.

Chapter 2
His Majesty, The Prince of Darkness

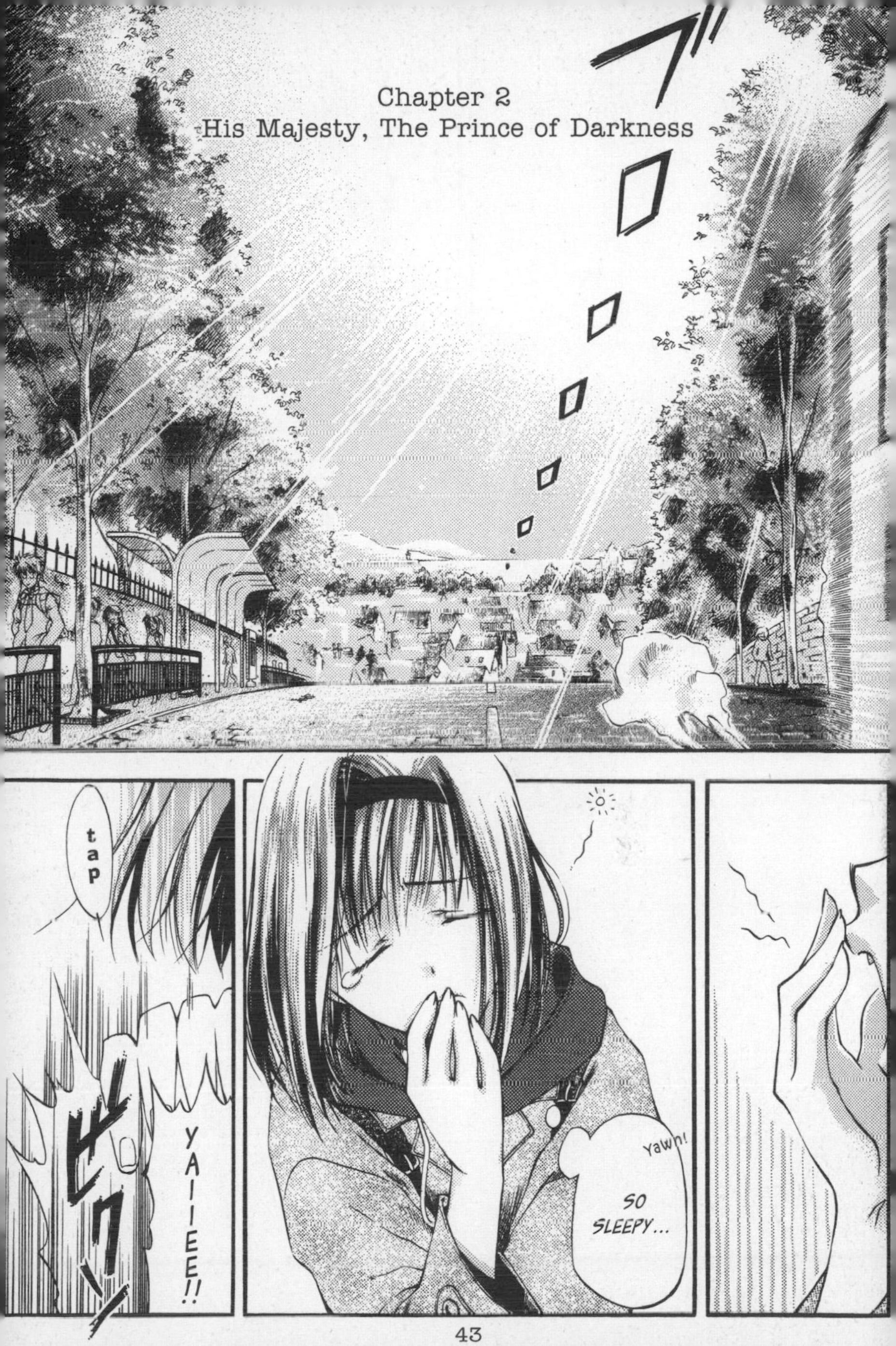
Yawn!
SO SLEEPY...
tap
YAIIEE!!

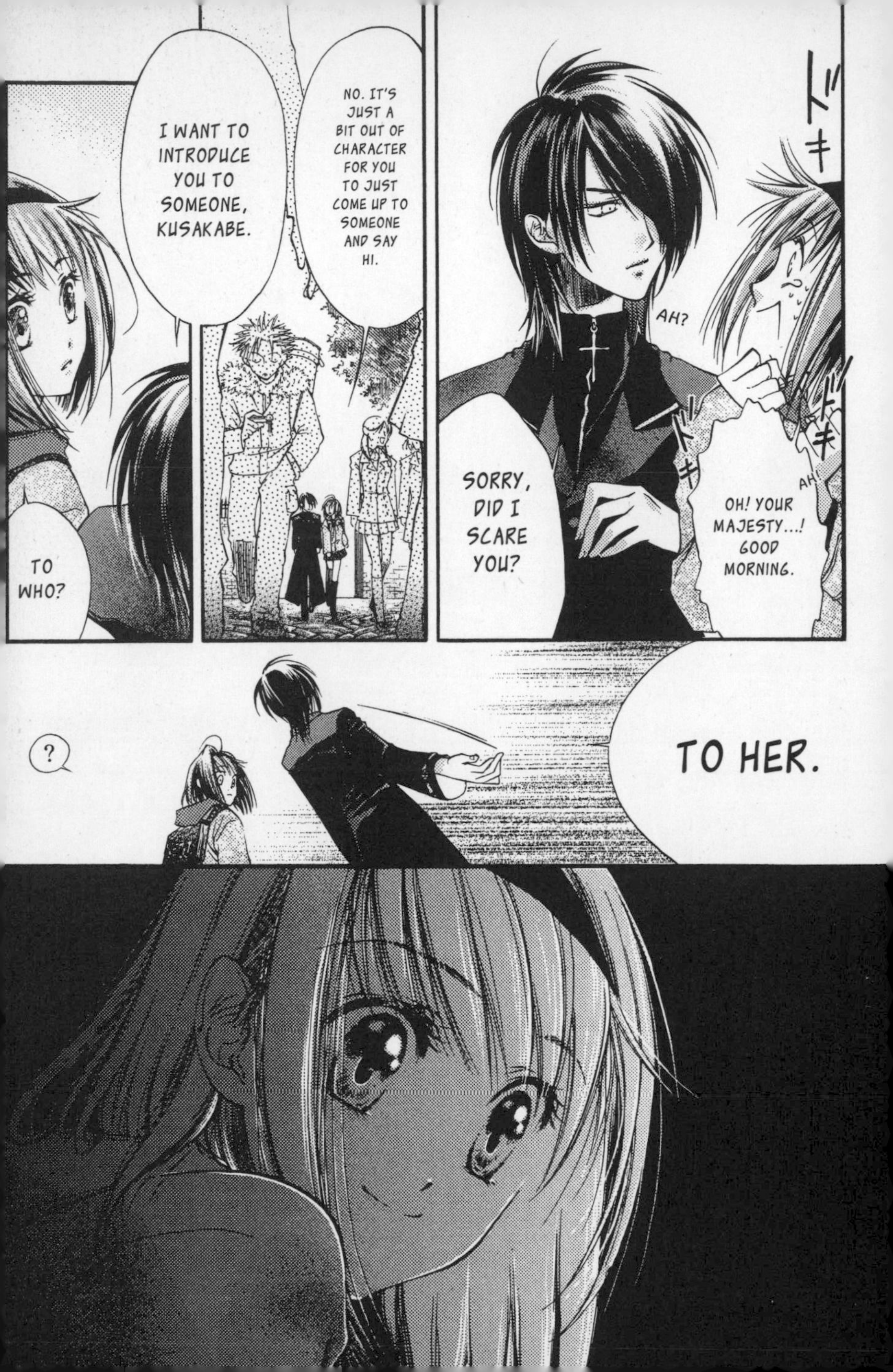
ドキ
AH?
ドキ
ドキ
AH
OH! YOUR MAJESTY...! GOOD MORNING.
SORRY, DID I SCARE YOU?
NO. IT'S JUST A BIT OUT OF CHARACTER FOR YOU TO JUST COME UP TO SOMEONE AND SAY HI.
I WANT TO INTRODUCE YOU TO SOMEONE, KUSAKABE.
TO WHO?
TO HER.
?

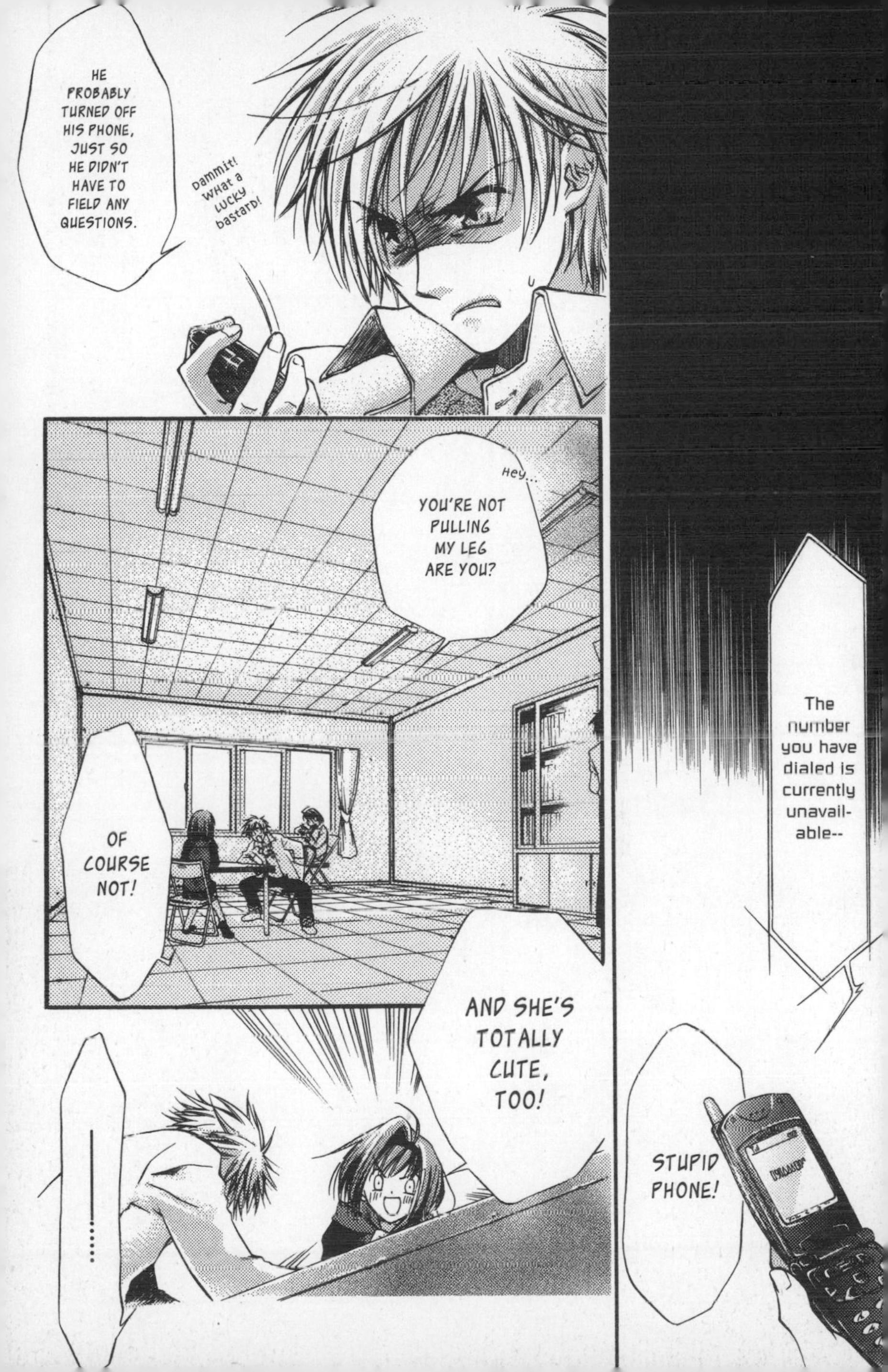
The number you have dialed is currently unavail-able--
STUPID PHONE!
HE PROBABLY TURNED OFF HIS PHONE, JUST SO HE DIDN'T HAVE TO FIELD ANY QUESTIONS.
Dammit! What a lucky bastard!
Hey...
YOU'RE NOT PULLING MY LEG ARE YOU?
OF COURSE NOT!
AND SHE'S TOTALLY CUTE, TOO!
......

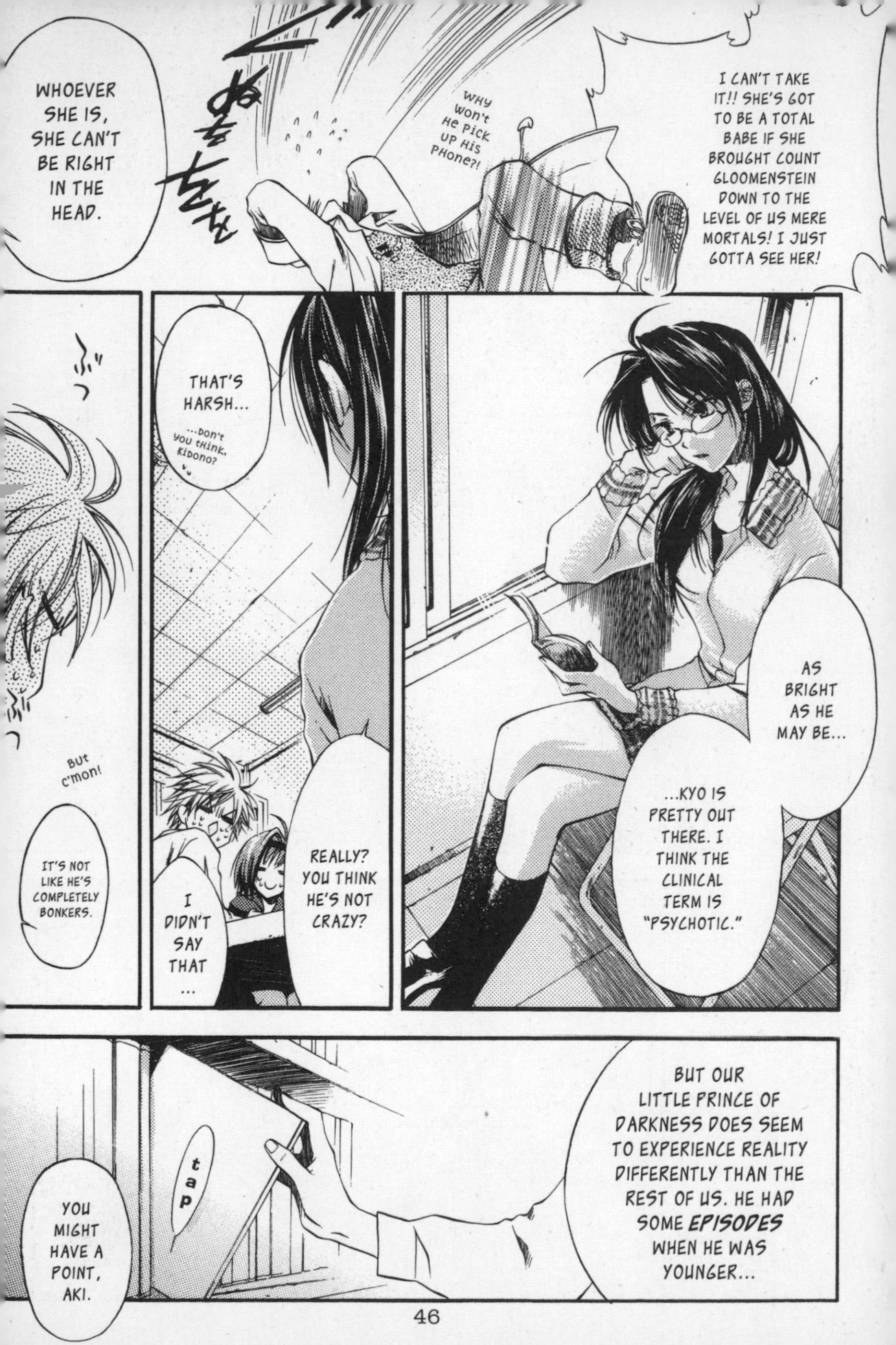
I CAN'T TAKE IT!! SHE'S GOT TO BE A TOTAL BABE IF SHE BROUGHT COUNT GLOOMENSTEIN DOWN TO THE LEVEL OF US MERE MORTALS! I JUST GOTTA SEE HER!
Why won't he pick up his phone?!
WHOEVER SHE IS, SHE CAN'T BE RIGHT IN THE HEAD.
AS BRIGHT AS HE MAY BE...
...KYO IS PRETTY OUT THERE. I THINK THE CLINICAL TERM IS "PSYCHOTIC."
THAT'S HARSH...
...don't you think, Kidono?
REALLY? YOU THINK HE'S NOT CRAZY?
I DIDN'T SAY THAT ...
But c'mon!
IT'S NOT LIKE HE'S COMPLETELY BONKERS.
BUT OUR LITTLE PRINCE OF DARKNESS DOES SEEM TO EXPERIENCE REALITY DIFFERENTLY THAN THE REST OF US. HE HAD SOME EPISODES WHEN HE WAS YOUNGER...
tap
YOU MIGHT HAVE A POINT, AKI.

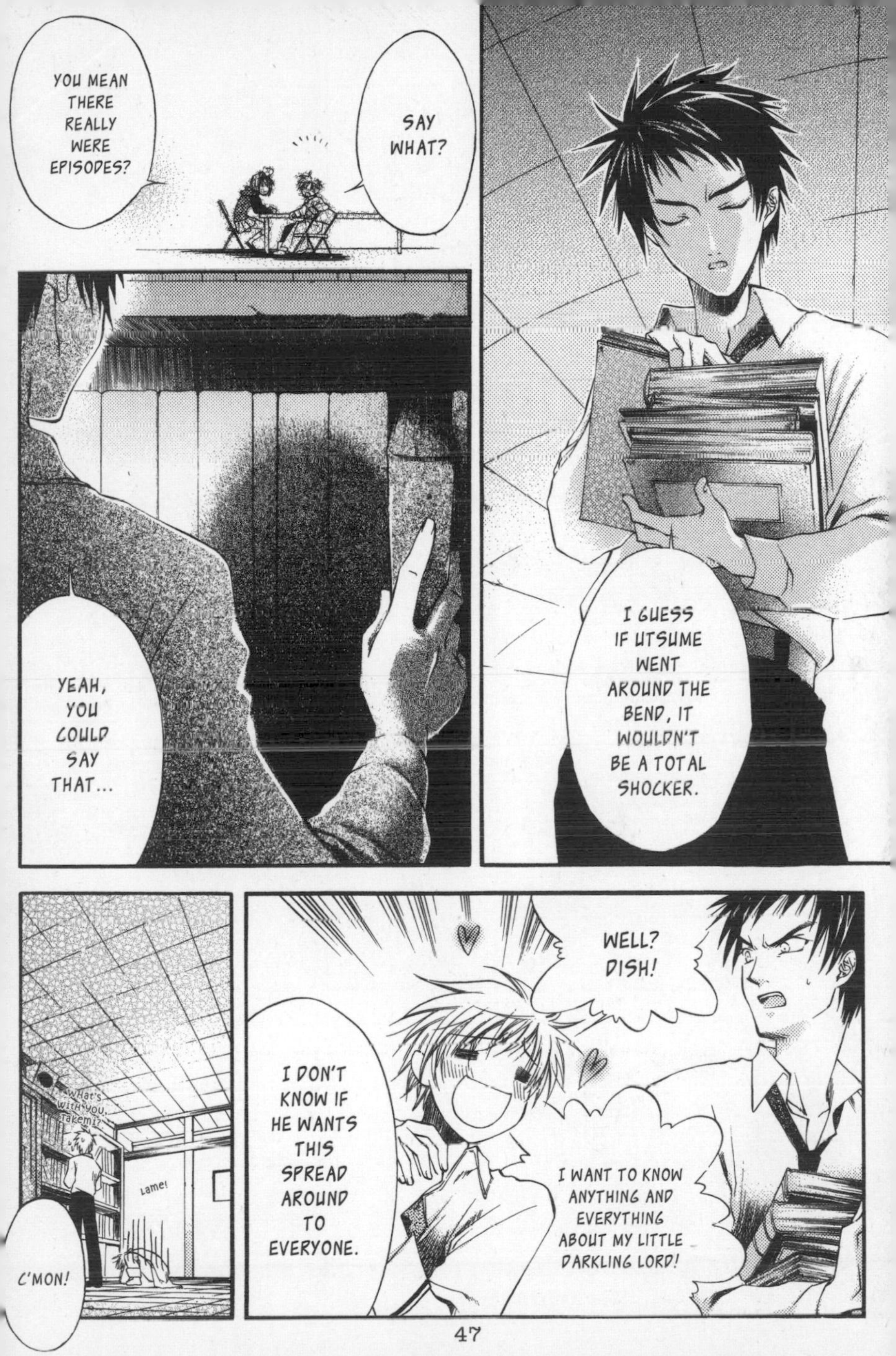
I GUESS IF UTSUME WENT AROUND THE BEND, IT WOULDN'T BE A TOTAL SHOCKER.
SAY WHAT?
YOU MEAN THERE REALLY WERE EPISODES?
YEAH, YOU COULD SAY THAT...
WELL? DISH!
I WANT TO KNOW ANYTHING AND EVERYTHING ABOUT MY LITTLE DARKLING LORD!
I DON'T KNOW IF HE WANTS THIS SPREAD AROUND TO EVERYONE.
What's with you, Takemi?
Lame!
C'MON!

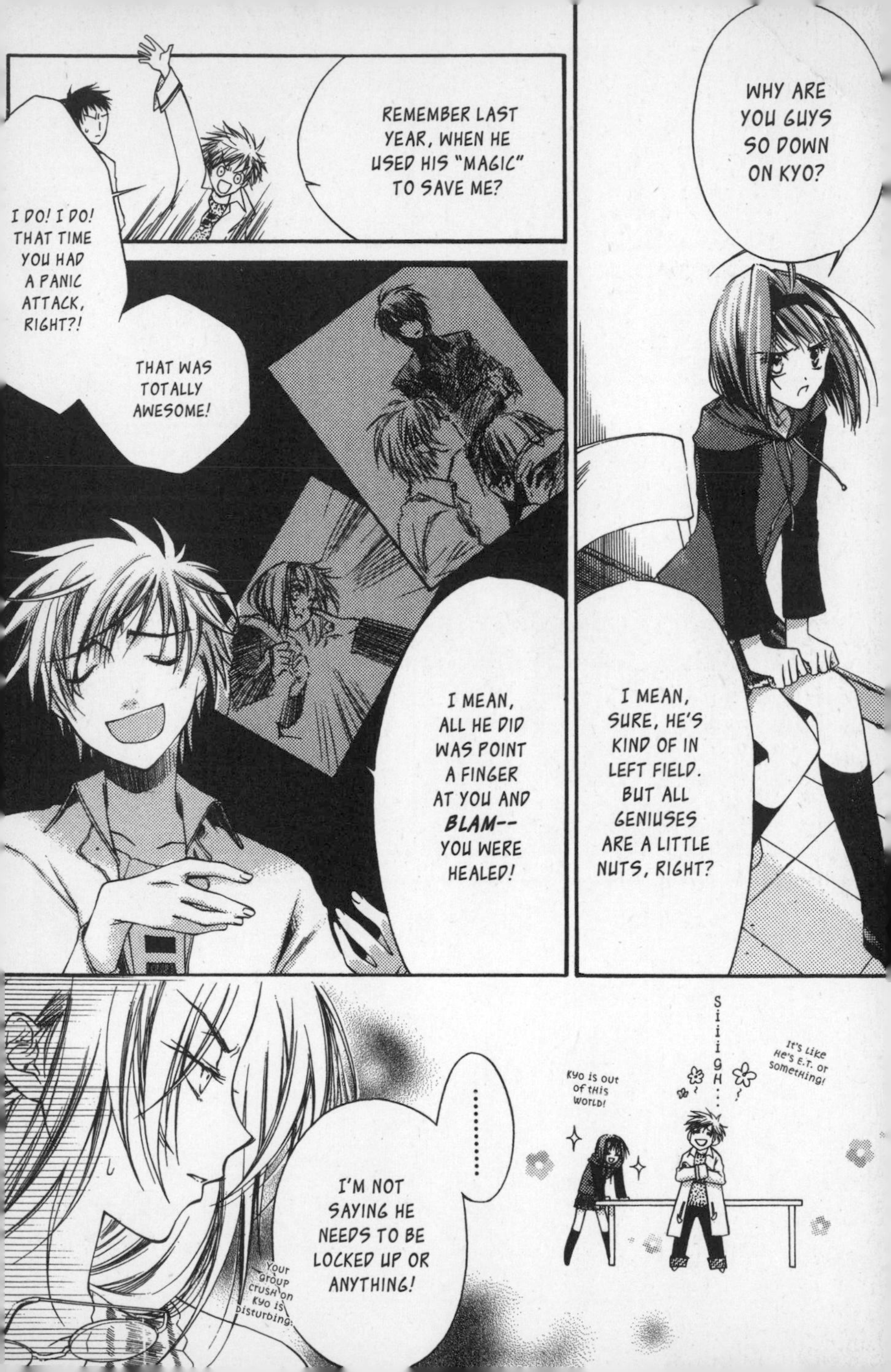
WHY ARE YOU GUYS SO DOWN ON KYO?
I MEAN, SURE, HE'S KIND OF IN LEFT FIELD. BUT ALL GENIUSES ARE A LITTLE NUTS, RIGHT?
REMEMBER LAST YEAR, WHEN HE USED HIS "MAGIC" TO SAVE ME?
I DO! I DO! THAT TIME YOU HAD A PANIC ATTACK, RIGHT?!
THAT WAS TOTALLY AWESOME!
I MEAN, ALL HE DID WAS POINT A FINGER AT YOU AND *BLAM*-- YOU WERE HEALED!
SIIIGH...
It's like he's E.T. or something!
Kyo is out of this world!
......
I'M NOT SAYING HE NEEDS TO BE LOCKED UP OR ANYTHING!
Your group crush on Kyo is disturbing.

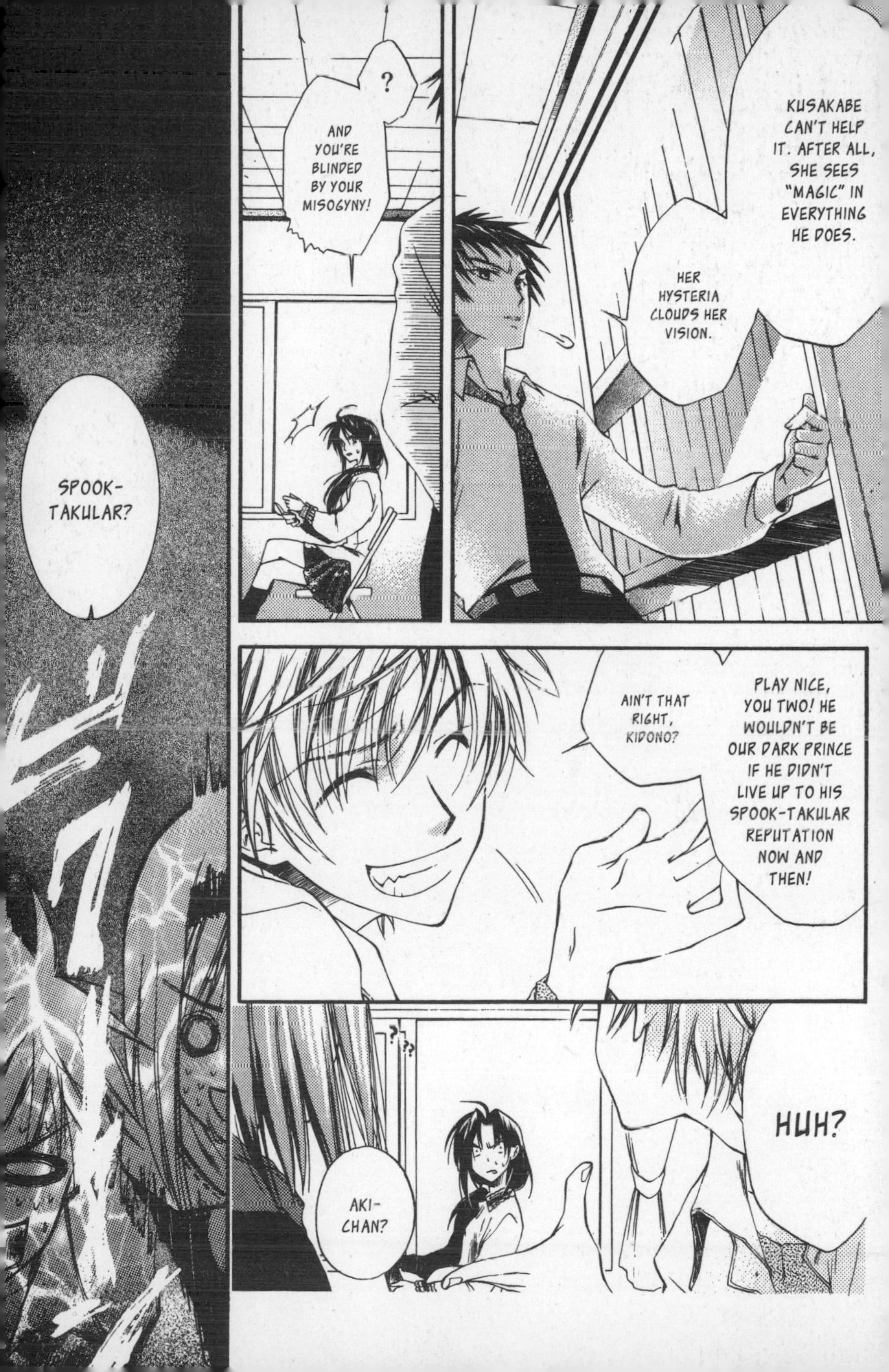
KUSAKABE CAN'T HELP IT. AFTER ALL, SHE SEES "MAGIC" IN EVERYTHING HE DOES.
HER HYSTERIA CLOUDS HER VISION.
?
AND YOU'RE BLINDED BY YOUR MISOGYNY!
PLAY NICE, YOU TWO! HE WOULDN'T BE OUR DARK PRINCE IF HE DIDN'T LIVE UP TO HIS SPOOK-TAKULAR REPUTATION NOW AND THEN!
AIN'T THAT RIGHT, KIDONO?
HUH?
???
AKI-CHAN?
SPOOK-TAKULAR?

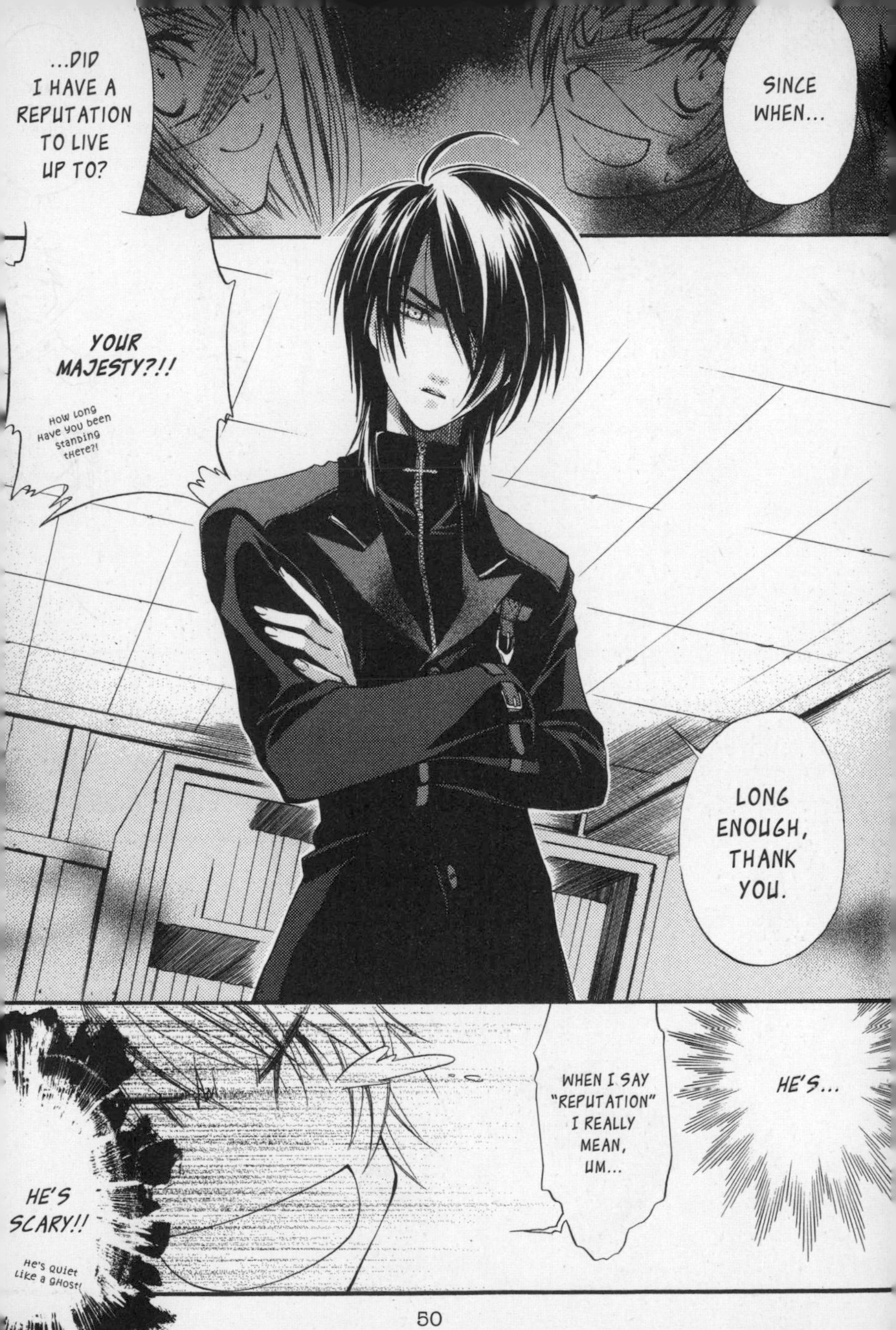
SINCE WHEN...
...DID I HAVE A REPUTATION TO LIVE UP TO?
YOUR MAJESTY?!!
How long have you been standing there?!
LONG ENOUGH, THANK YOU.
HE'S...
WHEN I SAY "REPUTATION" I REALLY MEAN, UM...
HE'S SCARY!!
He's quiet like a ghost!

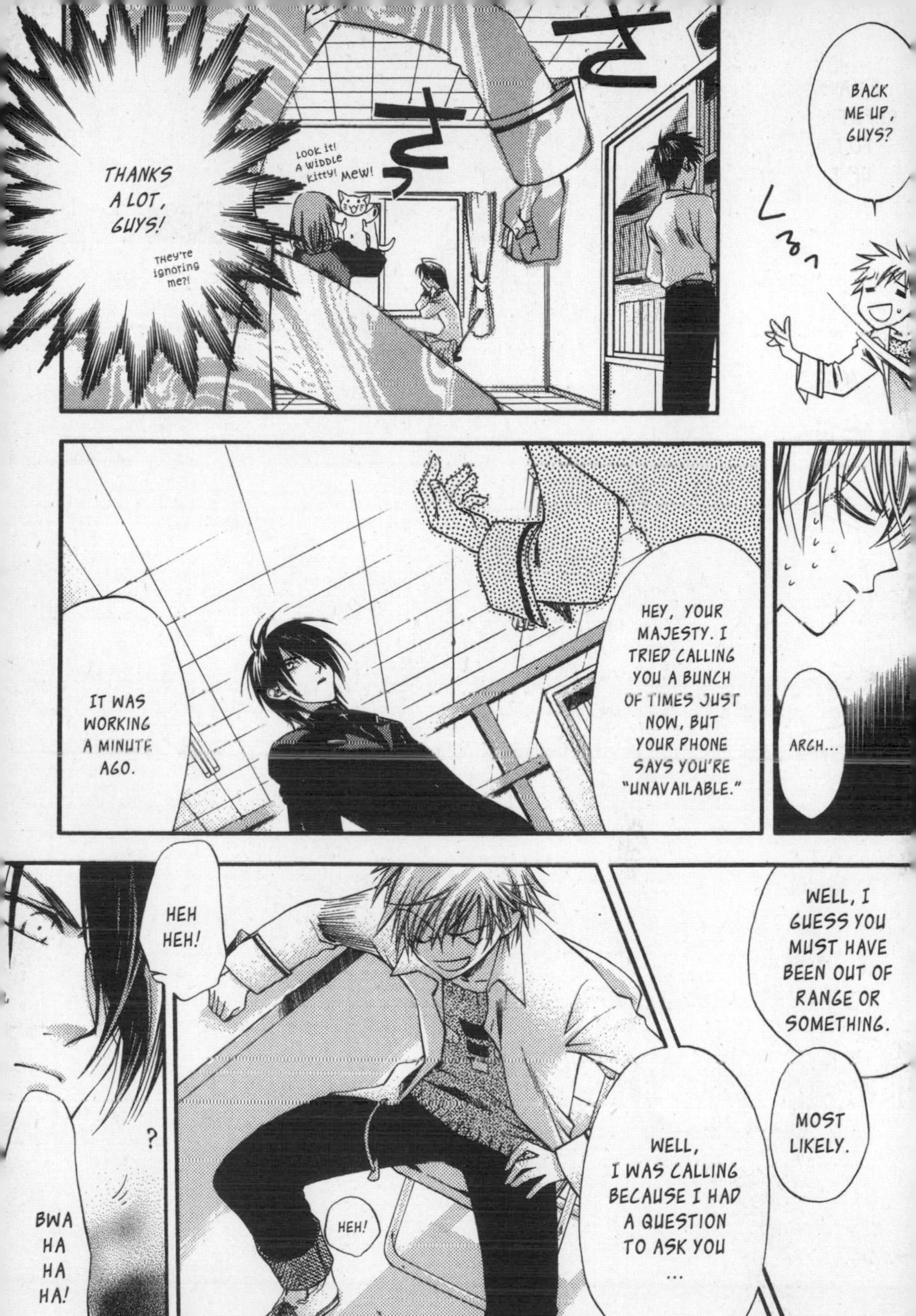
BACK ME UP, GUYS?
LOOK it! A widdle kitty!
MEW!
THANKS A LOT, GUYS!
They're ignoring me?!
ARCH...
HEY, YOUR MAJESTY. I TRIED CALLING YOU A BUNCH OF TIMES JUST NOW, BUT YOUR PHONE SAYS YOU'RE "UNAVAILABLE."
IT WAS WORKING A MINUTE AGO.
WELL, I GUESS YOU MUST HAVE BEEN OUT OF RANGE OR SOMETHING.
MOST LIKELY.
WELL, I WAS CALLING BECAUSE I HAD A QUESTION TO ASK YOU ...
HEH!
HEH HEH!
?
BWA HA HA HA!

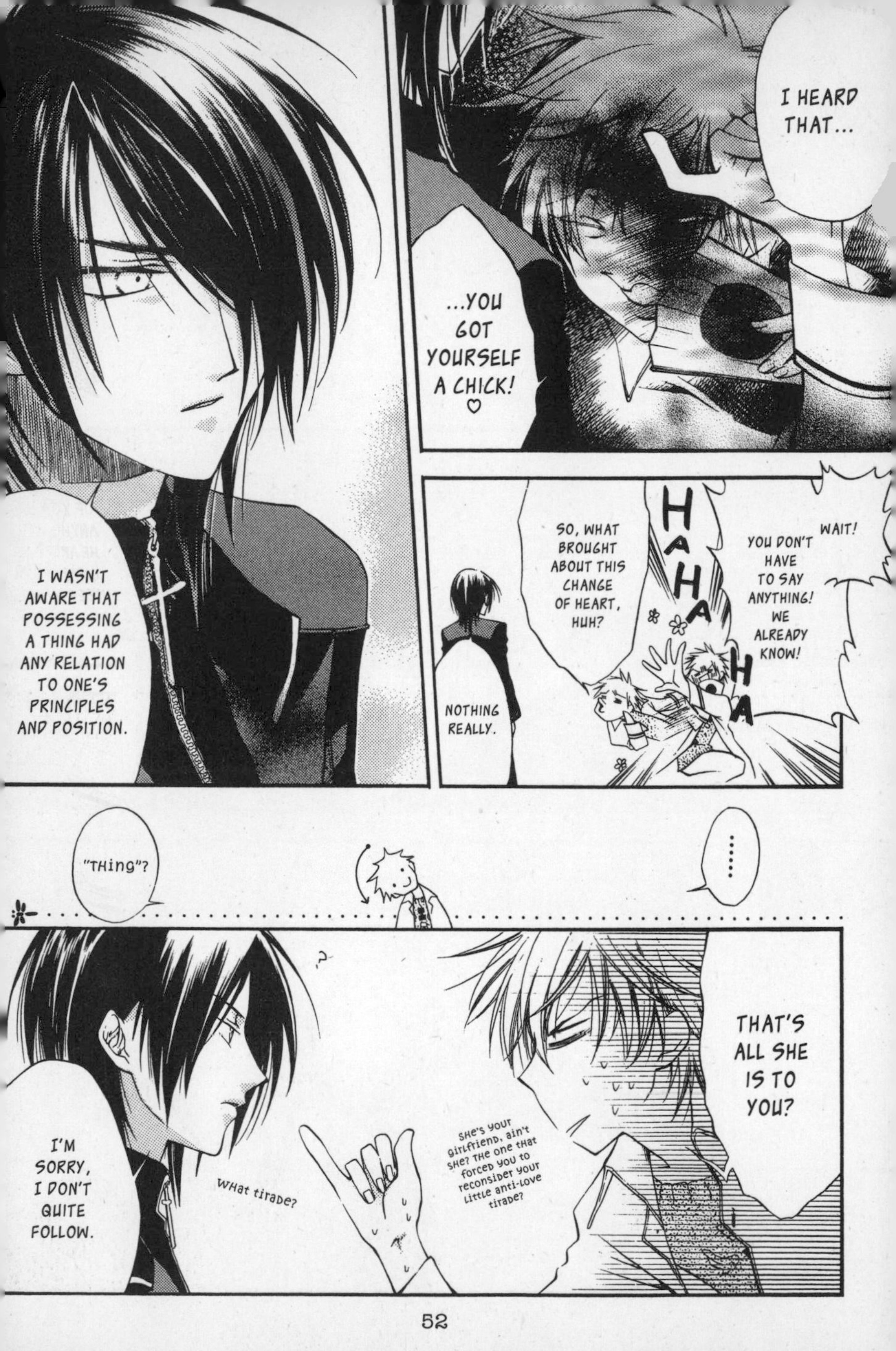
I HEARD THAT...
...YOU GOT YOURSELF A CHICK! ♡
WAIT!
YOU DON'T HAVE TO SAY ANYTHING! WE ALREADY KNOW!
HAHAHAHA
SO, WHAT BROUGHT ABOUT THIS CHANGE OF HEART, HUH?
NOTHING REALLY.
I WASN'T AWARE THAT POSSESSING A THING HAD ANY RELATION TO ONE'S PRINCIPLES AND POSITION.
......
"THING"?
THAT'S ALL SHE IS TO YOU?
SHE'S YOUR GIRLFRIEND, AIN'T SHE? THE ONE THAT FORCED YOU TO RECONSIDER YOUR LITTLE ANTI-LOVE TIRADE?
WHAT TIRADE?
I'M SORRY, I DON'T QUITE FOLLOW.

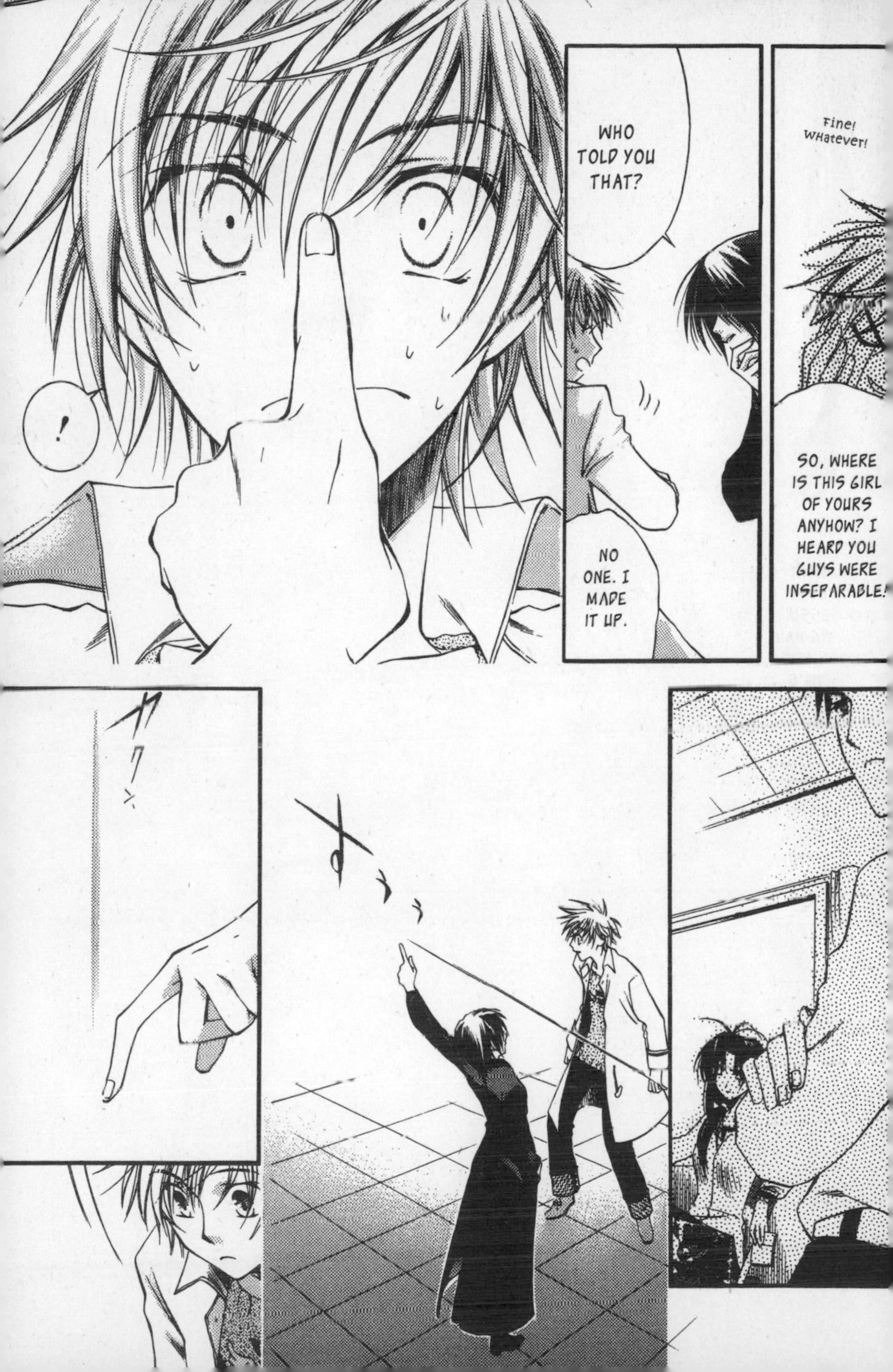
Fine! Whatever!
SO, WHERE IS THIS GIRL OF YOURS ANYHOW? I HEARD YOU GUYS WERE INSEPARABLE!
WHO TOLD YOU THAT?
NO ONE. I MADE IT UP.
!

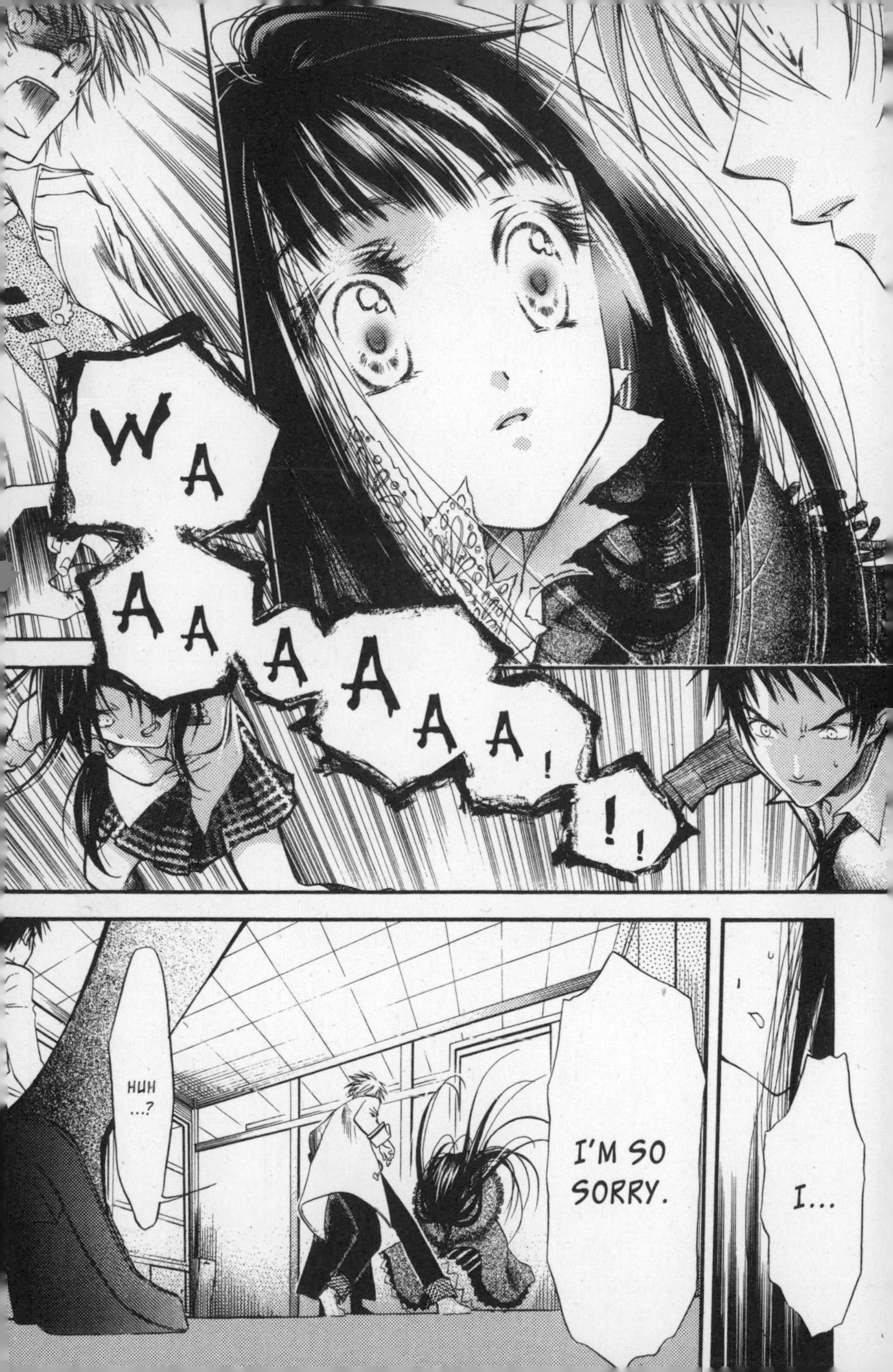
WAAAAAAAA!!!
I...
I'M SO SORRY.
HUH ...?

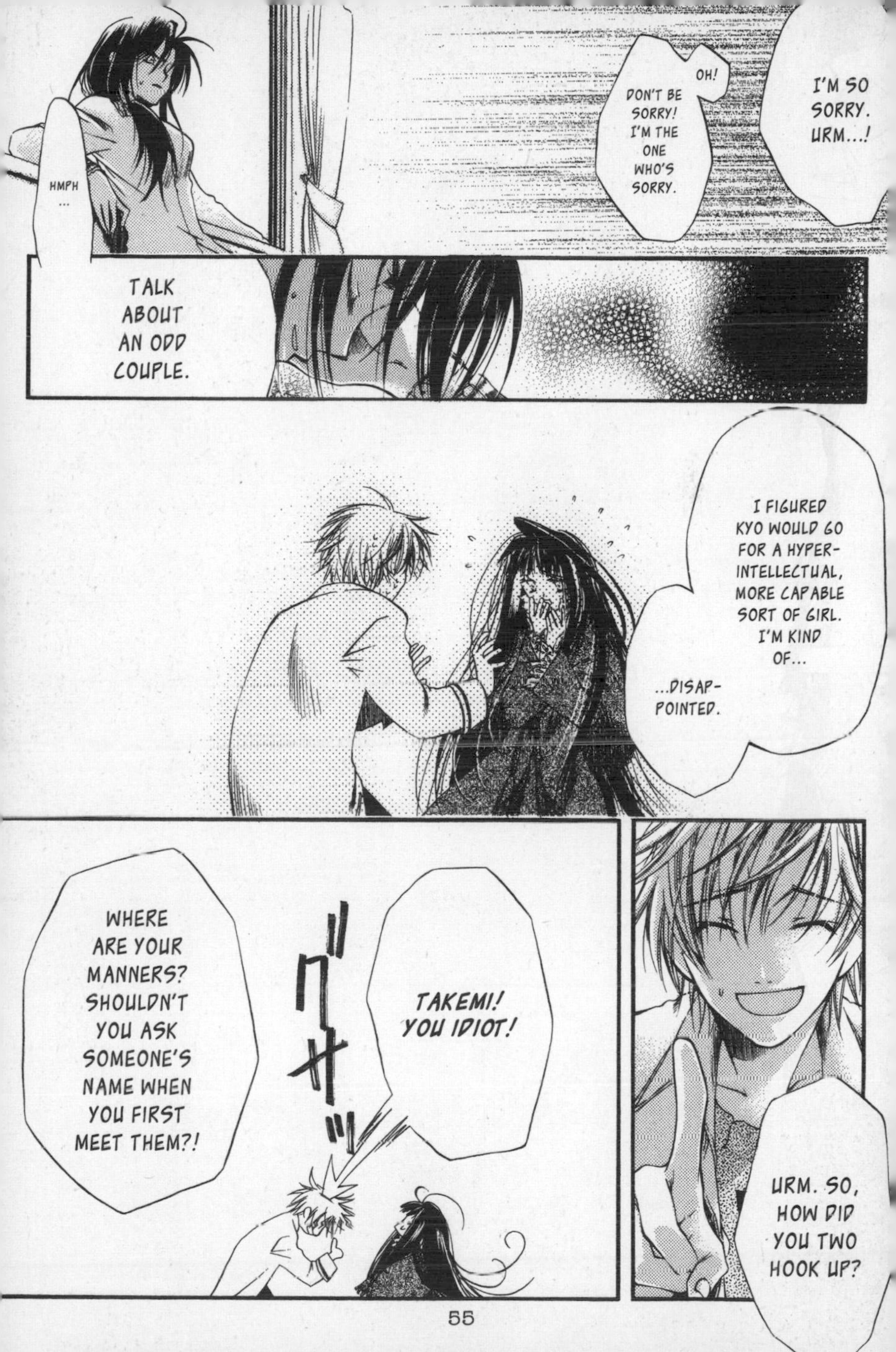
I'M SO SORRY. URM...!
OH!
DON'T BE SORRY! I'M THE ONE WHO'S SORRY.
HMPH ...
TALK ABOUT AN ODD COUPLE.
I FIGURED KYO WOULD GO FOR A HYPER-INTELLECTUAL, MORE CAPABLE SORT OF GIRL. I'M KIND OF...
...DISAP-POINTED.
URM. SO, HOW DID YOU TWO HOOK UP?
TAKEMI! YOU IDIOT!
WHERE ARE YOUR MANNERS? SHOULDN'T YOU ASK SOMEONE'S NAME WHEN YOU FIRST MEET THEM?!

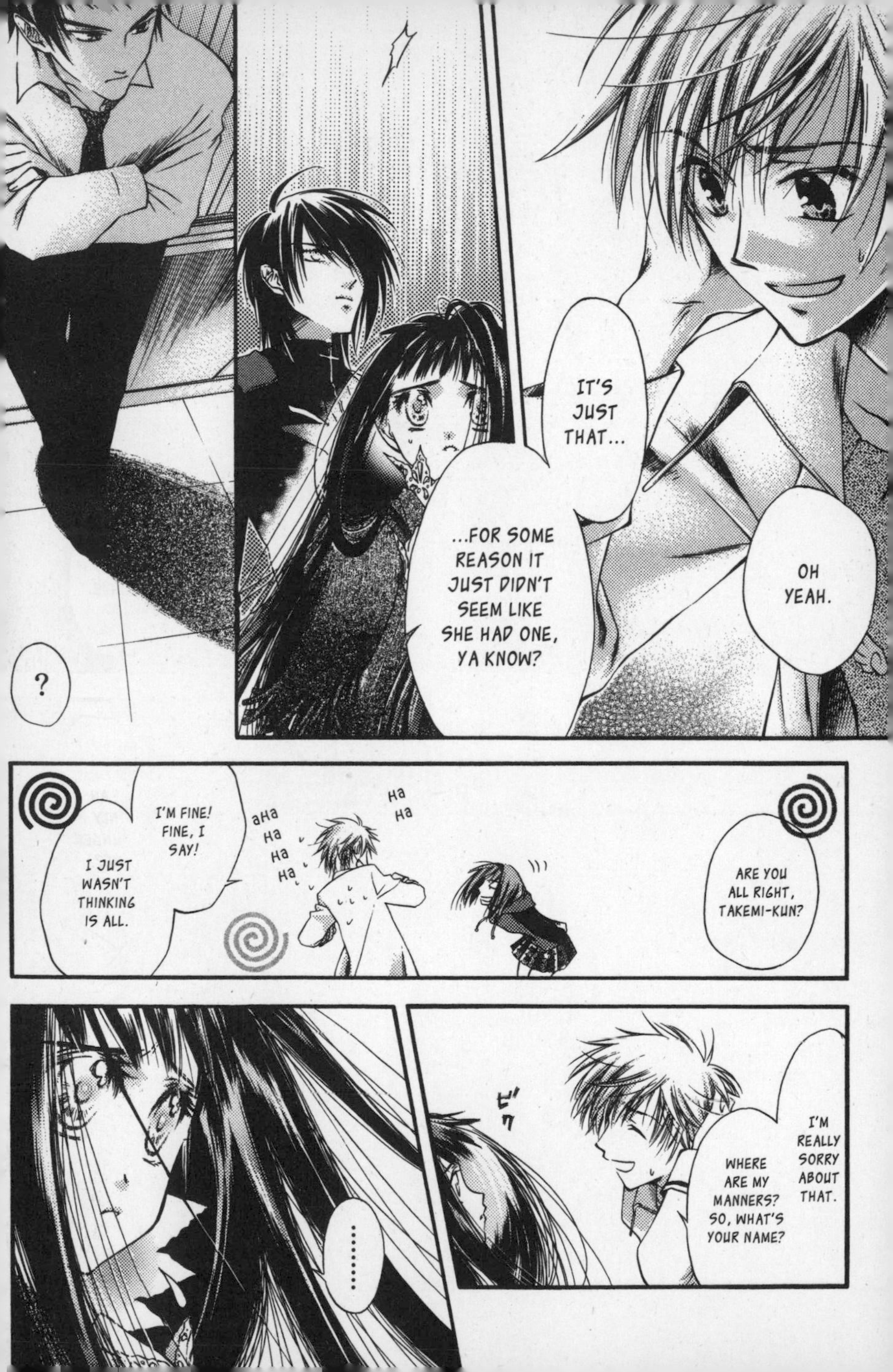
OH YEAH.
IT'S JUST THAT...
...FOR SOME REASON IT JUST DIDN'T SEEM LIKE SHE HAD ONE, YA KNOW?
?
ARE YOU ALL RIGHT, TAKEMI-KUN?
HA HA
AHA HA HA HA
I'M FINE! FINE, I SAY!
I JUST WASN'T THINKING IS ALL.
I'M REALLY SORRY ABOUT THAT.
WHERE ARE MY MANNERS? SO, WHAT'S YOUR NAME?
ビク
......

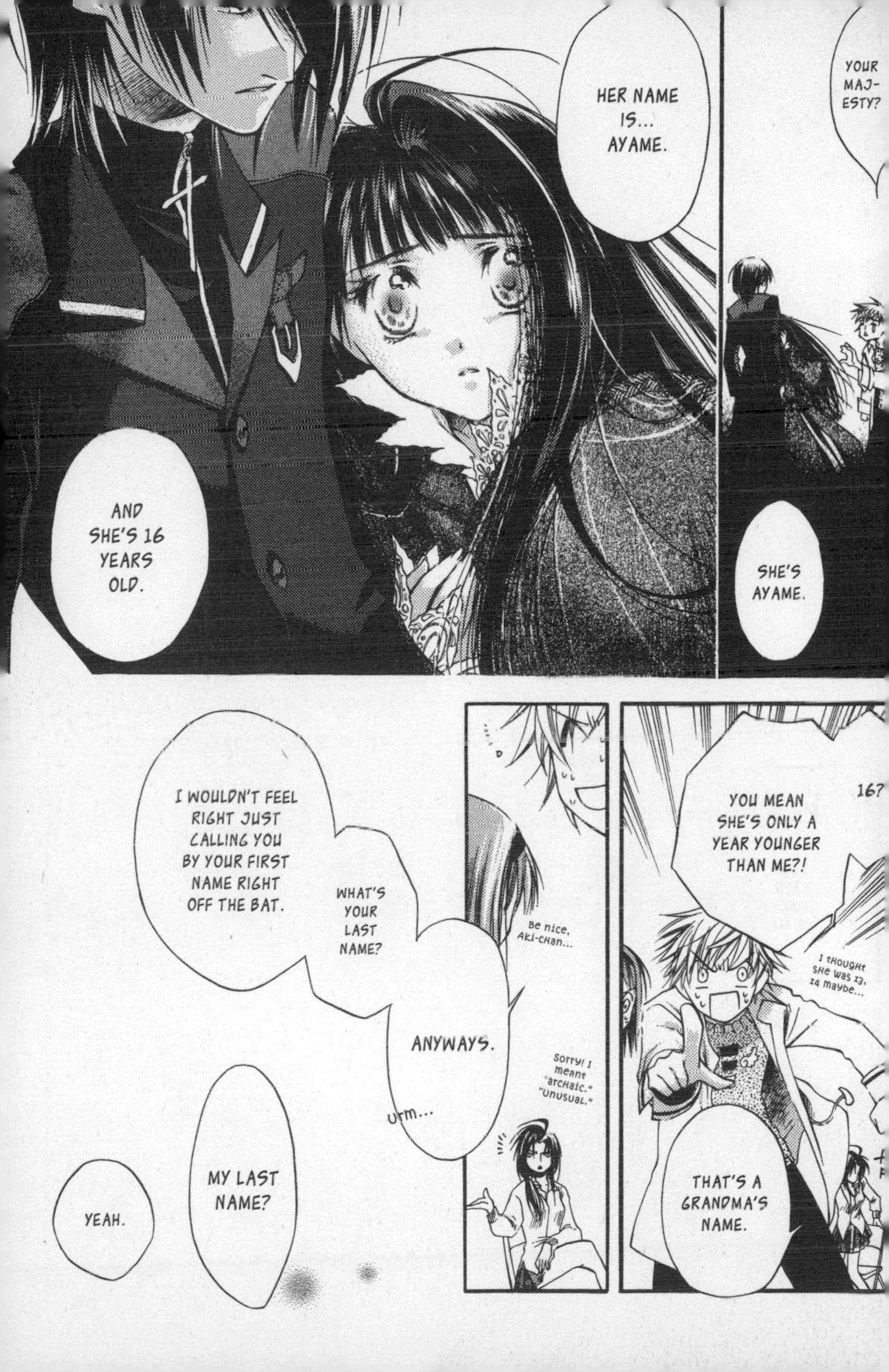
YOUR MAJ-ESTY?
SHE'S AYAME.
HER NAME IS... AYAME.
AND SHE'S 16 YEARS OLD.
16?
YOU MEAN SHE'S ONLY A YEAR YOUNGER THAN ME?!
I thought she was 13, 14 maybe...
THAT'S A GRANDMA'S NAME.
Be nice, Aki-chan...
Sorry! I meant "archaic." "Unusual."
ANYWAYS.
I WOULDN'T FEEL RIGHT JUST CALLING YOU BY YOUR FIRST NAME RIGHT OFF THE BAT.
WHAT'S YOUR LAST NAME?
urm...
MY LAST NAME?
YEAH.

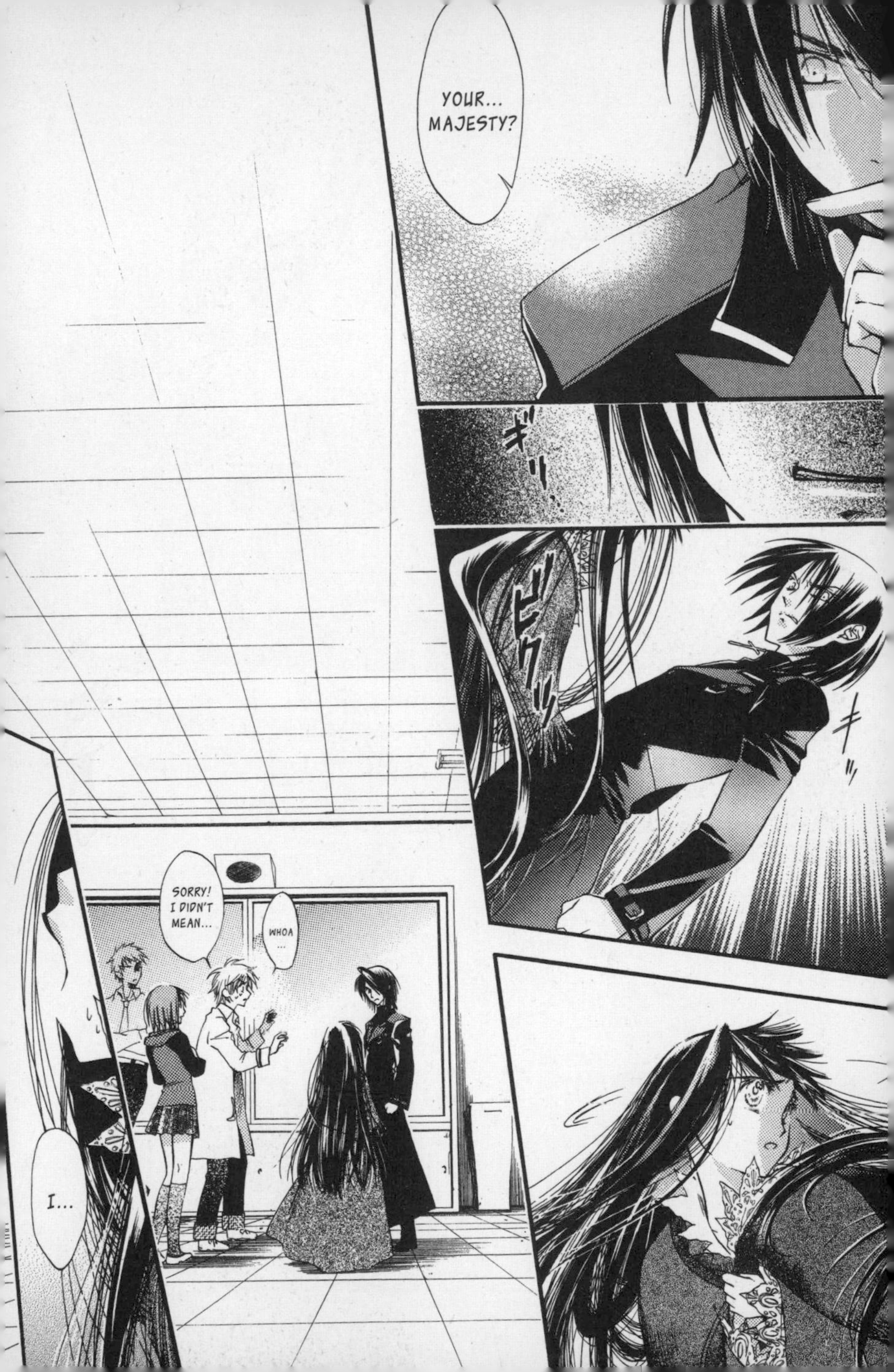
YOUR... MAJESTY?
ギリ…
ビクッ
キッ
WHOA ...
SORRY! I DIDN'T MEAN...
I...

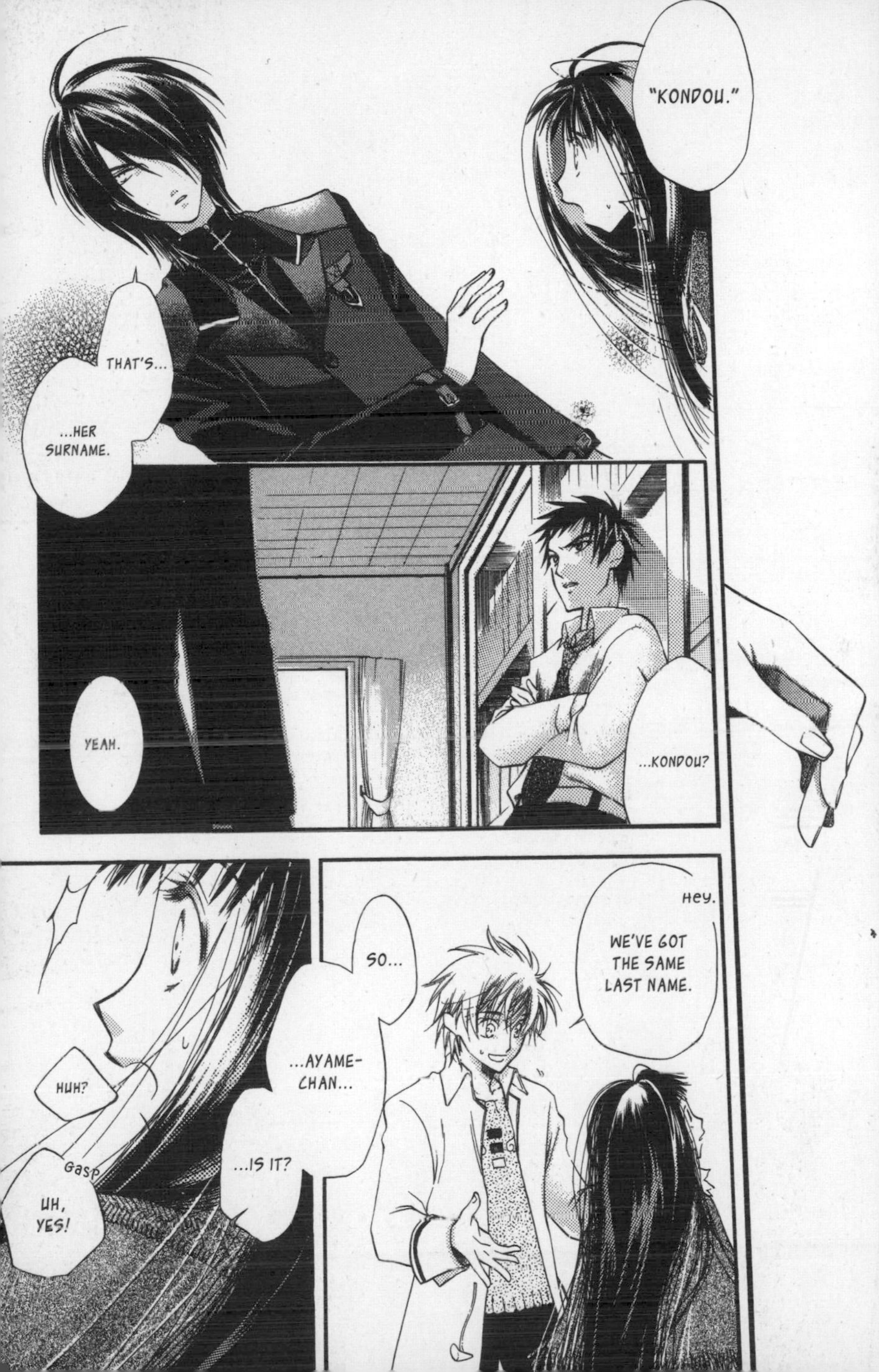
"KONDOU."
THAT'S...
...HER SURNAME.
...KONDOU?
YEAH.
Hey.
WE'VE GOT THE SAME LAST NAME.
SO...
...AYAME-CHAN...
...IS IT?
HUH?
Gasp
UH, YES!

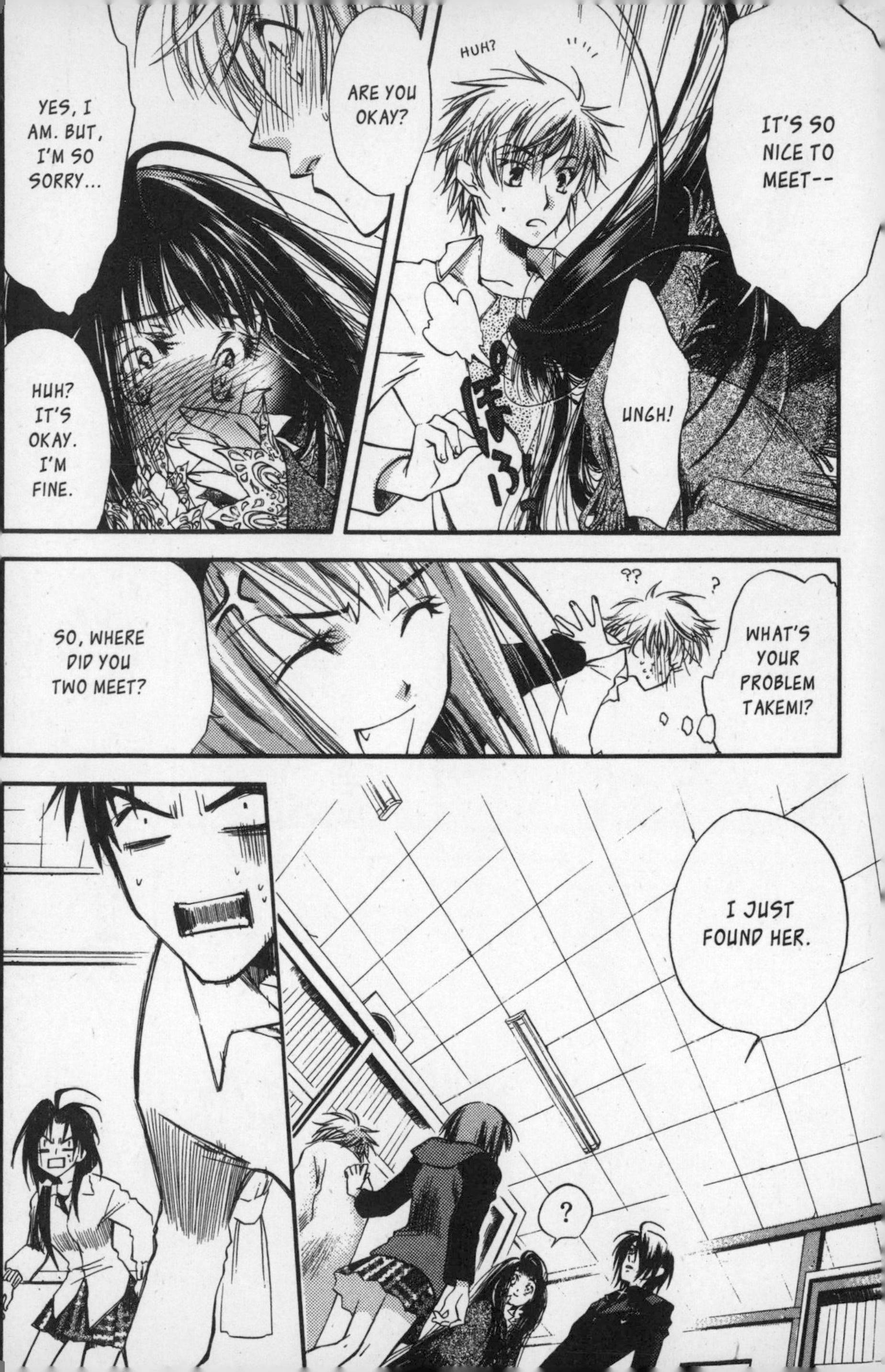
IT'S SO NICE TO MEET--
UNGH!
HUH?
ARE YOU OKAY?
YES, I AM. BUT, I'M SO SORRY...
HUH? IT'S OKAY. I'M FINE.
WHAT'S YOUR PROBLEM TAKEMI?
??
?
SO, WHERE DID YOU TWO MEET?
I JUST FOUND HER.
?

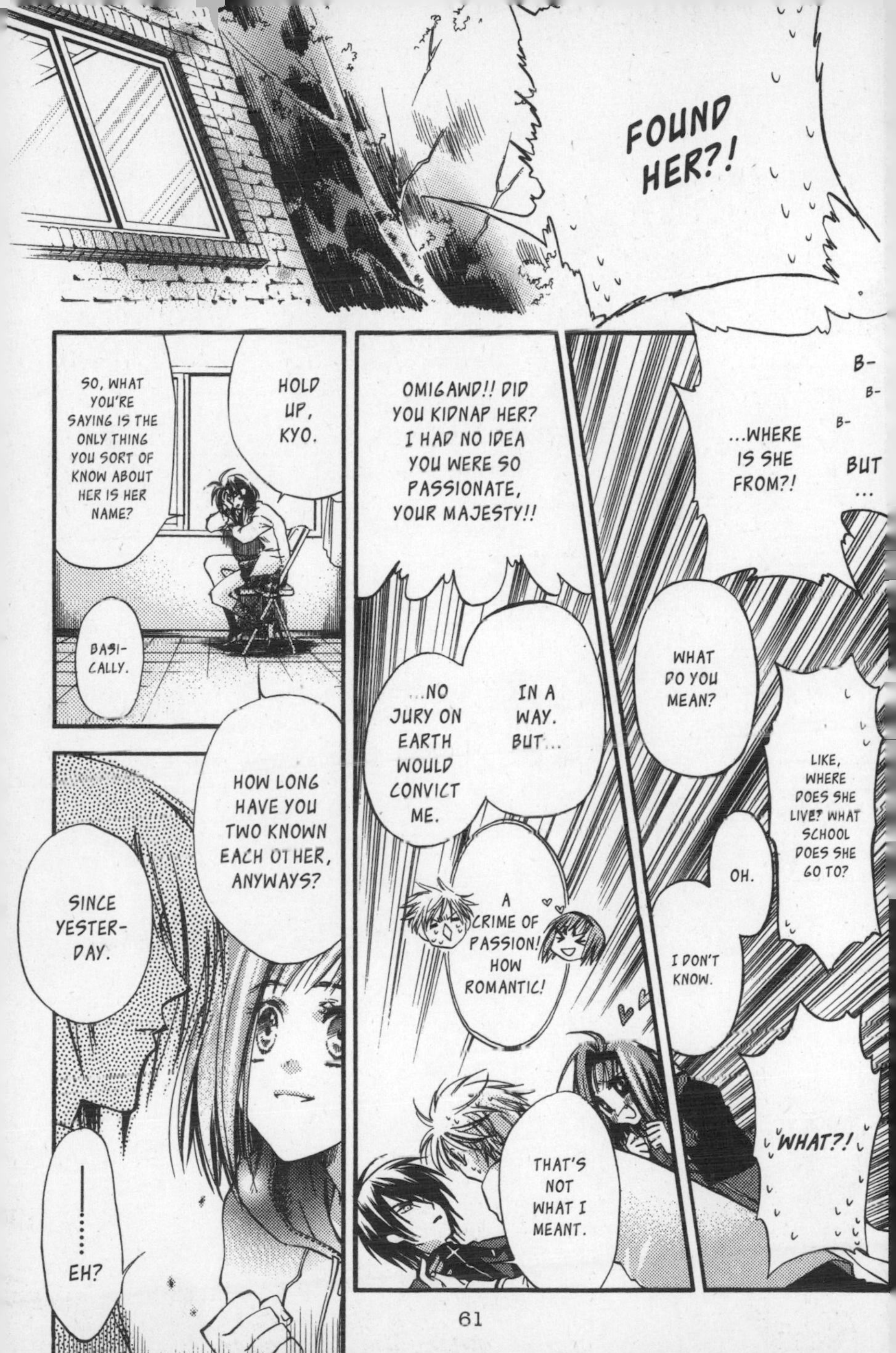
FOUND HER?!
B-B-B-BUT ...
...WHERE IS SHE FROM?!
WHAT DO YOU MEAN?
LIKE, WHERE DOES SHE LIVE? WHAT SCHOOL DOES SHE GO TO?
OH.
I DON'T KNOW.
WHAT?!
OMIGAWD!! DID YOU KIDNAP HER? I HAD NO IDEA YOU WERE SO PASSIONATE, YOUR MAJESTY!!
IN A WAY. BUT...
...NO JURY ON EARTH WOULD CONVICT ME.
A CRIME OF PASSION! HOW ROMANTIC!
THAT'S NOT WHAT I MEANT.
HOLD UP, KYO.
SO, WHAT YOU'RE SAYING IS THE ONLY THING YOU SORT OF KNOW ABOUT HER IS HER NAME?
BASI-CALLY.
HOW LONG HAVE YOU TWO KNOWN EACH OTHER, ANYWAYS?
SINCE YESTER-DAY.
......EH?

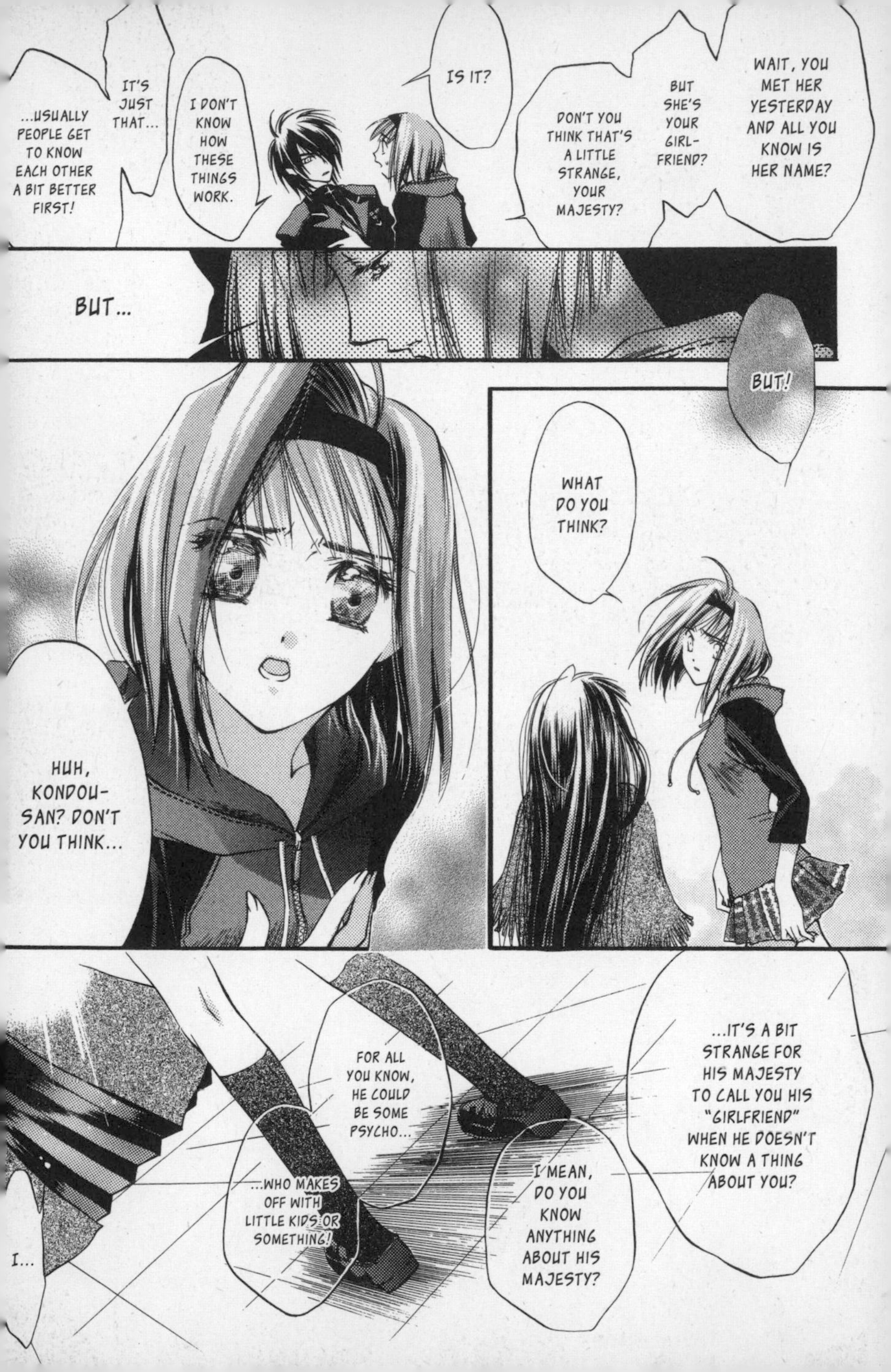
WAIT, YOU MET HER YESTERDAY AND ALL YOU KNOW IS HER NAME?
BUT SHE'S YOUR GIRL-FRIEND?
DON'T YOU THINK THAT'S A LITTLE STRANGE, YOUR MAJESTY?
IS IT?
I DON'T KNOW HOW THESE THINGS WORK.
IT'S JUST THAT...
...USUALLY PEOPLE GET TO KNOW EACH OTHER A BIT BETTER FIRST!
BUT...
BUT!
WHAT DO YOU THINK?
HUH, KONDOU-SAN? DON'T YOU THINK...
...IT'S A BIT STRANGE FOR HIS MAJESTY TO CALL YOU HIS "GIRLFRIEND" WHEN HE DOESN'T KNOW A THING ABOUT YOU?
I MEAN, DO YOU KNOW ANYTHING ABOUT HIS MAJESTY?
FOR ALL YOU KNOW, HE COULD BE SOME PSYCHO...
...WHO MAKES OFF WITH LITTLE KIDS OR SOMETHING!
I...

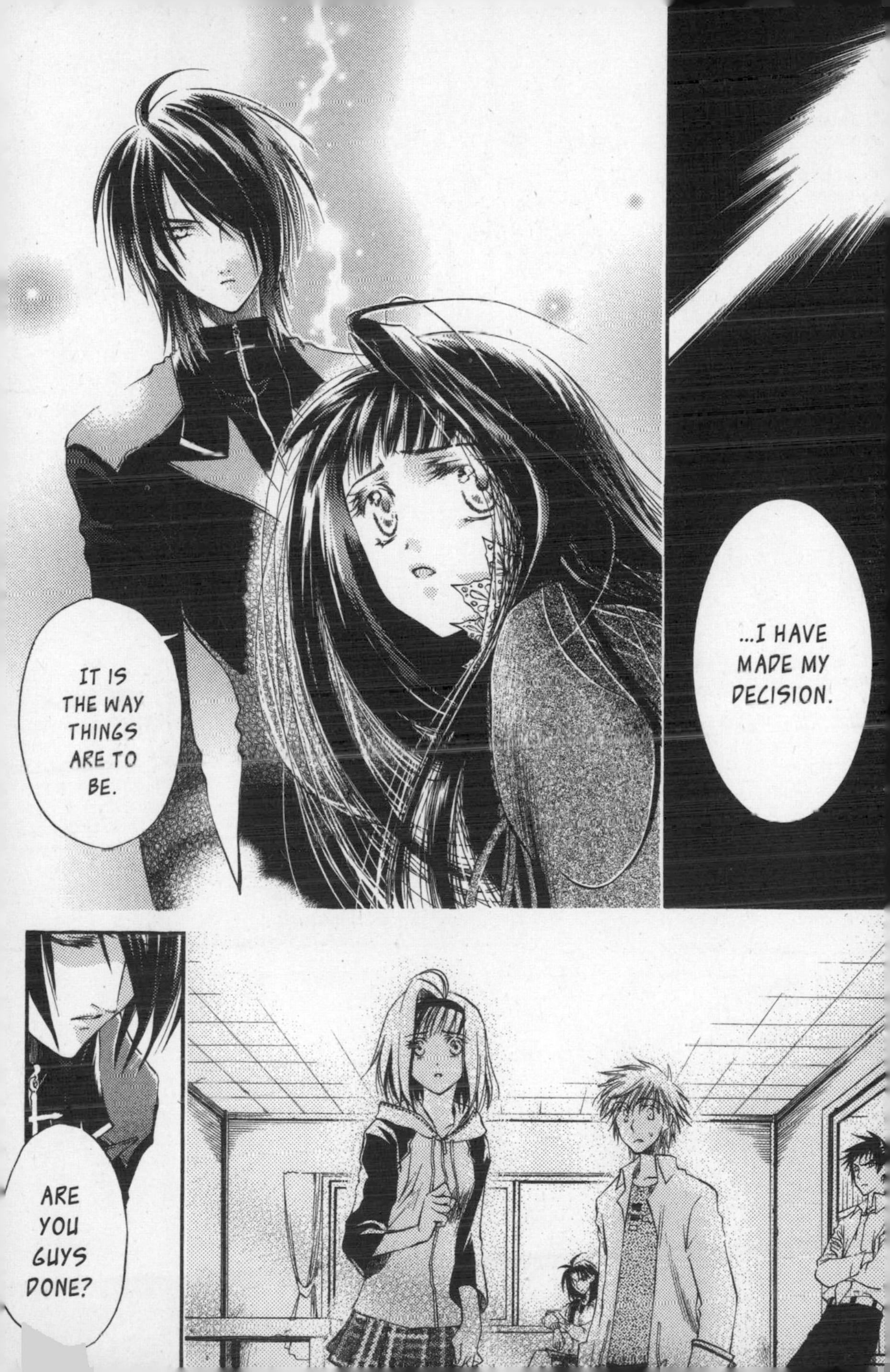
...I HAVE MADE MY DECISION.
IT IS THE WAY THINGS ARE TO BE.
ARE YOU GUYS DONE?

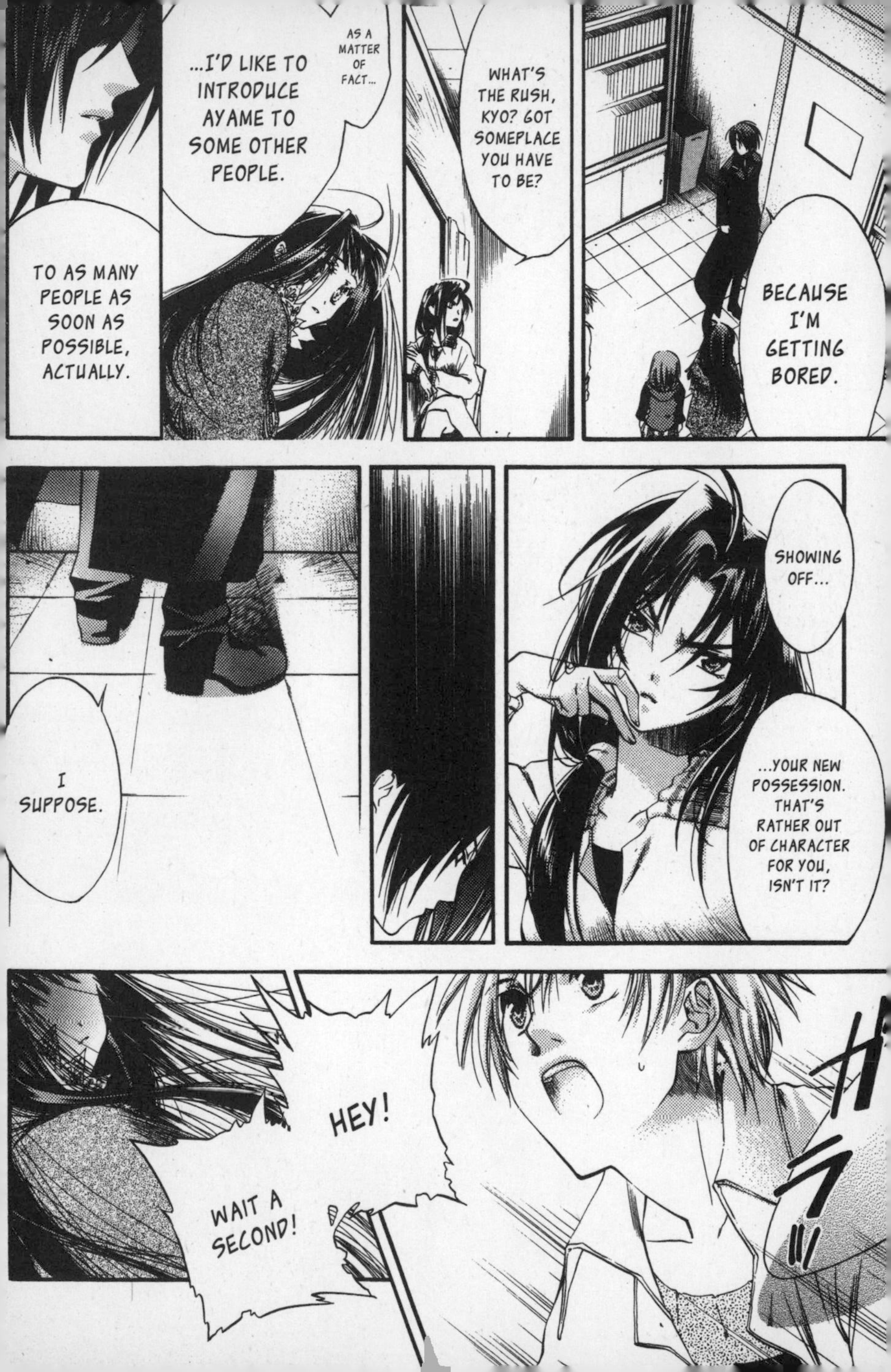
BECAUSE I'M GETTING BORED.
WHAT'S THE RUSH, KYO? GOT SOMEPLACE YOU HAVE TO BE?
AS A MATTER OF FACT...
...I'D LIKE TO INTRODUCE AYAME TO SOME OTHER PEOPLE.
TO AS MANY PEOPLE AS SOON AS POSSIBLE, ACTUALLY.
SHOWING OFF...
...YOUR NEW POSSESSION. THAT'S RATHER OUT OF CHARACTER FOR YOU, ISN'T IT?
I SUPPOSE.
ガラッ
HEY!
WAIT A SECOND!

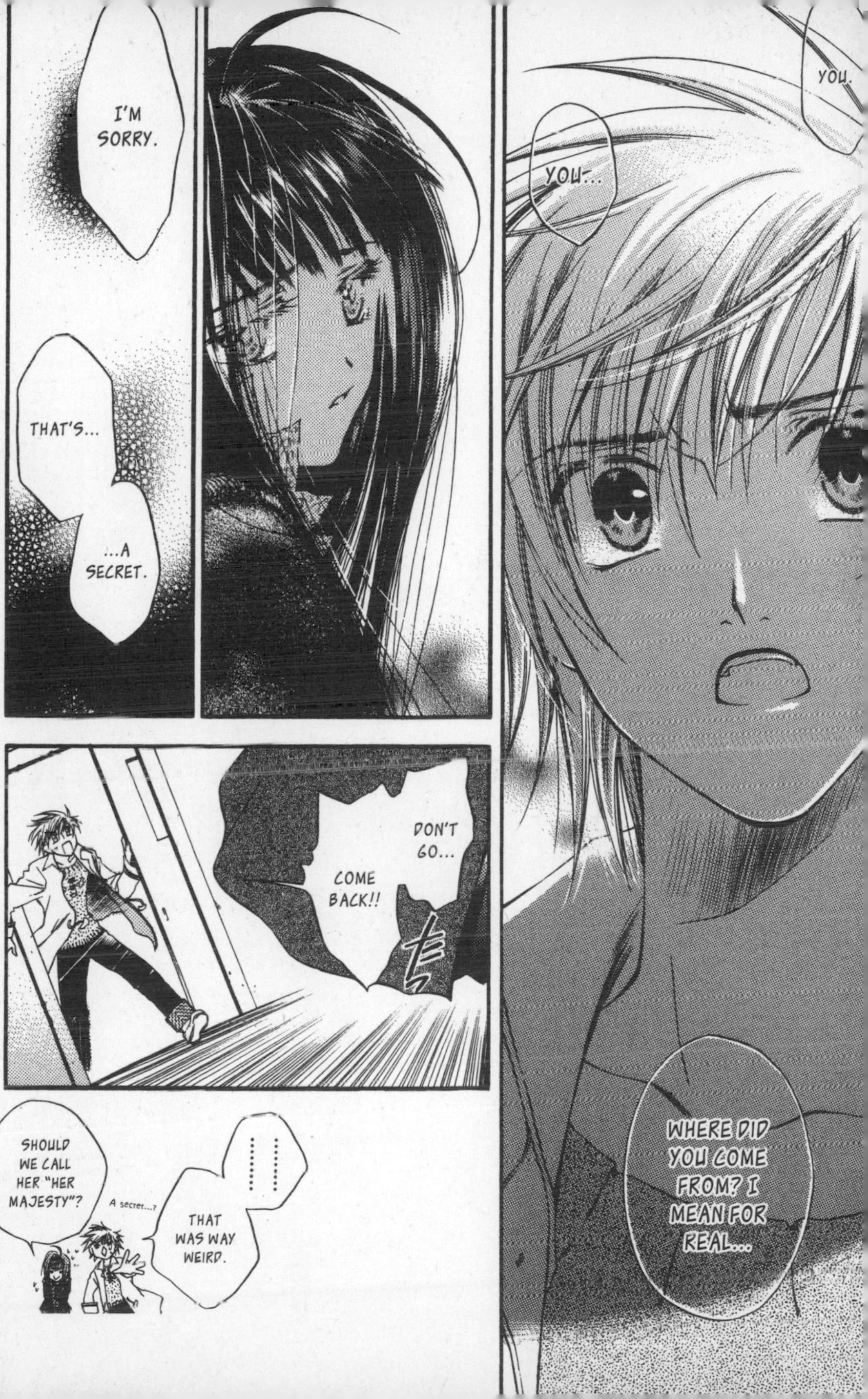
YOU.
YOU...
WHERE DID YOU COME FROM? I MEAN FOR REAL...
I'M SORRY.
THAT'S...
...A SECRET.
DON'T GO...
COME BACK!!
THAT WAS WAY WEIRD.
A secret...?
SHOULD WE CALL HER "HER MAJESTY"?

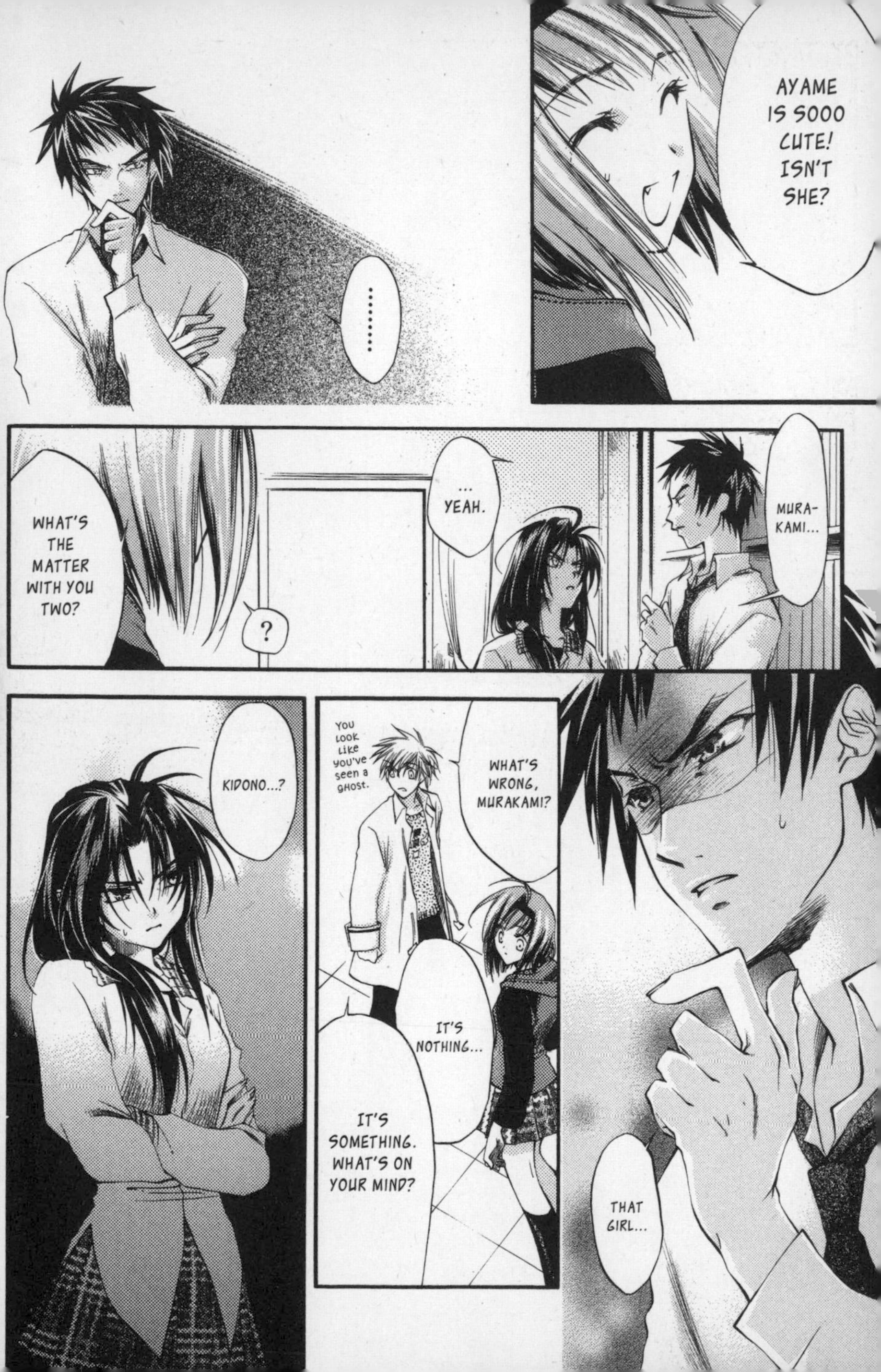
AYAME IS SOOO CUTE! ISN'T SHE?
......
MURA-KAMI...
... YEAH.
?
WHAT'S THE MATTER WITH YOU TWO?
THAT GIRL...
WHAT'S WRONG, MURAKAMI?
You look like you've seen a ghost.
IT'S NOTHING...
IT'S SOMETHING. WHAT'S ON YOUR MIND?
KIDONO...?

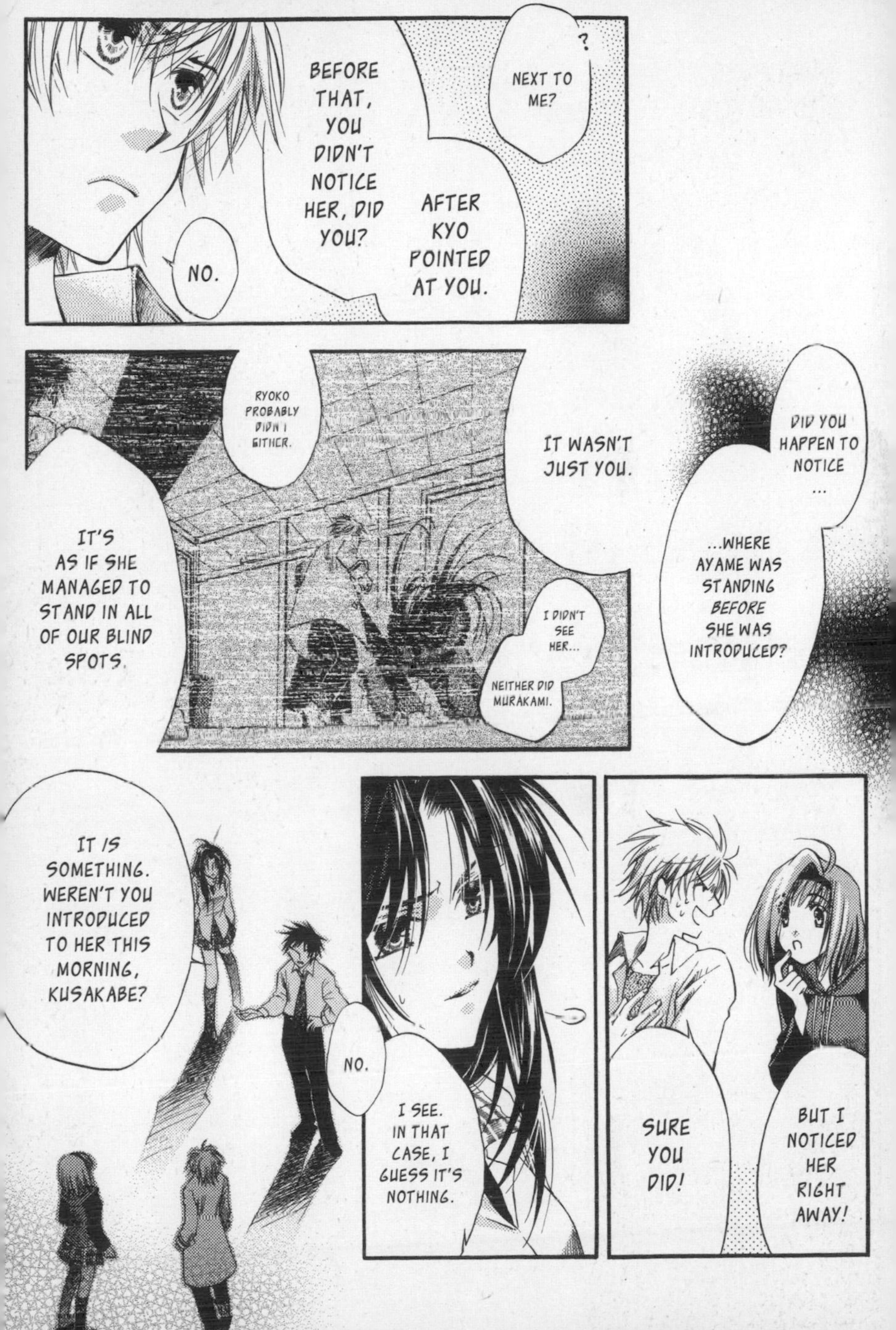
?
NEXT TO ME?
AFTER KYO POINTED AT YOU.
BEFORE THAT, YOU DIDN'T NOTICE HER, DID YOU?
NO.
DID YOU HAPPEN TO NOTICE ...
...WHERE AYAME WAS STANDING *BEFORE* SHE WAS INTRODUCED?
IT WASN'T JUST YOU.
RYOKO PROBABLY DIDN'T EITHER.
I DIDN'T SEE HER...
NEITHER DID MURAKAMI.
IT'S AS IF SHE MANAGED TO STAND IN ALL OF OUR BLIND SPOTS.
BUT I NOTICED HER RIGHT AWAY!
SURE YOU DID!
I SEE. IN THAT CASE, I GUESS IT'S NOTHING.
IT *IS* SOMETHING. WEREN'T YOU INTRODUCED TO HER THIS MORNING, KUSAKABE?
NO.

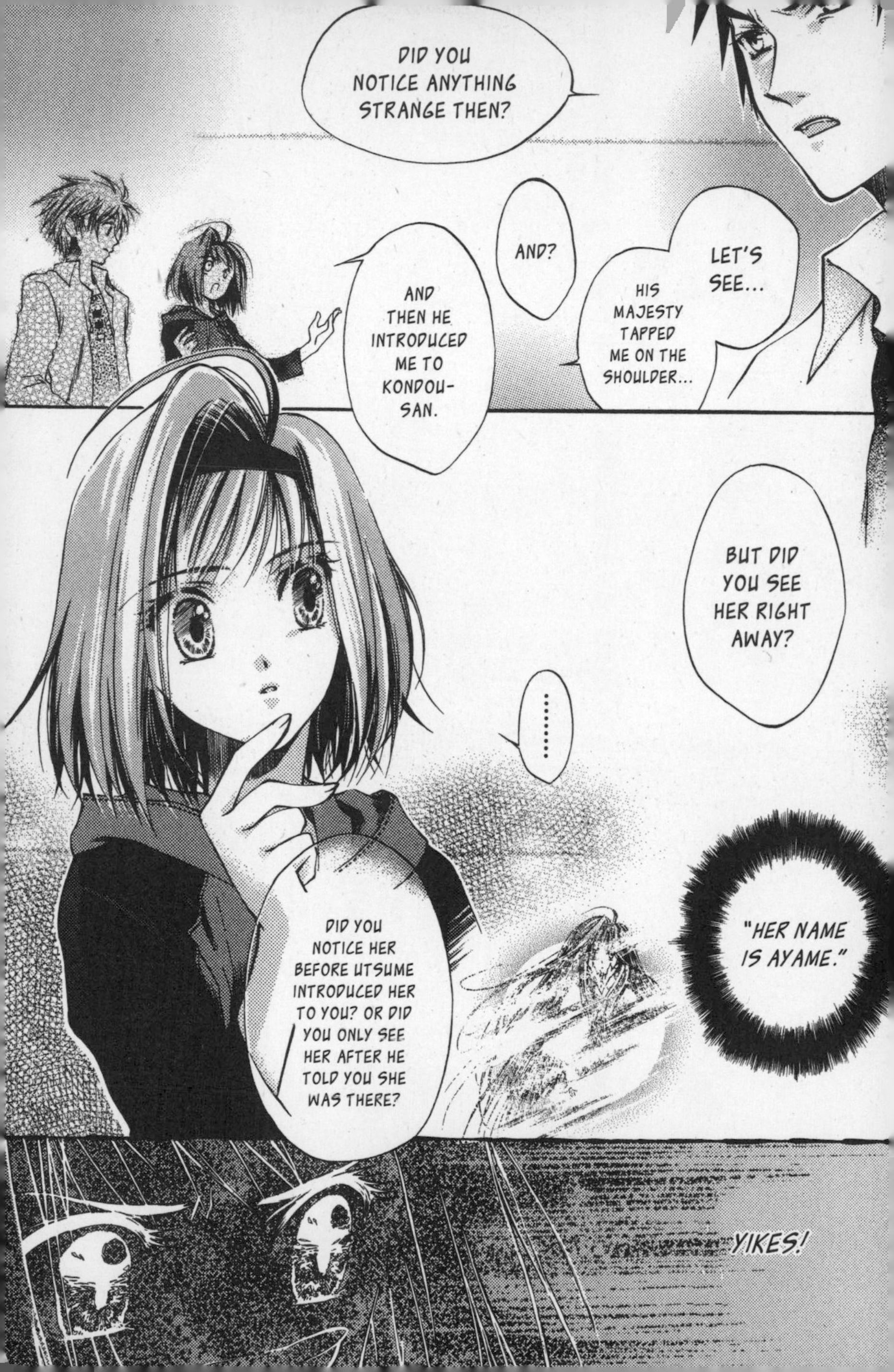
DID YOU NOTICE ANYTHING STRANGE THEN?
LET'S SEE...
HIS MAJESTY TAPPED ME ON THE SHOULDER...
AND?
AND THEN HE INTRODUCED ME TO KONDOU-SAN.
BUT DID YOU SEE HER RIGHT AWAY?
......
"HER NAME IS AYAME."
DID YOU NOTICE HER BEFORE UTSUME INTRODUCED HER TO YOU? OR DID YOU ONLY SEE HER AFTER HE TOLD YOU SHE WAS THERE?
YIKES!

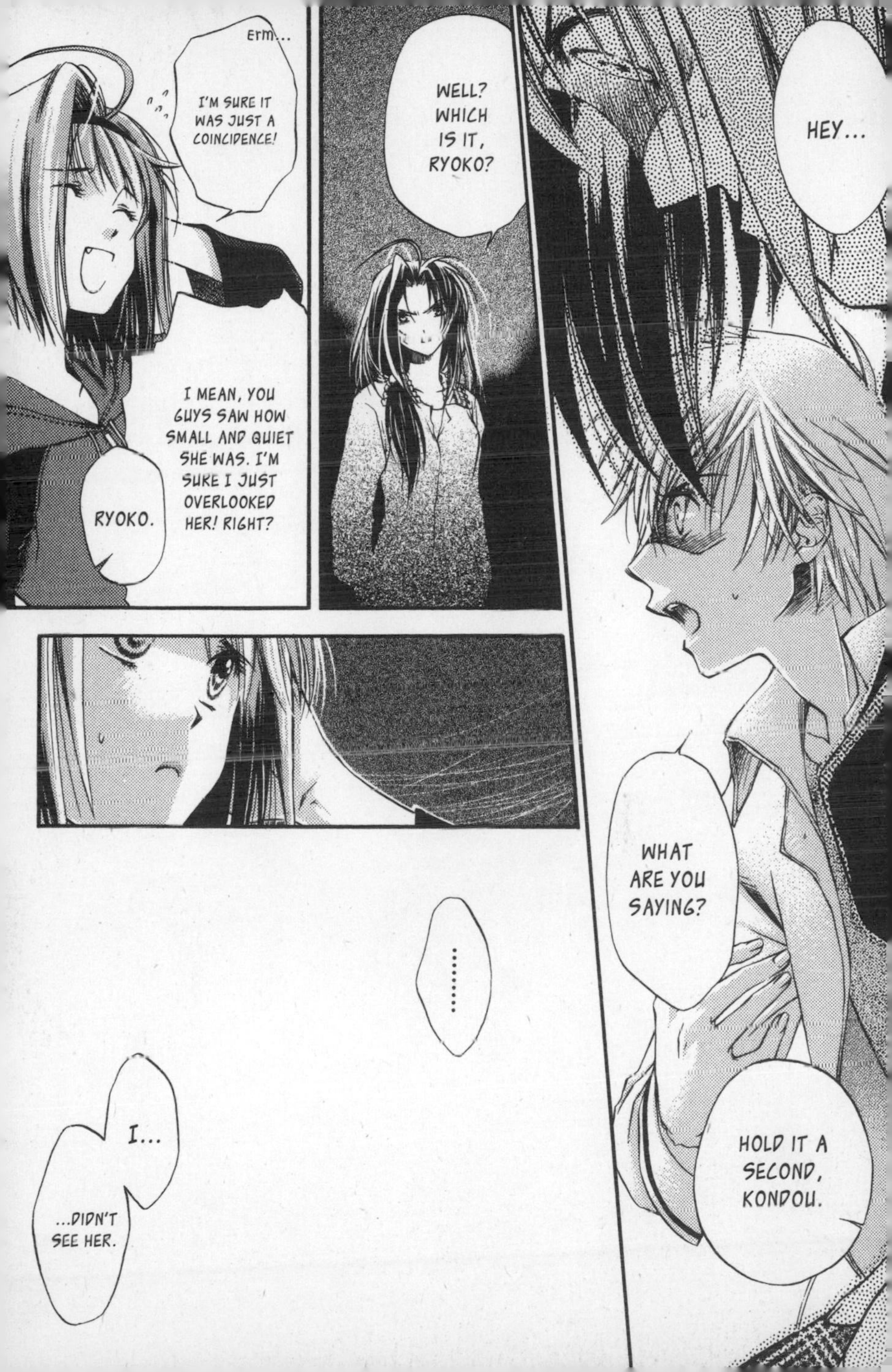
HEY...
WHAT ARE YOU SAYING?
HOLD IT A SECOND, KONDOU.
WELL? WHICH IS IT, RYOKO?
Erm...
I'M SURE IT WAS JUST A COINCIDENCE!
I MEAN, YOU GUYS SAW HOW SMALL AND QUIET SHE WAS. I'M SURE I JUST OVERLOOKED HER! RIGHT?
RYOKO.
....
I...
...DIDN'T SEE HER.

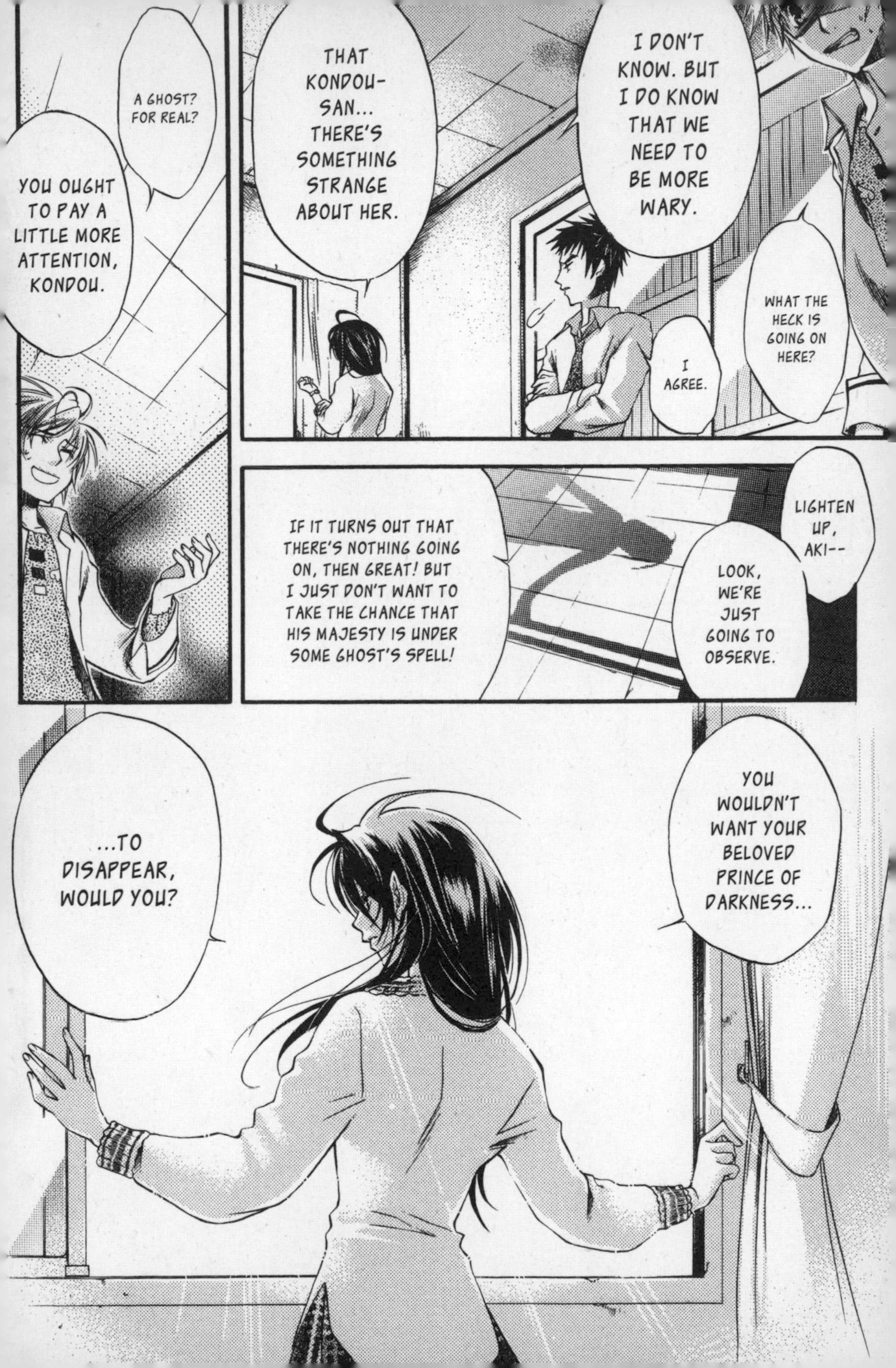
I DON'T KNOW. BUT I DO KNOW THAT WE NEED TO BE MORE WARY.
THAT KONDOU-SAN... THERE'S SOMETHING STRANGE ABOUT HER.
WHAT THE HECK IS GOING ON HERE?
I AGREE.
LIGHTEN UP, AKI--
LOOK, WE'RE JUST GOING TO OBSERVE.
IF IT TURNS OUT THAT THERE'S NOTHING GOING ON, THEN GREAT! BUT I JUST DON'T WANT TO TAKE THE CHANCE THAT HIS MAJESTY IS UNDER SOME GHOST'S SPELL!
YOU WOULDN'T WANT YOUR BELOVED PRINCE OF DARKNESS...
...TO DISAPPEAR, WOULD YOU?
A GHOST? FOR REAL?
YOU OUGHT TO PAY A LITTLE MORE ATTENTION, KONDOU.

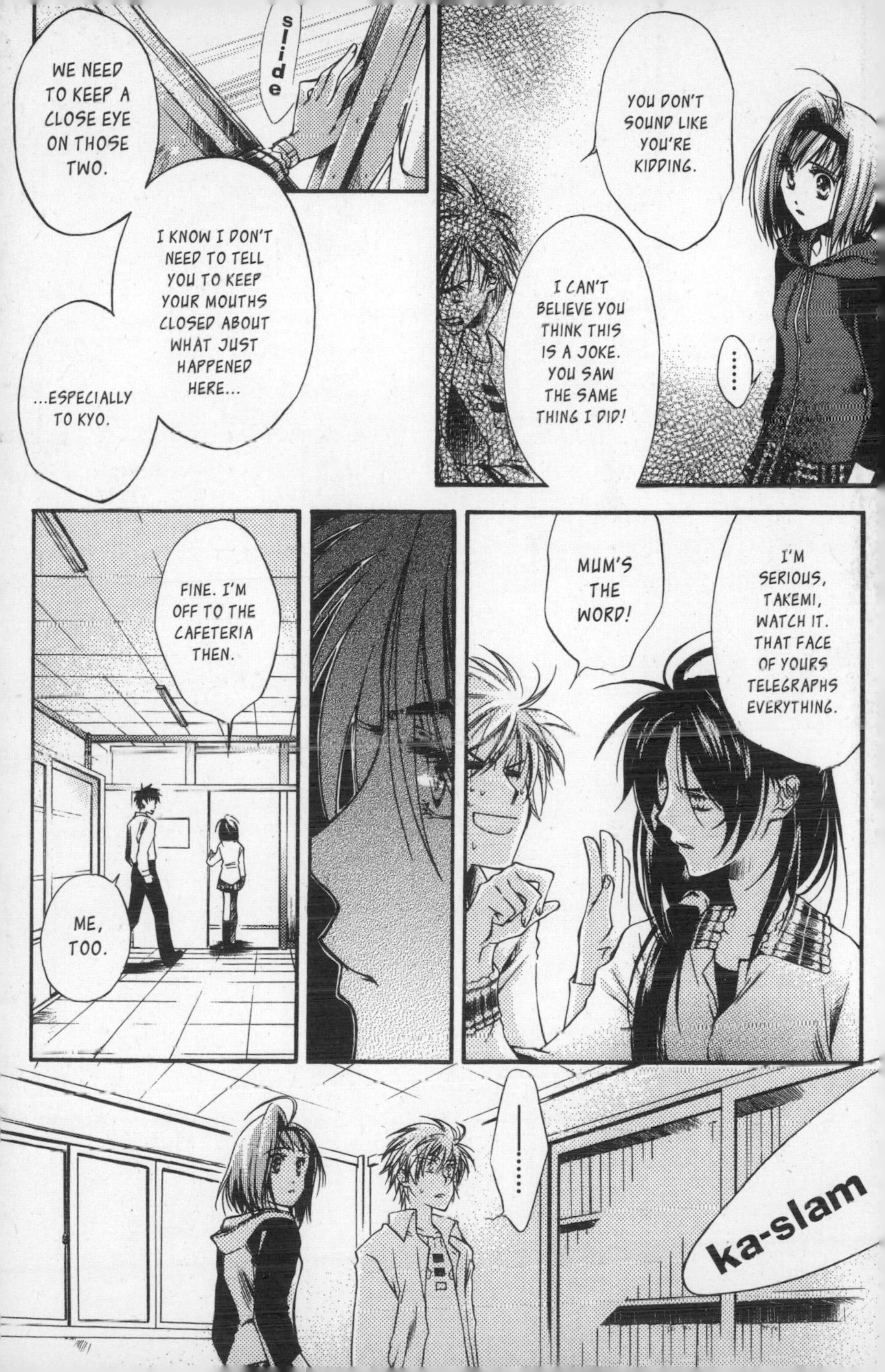
YOU DON'T SOUND LIKE YOU'RE KIDDING.
......
I CAN'T BELIEVE YOU THINK THIS IS A JOKE. YOU SAW THE SAME THING I DID!
slide
WE NEED TO KEEP A CLOSE EYE ON THOSE TWO.
I KNOW I DON'T NEED TO TELL YOU TO KEEP YOUR MOUTHS CLOSED ABOUT WHAT JUST HAPPENED HERE...
...ESPECIALLY TO KYO.
I'M SERIOUS, TAKEMI. WATCH IT. THAT FACE OF YOURS TELEGRAPHS EVERYTHING.
MUM'S THE WORD!
FINE. I'M OFF TO THE CAFETERIA THEN.
ME, TOO.
ka-slam
......

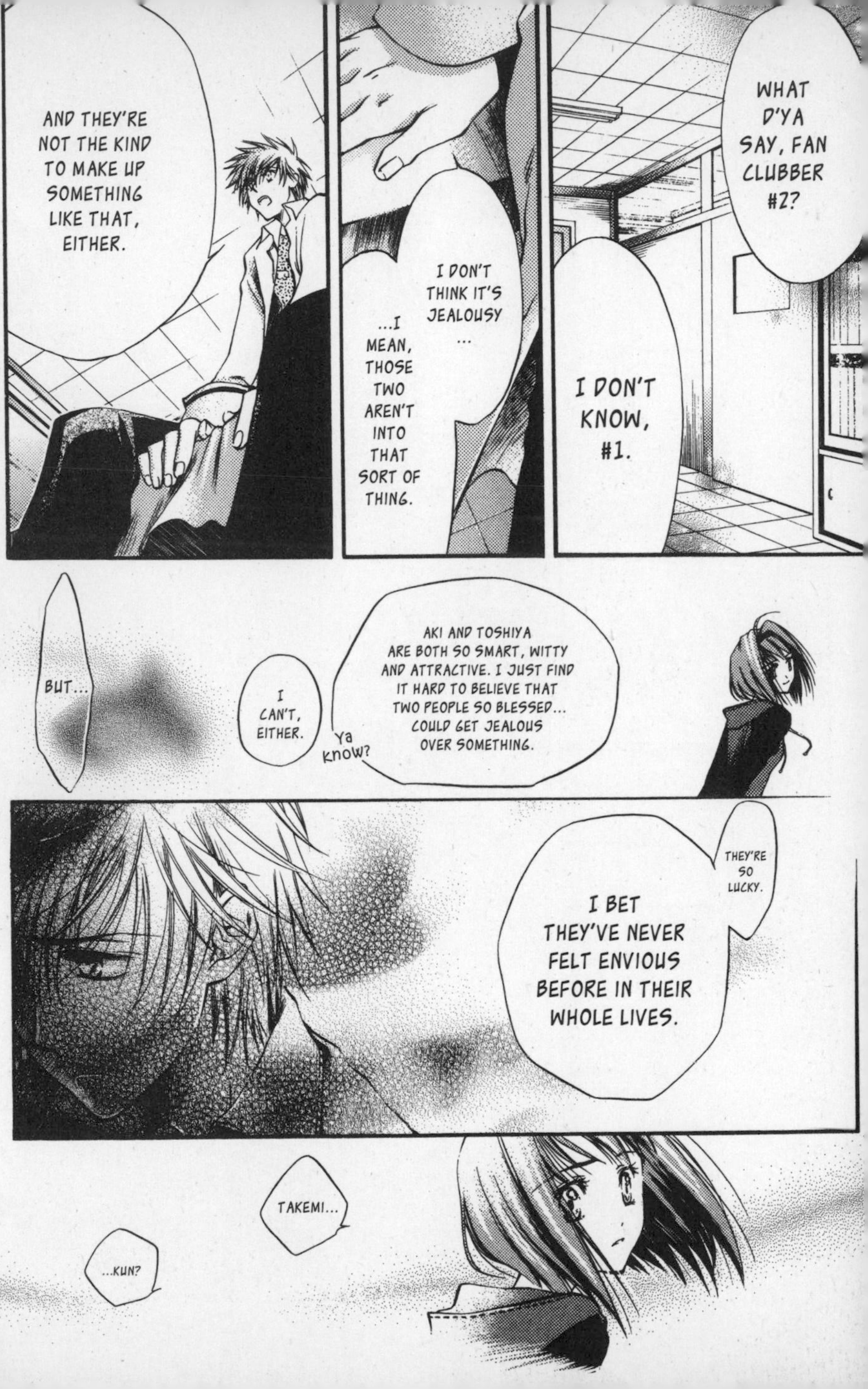
WHAT D'YA SAY, FAN CLUBBER #2?
I DON'T KNOW, #1.
I DON'T THINK IT'S JEALOUSY ...
...I MEAN, THOSE TWO AREN'T INTO THAT SORT OF THING.
AND THEY'RE NOT THE KIND TO MAKE UP SOMETHING LIKE THAT, EITHER.
AKI AND TOSHIYA ARE BOTH SO SMART, WITTY AND ATTRACTIVE. I JUST FIND IT HARD TO BELIEVE THAT TWO PEOPLE SO BLESSED... COULD GET JEALOUS OVER SOMETHING.
Ya know?
I CAN'T, EITHER.
BUT...
THEY'RE SO LUCKY.
I BET THEY'VE NEVER FELT ENVIOUS BEFORE IN THEIR WHOLE LIVES.
TAKEMI...
...KUN?

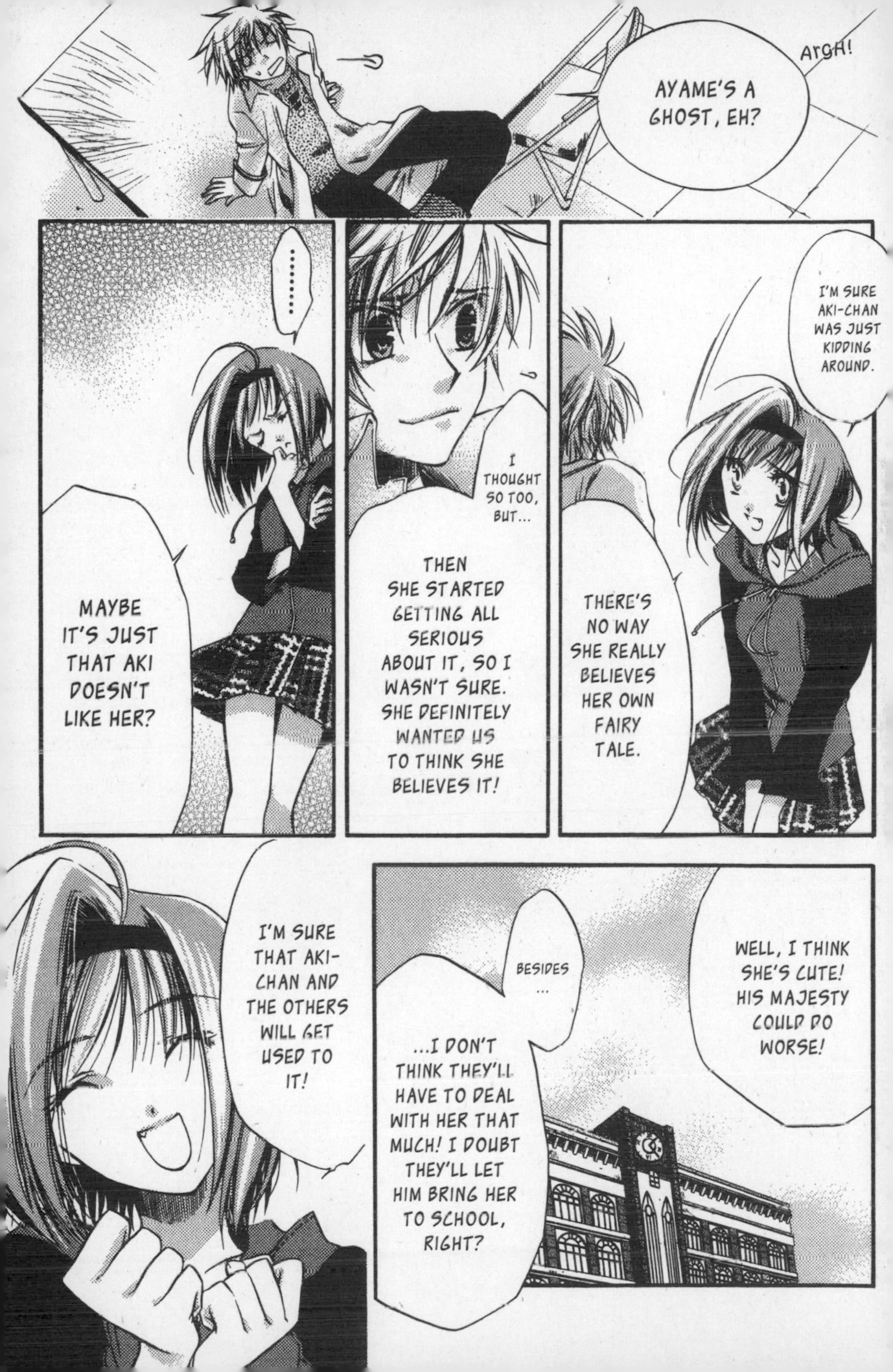

ARGH!
AYAME'S A GHOST, EH?
I'M SURE AKI-CHAN WAS JUST KIDDING AROUND.
THERE'S NO WAY SHE REALLY BELIEVES HER OWN FAIRY TALE.
I THOUGHT SO TOO, BUT...
THEN SHE STARTED GETTING ALL SERIOUS ABOUT IT, SO I WASN'T SURE. SHE DEFINITELY WANTED US TO THINK SHE BELIEVES IT!
....
MAYBE IT'S JUST THAT AKI DOESN'T LIKE HER?
WELL, I THINK SHE'S CUTE! HIS MAJESTY COULD DO WORSE!
BESIDES...
...I DON'T THINK THEY'LL HAVE TO DEAL WITH HER THAT MUCH! I DOUBT THEY'LL LET HIM BRING HER TO SCHOOL, RIGHT?
I'M SURE THAT AKI-CHAN AND THE OTHERS WILL GET USED TO IT!

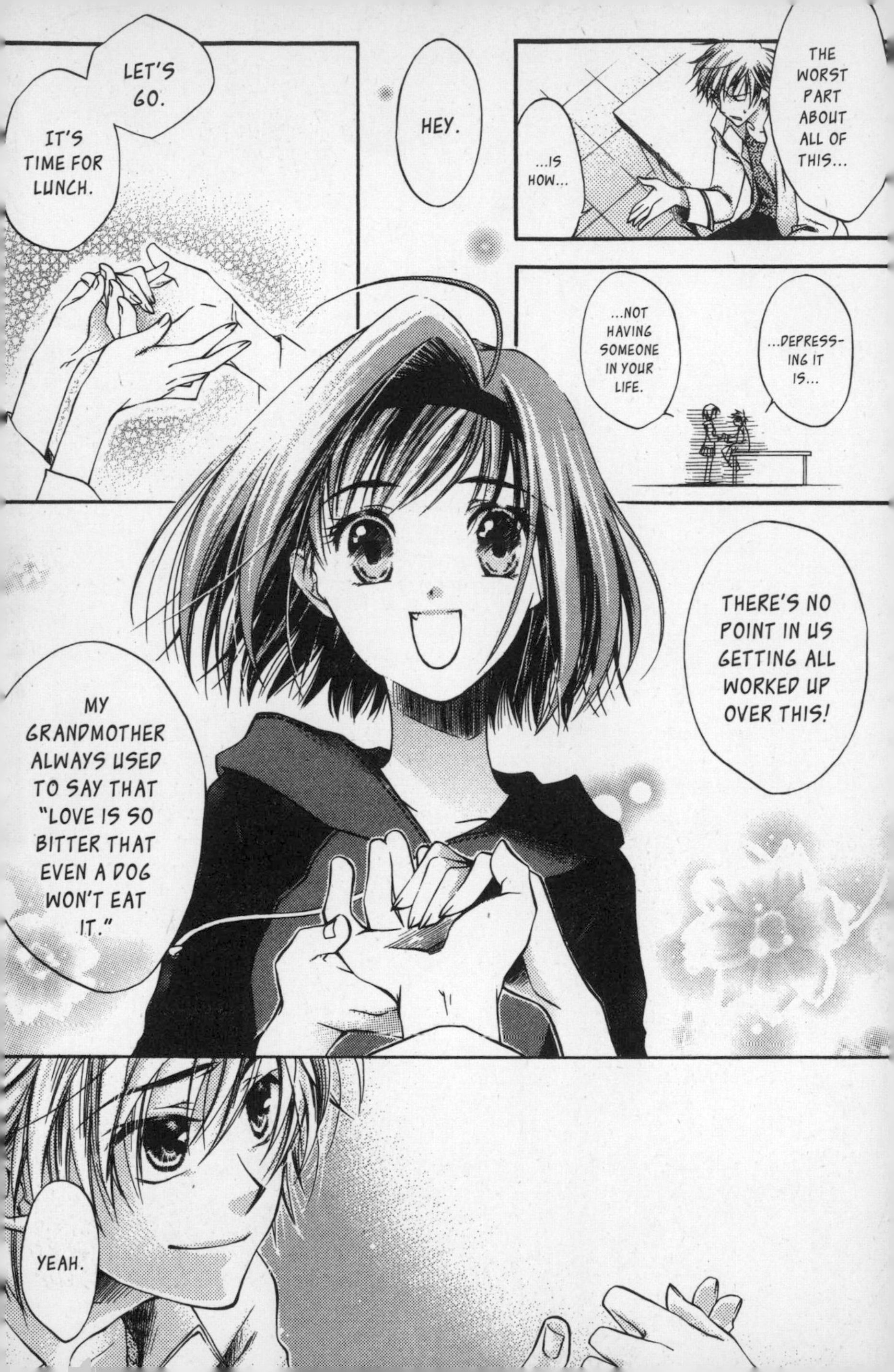
THE WORST PART ABOUT ALL OF THIS...
...IS HOW...
...DEPRESSING IT IS...
...NOT HAVING SOMEONE IN YOUR LIFE.
HEY.
LET'S GO.
IT'S TIME FOR LUNCH.
THERE'S NO POINT IN US GETTING ALL WORKED UP OVER THIS!
MY GRANDMOTHER ALWAYS USED TO SAY THAT "LOVE IS SO BITTER THAT EVEN A DOG WON'T EAT IT."
YEAH.

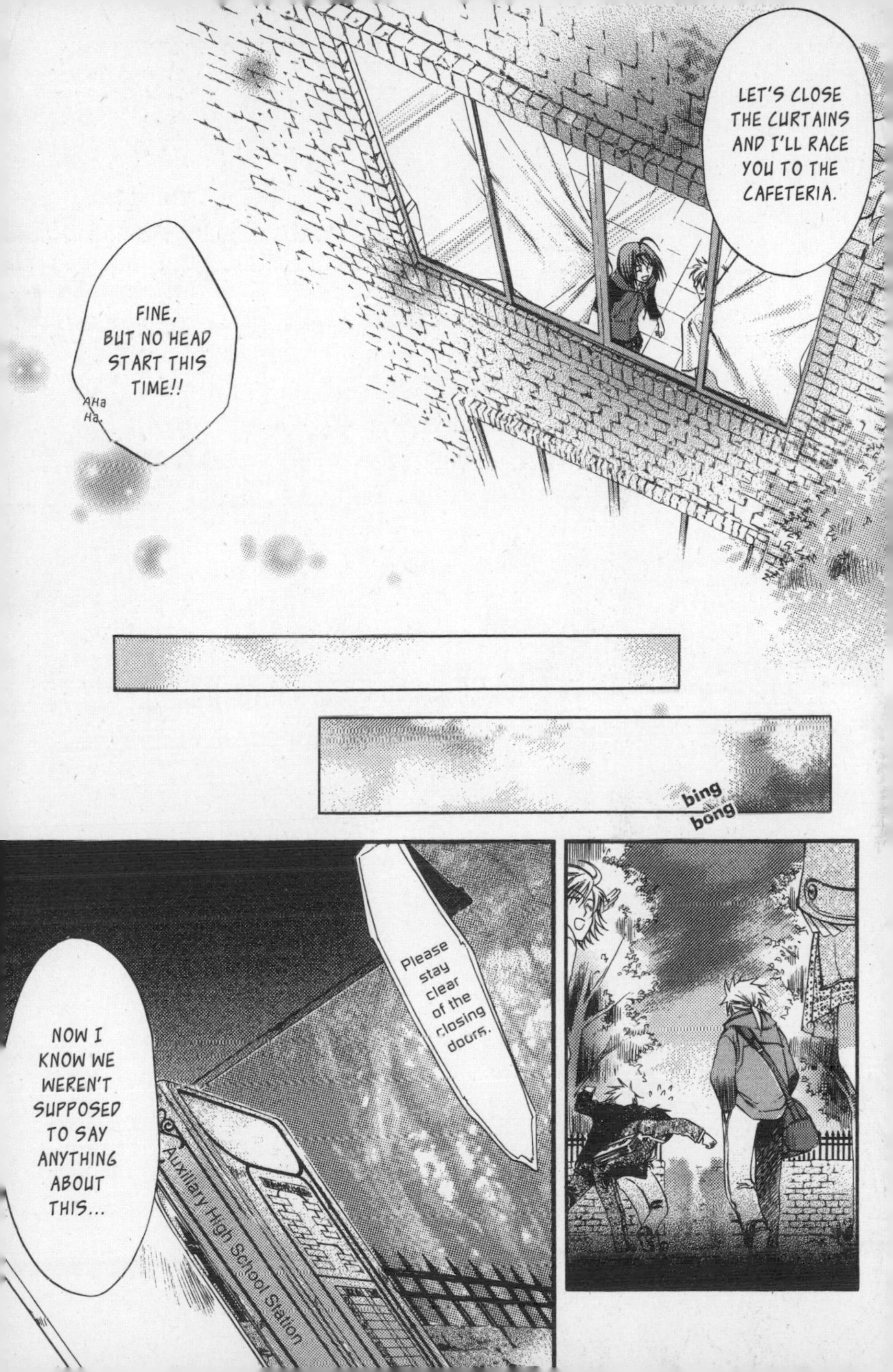

LET'S CLOSE THE CURTAINS AND I'LL RACE YOU TO THE CAFETERIA.
FINE, BUT NO HEAD START THIS TIME!!
AHa Ha.
bing bong
Please stay clear of the closing doors.
Auxiliary High School Station
NOW I KNOW WE WEREN'T SUPPOSED TO SAY ANYTHING ABOUT THIS...

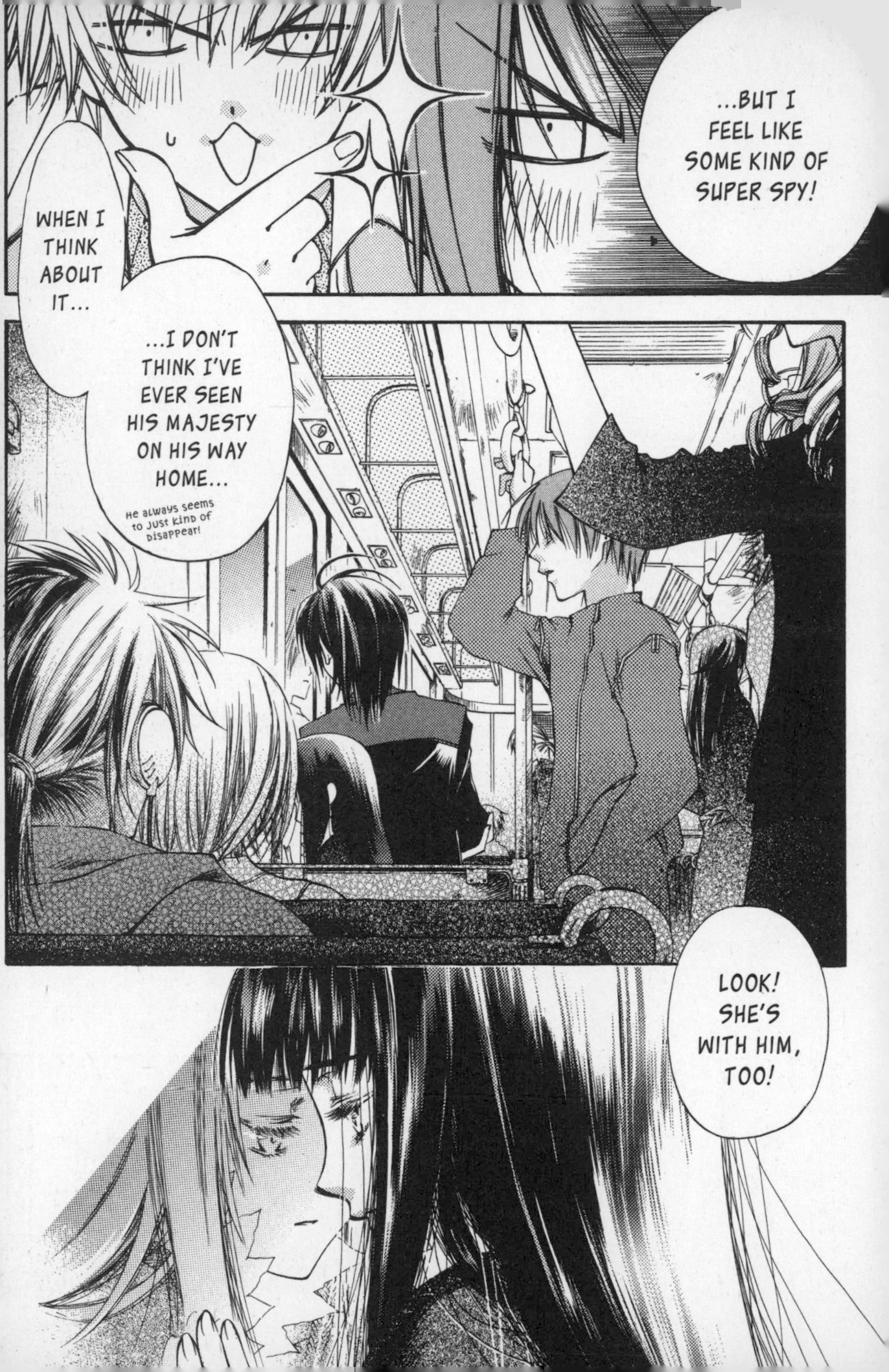
...BUT I FEEL LIKE SOME KIND OF SUPER SPY!
WHEN I THINK ABOUT IT...
...I DON'T THINK I'VE EVER SEEN HIS MAJESTY ON HIS WAY HOME...
He always seems to just kind of disappear!
LOOK! SHE'S WITH HIM, TOO!

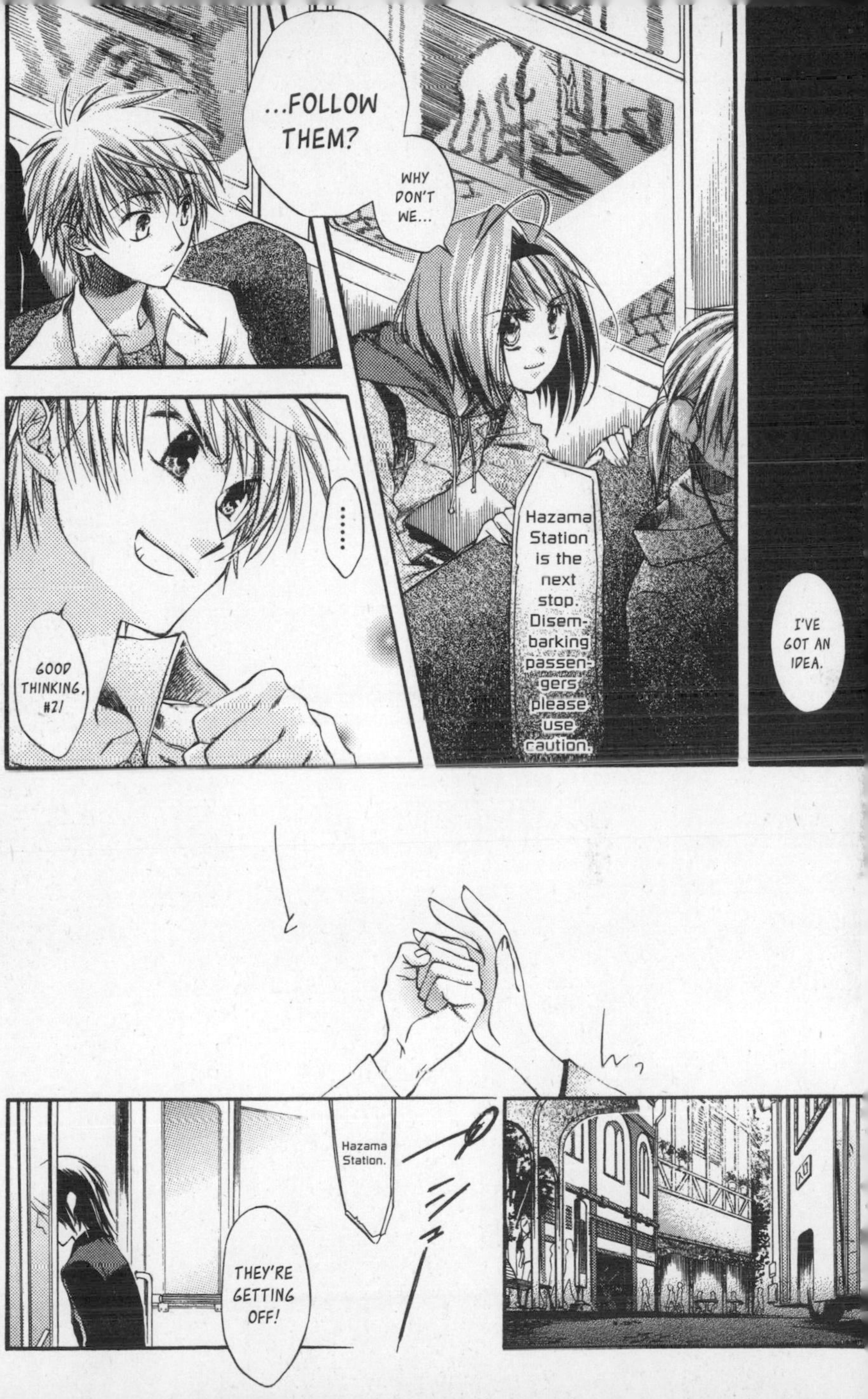
I'VE GOT AN IDEA.
WHY DON'T WE...
...FOLLOW THEM?
Hazama Station is the next stop. Disem-barking passen-gers please use caution.
......
GOOD THINKING, #2!
Hazama Station.
THEY'RE GETTING OFF!

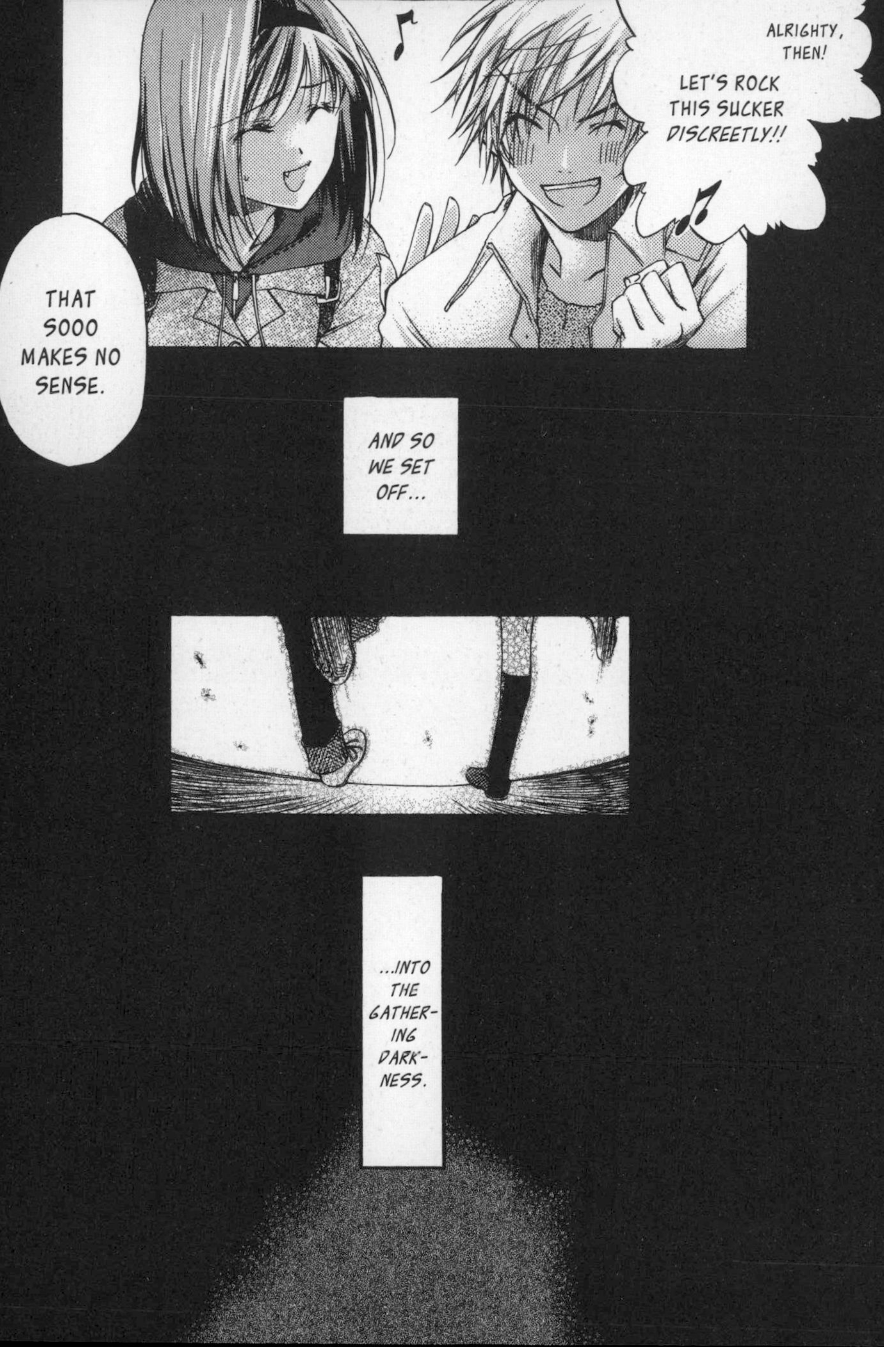
ALRIGHTY, THEN!
LET'S ROCK THIS SUCKER DISCREETLY!!
THAT SOOO MAKES NO SENSE.
AND SO WE SET OFF...
...INTO THE GATHERING DARKNESS.

Chapter 3
Waking Nightmares

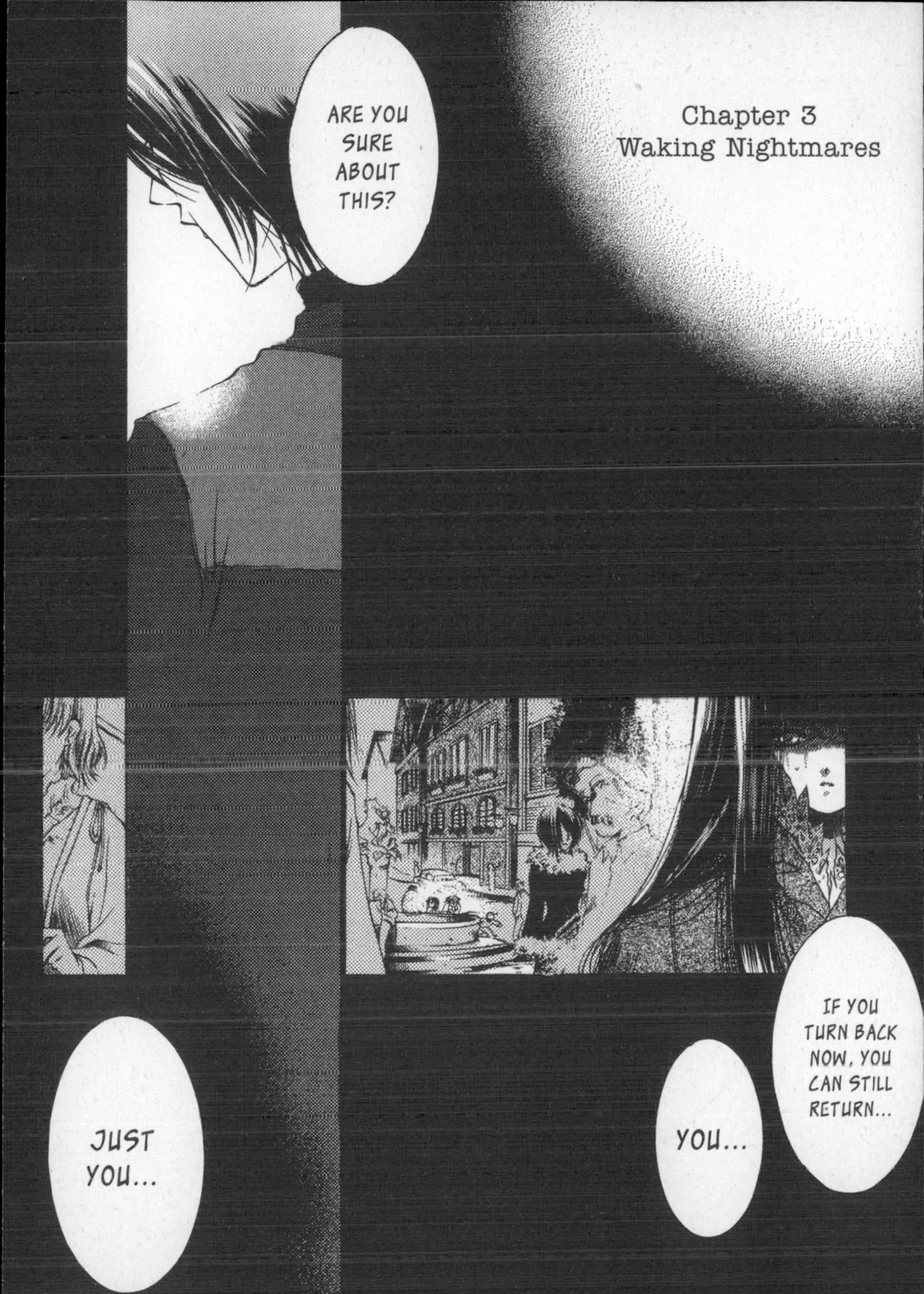
ARE YOU SURE ABOUT THIS?
IF YOU TURN BACK NOW, YOU CAN STILL RETURN...
YOU...
JUST YOU...

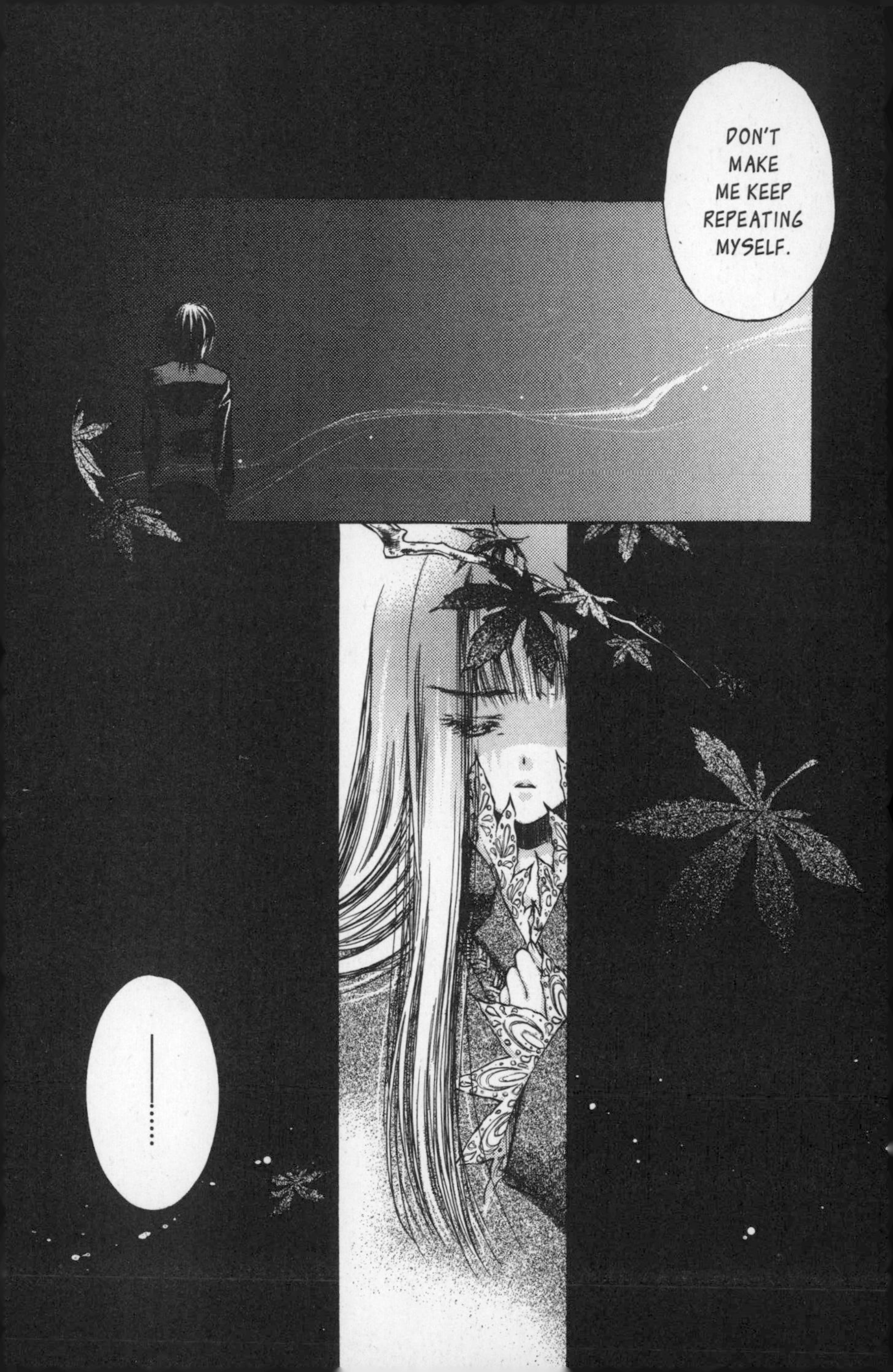
DON'T MAKE ME KEEP REPEATING MYSELF.
—......

I'M SORRY. SO SORRY.

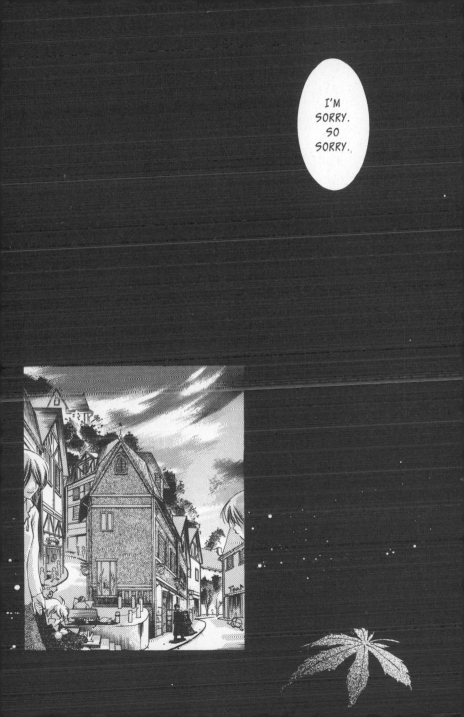

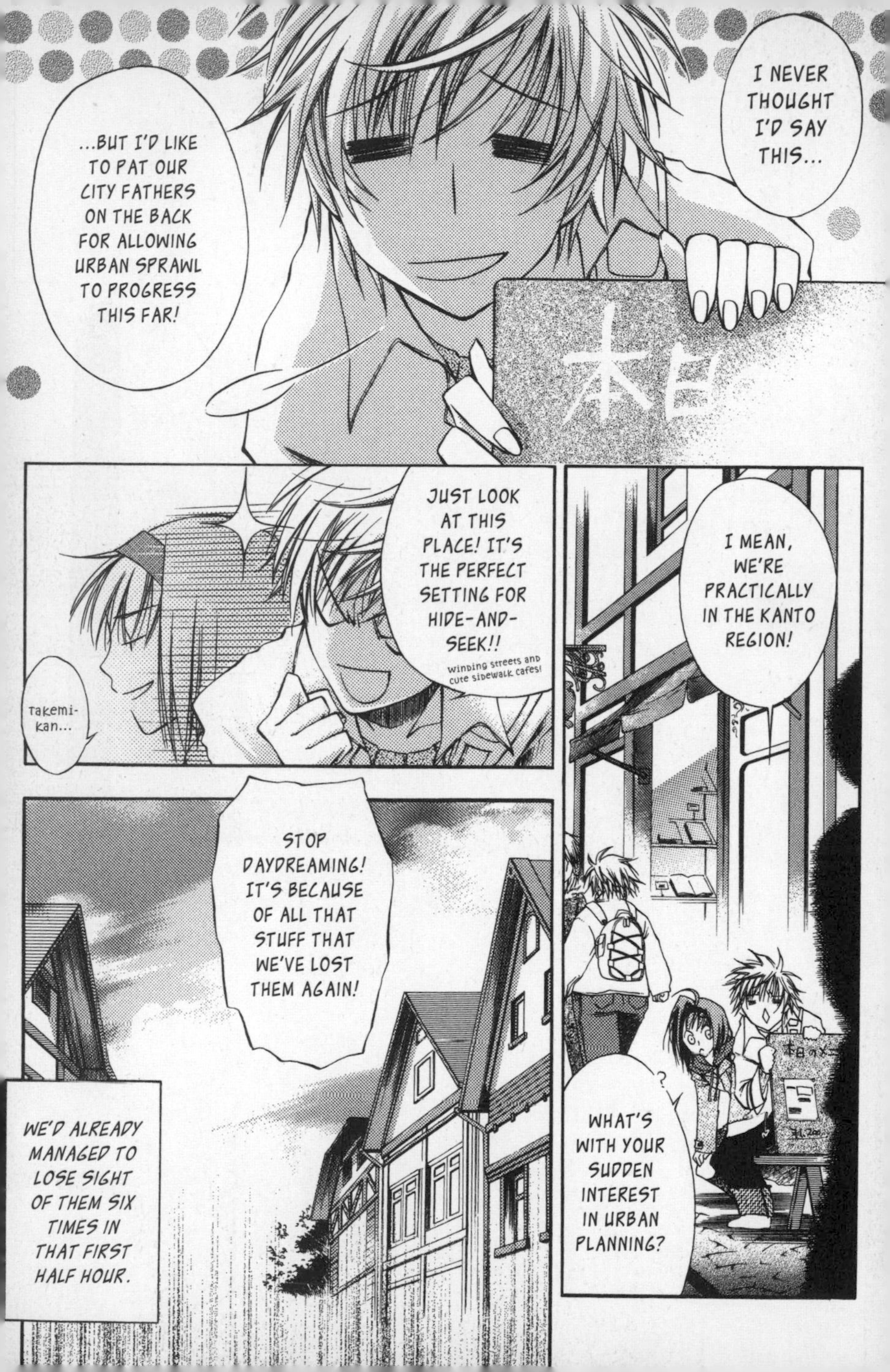
I NEVER THOUGHT I'D SAY THIS...
...BUT I'D LIKE TO PAT OUR CITY FATHERS ON THE BACK FOR ALLOWING URBAN SPRAWL TO PROGRESS THIS FAR!
I MEAN, WE'RE PRACTICALLY IN THE KANTO REGION!
WHAT'S WITH YOUR SUDDEN INTEREST IN URBAN PLANNING?
JUST LOOK AT THIS PLACE! IT'S THE PERFECT SETTING FOR HIDE-AND-SEEK!!
Winding streets and cute sidewalk cafes!
Takemi-kan...
STOP DAYDREAMING! IT'S BECAUSE OF ALL THAT STUFF THAT WE'VE LOST THEM AGAIN!
WE'D ALREADY MANAGED TO LOSE SIGHT OF THEM SIX TIMES IN THAT FIRST HALF HOUR.

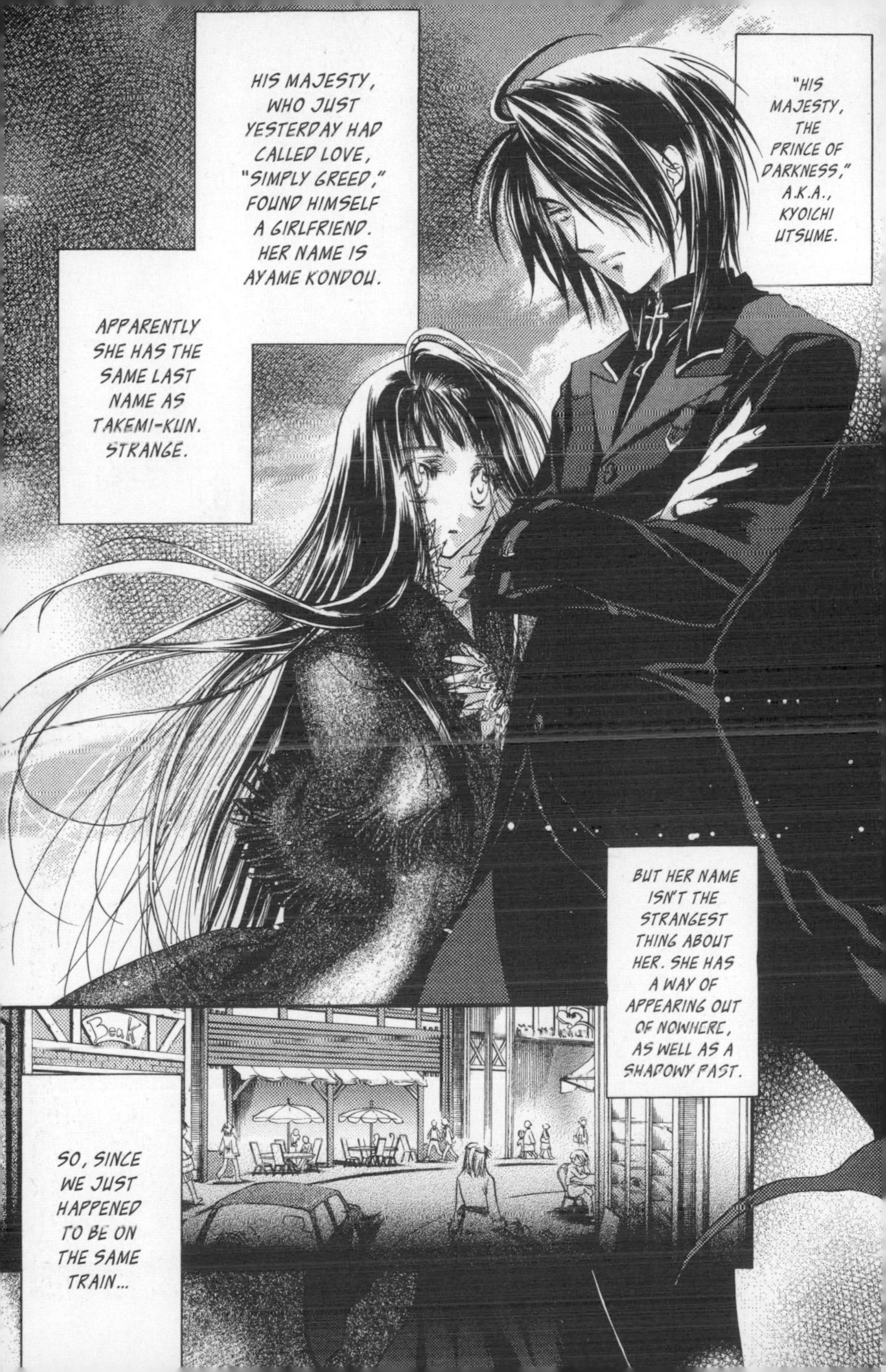
"HIS MAJESTY, THE PRINCE OF DARKNESS," A.K.A., KYOICHI UTSUME.
HIS MAJESTY, WHO JUST YESTERDAY HAD CALLED LOVE, "SIMPLY GREED," FOUND HIMSELF A GIRLFRIEND. HER NAME IS AYAME KONDOU.
APPARENTLY SHE HAS THE SAME LAST NAME AS TAKEMI-KUN. STRANGE.
BUT HER NAME ISN'T THE STRANGEST THING ABOUT HER. SHE HAS A WAY OF APPEARING OUT OF NOWHERE, AS WELL AS A SHADOWY PAST.
Bea K
SO, SINCE WE JUST HAPPENED TO BE ON THE SAME TRAIN...

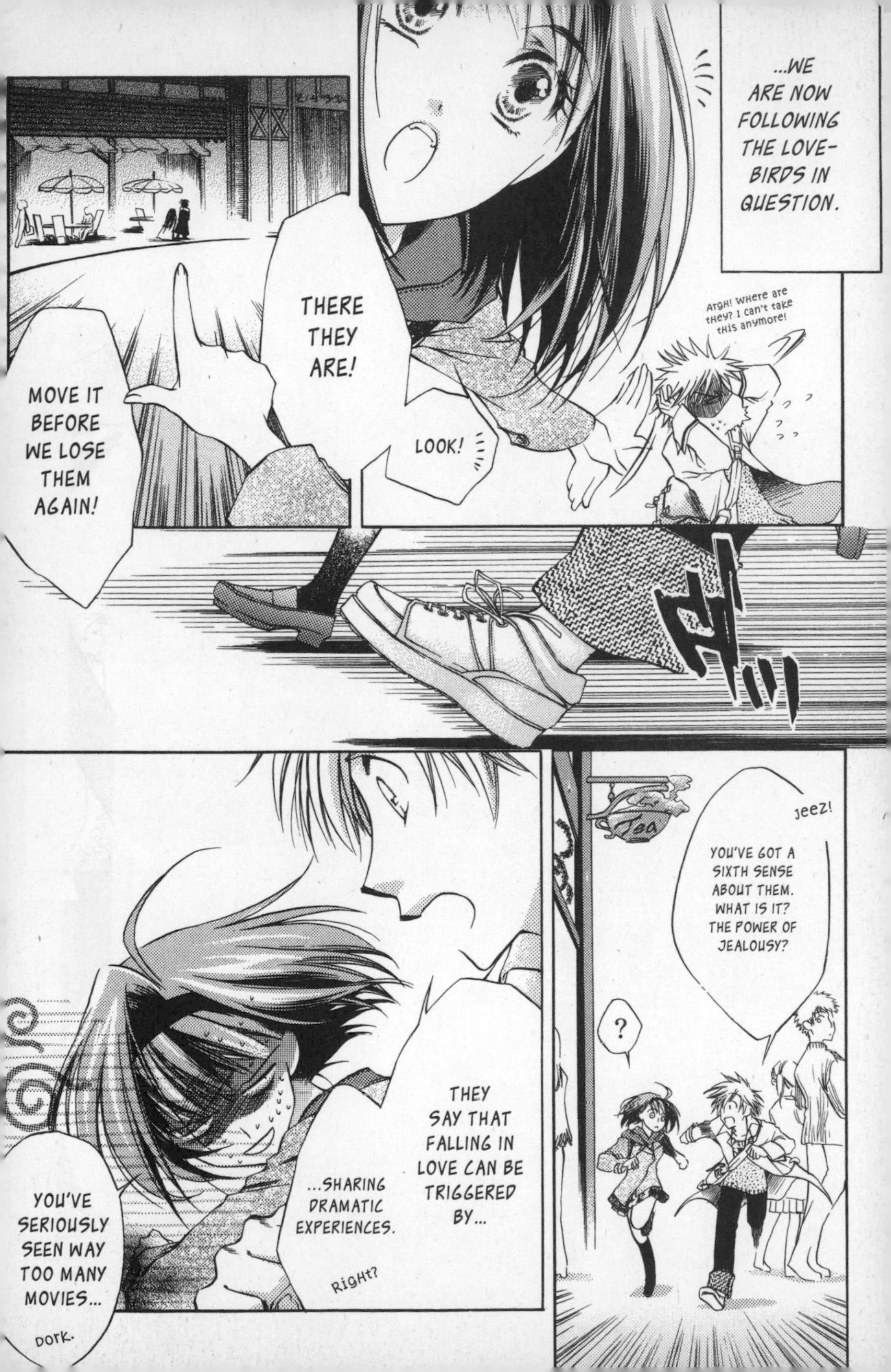
...WE ARE NOW FOLLOWING THE LOVE-BIRDS IN QUESTION.
Argh! Where are they? I can't take this anymore!
THERE THEY ARE!
LOOK!
MOVE IT BEFORE WE LOSE THEM AGAIN!
Jeez!
YOU'VE GOT A SIXTH SENSE ABOUT THEM. WHAT IS IT? THE POWER OF JEALOUSY?
?
THEY SAY THAT FALLING IN LOVE CAN BE TRIGGERED BY...
...SHARING DRAMATIC EXPERIENCES.
Right?
YOU'VE SERIOUSLY SEEN WAY TOO MANY MOVIES...
Dork.

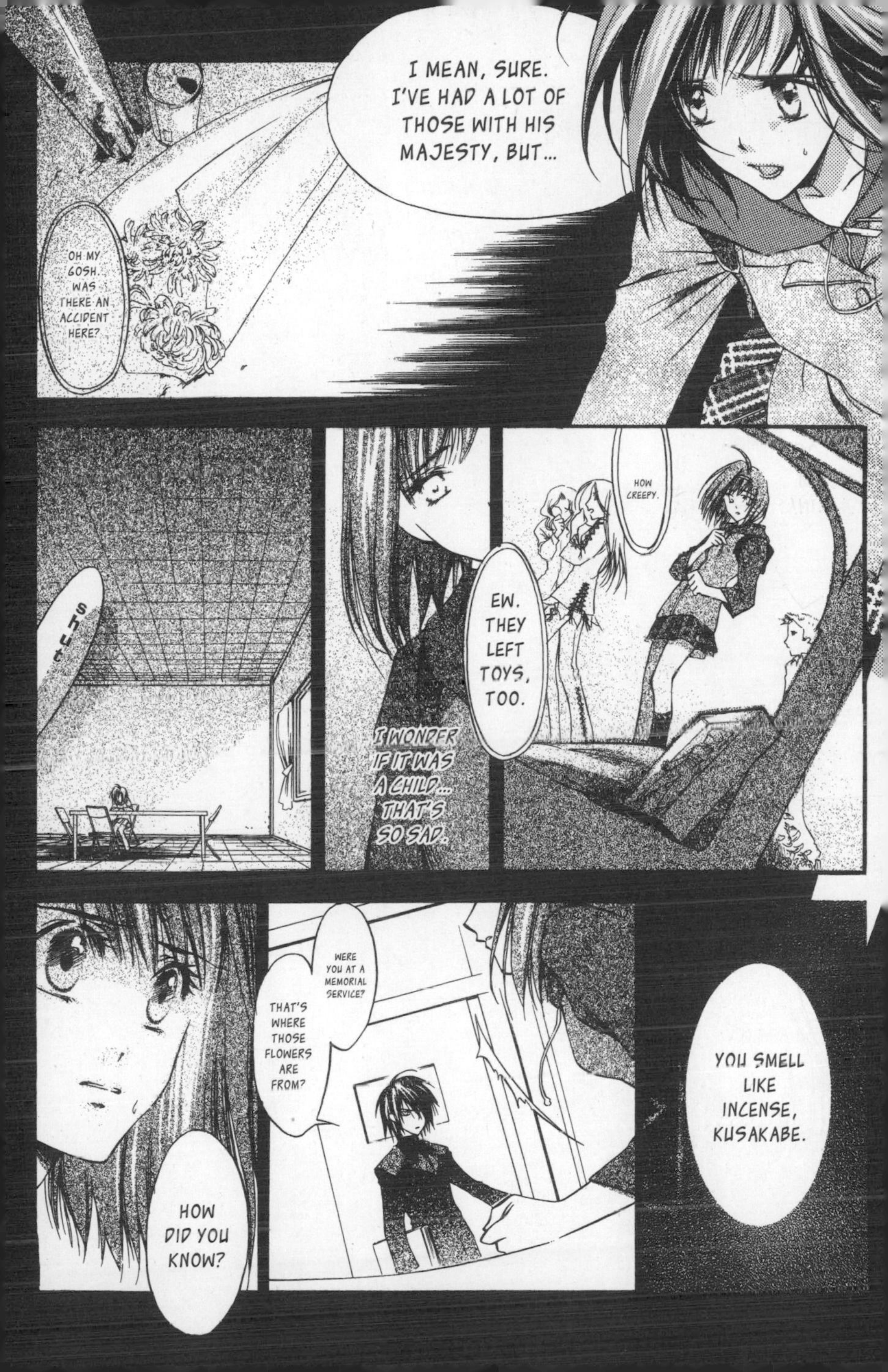
I MEAN, SURE. I'VE HAD A LOT OF THOSE WITH HIS MAJESTY, BUT...
OH MY GOSH. WAS THERE AN ACCIDENT HERE?
HOW CREEPY.
EW. THEY LEFT TOYS, TOO.
I WONDER IF IT WAS A CHILD... THAT'S SO SAD..
shut
YOU SMELL LIKE INCENSE, KUSAKABE.
WERE YOU AT A MEMORIAL SERVICE?
THAT'S WHERE THOSE FLOWERS ARE FROM?
HOW DID YOU KNOW?

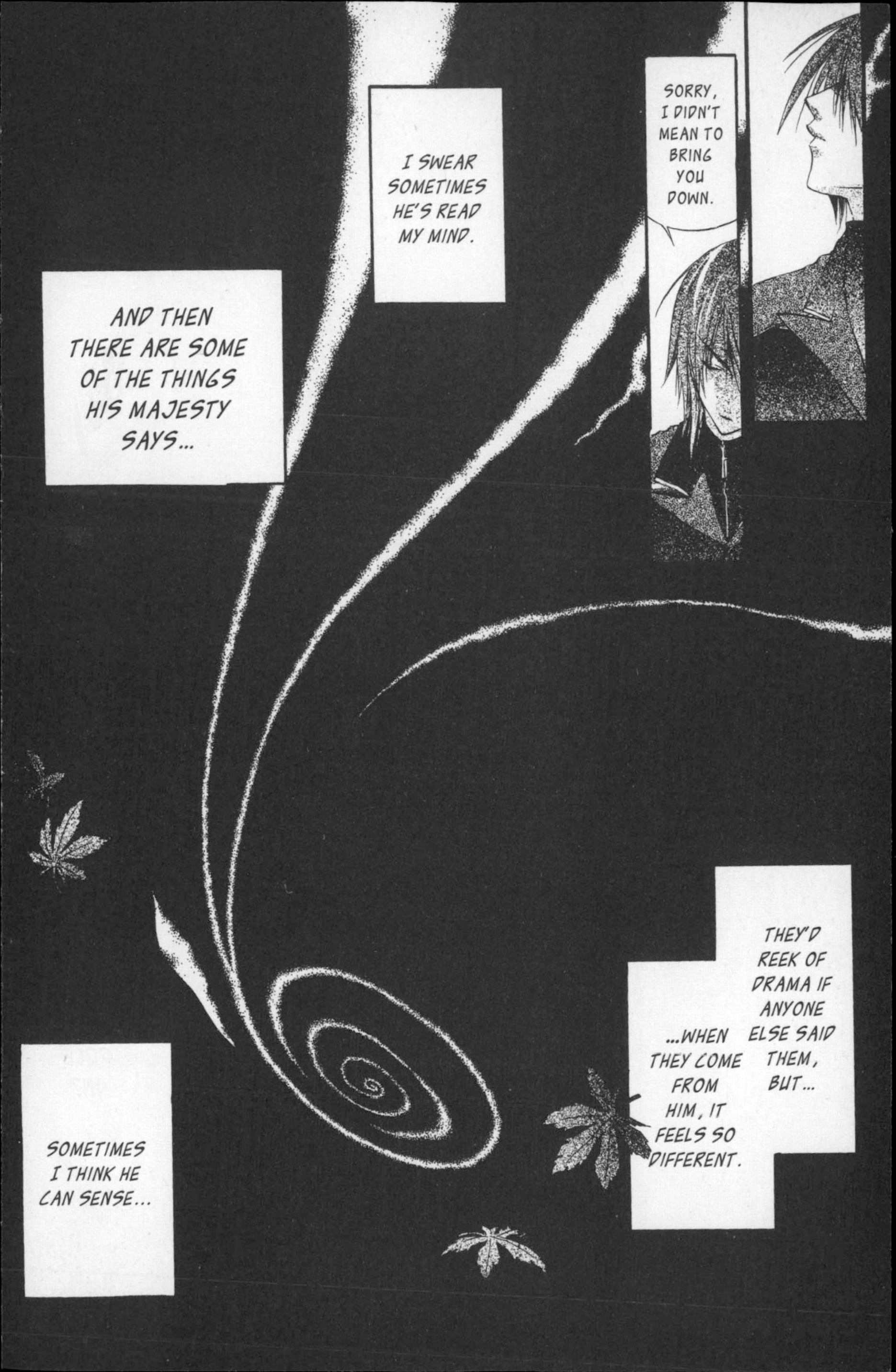
SORRY, I DIDN'T MEAN TO BRING YOU DOWN.
I SWEAR SOMETIMES HE'S READ MY MIND.
AND THEN THERE ARE SOME OF THE THINGS HIS MAJESTY SAYS...
THEY'D REEK OF DRAMA IF ANYONE ELSE SAID THEM, BUT...
...WHEN THEY COME FROM HIM, IT FEELS SO DIFFERENT.
SOMETIMES I THINK HE CAN SENSE...

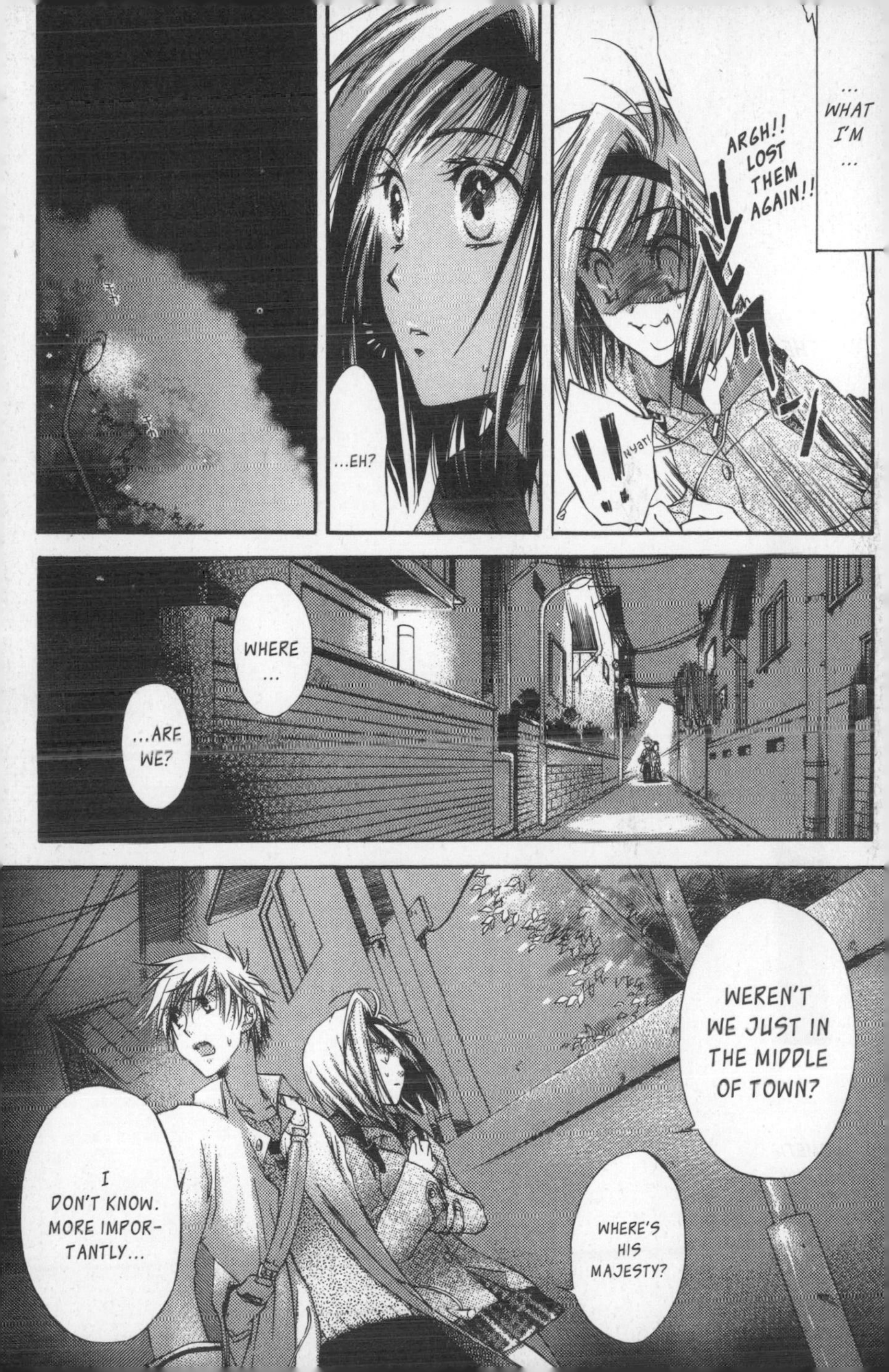
... WHAT I'M ...
ARGH!! LOST THEM AGAIN!!
Nyar!
...EH?
WHERE ...
...ARE WE?
WEREN'T WE JUST IN THE MIDDLE OF TOWN?
WHERE'S HIS MAJESTY?
I DON'T KNOW. MORE IMPOR-TANTLY...

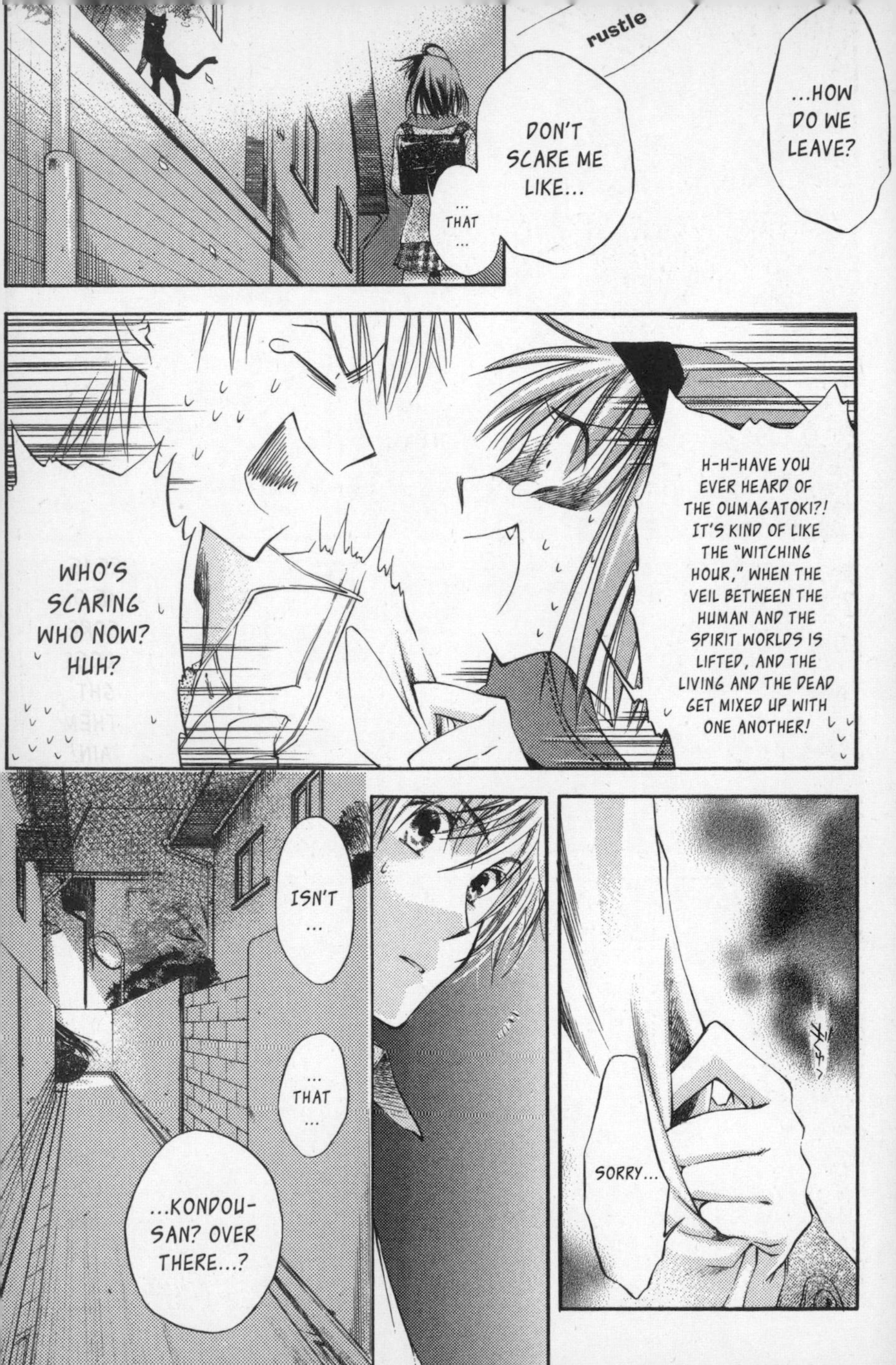
rustle
...HOW DO WE LEAVE?
DON'T SCARE ME LIKE...
... THAT ...
H-H-HAVE YOU EVER HEARD OF THE OUMAGATOKI?! IT'S KIND OF LIKE THE "WITCHING HOUR," WHEN THE VEIL BETWEEN THE HUMAN AND THE SPIRIT WORLDS IS LIFTED, AND THE LIVING AND THE DEAD GET MIXED UP WITH ONE ANOTHER!
WHO'S SCARING WHO NOW? HUH?
SORRY...
ISN'T ...
... THAT ...
...KONDOU-SAN? OVER THERE...?

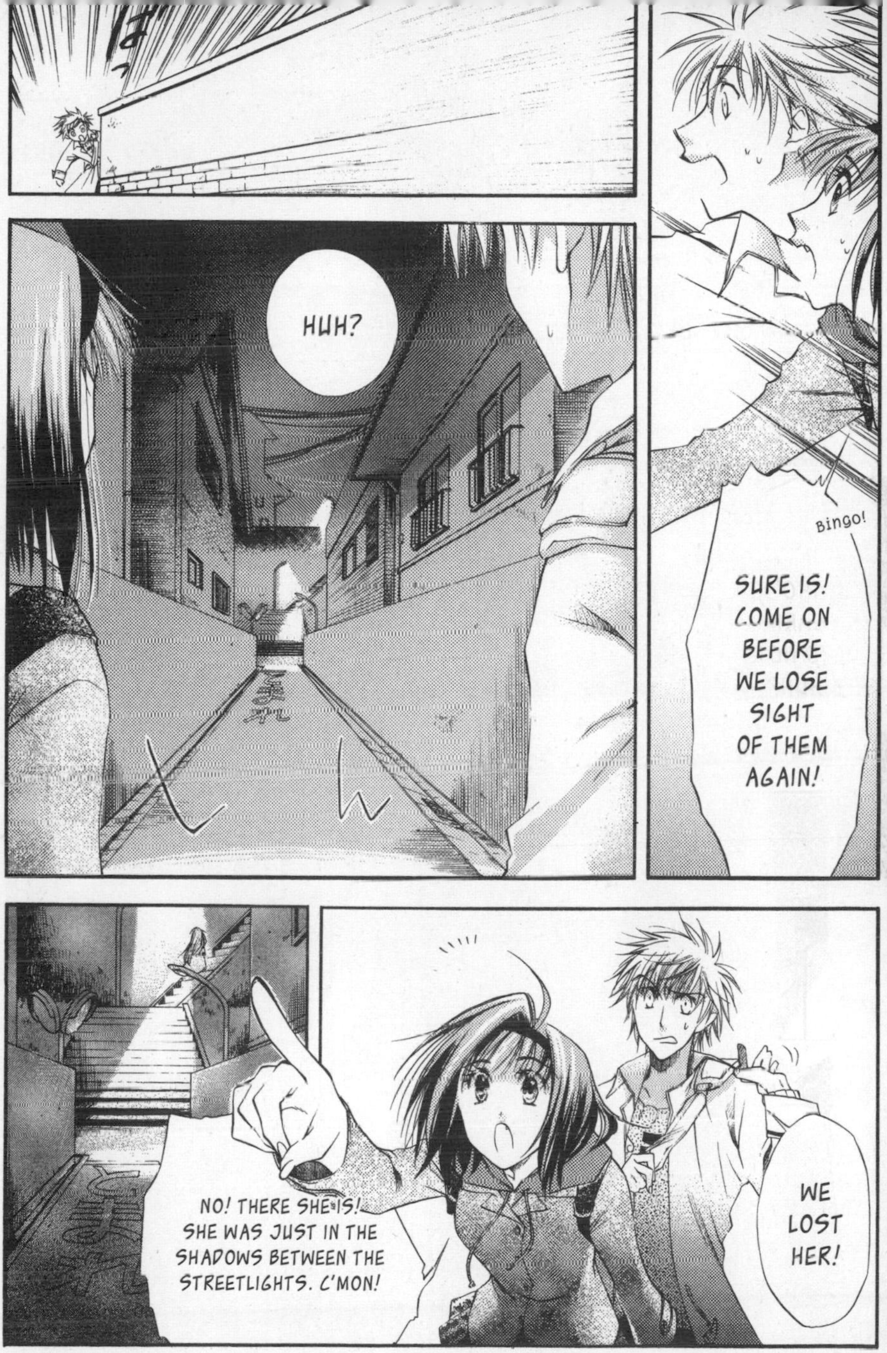
Bingo!
SURE IS! COME ON BEFORE WE LOSE SIGHT OF THEM AGAIN!
HUH?
WE LOST HER!
NO! THERE SHE IS! SHE WAS JUST IN THE SHADOWS BETWEEN THE STREETLIGHTS. C'MON!

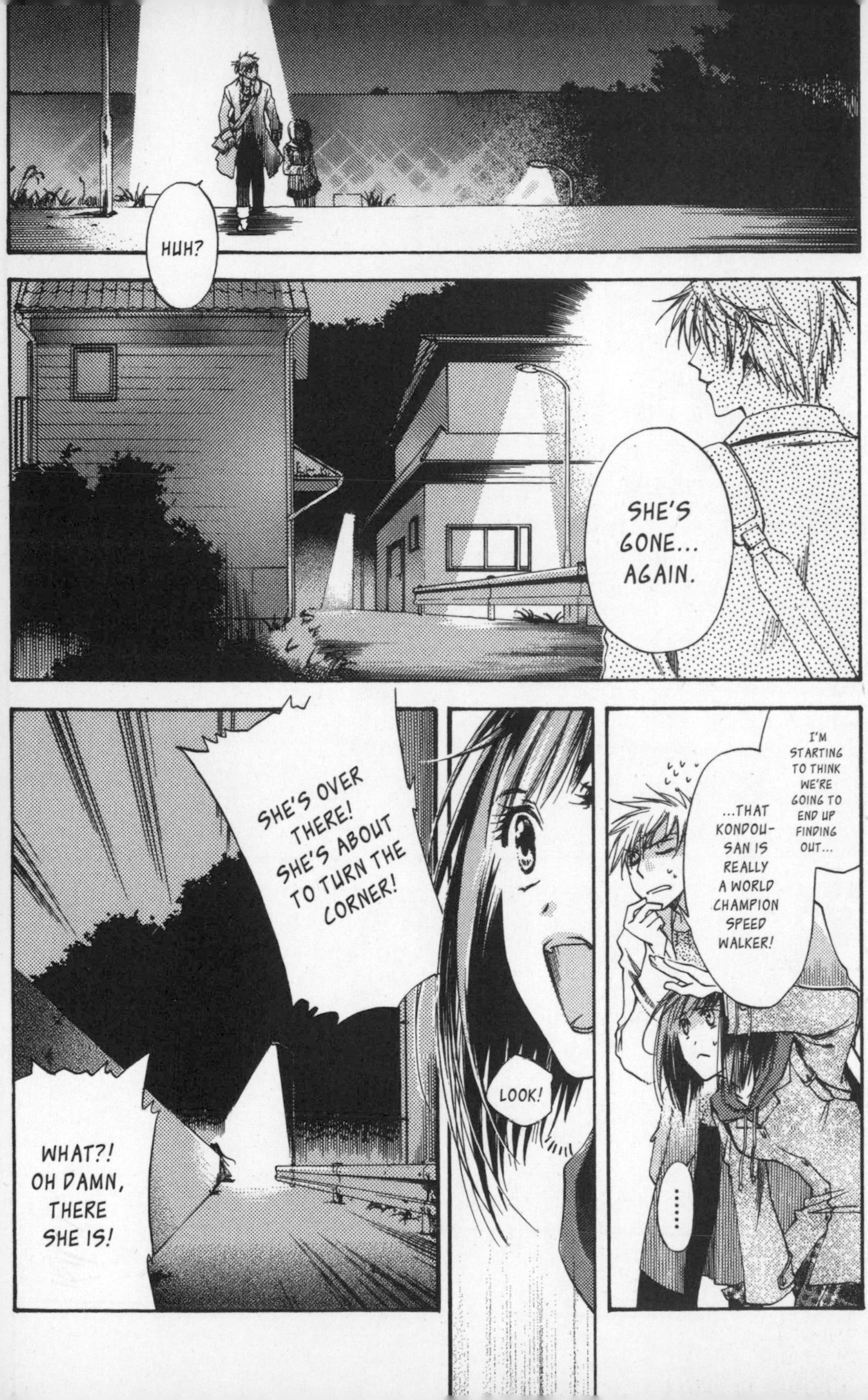
HUH?
SHE'S GONE... AGAIN.
I'M STARTING TO THINK WE'RE GOING TO END UP FINDING OUT...
...THAT KONDOU-SAN IS REALLY A WORLD CHAMPION SPEED WALKER!
......
LOOK!
SHE'S OVER THERE! SHE'S ABOUT TO TURN THE CORNER!
WHAT?! OH DAMN, THERE SHE IS!

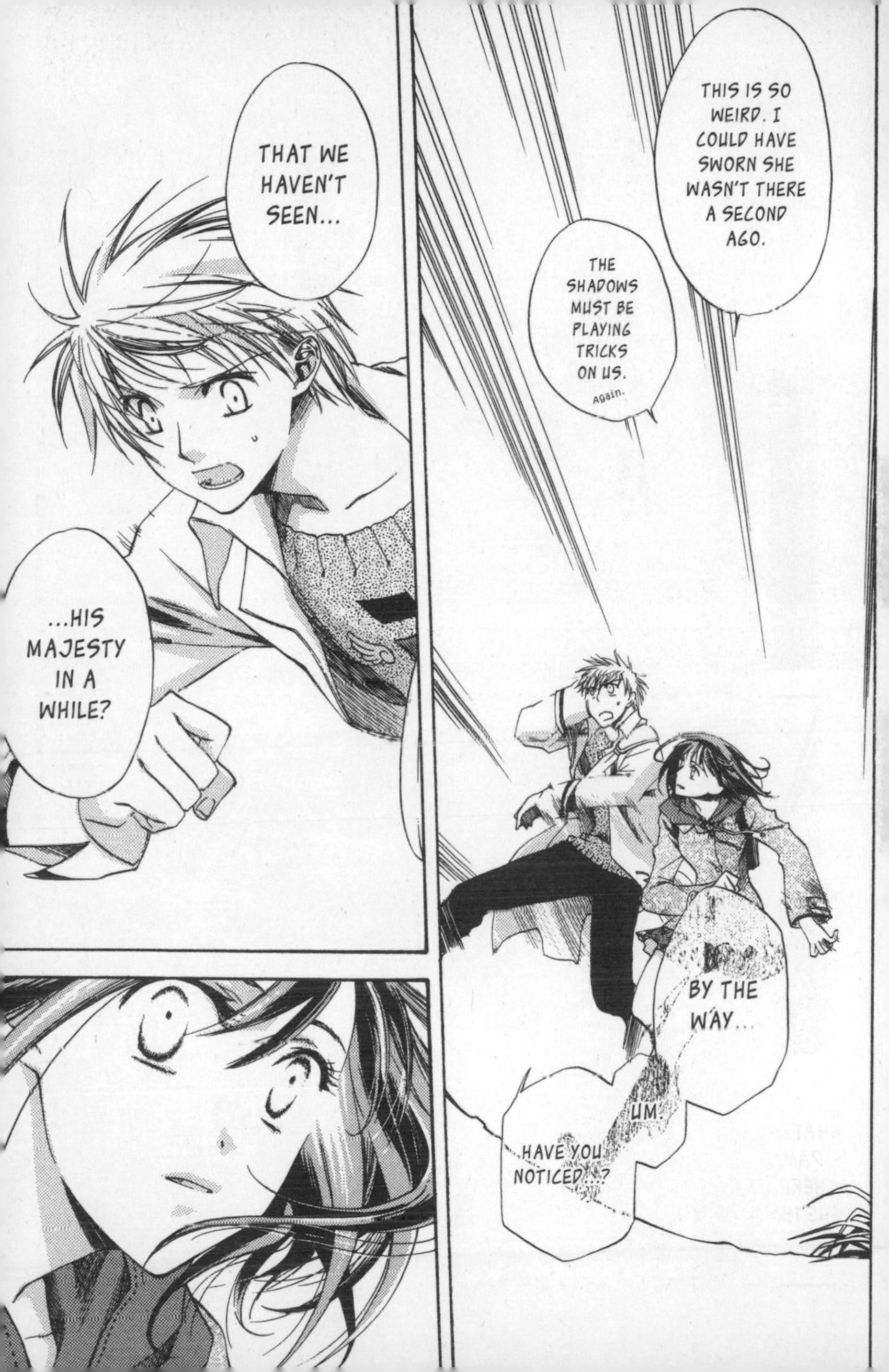
THIS IS SO WEIRD. I COULD HAVE SWORN SHE WASN'T THERE A SECOND AGO.
THE SHADOWS MUST BE PLAYING TRICKS ON US.
Again.
BY THE WAY...
UM.
HAVE YOU NOTICED...?
THAT WE HAVEN'T SEEN...
...HIS MAJESTY IN A WHILE?

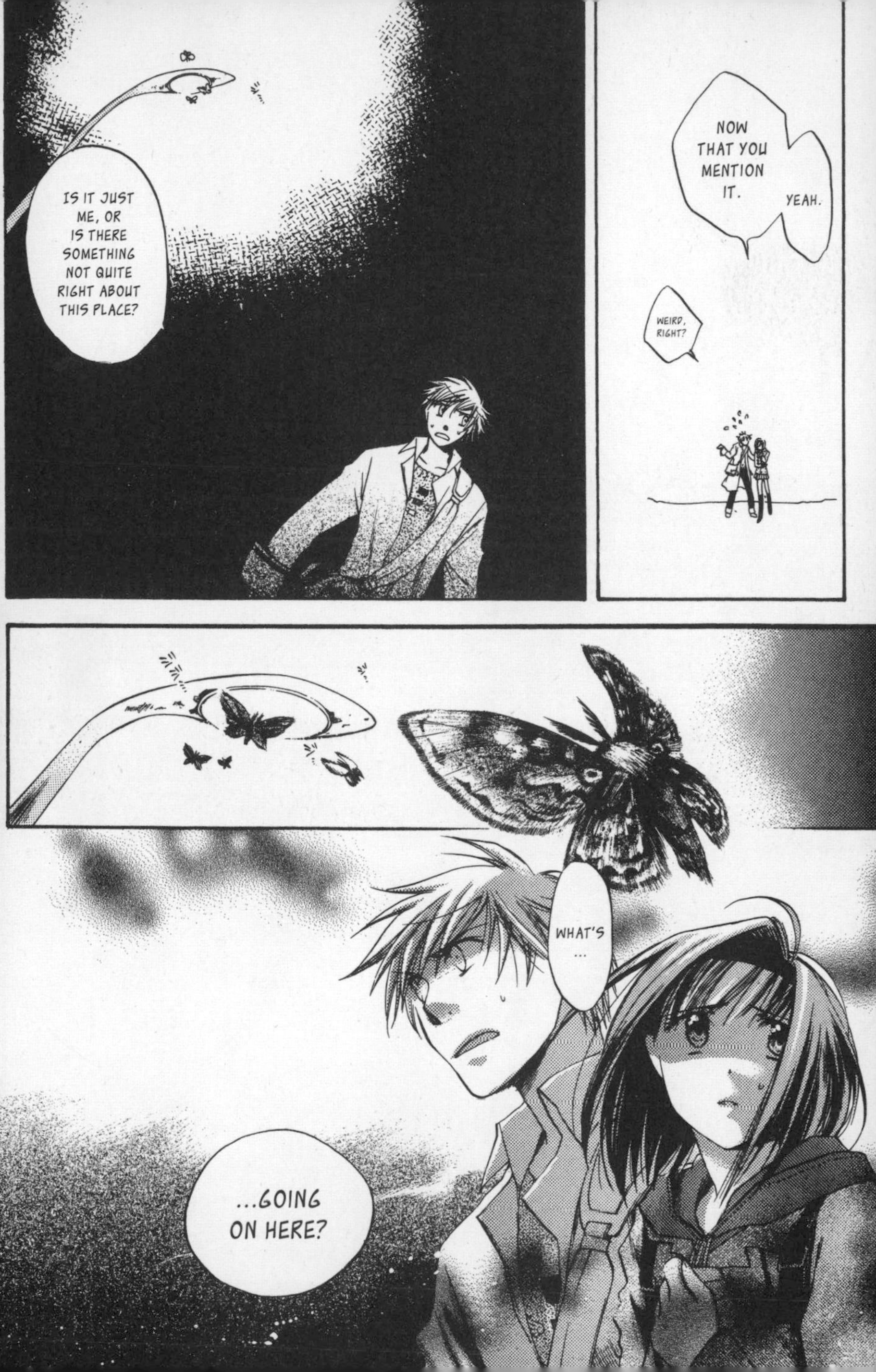
NOW THAT YOU MENTION IT.
YEAH.
WEIRD, RIGHT?
IS IT JUST ME, OR IS THERE SOMETHING NOT QUITE RIGHT ABOUT THIS PLACE?
WHAT'S ...
...GOING ON HERE?

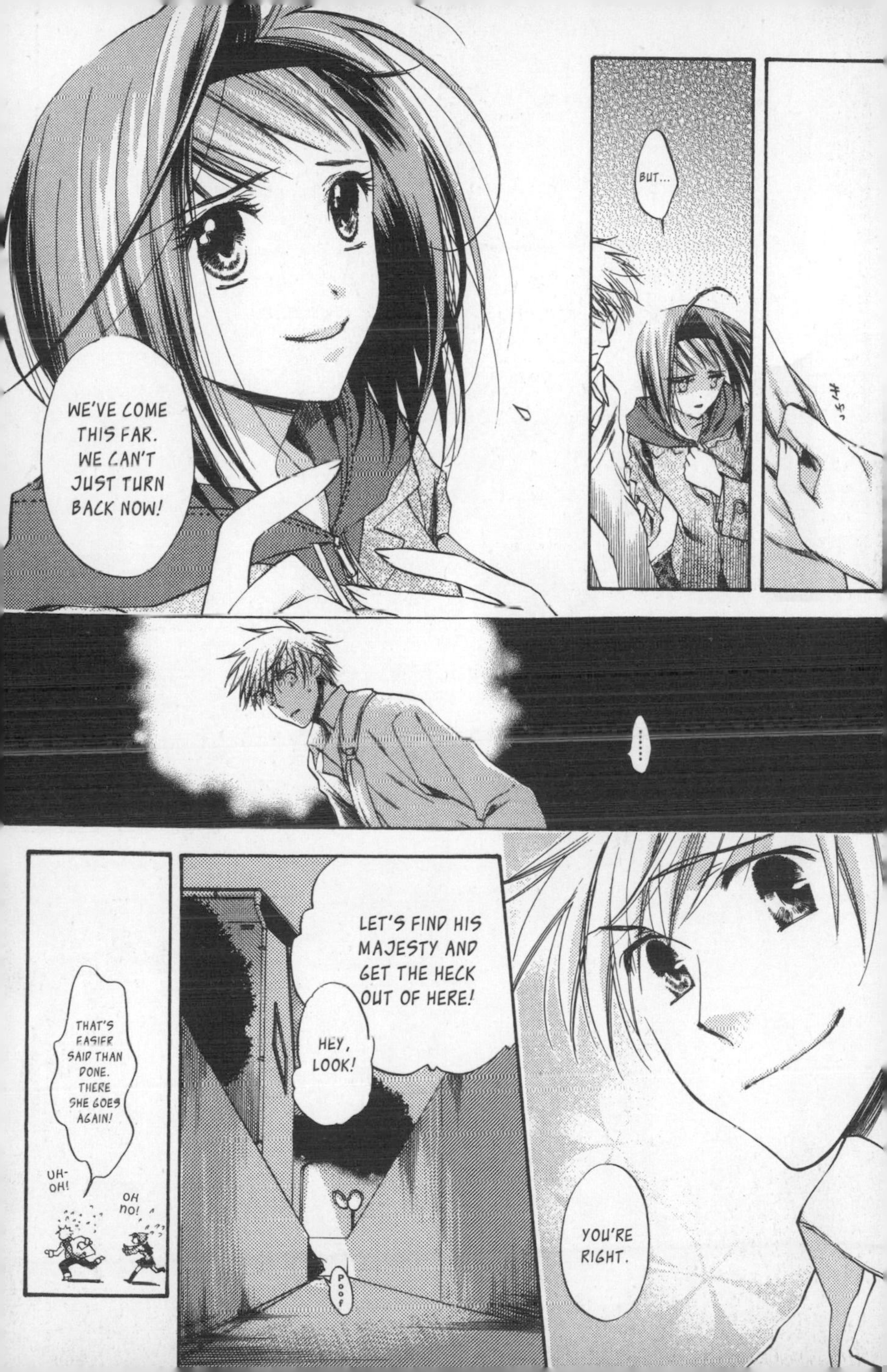
BUT...
WE'VE COME THIS FAR. WE CAN'T JUST TURN BACK NOW!
......
YOU'RE RIGHT.
LET'S FIND HIS MAJESTY AND GET THE HECK OUT OF HERE!
HEY, LOOK!
Poof
THAT'S EASIER SAID THAN DONE. THERE SHE GOES AGAIN!
UH-OH!
OH NO!

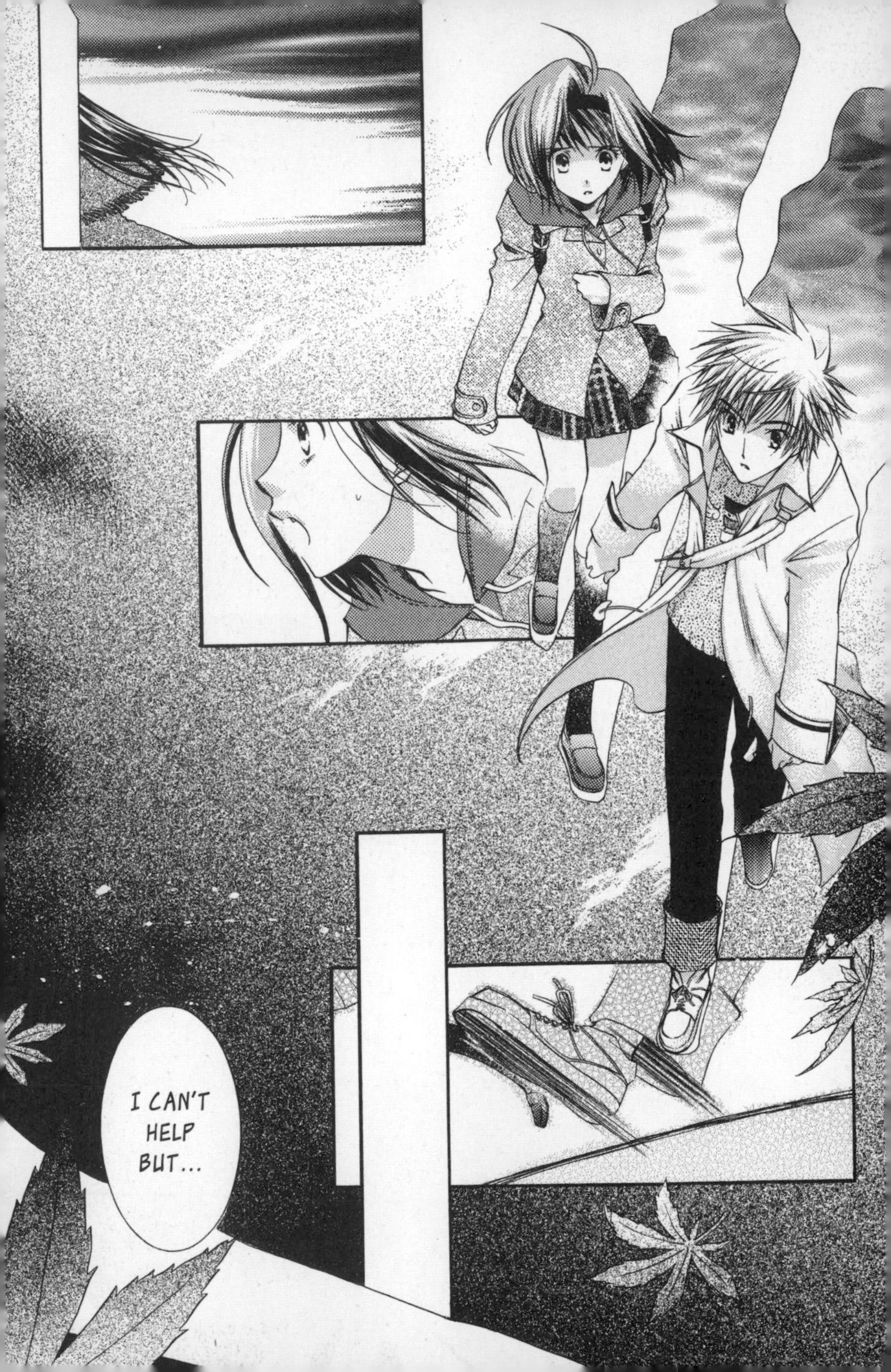
I CAN'T HELP BUT...

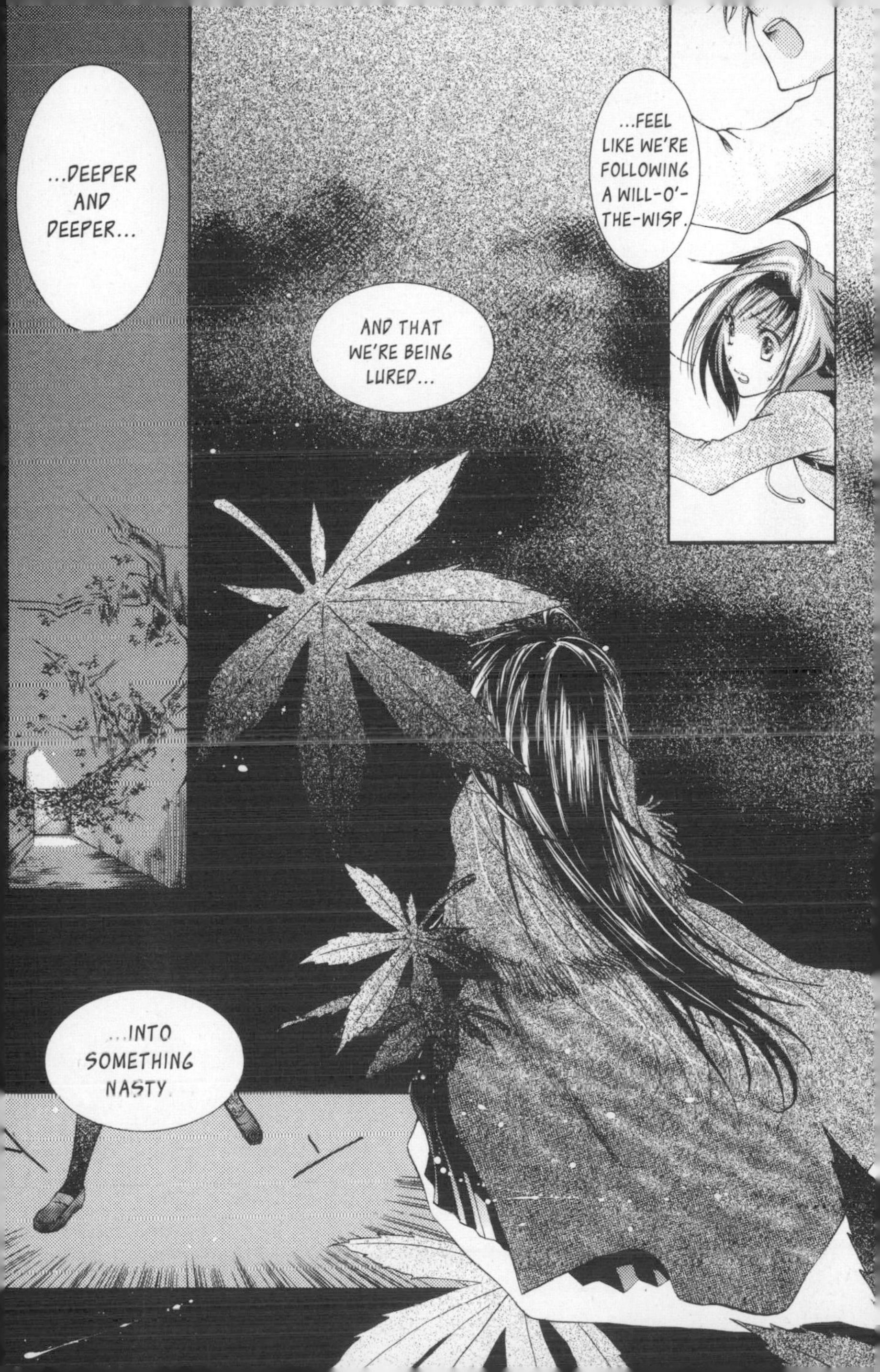
...FEEL LIKE WE'RE FOLLOWING A WILL-O'-THE-WISP.
AND THAT WE'RE BEING LURED...
...DEEPER AND DEEPER...
...INTO SOMETHING NASTY.

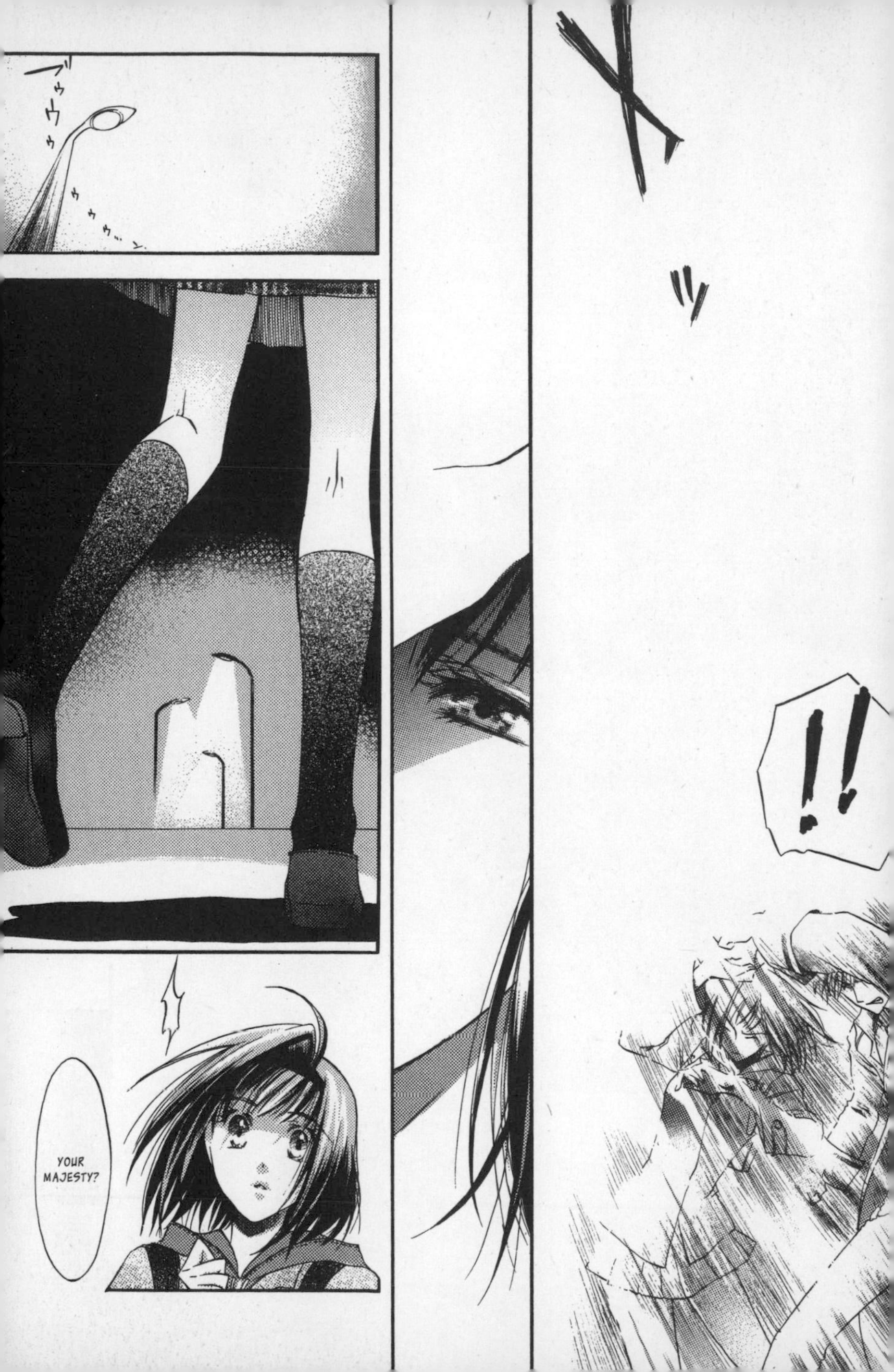
!!
YOUR MAJESTY?

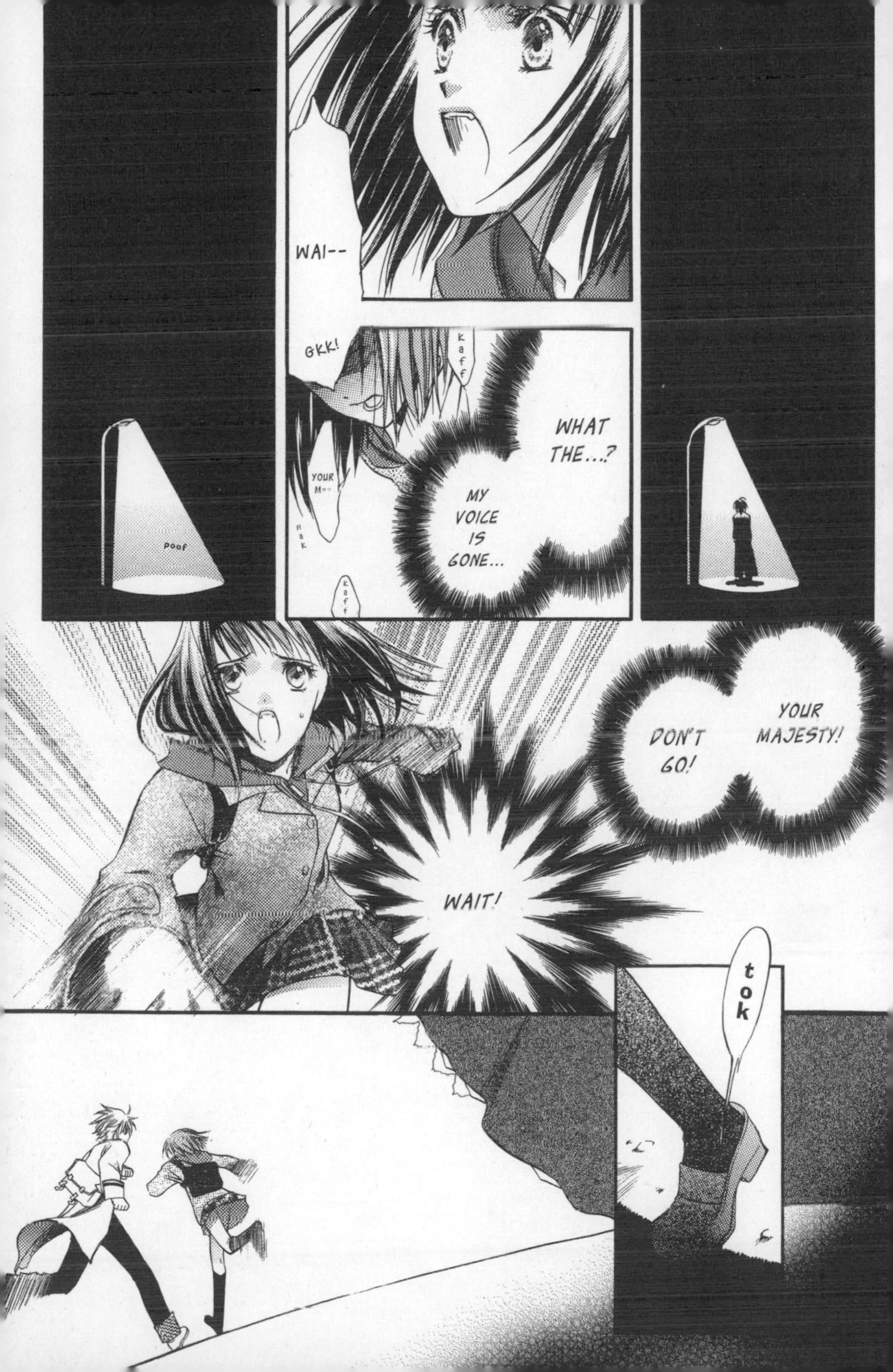
WAI--
WHAT THE...?
kaff
GKK!
MY VOICE IS GONE...
YOUR M--
hak
kaff
poof
YOUR MAJESTY!
DON'T GO!
WAIT!
tok

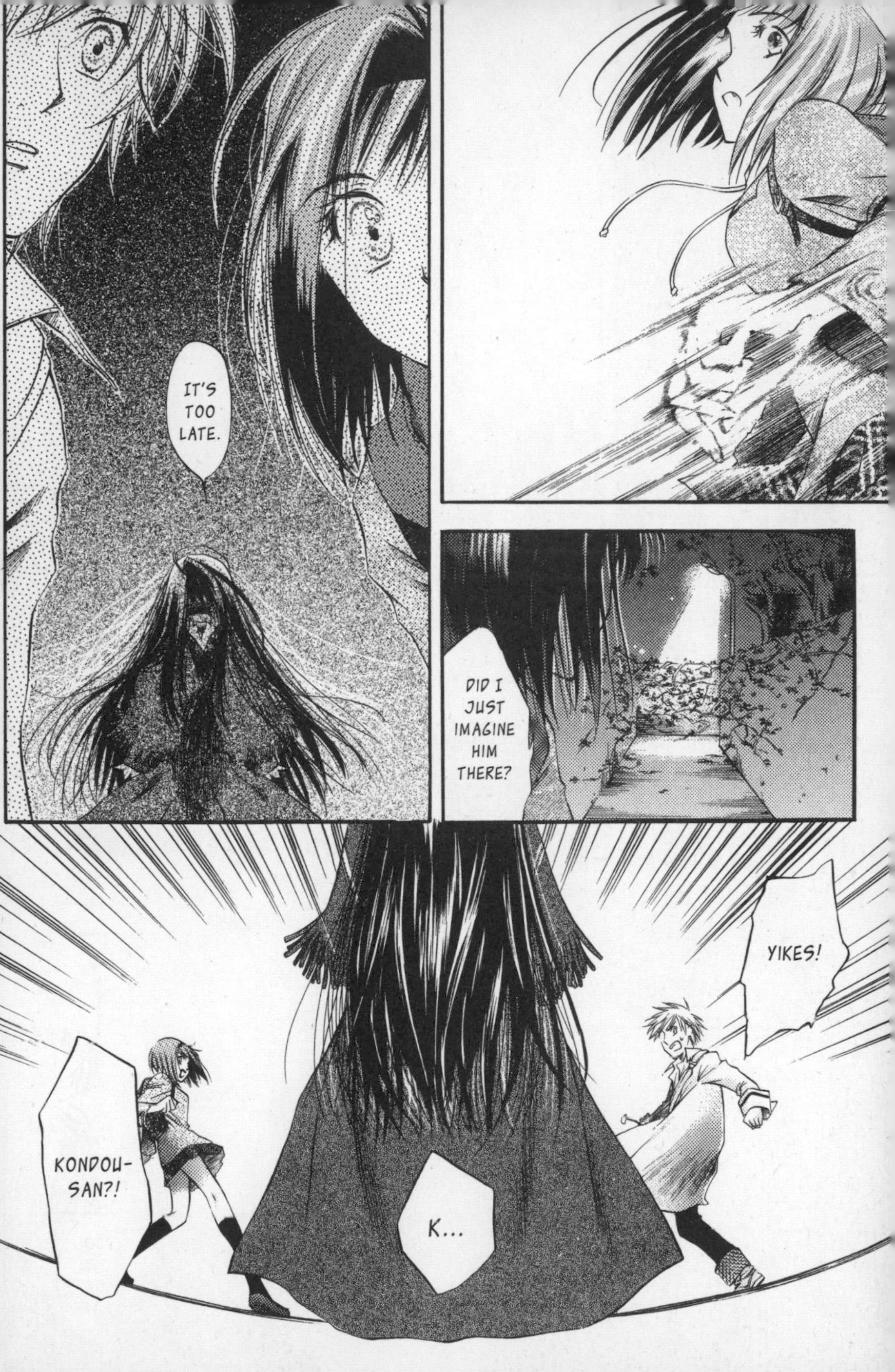
DID I JUST IMAGINE HIM THERE?
IT'S TOO LATE.
YIKES!
K...
KONDOU-SAN?!

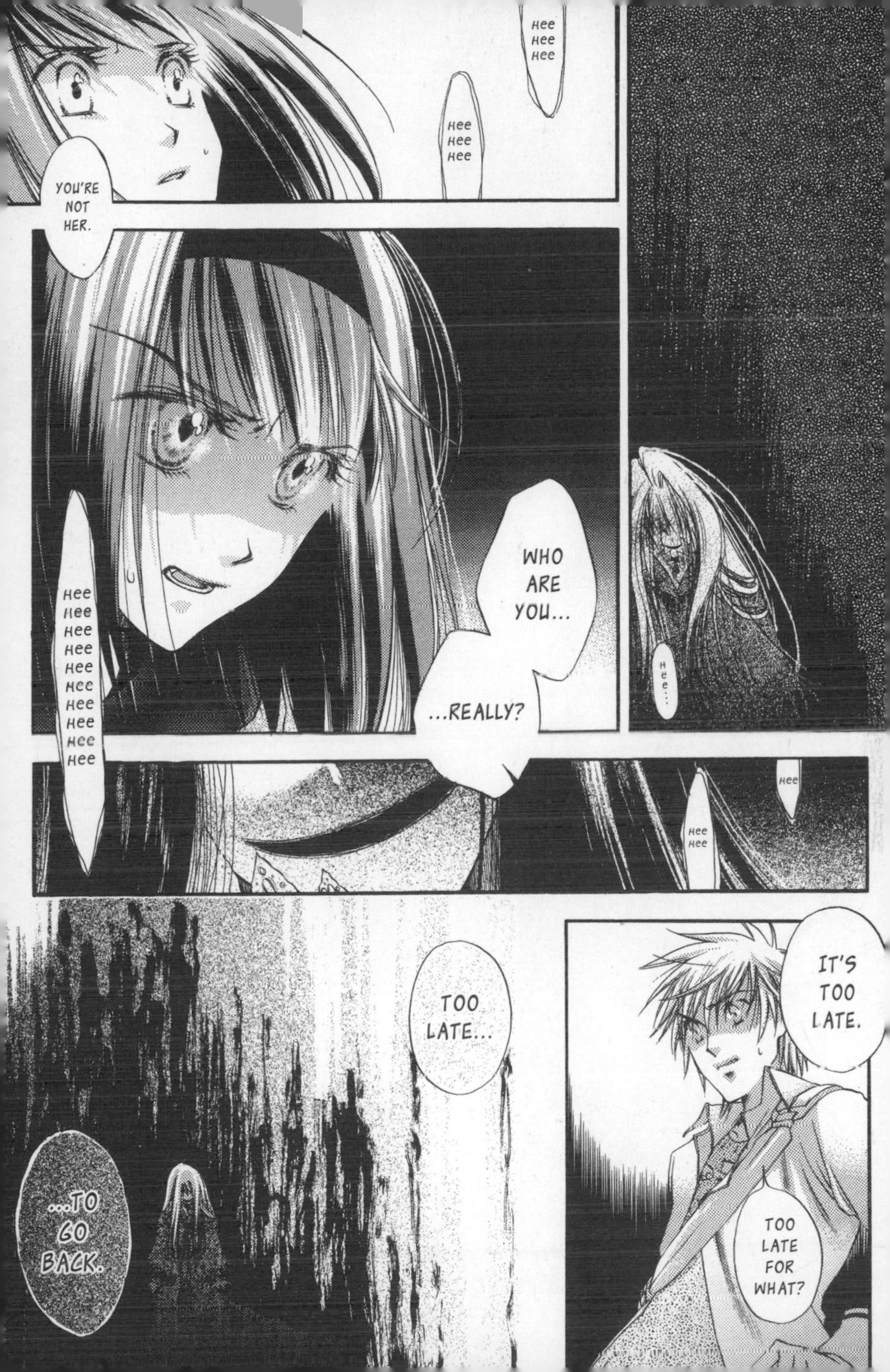
HEE...
HEE HEE HEE
HEE HEE HEE
YOU'RE NOT HER.
WHO ARE YOU...
...REALLY?
HEE HEE HEE HEE HEE HEE HEE HEE HEE HEE
HEE
HEE HEE
IT'S TOO LATE.
TOO LATE FOR WHAT?
TOO LATE...
...TO GO BACK.

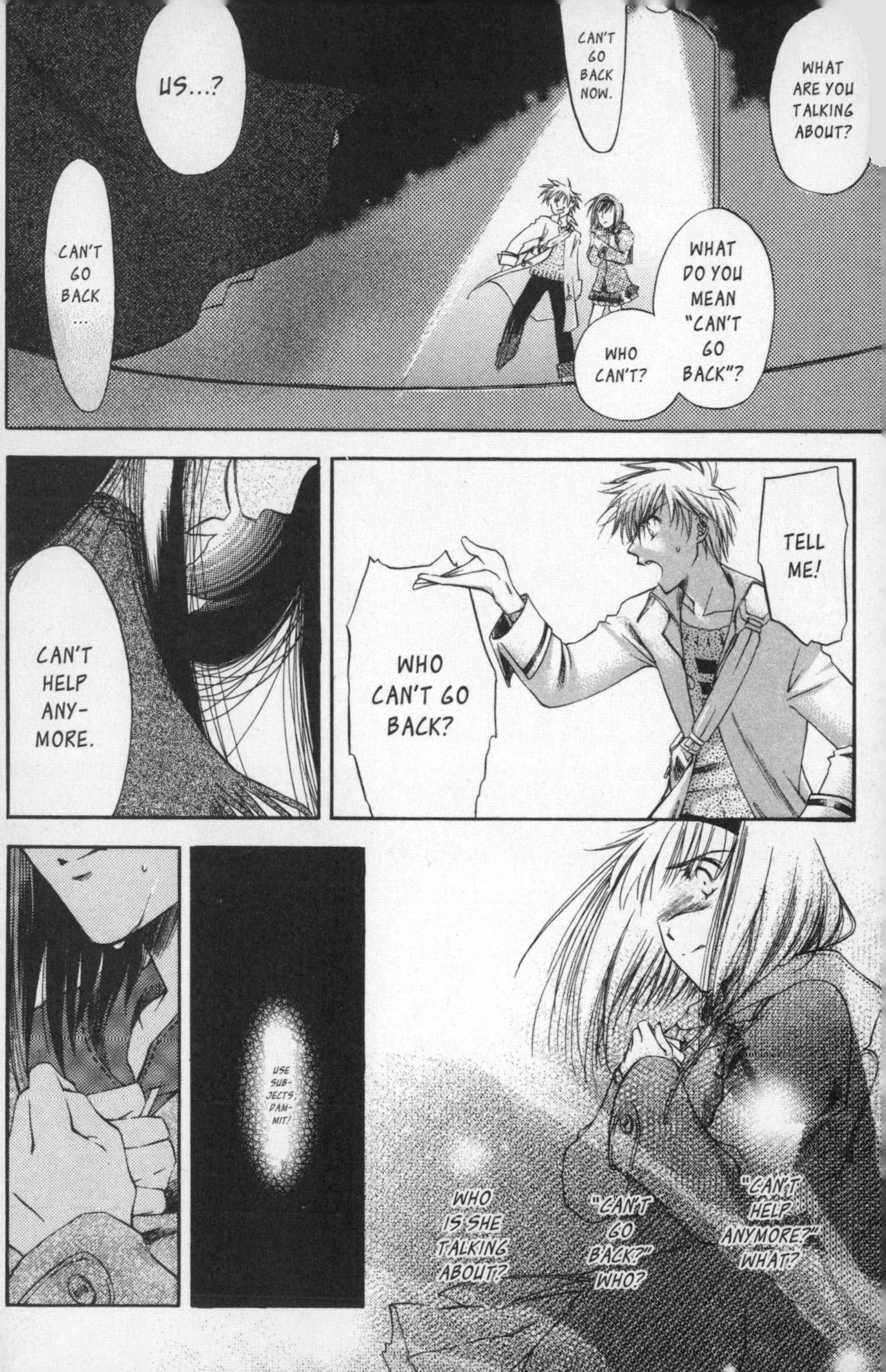
WHAT ARE YOU TALKING ABOUT?
CAN'T GO BACK NOW.
US...?
WHAT DO YOU MEAN "CAN'T GO BACK"?
WHO CAN'T?
CAN'T GO BACK ...
TELL ME!
WHO CAN'T GO BACK?
CAN'T HELP ANY-MORE.
"CAN'T HELP ANYMORE?" WHAT?
"CAN'T GO BACK?" WHO?
WHO IS SHE TALKING ABOUT?
USE SUB-JECTS, DAM-MIT!

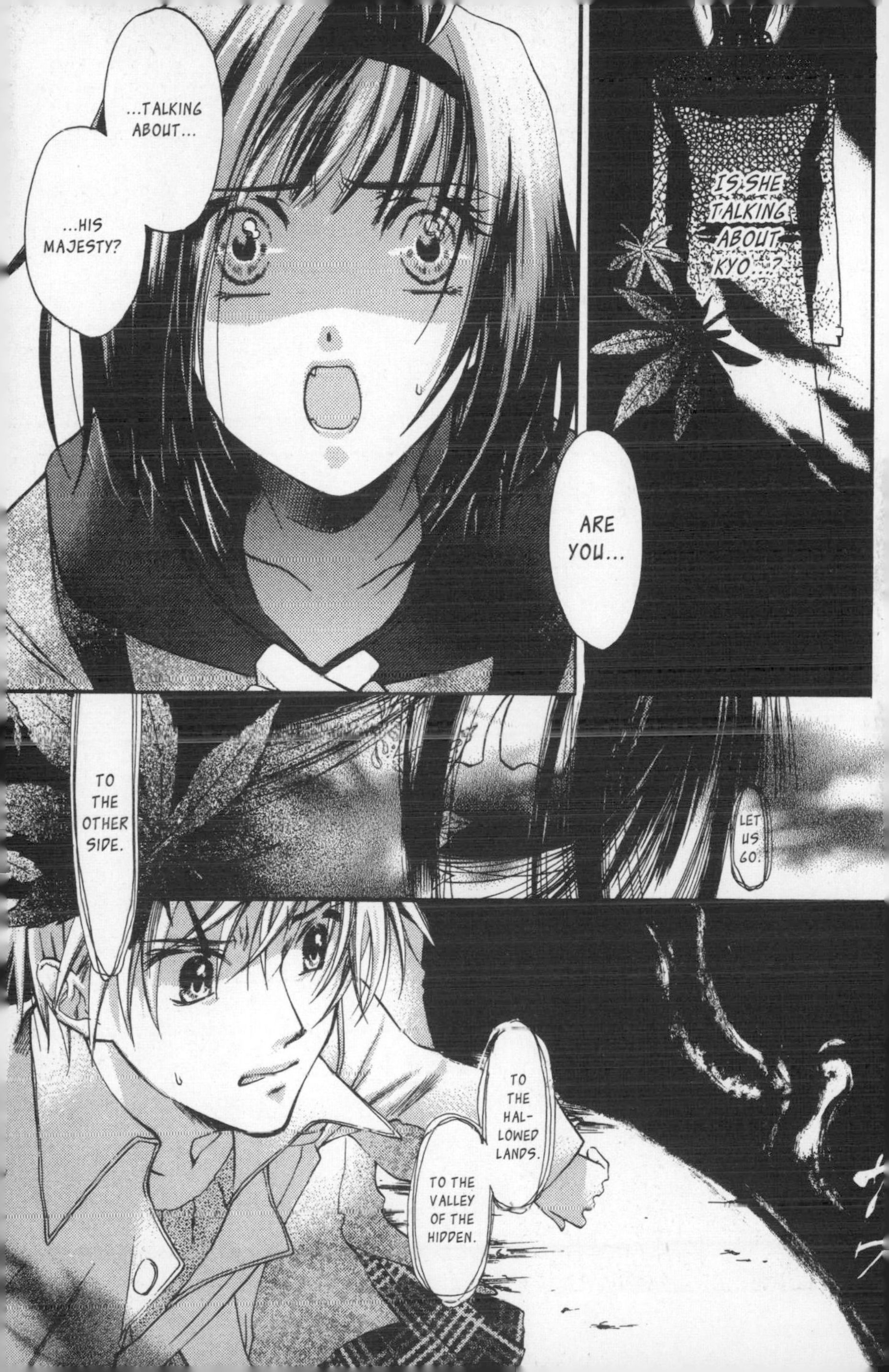
IS SHE TALKING ABOUT KYO...?
ARE YOU...
...TALKING ABOUT...
...HIS MAJESTY?
LET US GO.
TO THE OTHER SIDE.
TO THE HAL-LOWED LANDS.
TO THE VALLEY OF THE HIDDEN.

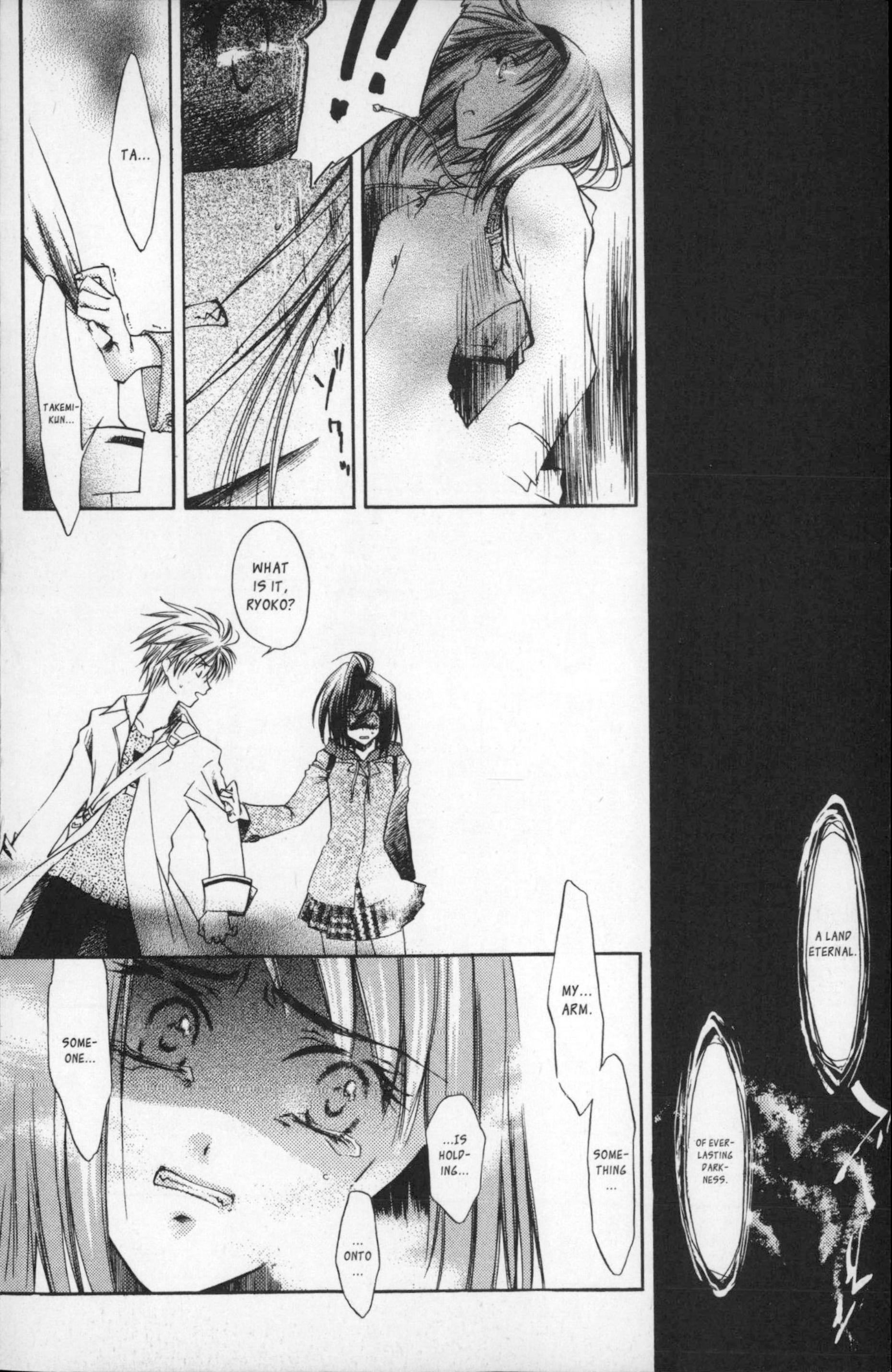
A LAND ETERNAL.
OF EVER-LASTING DARK-NESS.
!!
TA...
TAKEMI-KUN...
WHAT IS IT, RYOKO?
MY... ARM.
SOME-THING...
...IS HOLD-ING...
...ONTO...
SOME-ONE...

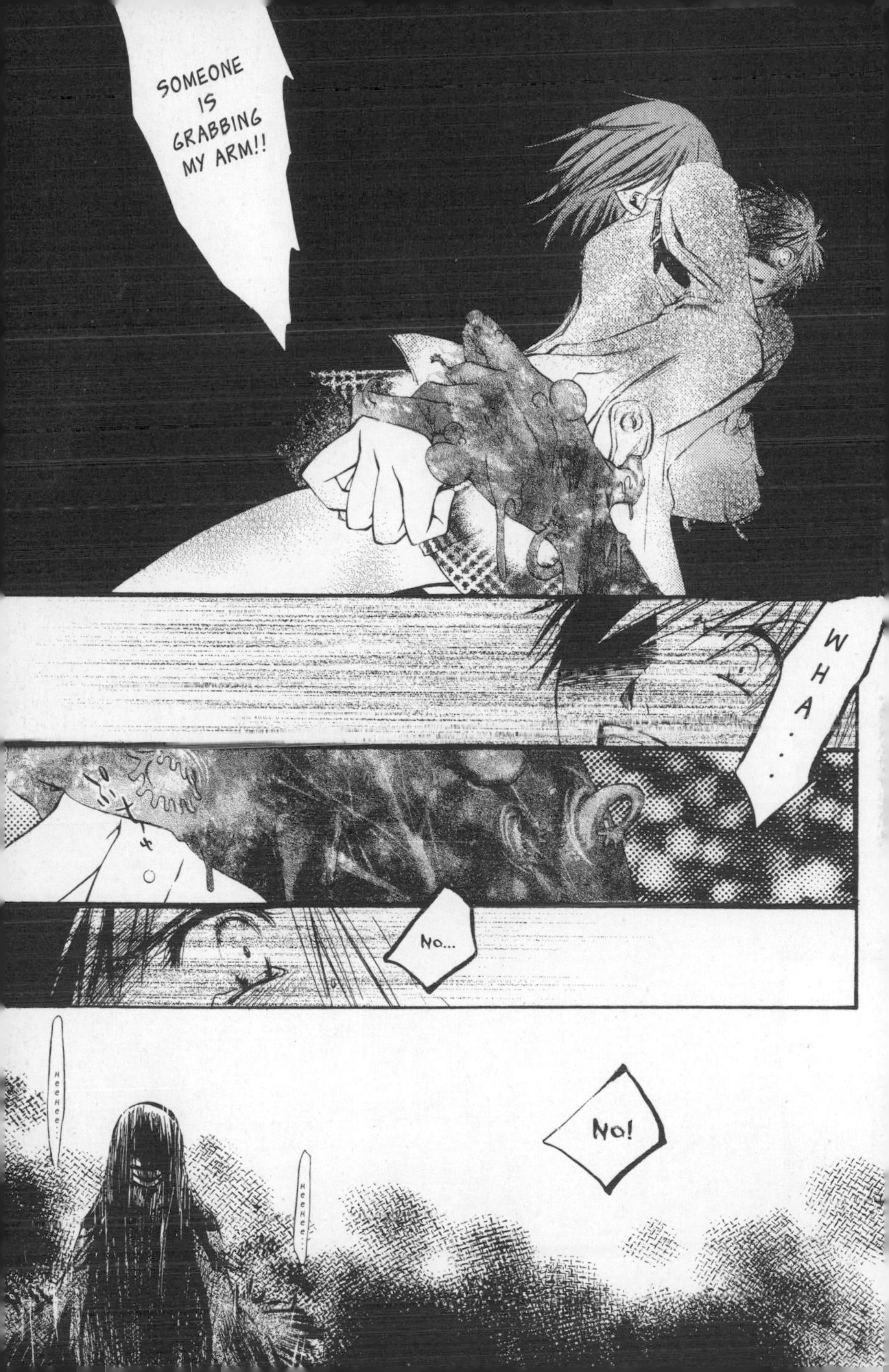
SOMEONE IS GRABBING MY ARM!!
WHA...
No...
No!
Heehee...
Heehee...

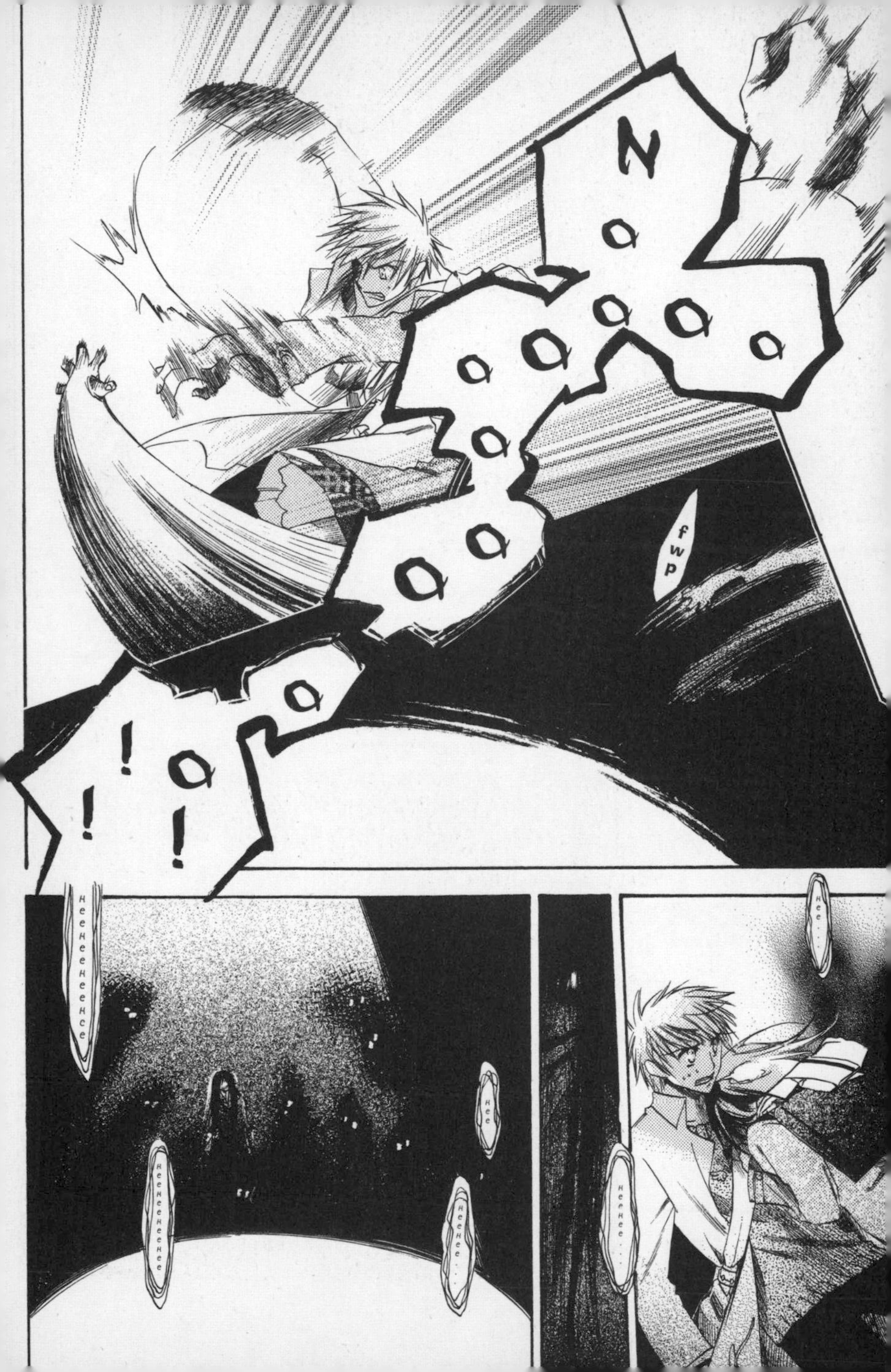
Naaaaaaaaaaaa!!!!
fwp
Hee...
HeeHee...
HeeHeeHeeHee
Hee
HeeHeeHeeHee
HeeHee...

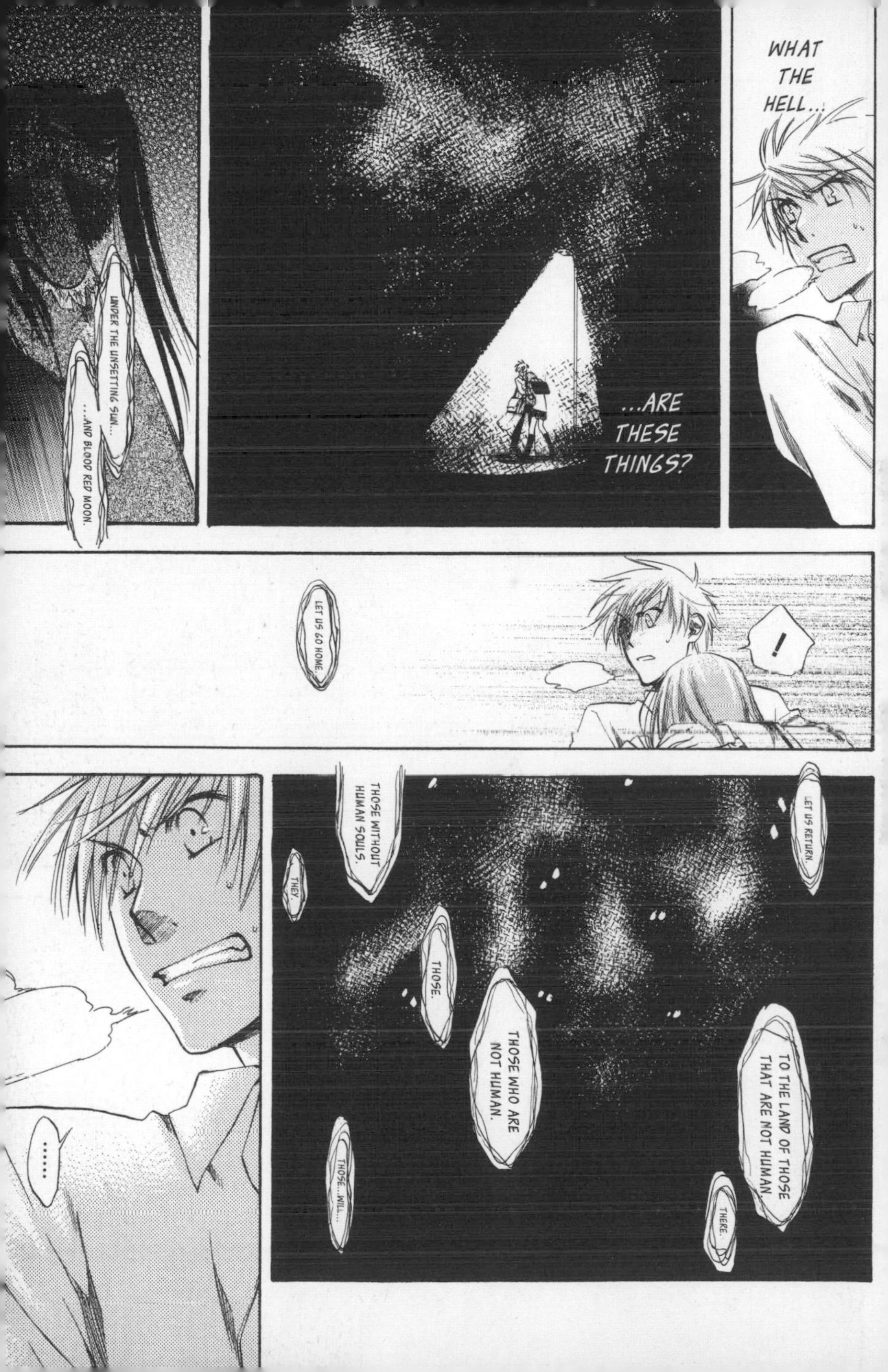
WHAT THE HELL...
...ARE THESE THINGS?
UNDER THE UNSETTING SUN...
...AND BLOOD RED MOON.
!
LET US GO HOME.
LET US RETURN.
TO THE LAND OF THOSE THAT ARE NOT HUMAN.
THERE.
THOSE WHO ARE NOT HUMAN.
THOSE.
THOSE WITHOUT HUMAN SOULS.
THEY.
THOSE...WILL...
......

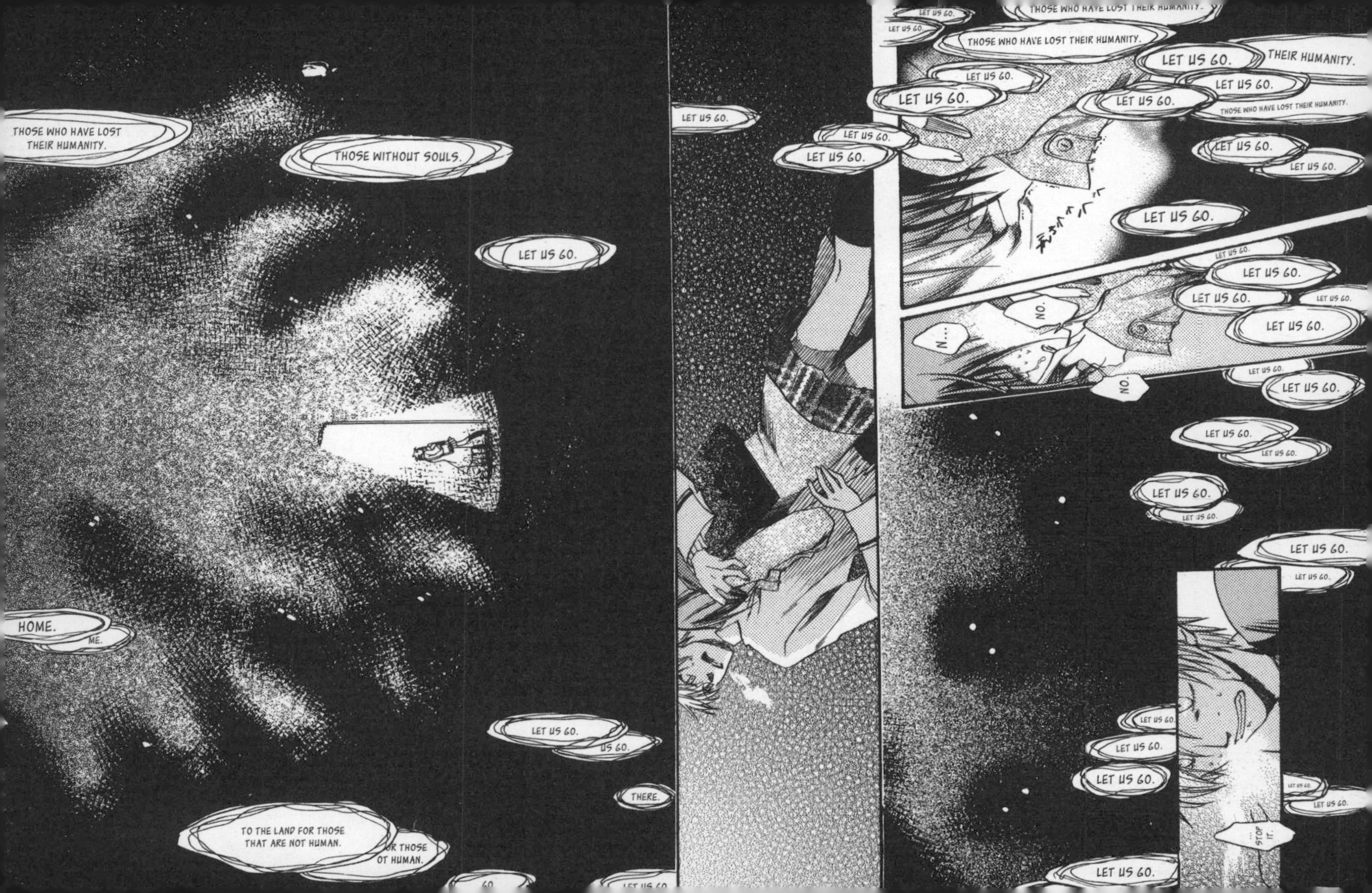
THOSE WHO HAVE LOST THEIR HUMANITY.
THOSE WHO HAVE LOST THEIR HUMANITY.
LET US GO.
LET US GO.
THEIR HUMANITY.
LET US GO.
LET US GO.
LET US GO.
THOSE WHO HAVE LOST THEIR HUMANITY.
LET US GO.
LET US GO.
LET US GO.
LET US GO.
LET US GO.
LET US GO.
LET US GO.
LET US GO.
N...
NO.
NO.
LET US GO.
LET US GO.
LET US GO.
LET US GO.
LET US GO.
LET US GO.
LET US GO.
...STOP IT.
LET US GO.
LET US GO.
LET US GO.
LET US GO.
THOSE WHO HAVE LOST THEIR HUMANITY.
THOSE WITHOUT SOULS.
LET US GO.
HOME.
ME.
LET US GO.
THERE.
TO THE LAND FOR THOSE THAT ARE NOT HUMAN.

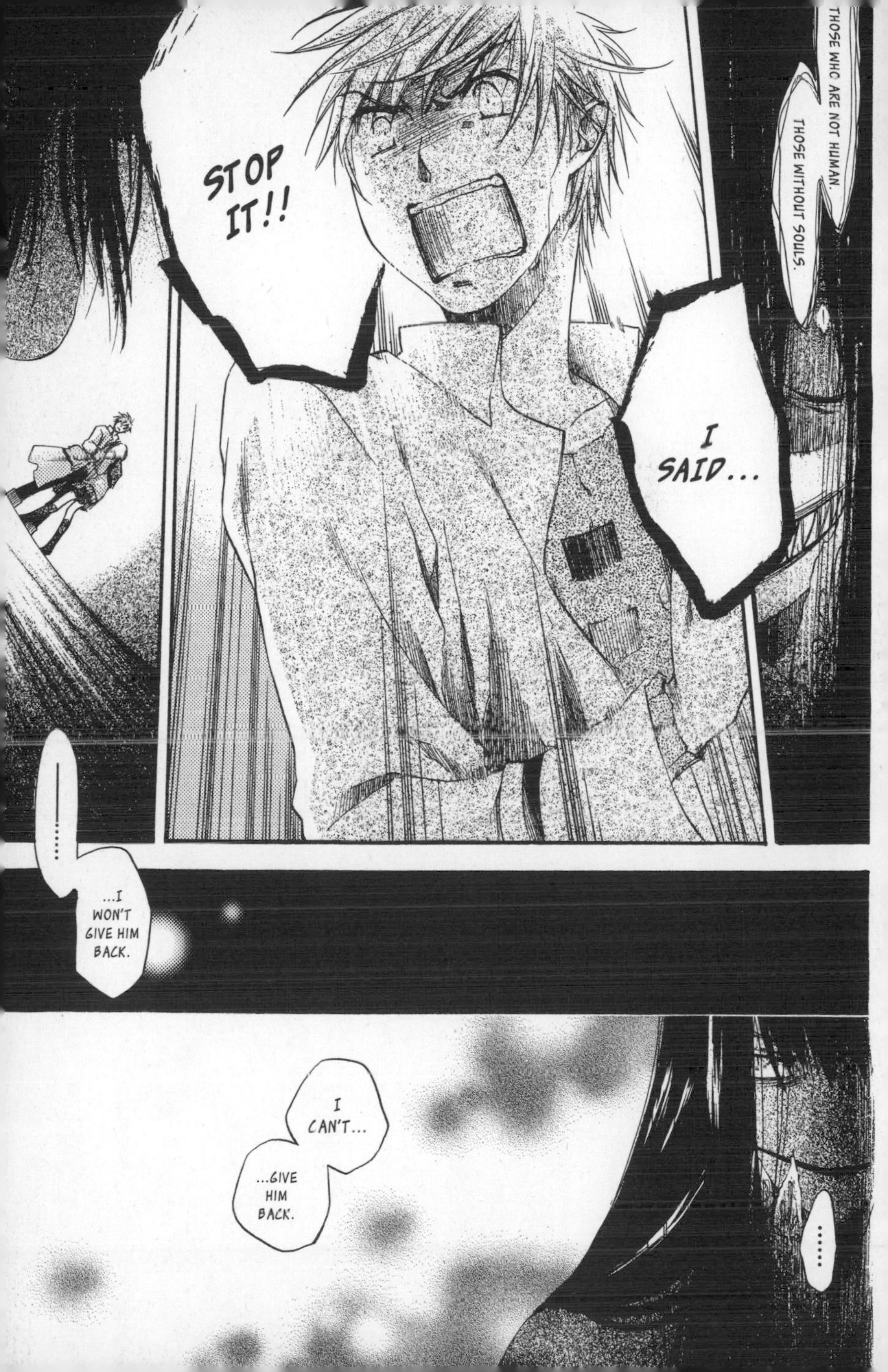
THOSE WHO ARE NOT HUMAN.
THOSE WITHOUT SOULS.
I SAID...
STOP IT!!
......
...I WON'T GIVE HIM BACK.
......
I CAN'T...
...GIVE HIM BACK.

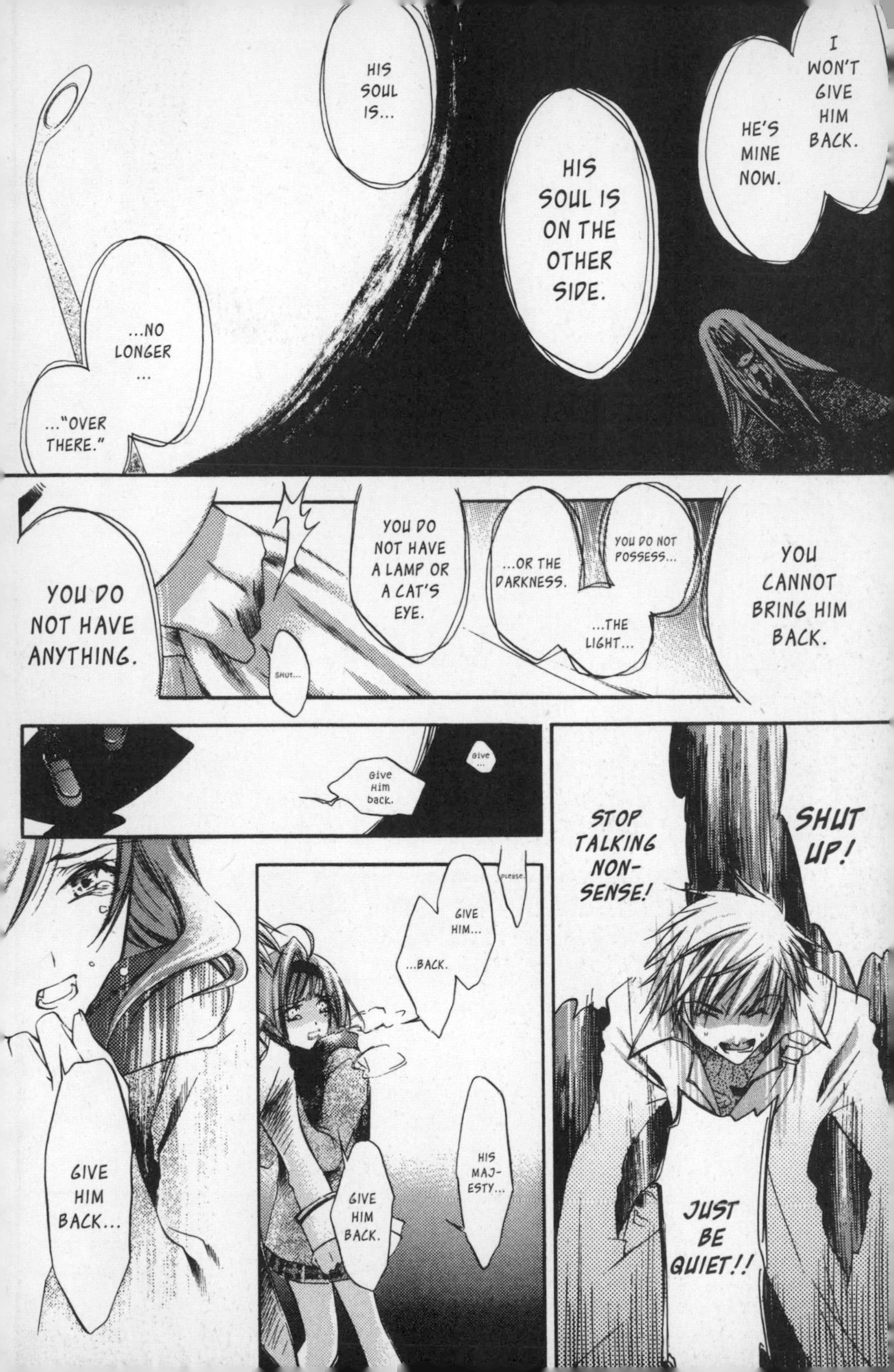
I WON'T GIVE HIM BACK.
HE'S MINE NOW.
HIS SOUL IS ON THE OTHER SIDE.
HIS SOUL IS...
...NO LONGER...
..."OVER THERE."
YOU CANNOT BRING HIM BACK.
YOU DO NOT POSSESS...
...THE LIGHT...
...OR THE DARKNESS.
YOU DO NOT HAVE A LAMP OR A CAT'S EYE.
Shut...
YOU DO NOT HAVE ANYTHING.
SHUT UP!
STOP TALKING NON-SENSE!
JUST BE QUIET!!
Give...
Give him back.
Please.
GIVE HIM...
...BACK.
HIS MAJ-ESTY...
GIVE HIM BACK.
GIVE HIM BACK...

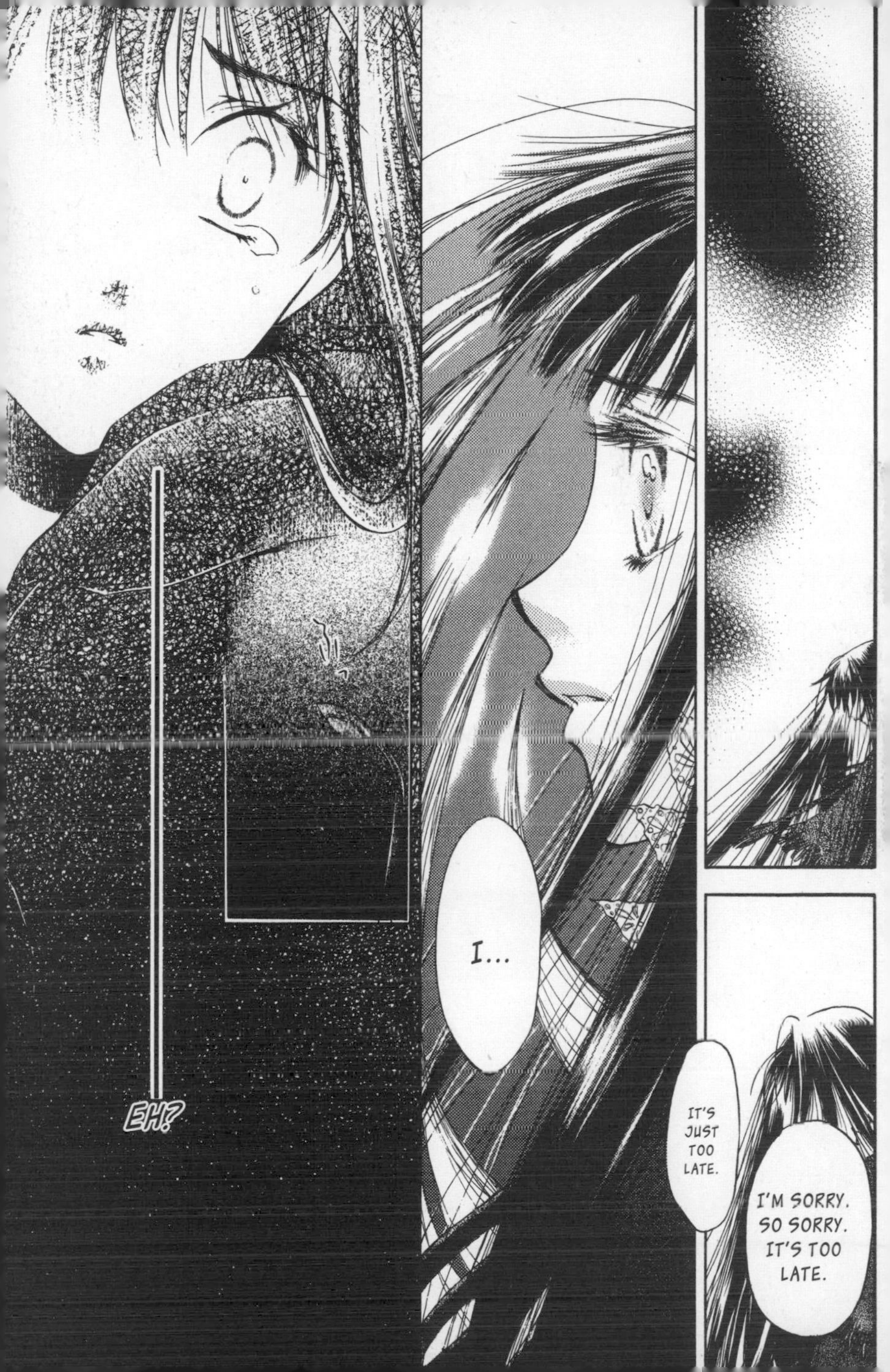
I'M SORRY. SO SORRY. IT'S TOO LATE.
IT'S JUST TOO LATE.
I...
EH?

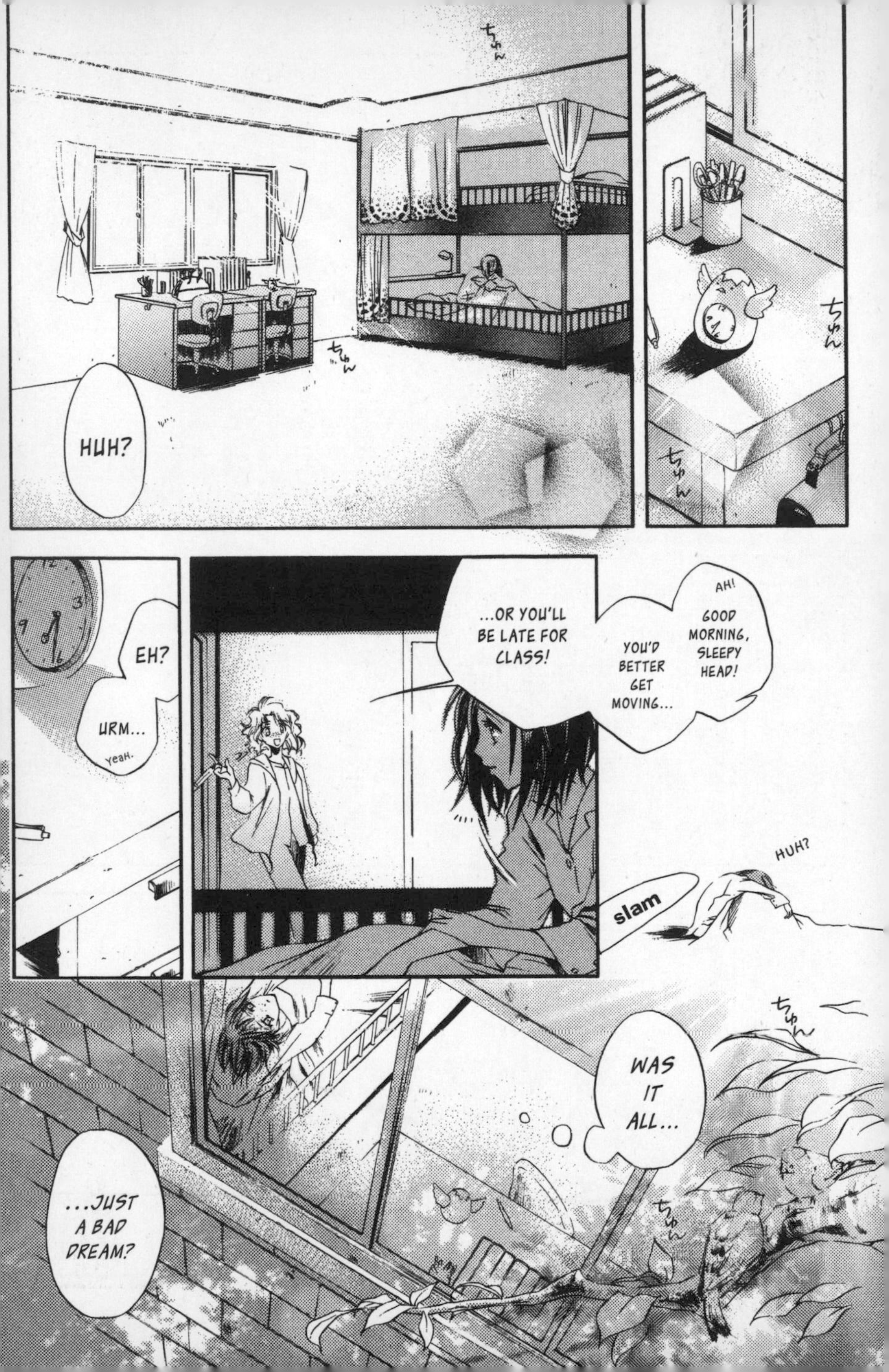
ちゅん
ちゅん
ちゅん
ちゅん
HUH?
HUH?
AH! GOOD MORNING, SLEEPY HEAD!
YOU'D BETTER GET MOVING...
...OR YOU'LL BE LATE FOR CLASS!
slam
EH?
URM... yeah.
ちゅん
WAS IT ALL...
ちゅん
...JUST A BAD DREAM?

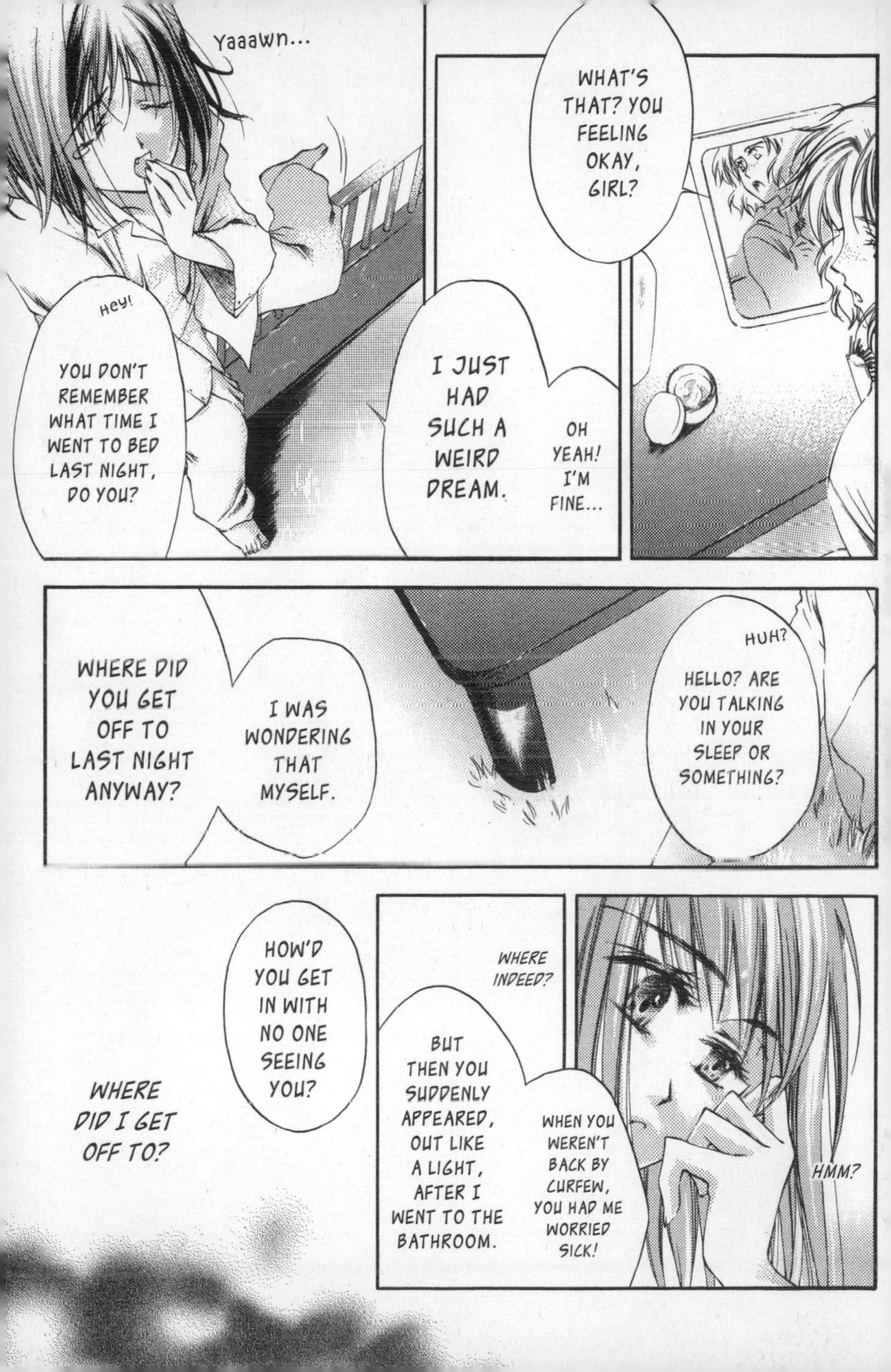
WHAT'S THAT? YOU FEELING OKAY, GIRL?
OH YEAH! I'M FINE...
I JUST HAD SUCH A WEIRD DREAM.
Yaaawn...
Hey!
YOU DON'T REMEMBER WHAT TIME I WENT TO BED LAST NIGHT, DO YOU?
HUH?
HELLO? ARE YOU TALKING IN YOUR SLEEP OR SOMETHING?
I WAS WONDERING THAT MYSELF.
WHERE DID YOU GET OFF TO LAST NIGHT ANYWAY?
HMM?
WHERE INDEED?
WHEN YOU WEREN'T BACK BY CURFEW, YOU HAD ME WORRIED SICK!
BUT THEN YOU SUDDENLY APPEARED, OUT LIKE A LIGHT, AFTER I WENT TO THE BATHROOM.
HOW'D YOU GET IN WITH NO ONE SEEING YOU?
WHERE DID I GET OFF TO?

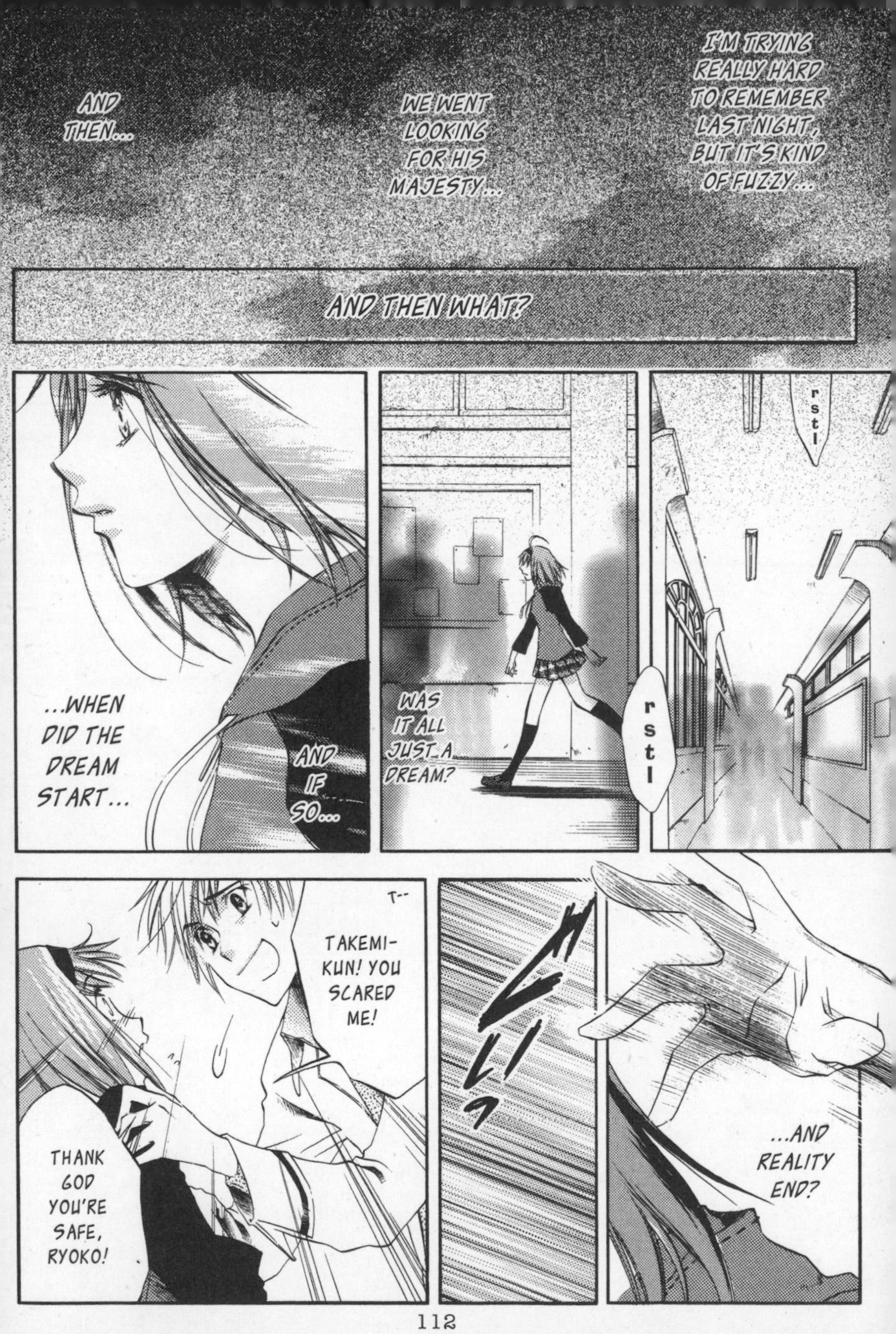
I'M TRYING REALLY HARD TO REMEMBER LAST NIGHT, BUT IT'S KIND OF FUZZY...
WE WENT LOOKING FOR HIS MAJESTY...
AND THEN...
AND THEN WHAT?
rstl
rstl
WAS IT ALL JUST A DREAM?
AND IF SO...
...WHEN DID THE DREAM START...
...AND REALITY END?
T--
TAKEMI-KUN! YOU SCARED ME!
THANK GOD YOU'RE SAFE, RYOKO!

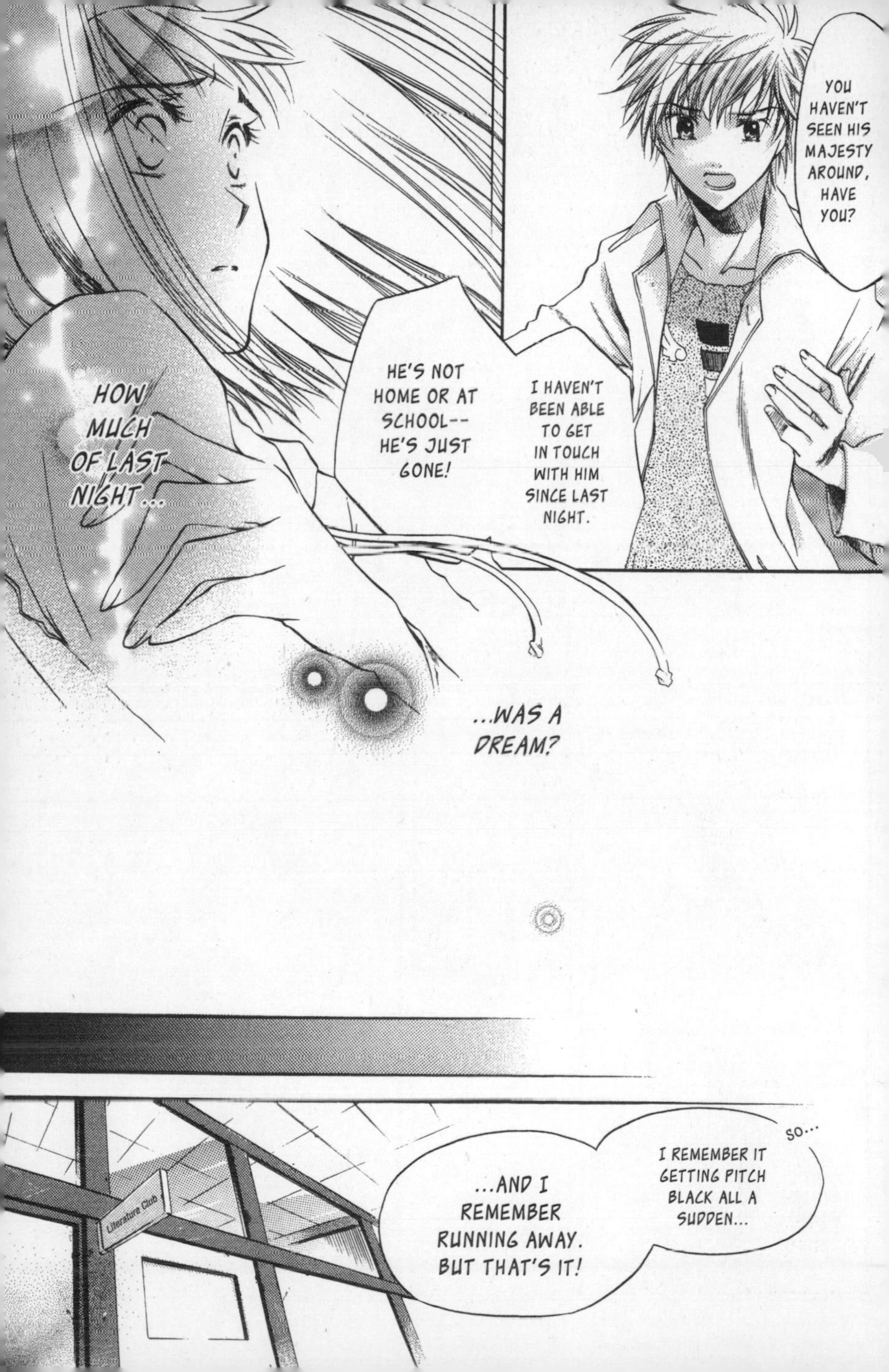
YOU HAVEN'T SEEN HIS MAJESTY AROUND, HAVE YOU?
I HAVEN'T BEEN ABLE TO GET IN TOUCH WITH HIM SINCE LAST NIGHT.
HE'S NOT HOME OR AT SCHOOL-- HE'S JUST GONE!
HOW MUCH OF LAST NIGHT...
...WAS A DREAM?
Literature Club
SO...
I REMEMBER IT GETTING PITCH BLACK ALL A SUDDEN...
...AND I REMEMBER RUNNING AWAY. BUT THAT'S IT!

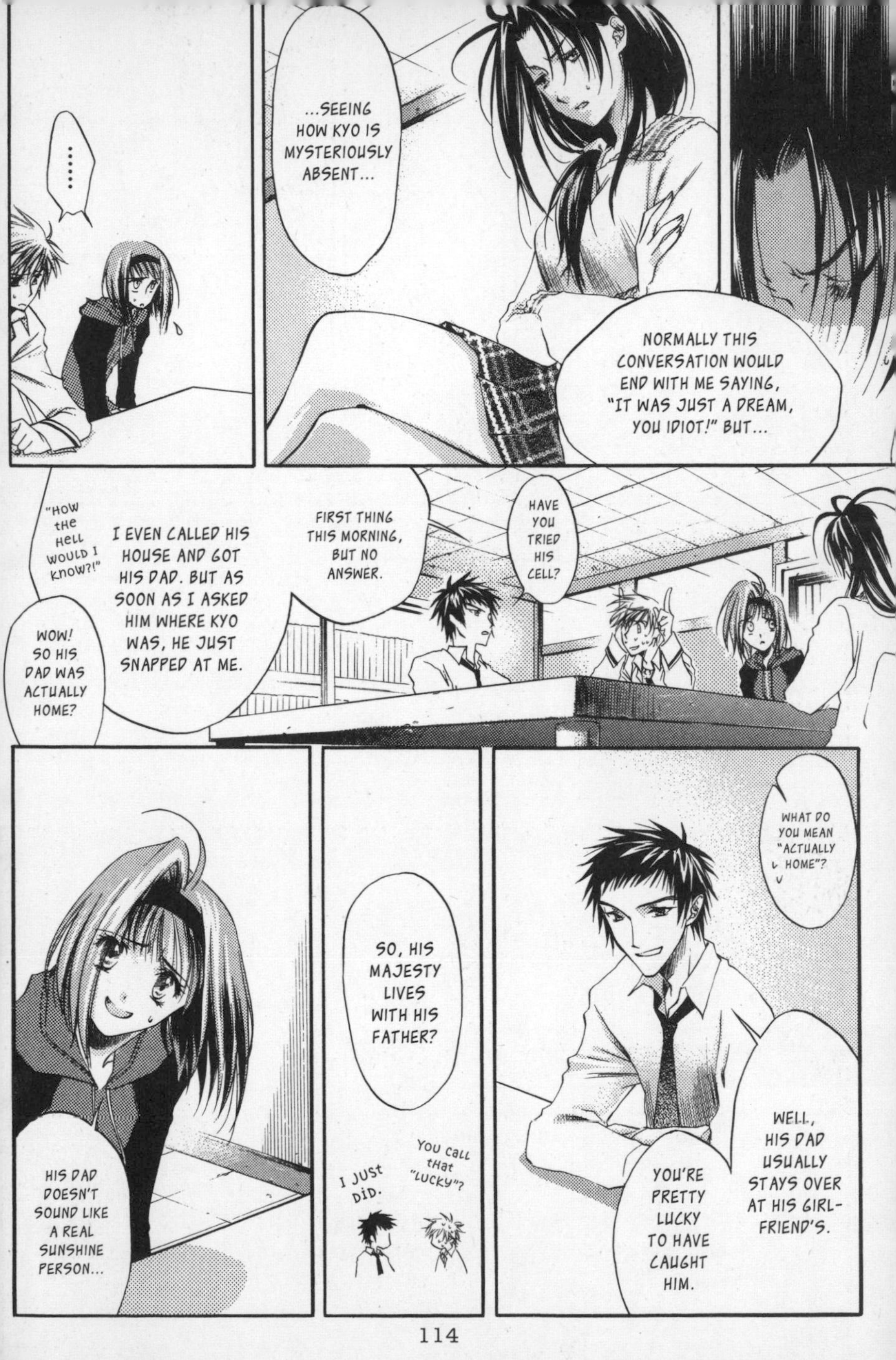
NORMALLY THIS CONVERSATION WOULD END WITH ME SAYING, "IT WAS JUST A DREAM, YOU IDIOT!" BUT...
...SEEING HOW KYO IS MYSTERIOUSLY ABSENT...
......
HAVE YOU TRIED HIS CELL?
FIRST THING THIS MORNING, BUT NO ANSWER.
I EVEN CALLED HIS HOUSE AND GOT HIS DAD. BUT AS SOON AS I ASKED HIM WHERE KYO WAS, HE JUST SNAPPED AT ME.
"HOW THE HELL WOULD I KNOW?!"
WOW! SO HIS DAD WAS ACTUALLY HOME?
WHAT DO YOU MEAN "ACTUALLY HOME"?
WELL, HIS DAD USUALLY STAYS OVER AT HIS GIRL-FRIEND'S.
YOU'RE PRETTY LUCKY TO HAVE CAUGHT HIM.
SO, HIS MAJESTY LIVES WITH HIS FATHER?
YOU CALL THAT "LUCKY"?
I JUST DID.
HIS DAD DOESN'T SOUND LIKE A REAL SUNSHINE PERSON...

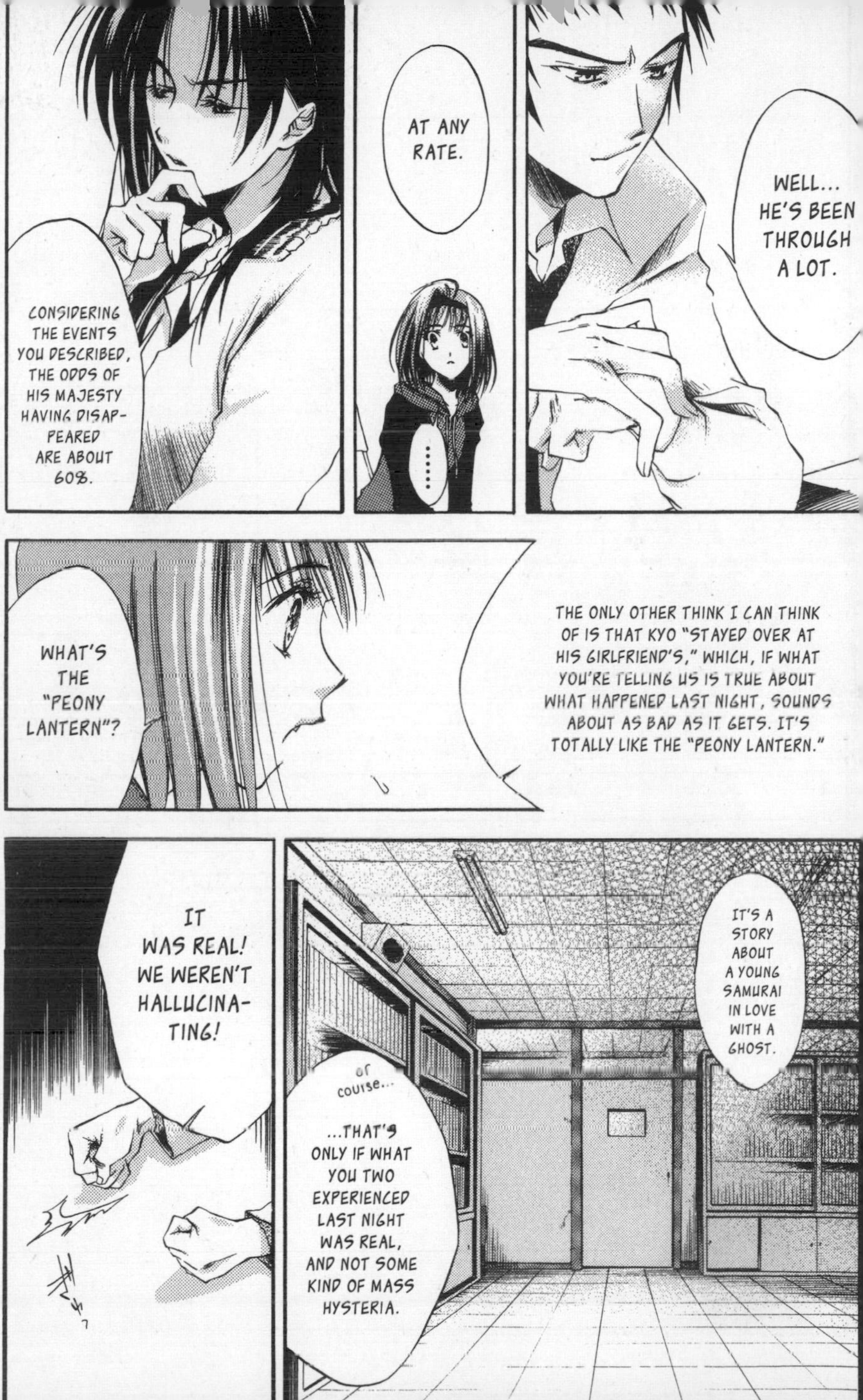
WELL... HE'S BEEN THROUGH A LOT.
AT ANY RATE.
......
CONSIDERING THE EVENTS YOU DESCRIBED, THE ODDS OF HIS MAJESTY HAVING DISAP-PEARED ARE ABOUT 60%.
THE ONLY OTHER THINK I CAN THINK OF IS THAT KYO "STAYED OVER AT HIS GIRLFRIEND'S," WHICH, IF WHAT YOU'RE TELLING US IS TRUE ABOUT WHAT HAPPENED LAST NIGHT, SOUNDS ABOUT AS BAD AS IT GETS. IT'S TOTALLY LIKE THE "PEONY LANTERN."
WHAT'S THE "PEONY LANTERN"?
IT'S A STORY ABOUT A YOUNG SAMURAI IN LOVE WITH A GHOST.
OF COURSE...
...THAT'S ONLY IF WHAT YOU TWO EXPERIENCED LAST NIGHT WAS REAL, AND NOT SOME KIND OF MASS HYSTERIA.
IT WAS REAL! WE WEREN'T HALLUCINA-TING!

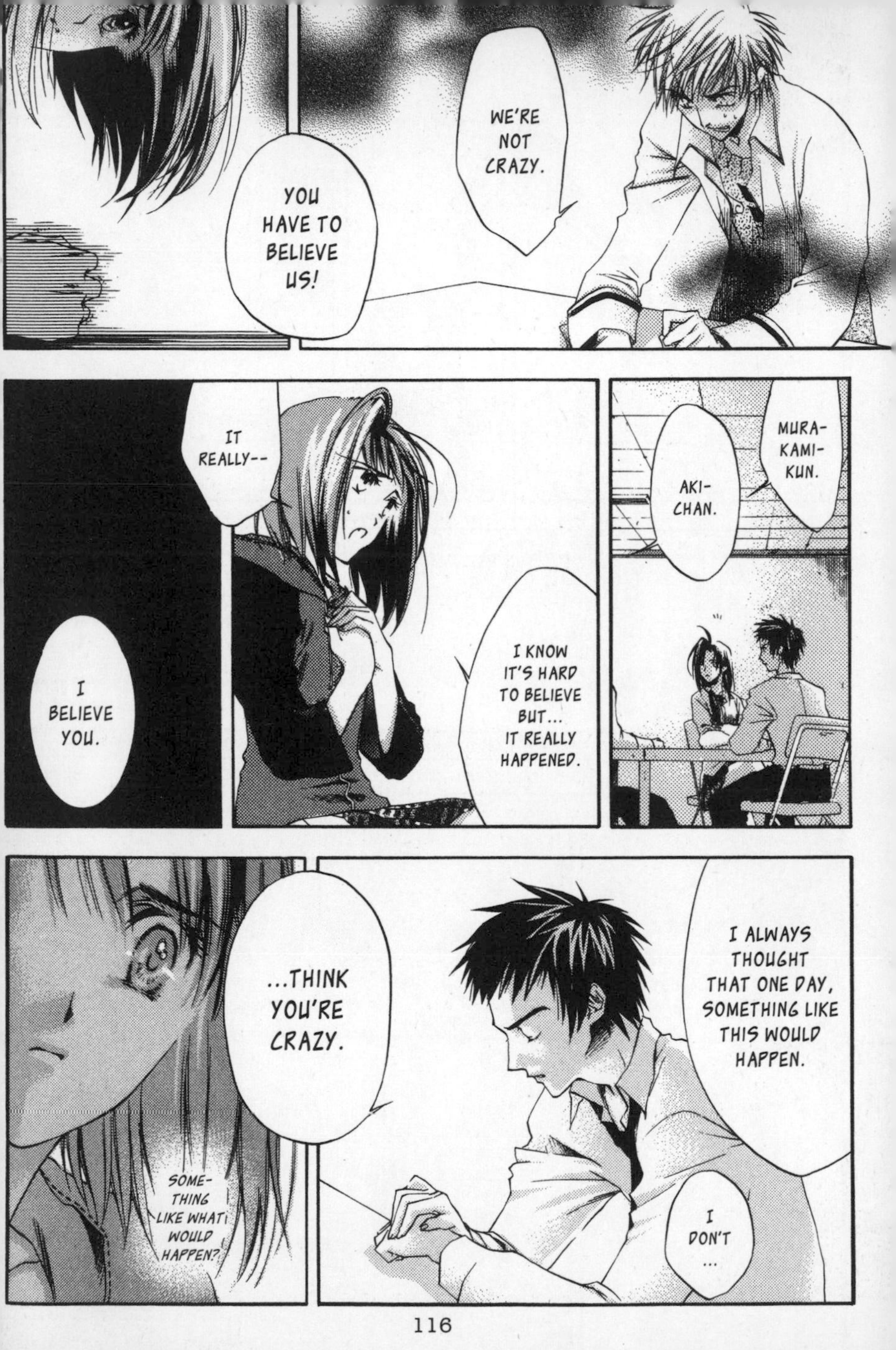
WE'RE NOT CRAZY.
YOU HAVE TO BELIEVE US!
MURA-KAMI-KUN.
AKI-CHAN.
I KNOW IT'S HARD TO BELIEVE BUT... IT REALLY HAPPENED.
IT REALLY--
I BELIEVE YOU.
I ALWAYS THOUGHT THAT ONE DAY, SOMETHING LIKE THIS WOULD HAPPEN.
I DON'T ...
...THINK YOU'RE CRAZY.
SOME-THING LIKE WHAT WOULD HAPPEN?

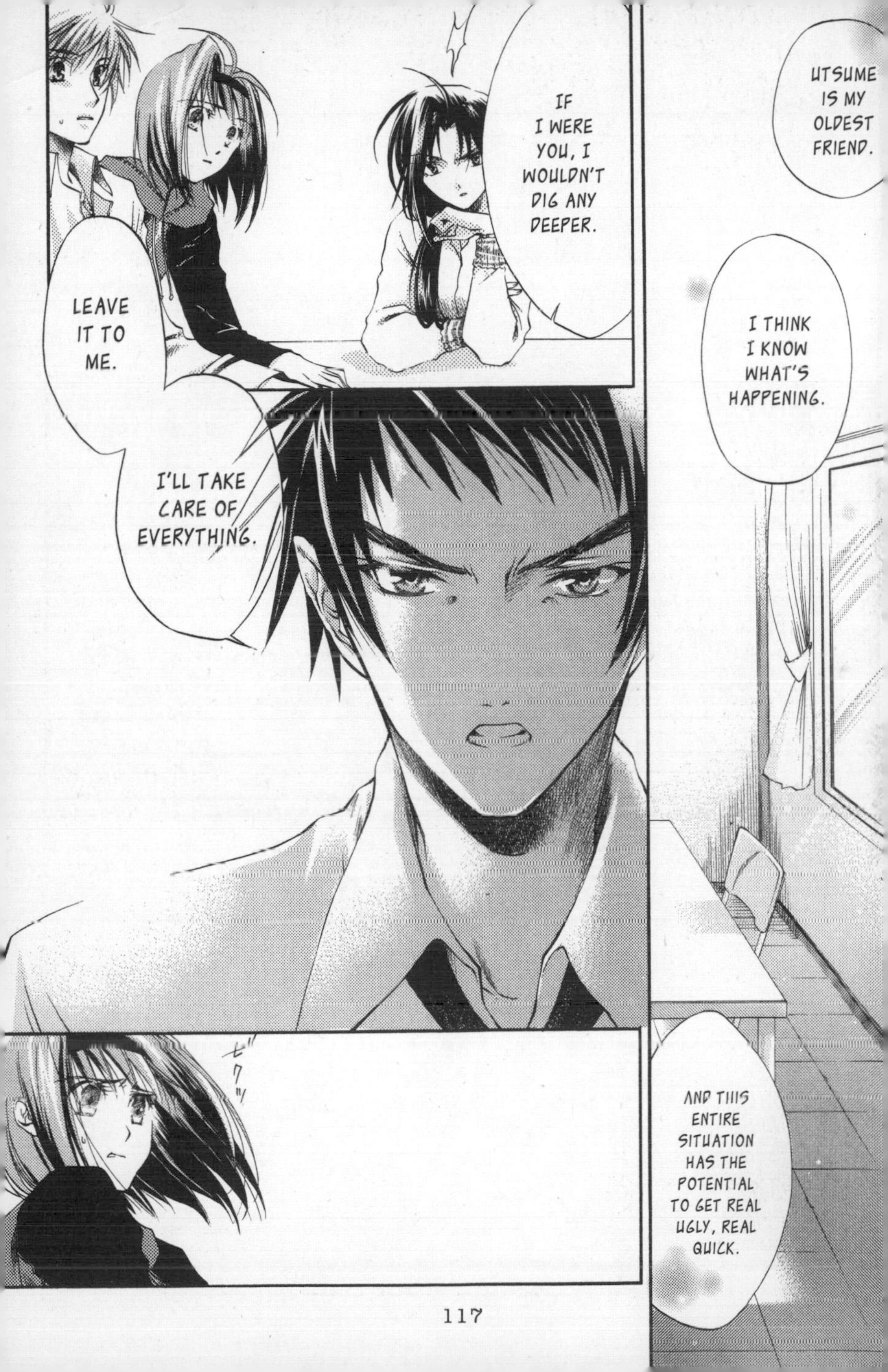
UTSUME IS MY OLDEST FRIEND.
I THINK I KNOW WHAT'S HAPPENING.
AND THIS ENTIRE SITUATION HAS THE POTENTIAL TO GET REAL UGLY, REAL QUICK.
IF I WERE YOU, I WOULDN'T DIG ANY DEEPER.
LEAVE IT TO ME.
I'LL TAKE CARE OF EVERYTHING.
ビクッ

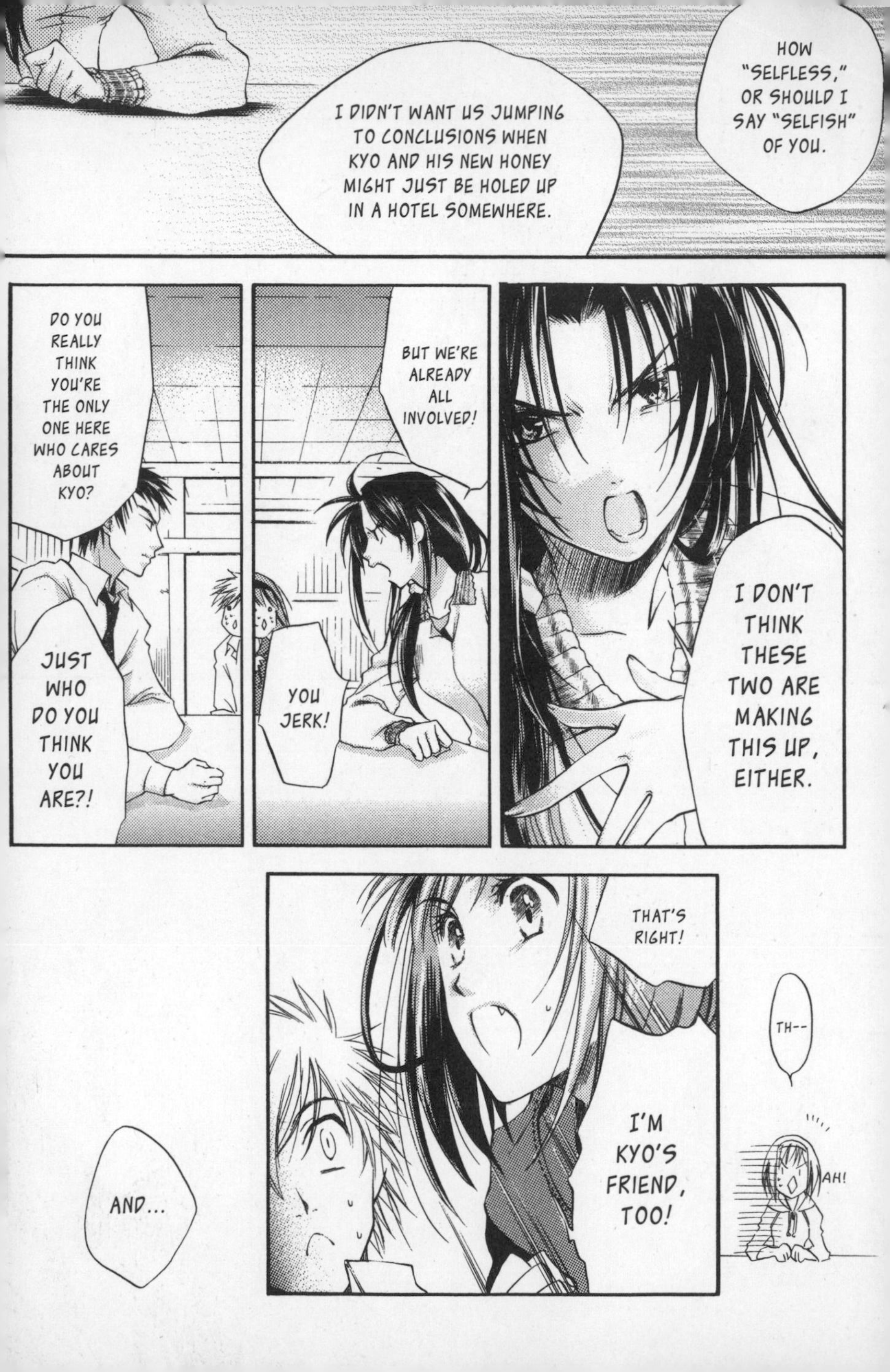
HOW "SELFLESS," OR SHOULD I SAY "SELFISH" OF YOU.
I DIDN'T WANT US JUMPING TO CONCLUSIONS WHEN KYO AND HIS NEW HONEY MIGHT JUST BE HOLED UP IN A HOTEL SOMEWHERE.
I DON'T THINK THESE TWO ARE MAKING THIS UP, EITHER.
BUT WE'RE ALREADY ALL INVOLVED!
YOU JERK!
DO YOU REALLY THINK YOU'RE THE ONLY ONE HERE WHO CARES ABOUT KYO?
JUST WHO DO YOU THINK YOU ARE?!
TH--
AH!
THAT'S RIGHT!
I'M KYO'S FRIEND, TOO!
AND...

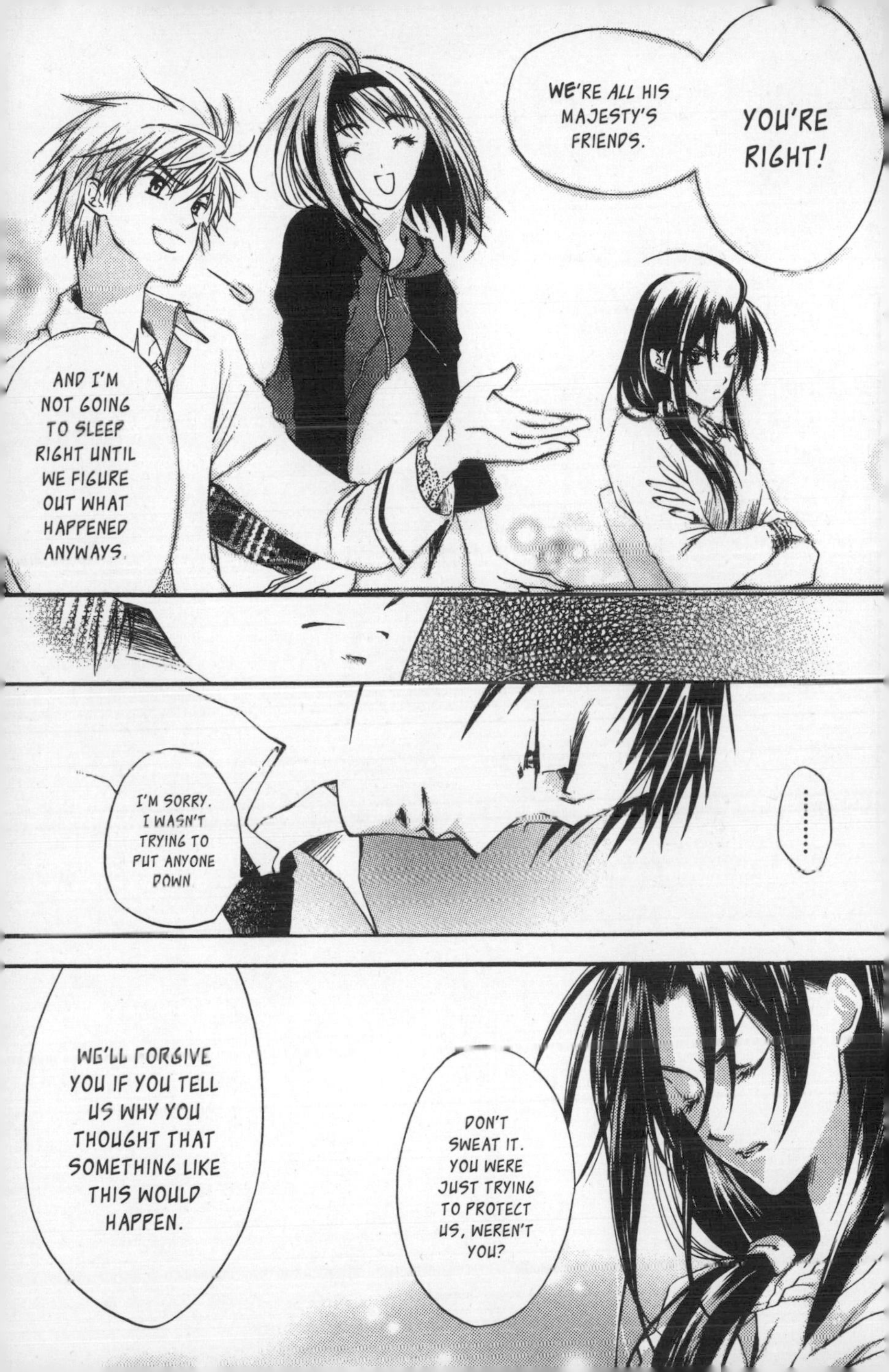
YOU'RE RIGHT! WE'RE ALL HIS MAJESTY'S FRIENDS.
AND I'M NOT GOING TO SLEEP RIGHT UNTIL WE FIGURE OUT WHAT HAPPENED ANYWAYS.
......
I'M SORRY. I WASN'T TRYING TO PUT ANYONE DOWN
DON'T SWEAT IT. YOU WERE JUST TRYING TO PROTECT US, WEREN'T YOU?
WE'LL FORGIVE YOU IF YOU TELL US WHY YOU THOUGHT THAT SOMETHING LIKE THIS WOULD HAPPEN.

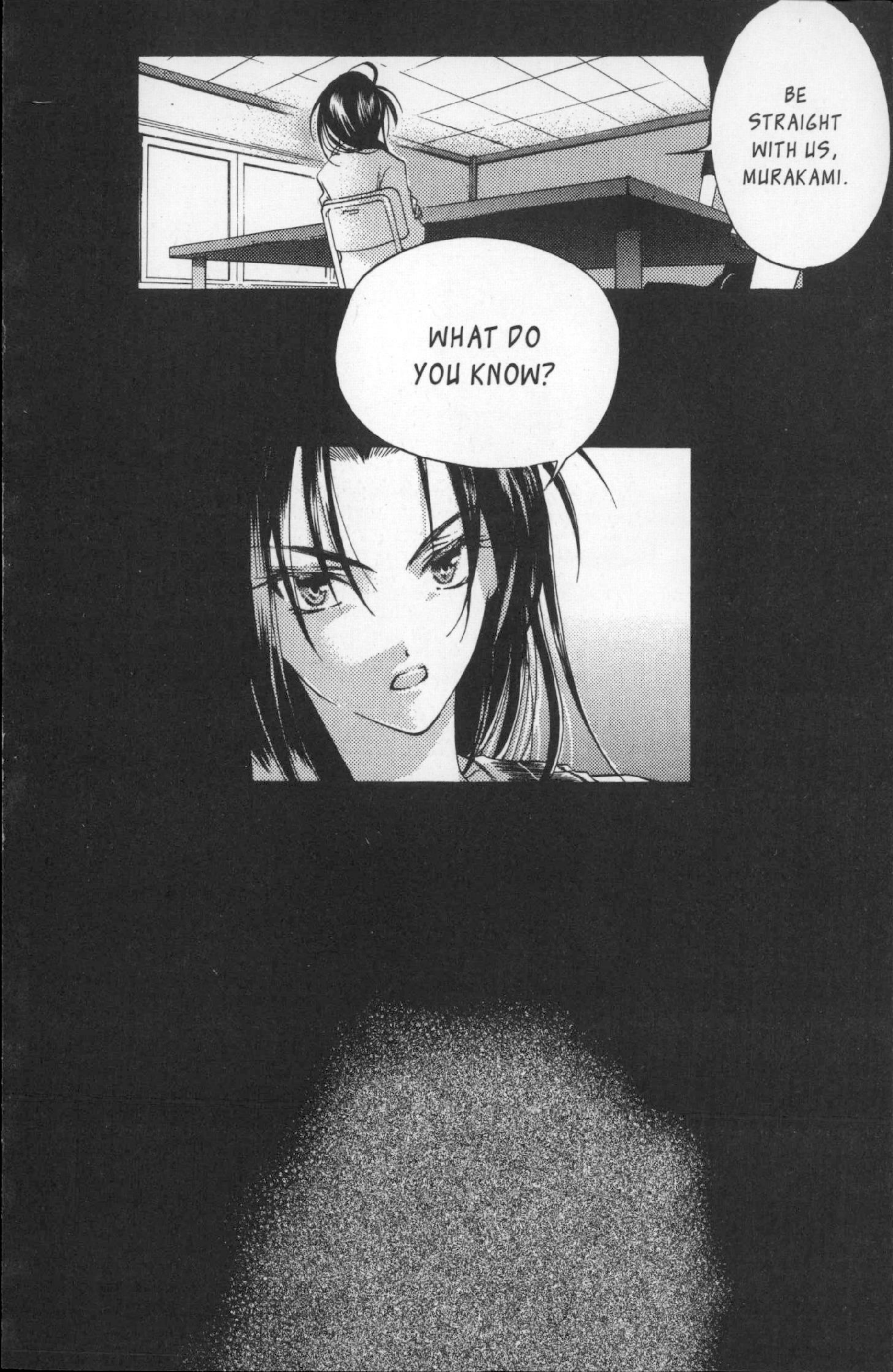
BE STRAIGHT WITH US, MURAKAMI.
WHAT DO YOU KNOW?

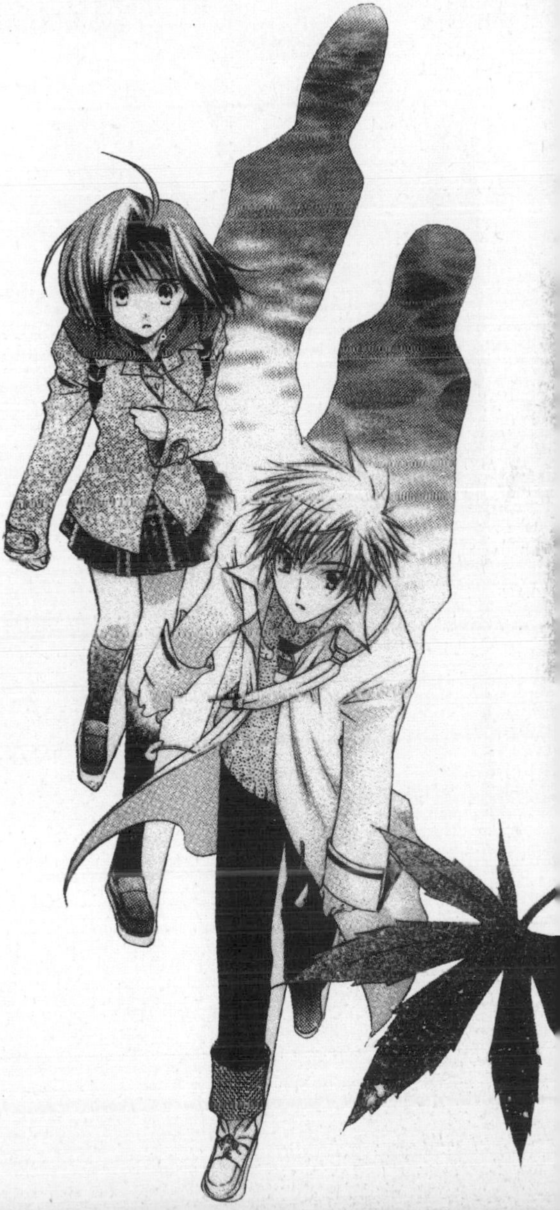

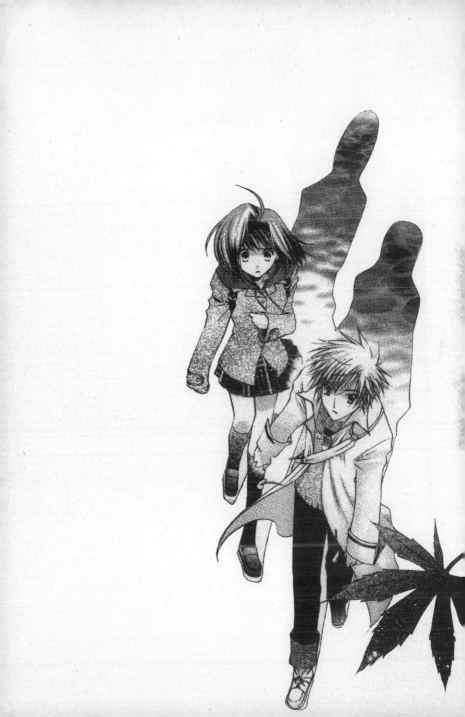

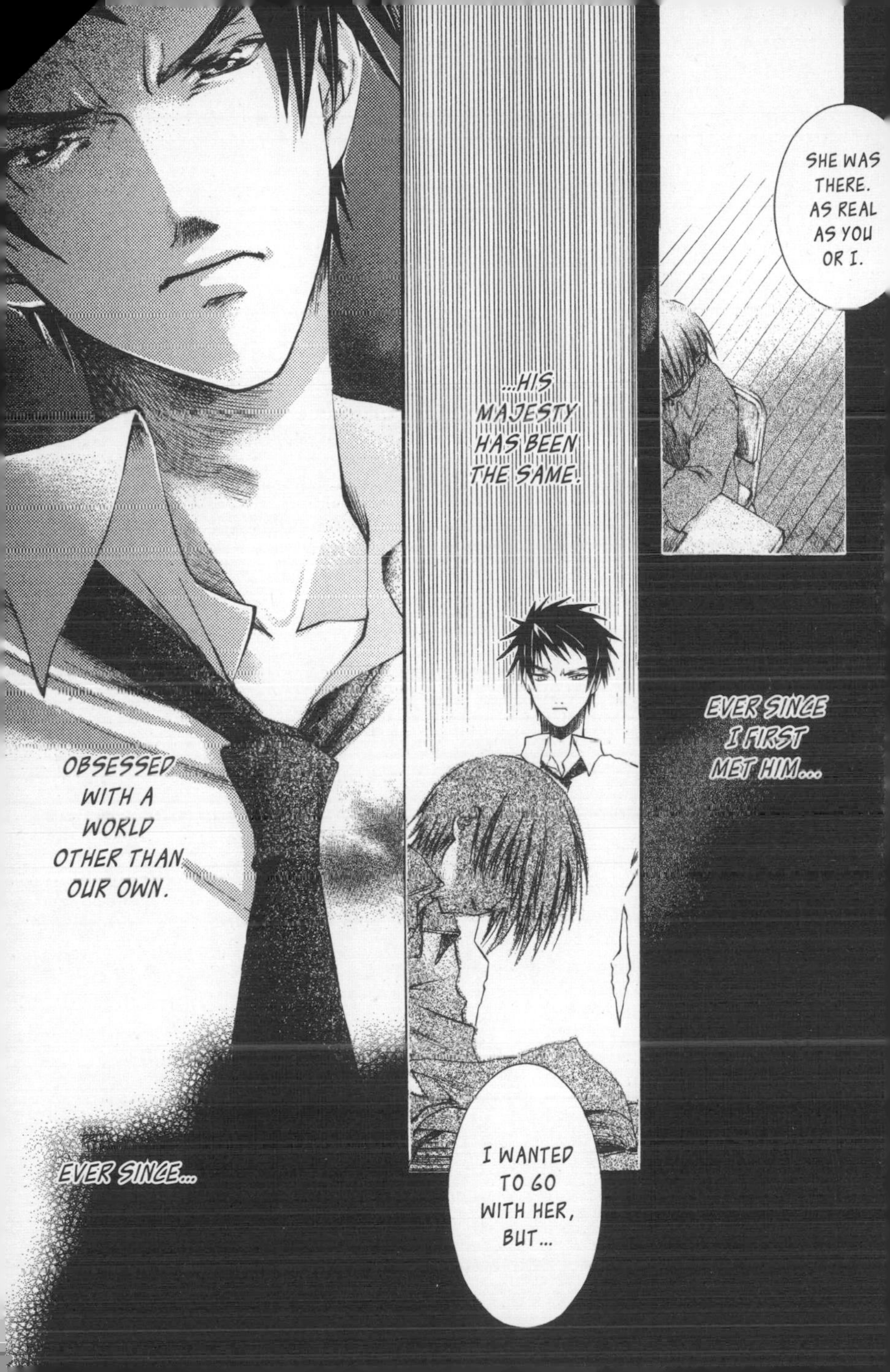
SHE WAS THERE. AS REAL AS YOU OR I.
I WANTED TO GO WITH HER, BUT...
EVER SINCE I FIRST MET HIM...
...HIS MAJESTY HAS BEEN THE SAME.
OBSESSED WITH A WORLD OTHER THAN OUR OWN.
EVER SINCE...

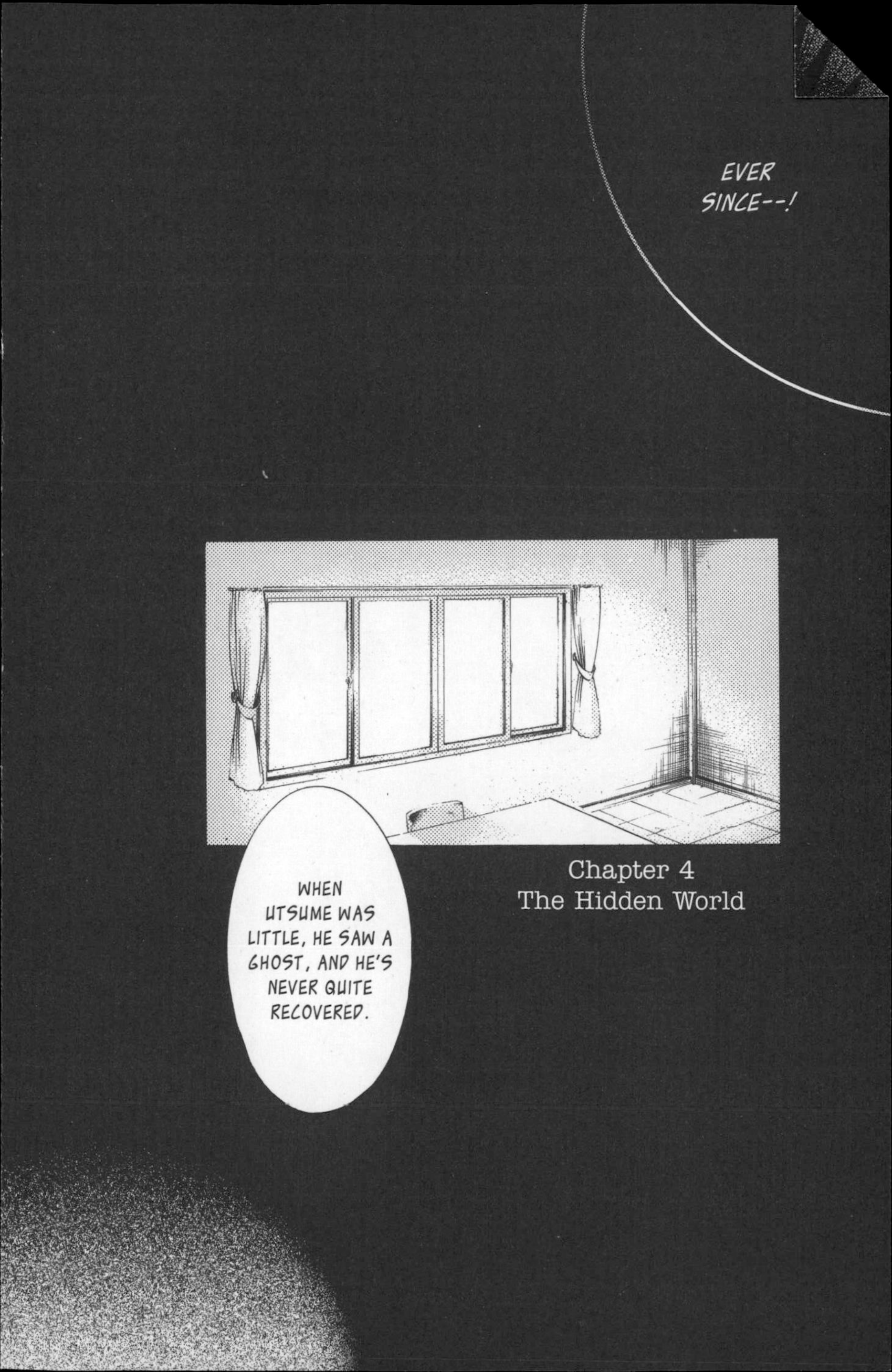
EVER SINCE--!
WHEN UTSUME WAS LITTLE, HE SAW A GHOST, AND HE'S NEVER QUITE RECOVERED.

Chapter 4
The Hidden World

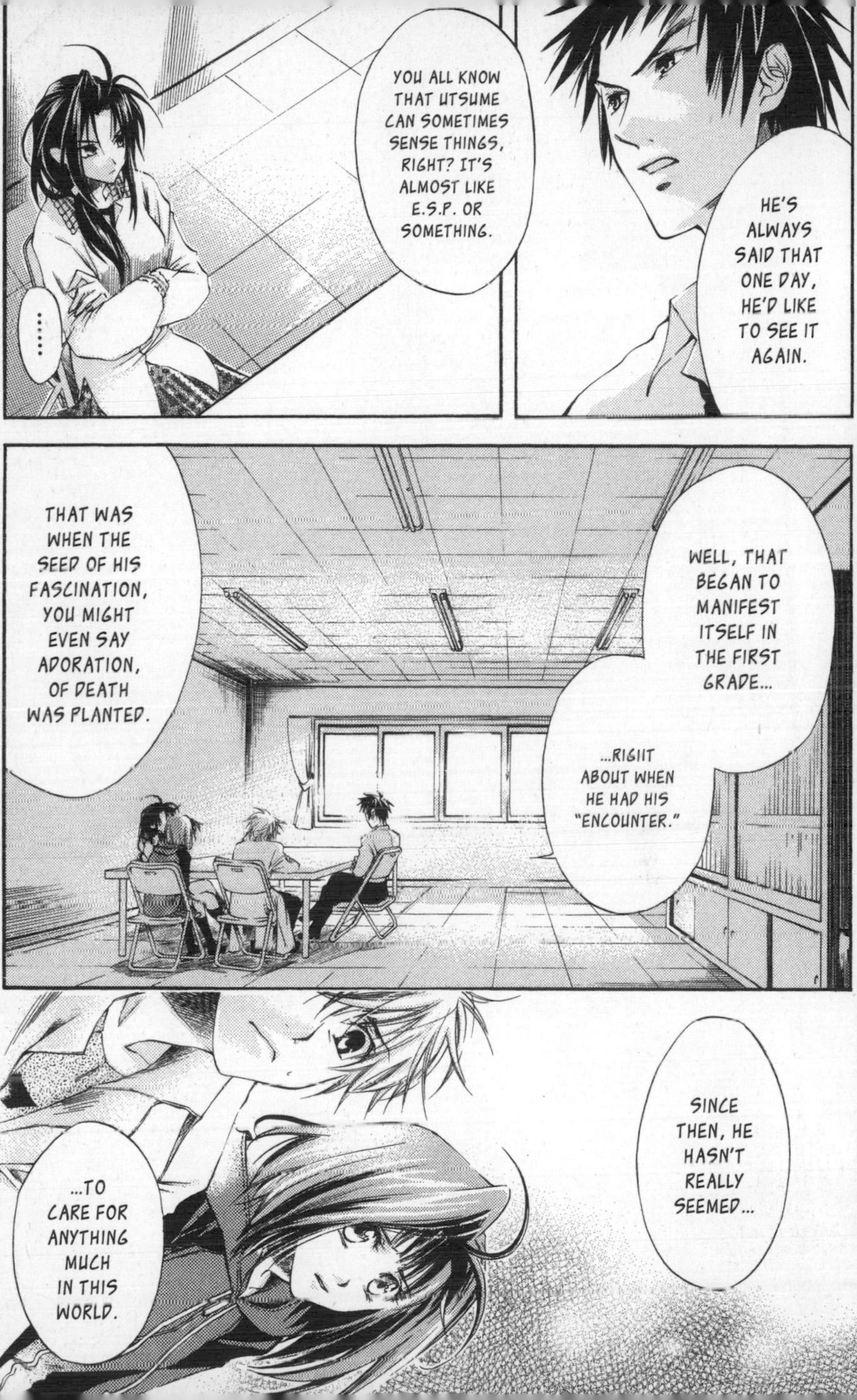
HE'S ALWAYS SAID THAT ONE DAY, HE'D LIKE TO SEE IT AGAIN.
YOU ALL KNOW THAT UTSUME CAN SOMETIMES SENSE THINGS, RIGHT? IT'S ALMOST LIKE E.S.P. OR SOMETHING.
......
WELL, THAT BEGAN TO MANIFEST ITSELF IN THE FIRST GRADE...
...RIGHT ABOUT WHEN HE HAD HIS "ENCOUNTER."
THAT WAS WHEN THE SEED OF HIS FASCINATION, YOU MIGHT EVEN SAY ADORATION, OF DEATH WAS PLANTED.
SINCE THEN, HE HASN'T REALLY SEEMED...
...TO CARE FOR ANYTHING MUCH IN THIS WORLD.

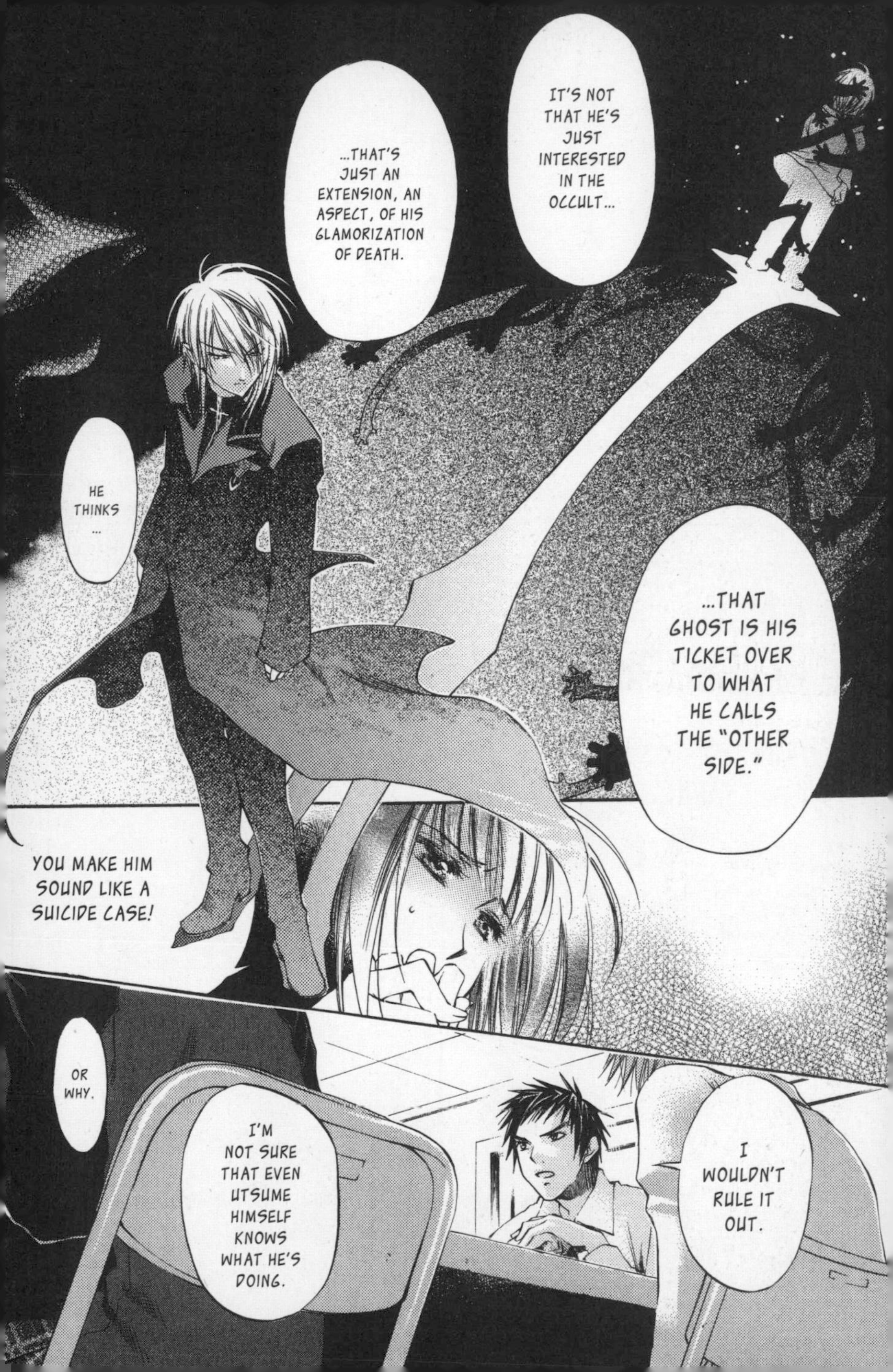
IT'S NOT THAT HE'S JUST INTERESTED IN THE OCCULT...
...THAT'S JUST AN EXTENSION, AN ASPECT, OF HIS GLAMORIZATION OF DEATH.
HE THINKS ...
...THAT GHOST IS HIS TICKET OVER TO WHAT HE CALLS THE "OTHER SIDE."
YOU MAKE HIM SOUND LIKE A SUICIDE CASE!
I WOULDN'T RULE IT OUT.
I'M NOT SURE THAT EVEN UTSUME HIMSELF KNOWS WHAT HE'S DOING.
OR WHY.

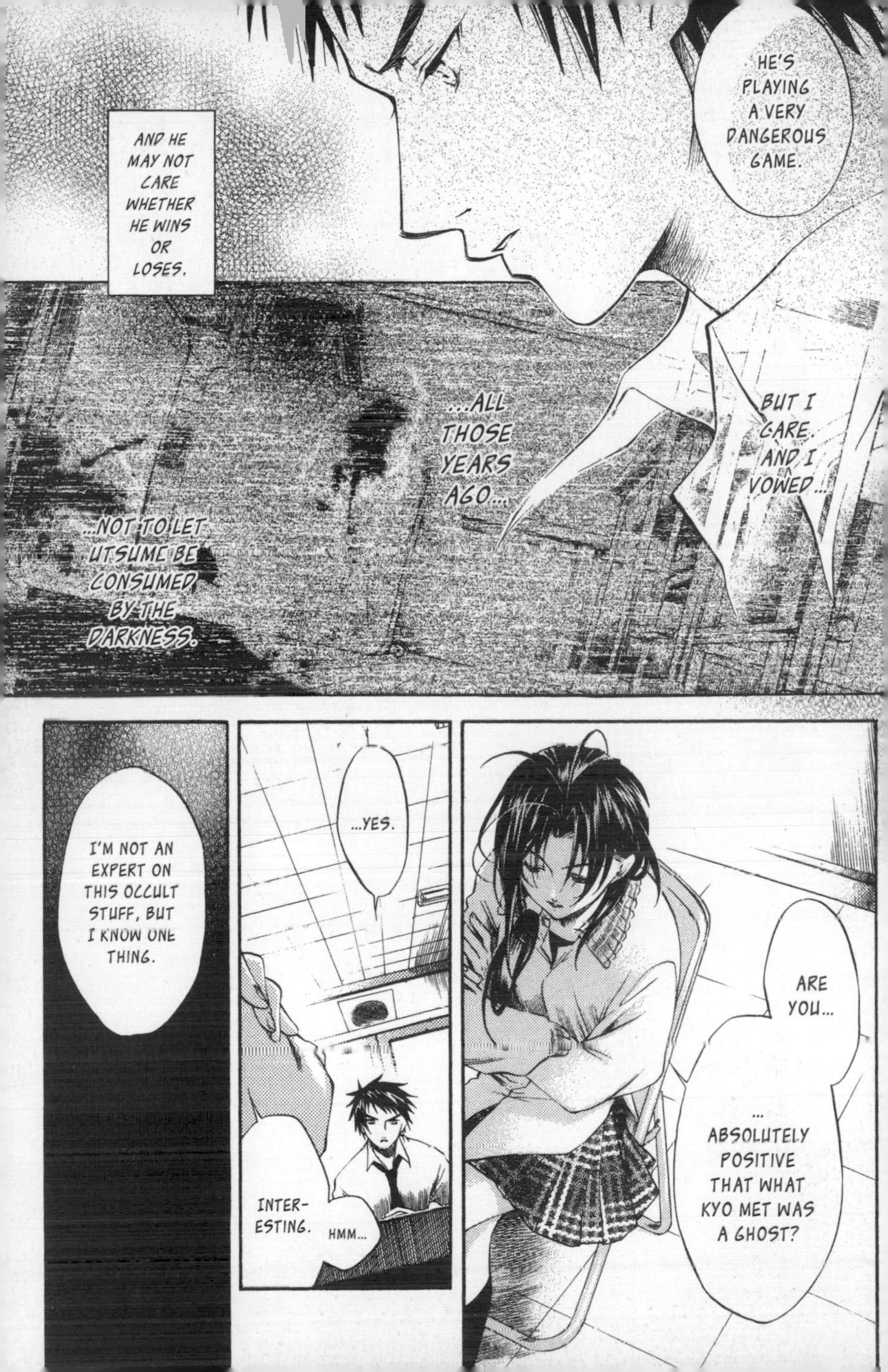
HE'S PLAYING A VERY DANGEROUS GAME.
AND HE MAY NOT CARE WHETHER HE WINS OR LOSES.
BUT I CARE. AND I VOWED...
...ALL THOSE YEARS AGO...
...NOT TO LET UTSUME BE CONSUMED BY THE DARKNESS.
ARE YOU...
...ABSOLUTELY POSITIVE THAT WHAT KYO MET WAS A GHOST?
...YES.
HMM...
INTER-ESTING.
I'M NOT AN EXPERT ON THIS OCCULT STUFF, BUT I KNOW ONE THING.

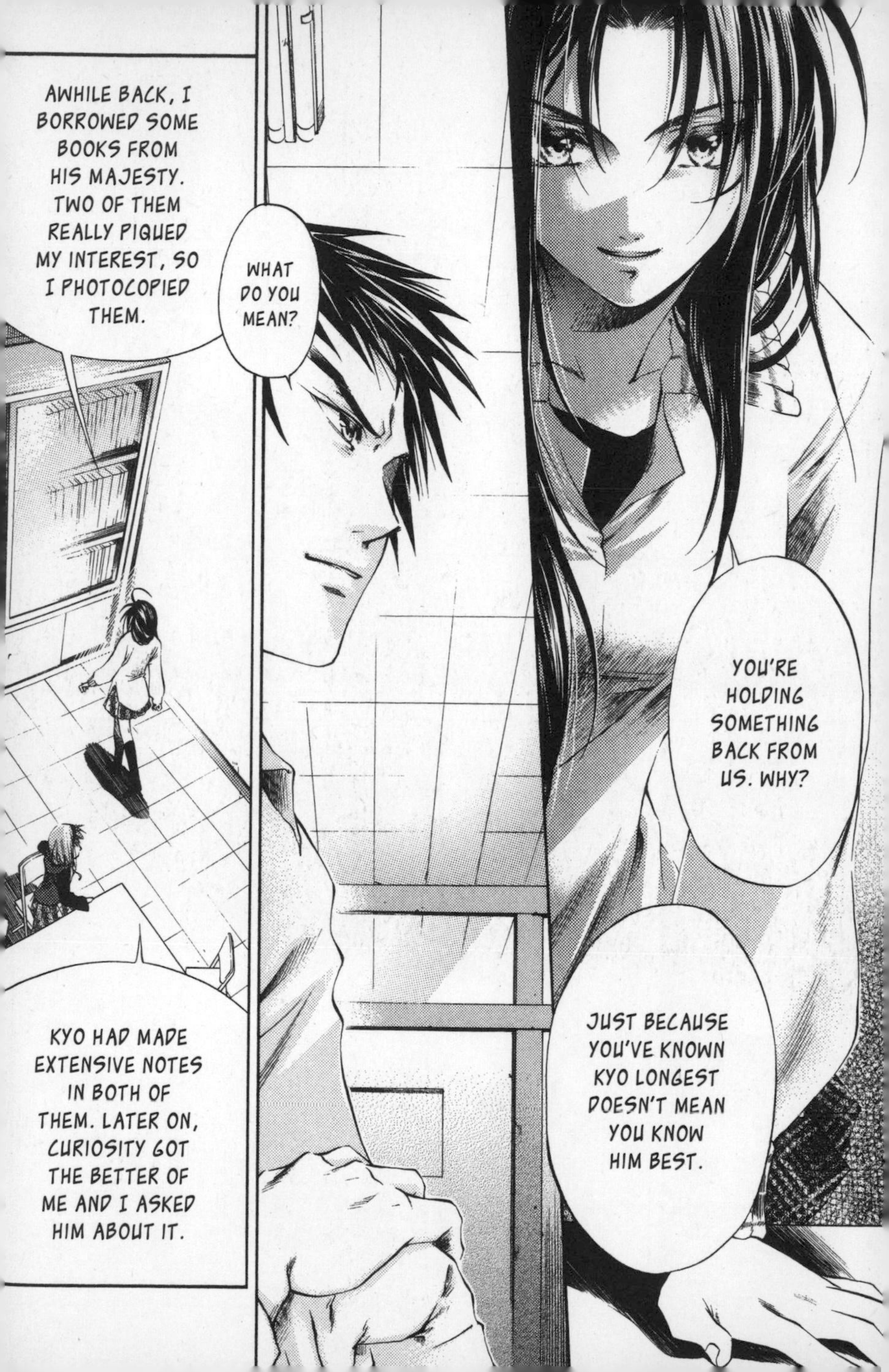
YOU'RE HOLDING SOMETHING BACK FROM US. WHY?
JUST BECAUSE YOU'VE KNOWN KYO LONGEST DOESN'T MEAN YOU KNOW HIM BEST.
WHAT DO YOU MEAN?
AWHILE BACK, I BORROWED SOME BOOKS FROM HIS MAJESTY. TWO OF THEM REALLY PIQUED MY INTEREST, SO I PHOTOCOPIED THEM.
KYO HAD MADE EXTENSIVE NOTES IN BOTH OF THEM. LATER ON, CURIOSITY GOT THE BETTER OF ME AND I ASKED HIM ABOUT IT.

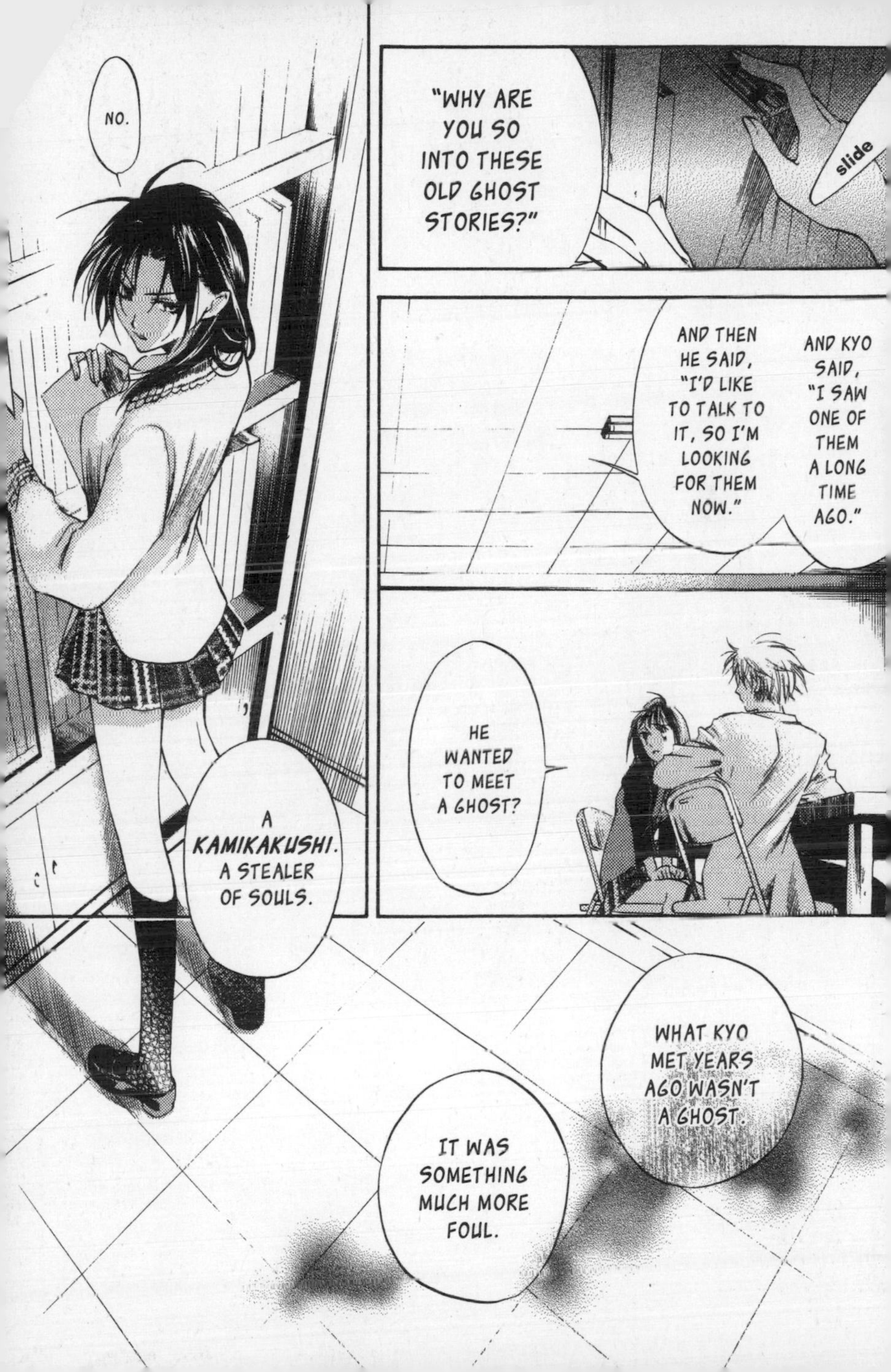
slide
"WHY ARE YOU SO INTO THESE OLD GHOST STORIES?"
AND KYO SAID, "I SAW ONE OF THEM A LONG TIME AGO."
AND THEN HE SAID, "I'D LIKE TO TALK TO IT, SO I'M LOOKING FOR THEM NOW."
HE WANTED TO MEET A GHOST?
NO.
A *KAMIKAKUSHI*. A STEALER OF SOULS.
WHAT KYO MET YEARS AGO WASN'T A GHOST.
IT WAS SOMETHING MUCH MORE FOUL.

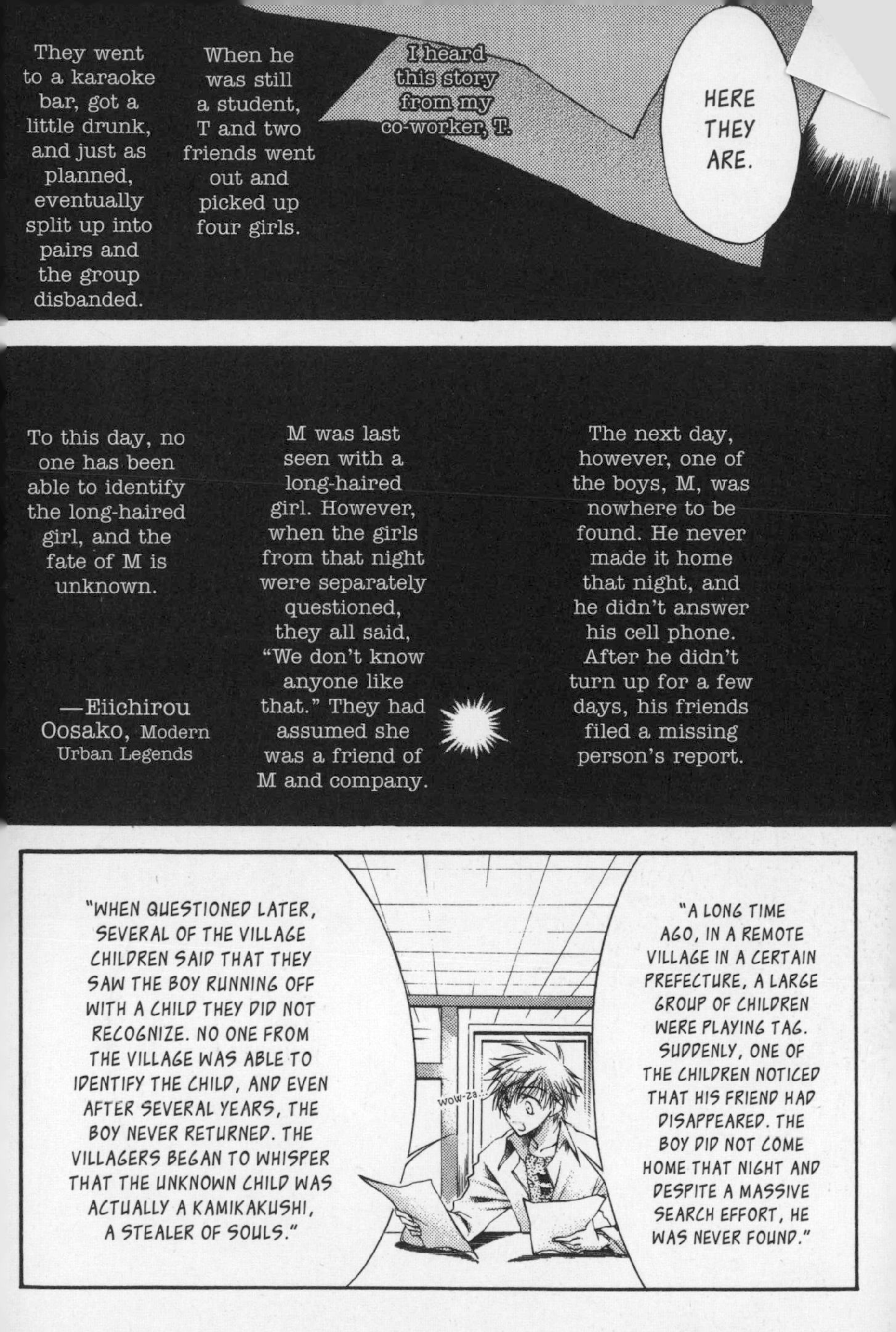
HERE THEY ARE.
I heard this story from my co-worker, T.
When he was still a student, T and two friends went out and picked up four girls.
They went to a karaoke bar, got a little drunk, and just as planned, eventually split up into pairs and the group disbanded.
The next day, however, one of the boys, M, was nowhere to be found. He never made it home that night, and he didn't answer his cell phone. After he didn't turn up for a few days, his friends filed a missing person's report.
M was last seen with a long-haired girl. However, when the girls from that night were separately questioned, they all said, "We don't know anyone like that." They had assumed she was a friend of M and company.
To this day, no one has been able to identify the long-haired girl, and the fate of M is unknown.
—Eiichirou Oosako, Modern Urban Legends
"A LONG TIME AGO, IN A REMOTE VILLAGE IN A CERTAIN PREFECTURE, A LARGE GROUP OF CHILDREN WERE PLAYING TAG. SUDDENLY, ONE OF THE CHILDREN NOTICED THAT HIS FRIEND HAD DISAPPEARED. THE BOY DID NOT COME HOME THAT NIGHT AND DESPITE A MASSIVE SEARCH EFFORT, HE WAS NEVER FOUND."
WOW-ZA...
"WHEN QUESTIONED LATER, SEVERAL OF THE VILLAGE CHILDREN SAID THAT THEY SAW THE BOY RUNNING OFF WITH A CHILD THEY DID NOT RECOGNIZE. NO ONE FROM THE VILLAGE WAS ABLE TO IDENTIFY THE CHILD, AND EVEN AFTER SEVERAL YEARS, THE BOY NEVER RETURNED. THE VILLAGERS BEGAN TO WHISPER THAT THE UNKNOWN CHILD WAS ACTUALLY A KAMIKAKUSHI, A STEALER OF SOULS."

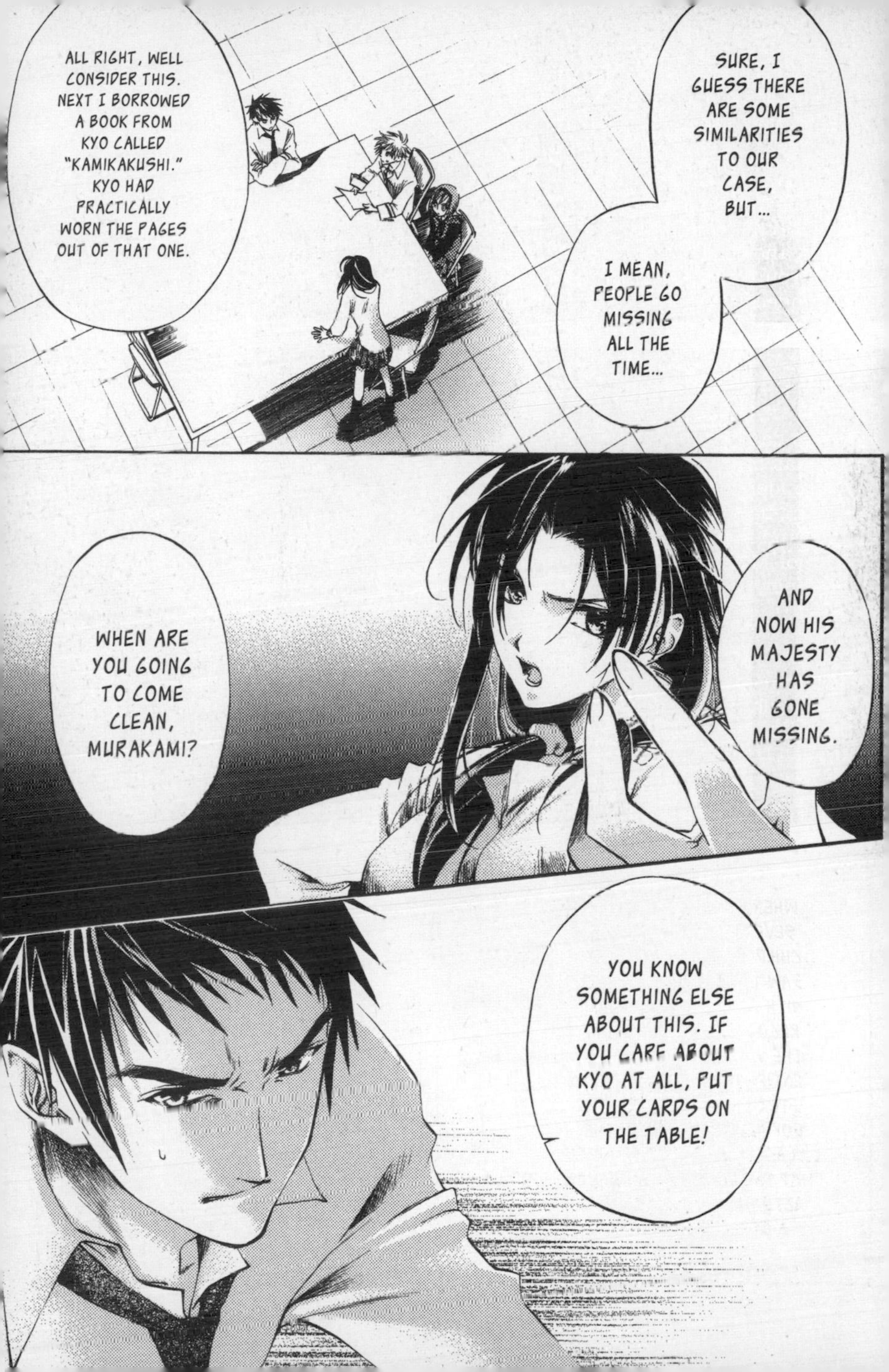

SURE, I GUESS THERE ARE SOME SIMILARITIES TO OUR CASE, BUT...
I MEAN, PEOPLE GO MISSING ALL THE TIME...
ALL RIGHT, WELL CONSIDER THIS. NEXT I BORROWED A BOOK FROM KYO CALLED "KAMIKAKUSHI." KYO HAD PRACTICALLY WORN THE PAGES OUT OF THAT ONE.
AND NOW HIS MAJESTY HAS GONE MISSING.
WHEN ARE YOU GOING TO COME CLEAN, MURAKAMI?
YOU KNOW SOMETHING ELSE ABOUT THIS. IF YOU CARE ABOUT KYO AT ALL, PUT YOUR CARDS ON THE TABLE!

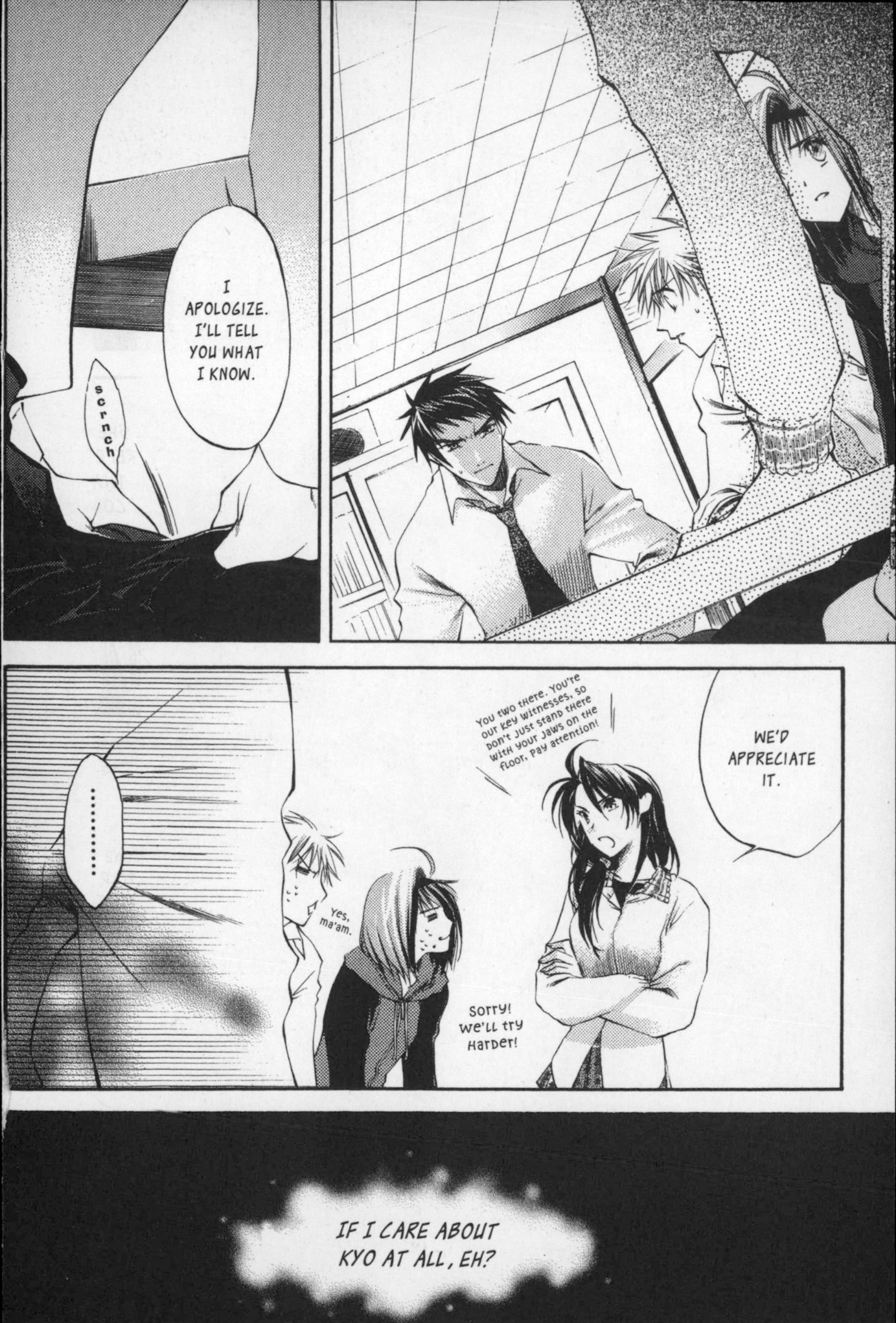
I APOLOGIZE. I'LL TELL YOU WHAT I KNOW.
scrnch
WE'D APPRECIATE IT.
You two there. You're our key witnesses, so don't just stand there with your jaws on the floor. Pay attention!
Yes, ma'am.
Sorry! We'll try harder!
......
IF I CARE ABOUT KYO AT ALL, EH?

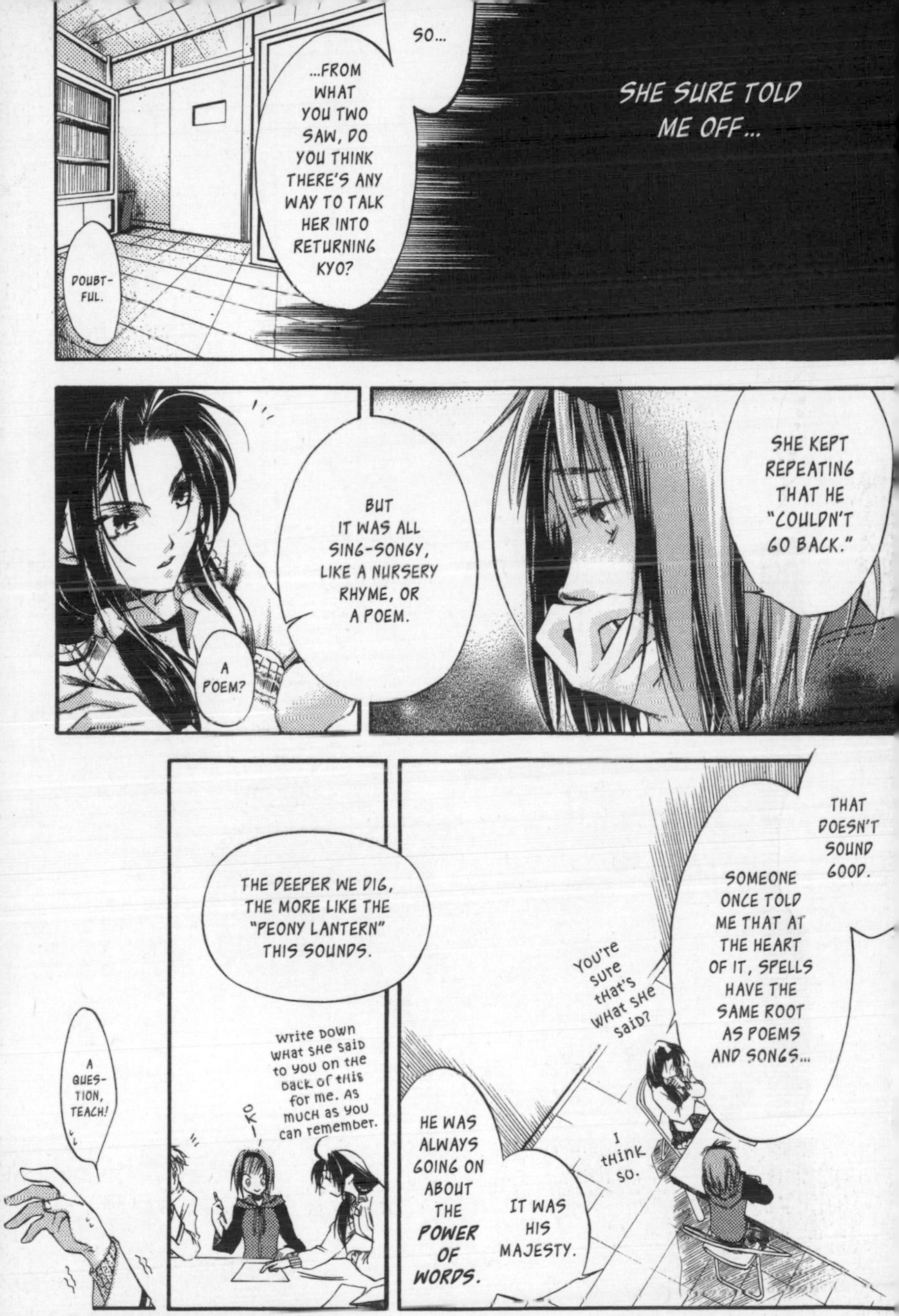
SHE SURE TOLD ME OFF...
SO...
...FROM WHAT YOU TWO SAW, DO YOU THINK THERE'S ANY WAY TO TALK HER INTO RETURNING KYO?
DOUBT-FUL.
SHE KEPT REPEATING THAT HE "COULDN'T GO BACK."
BUT IT WAS ALL SING-SONGY, LIKE A NURSERY RHYME, OR A POEM.
A POEM?
THAT DOESN'T SOUND GOOD.
SOMEONE ONCE TOLD ME THAT AT THE HEART OF IT, SPELLS HAVE THE SAME ROOT AS POEMS AND SONGS...
YOU'RE SURE THAT'S WHAT SHE SAID?
I THINK SO.
IT WAS HIS MAJESTY.
HE WAS ALWAYS GOING ON ABOUT THE *POWER OF WORDS*.
THE DEEPER WE DIG, THE MORE LIKE THE "PEONY LANTERN" THIS SOUNDS.
Write down what she said to you on the back of this for me. As much as you can remember.
OK—
A QUES-TION, TEACH!

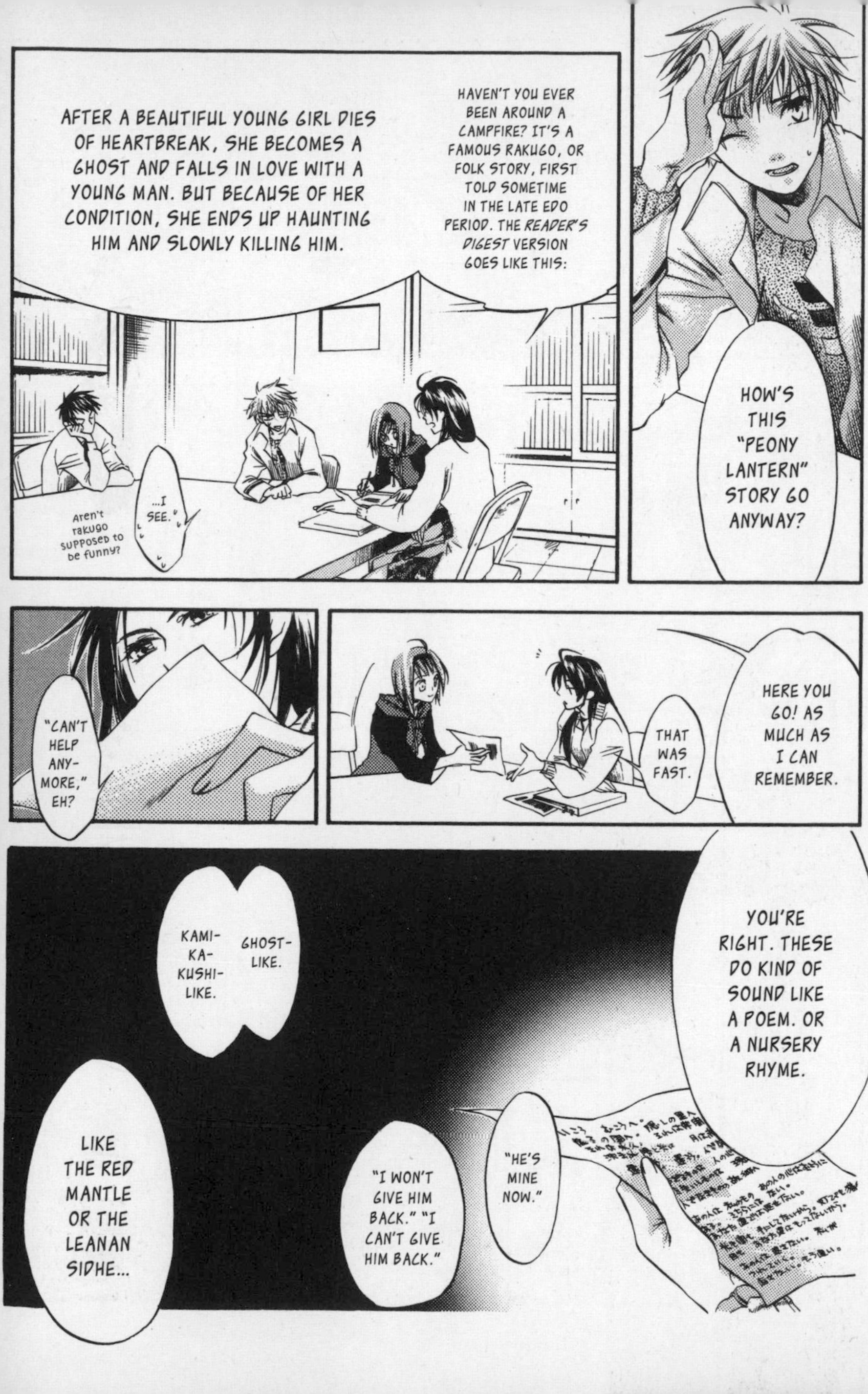
HOW'S THIS "PEONY LANTERN" STORY GO ANYWAY?
HAVEN'T YOU EVER BEEN AROUND A CAMPFIRE? IT'S A FAMOUS RAKUGO, OR FOLK STORY, FIRST TOLD SOMETIME IN THE LATE EDO PERIOD. THE *READER'S DIGEST* VERSION GOES LIKE THIS:
AFTER A BEAUTIFUL YOUNG GIRL DIES OF HEARTBREAK, SHE BECOMES A GHOST AND FALLS IN LOVE WITH A YOUNG MAN. BUT BECAUSE OF HER CONDITION, SHE ENDS UP HAUNTING HIM AND SLOWLY KILLING HIM.
...I SEE.
Aren't rakugo supposed to be funny?
HERE YOU GO! AS MUCH AS I CAN REMEMBER.
THAT WAS FAST.
"CAN'T HELP ANYMORE," EH?
YOU'RE RIGHT. THESE DO KIND OF SOUND LIKE A POEM. OR A NURSERY RHYME.
"HE'S MINE NOW."
"I WON'T GIVE HIM BACK." "I CAN'T GIVE HIM BACK."
GHOST-LIKE.
KAMI-KA-KUSHI-LIKE.
LIKE THE RED MANTLE OR THE LEANAN SIDHE...

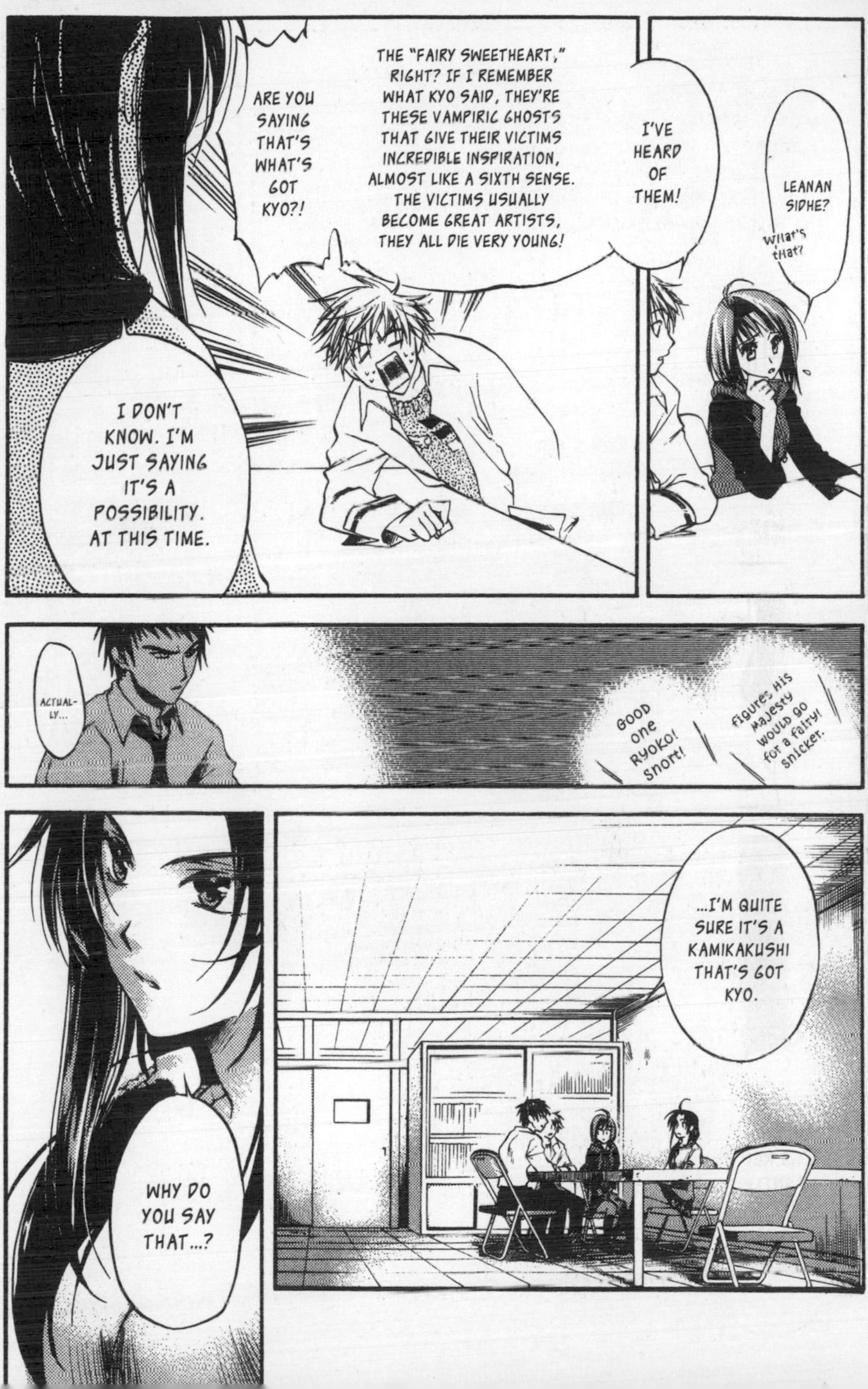
LEANAN SIDHE?
What's that?
I'VE HEARD OF THEM!
THE "FAIRY SWEETHEART," RIGHT? IF I REMEMBER WHAT KYO SAID, THEY'RE THESE VAMPIRIC GHOSTS THAT GIVE THEIR VICTIMS INCREDIBLE INSPIRATION, ALMOST LIKE A SIXTH SENSE. THE VICTIMS USUALLY BECOME GREAT ARTISTS, THEY ALL DIE VERY YOUNG!
ARE YOU SAYING THAT'S WHAT'S GOT KYO?!
I DON'T KNOW. I'M JUST SAYING IT'S A POSSIBILITY. AT THIS TIME.
figures His Majesty would go for a fairy! snicker.
GOOD one Ryoko! Snort!
Actual-ly...
...I'M QUITE SURE IT'S A KAMIKAKUSHI THAT'S GOT KYO.
WHY DO YOU SAY THAT...?

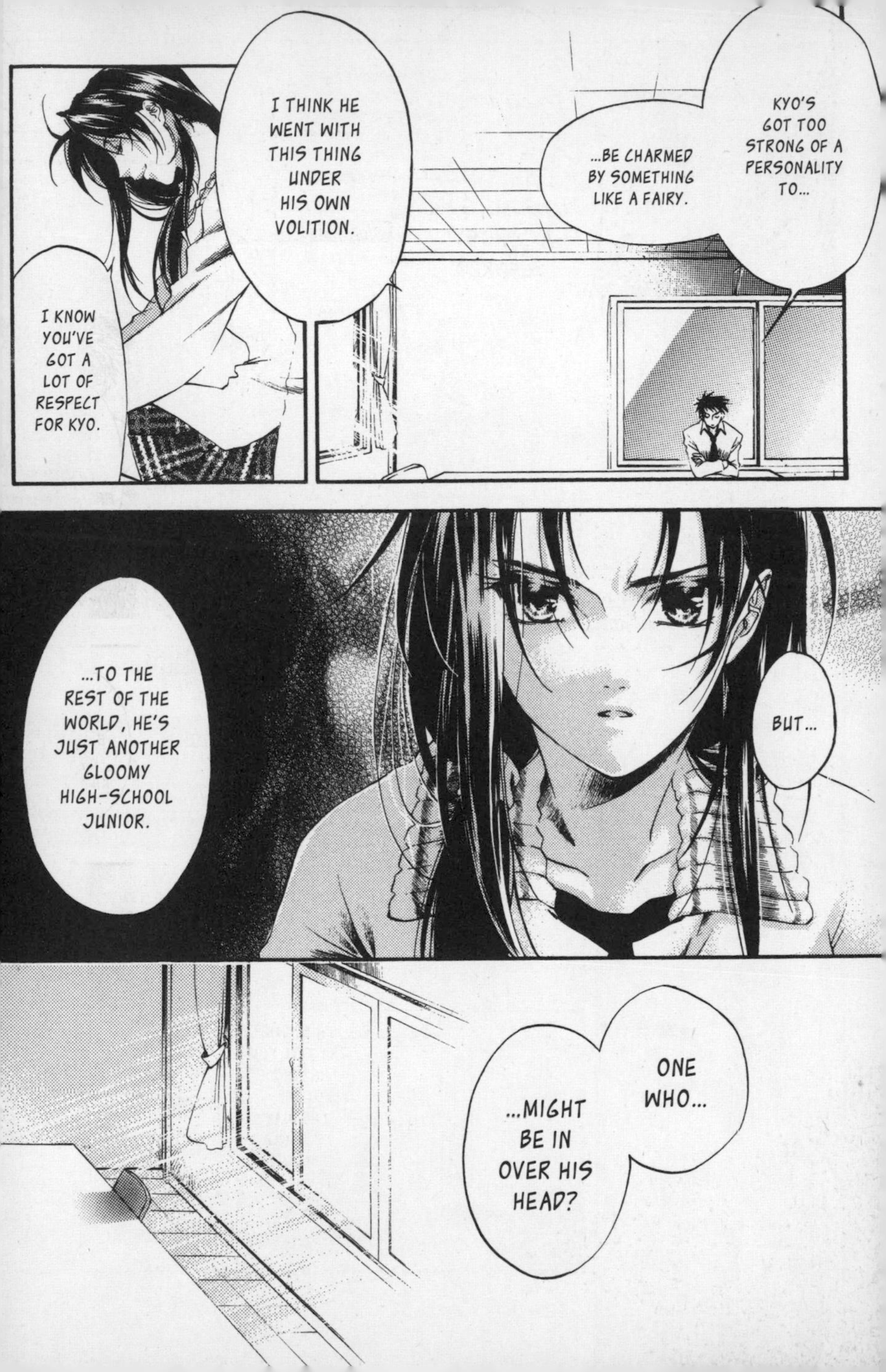
KYO'S GOT TOO STRONG OF A PERSONALITY TO...
...BE CHARMED BY SOMETHING LIKE A FAIRY.
I THINK HE WENT WITH THIS THING UNDER HIS OWN VOLITION.
I KNOW YOU'VE GOT A LOT OF RESPECT FOR KYO.
BUT...
...TO THE REST OF THE WORLD, HE'S JUST ANOTHER GLOOMY HIGH-SCHOOL JUNIOR.
ONE WHO...
...MIGHT BE IN OVER HIS HEAD?

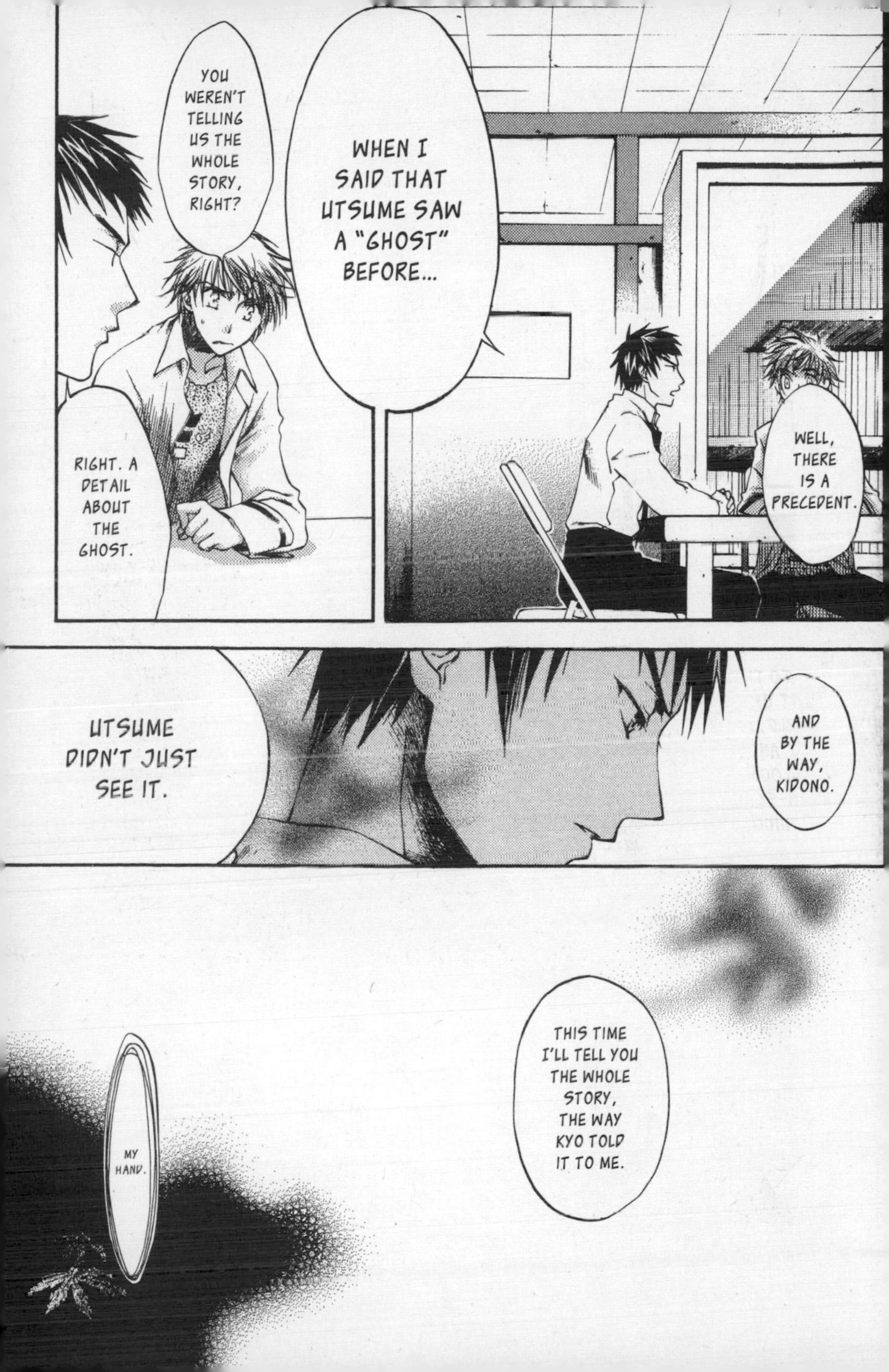
WELL, THERE IS A PRECEDENT.
WHEN I SAID THAT UTSUME SAW A "GHOST" BEFORE...
YOU WEREN'T TELLING US THE WHOLE STORY, RIGHT?
RIGHT. A DETAIL ABOUT THE GHOST.
AND BY THE WAY, KIDONO.
UTSUME DIDN'T JUST SEE IT.
THIS TIME I'LL TELL YOU THE WHOLE STORY, THE WAY KYO TOLD IT TO ME.
MY HAND.

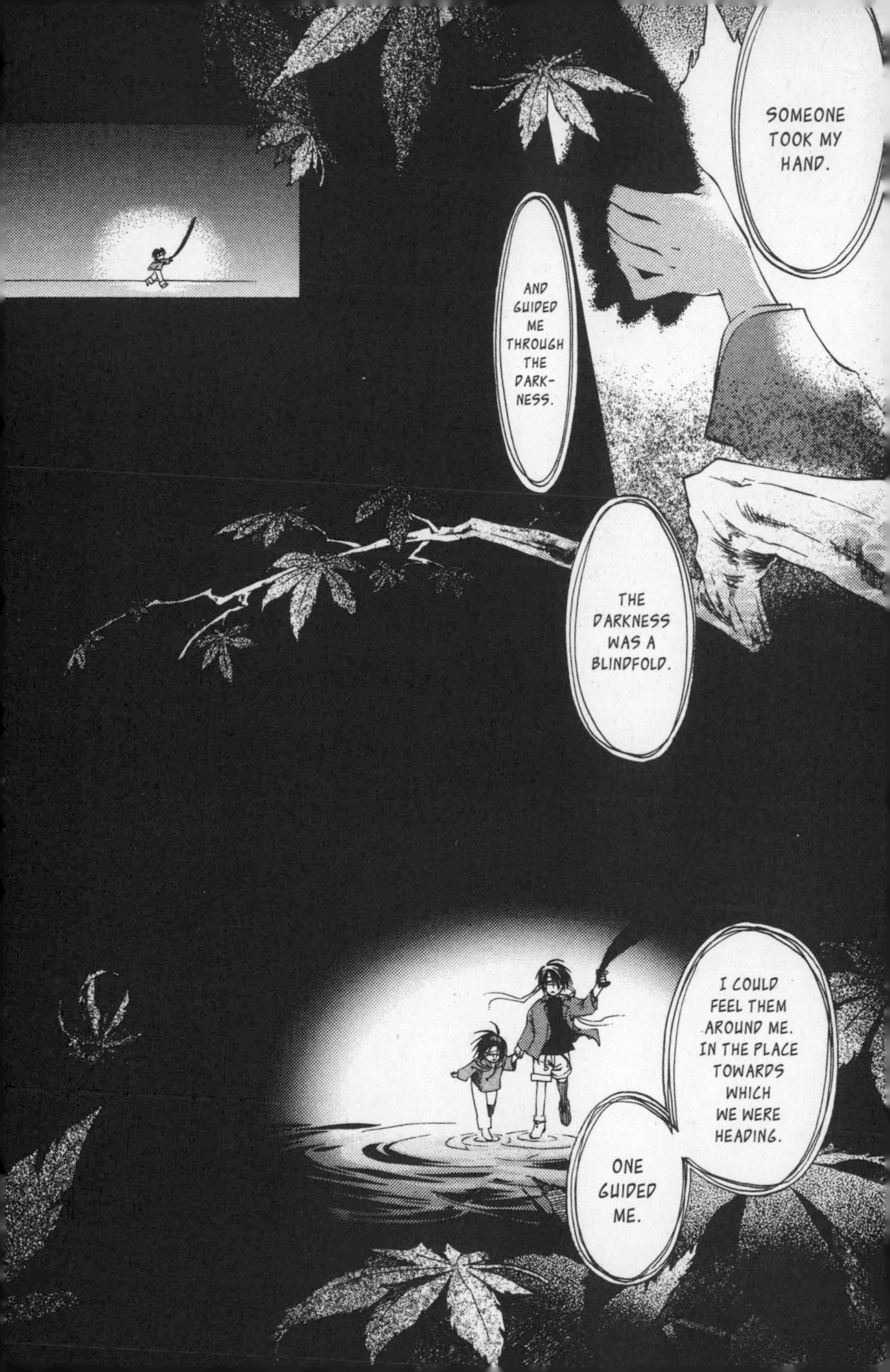
SOMEONE TOOK MY HAND.
AND GUIDED ME THROUGH THE DARK-NESS.
THE DARKNESS WAS A BLINDFOLD.
I COULD FEEL THEM AROUND ME. IN THE PLACE TOWARDS WHICH WE WERE HEADING.
ONE GUIDED ME.

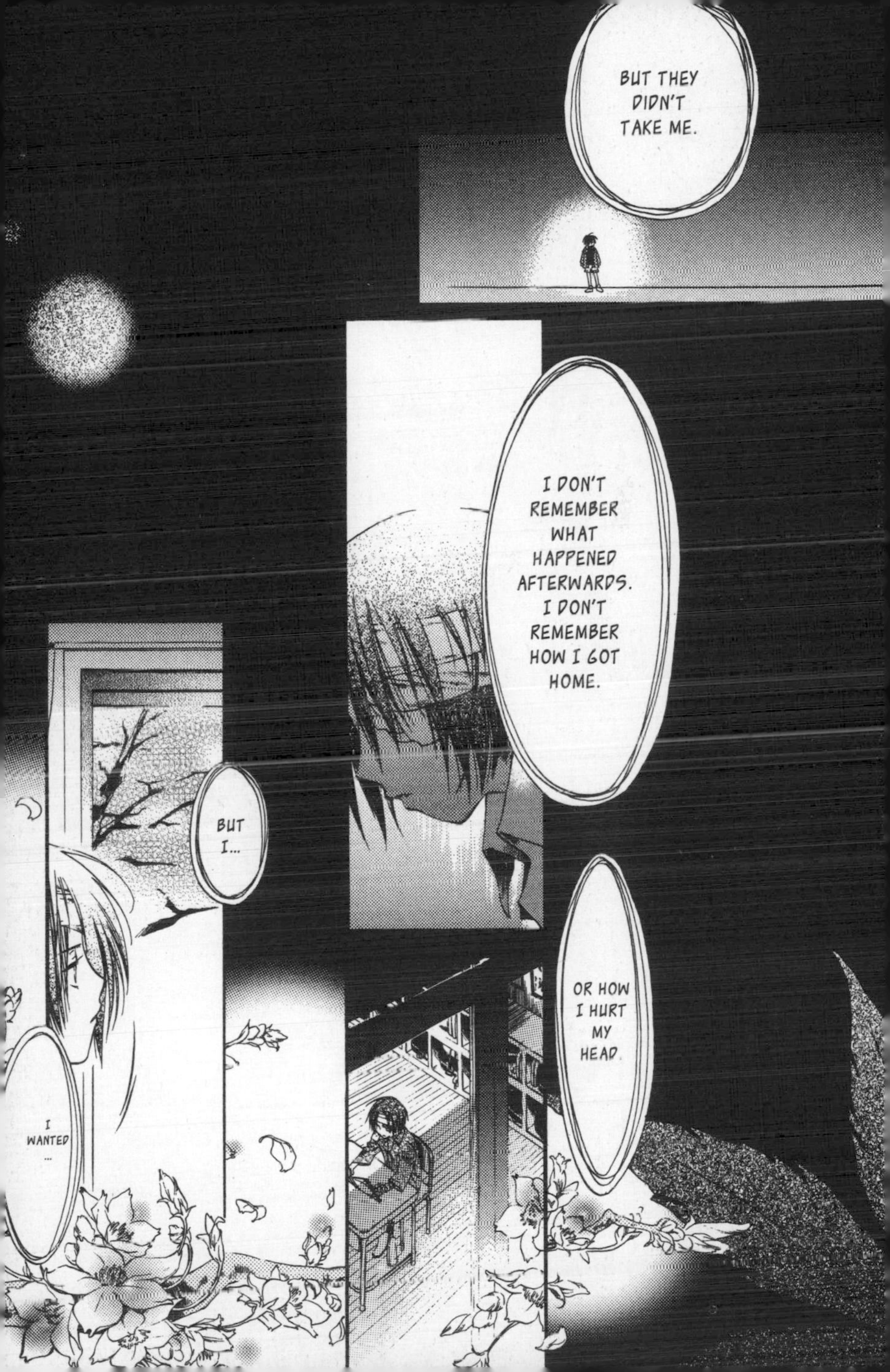
BUT THEY DIDN'T TAKE ME.
I DON'T REMEMBER WHAT HAPPENED AFTERWARDS. I DON'T REMEMBER HOW I GOT HOME.
OR HOW I HURT MY HEAD.
BUT I...
I WANTED ...

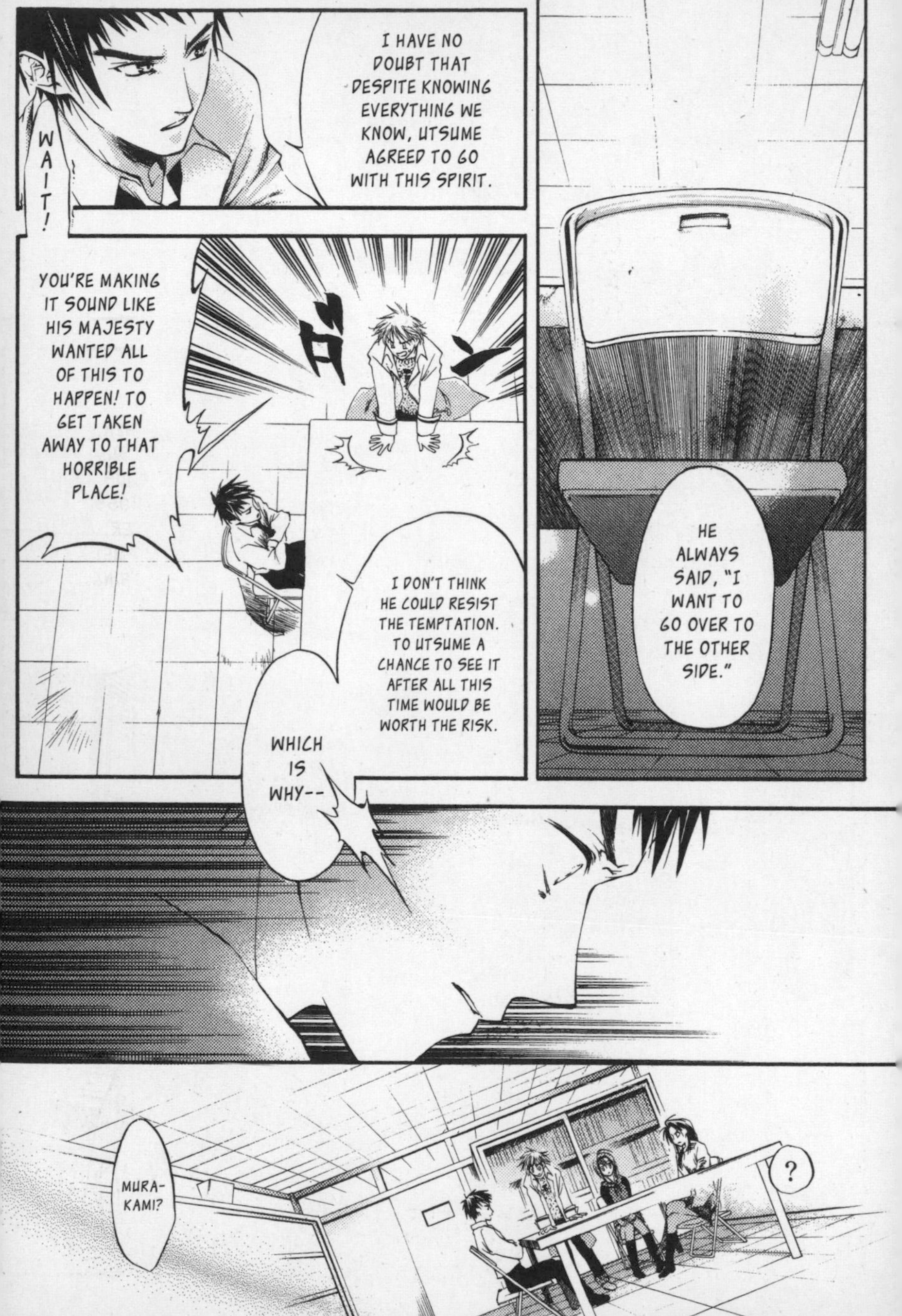
I HAVE NO DOUBT THAT DESPITE KNOWING EVERYTHING WE KNOW, UTSUME AGREED TO GO WITH THIS SPIRIT.
WAIT!
YOU'RE MAKING IT SOUND LIKE HIS MAJESTY WANTED ALL OF THIS TO HAPPEN! TO GET TAKEN AWAY TO THAT HORRIBLE PLACE!
I DON'T THINK HE COULD RESIST THE TEMPTATION. TO UTSUME A CHANCE TO SEE IT AFTER ALL THIS TIME WOULD BE WORTH THE RISK.
HE ALWAYS SAID, "I WANT TO GO OVER TO THE OTHER SIDE."
WHICH IS WHY--
?
MURA-KAMI?

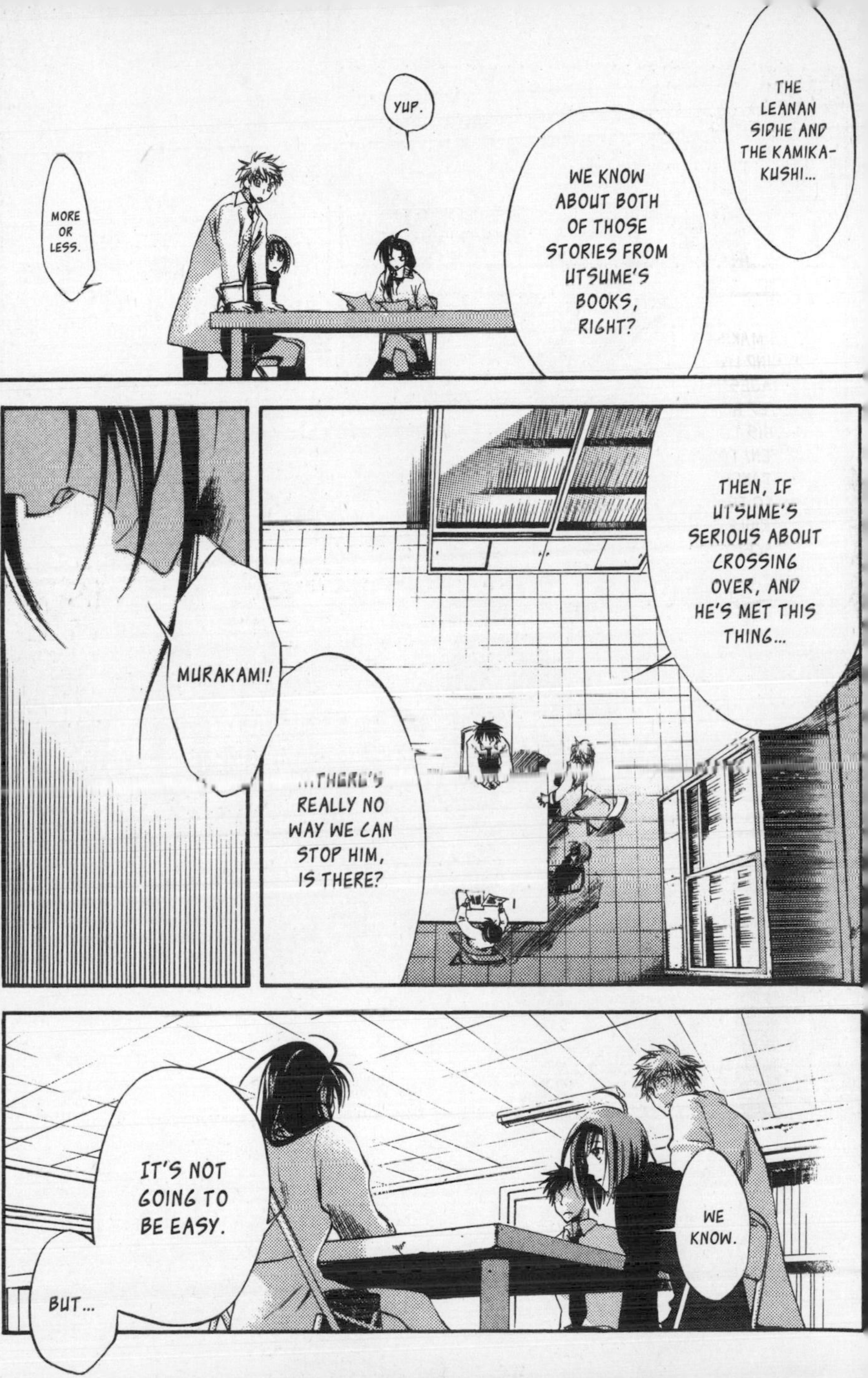
THE LEANAN SIDHE AND THE KAMIKA-KUSHI...
WE KNOW ABOUT BOTH OF THOSE STORIES FROM UTSUME'S BOOKS, RIGHT?
YUP.
MORE OR LESS.
THEN, IF UTSUME'S SERIOUS ABOUT CROSSING OVER, AND HE'S MET THIS THING...
...THERE'S REALLY NO WAY WE CAN STOP HIM, IS THERE?
MURAKAMI!
WE KNOW.
IT'S NOT GOING TO BE EASY.
BUT...

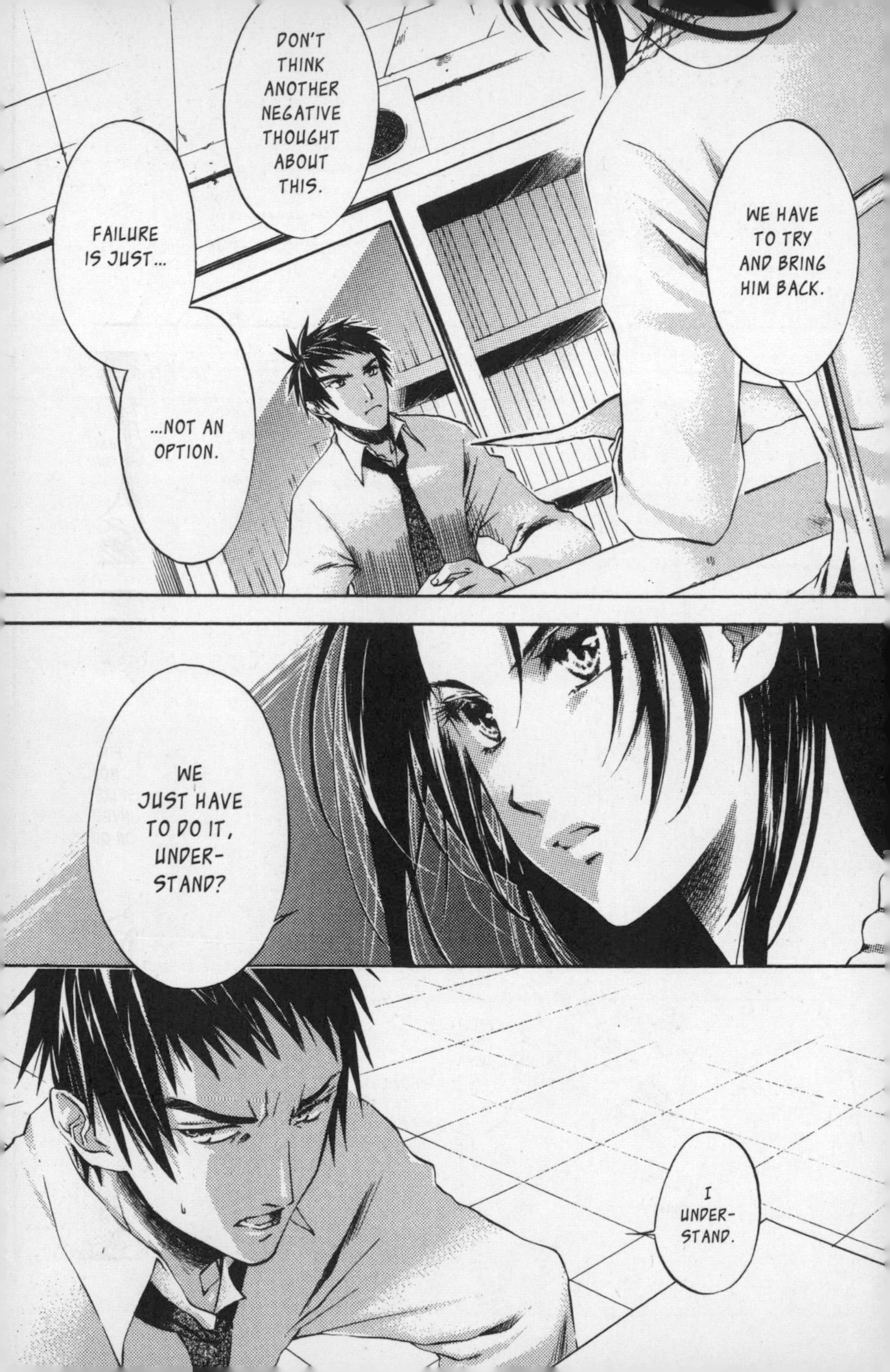
WE HAVE TO TRY AND BRING HIM BACK.
DON'T THINK ANOTHER NEGATIVE THOUGHT ABOUT THIS.
FAILURE IS JUST...
...NOT AN OPTION.
WE JUST HAVE TO DO IT, UNDER-STAND?
I UNDER-STAND.

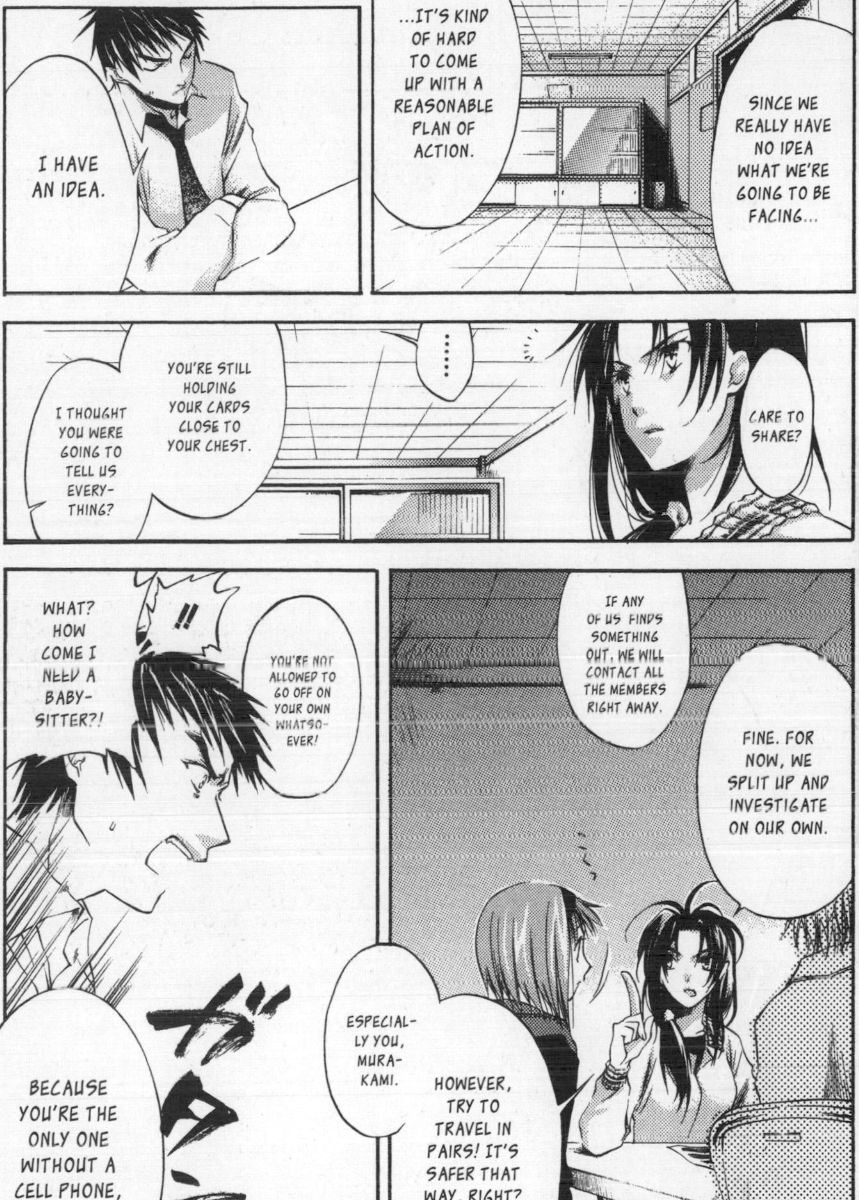
SINCE WE REALLY HAVE NO IDEA WHAT WE'RE GOING TO BE FACING...
...IT'S KIND OF HARD TO COME UP WITH A REASONABLE PLAN OF ACTION.
I HAVE AN IDEA.
CARE TO SHARE?
......
YOU'RE STILL HOLDING YOUR CARDS CLOSE TO YOUR CHEST.
I THOUGHT YOU WERE GOING TO TELL US EVERY-THING?
FINE. FOR NOW, WE SPLIT UP AND INVESTIGATE ON OUR OWN.
IF ANY OF US FINDS SOMETHING OUT, WE WILL CONTACT ALL THE MEMBERS RIGHT AWAY.
HOWEVER, TRY TO TRAVEL IN PAIRS! IT'S SAFER THAT WAY, RIGHT?
ESPECIAL-LY YOU, MURA-KAMI.
YOU'RE NOT ALLOWED TO GO OFF ON YOUR OWN WHATSO-EVER!
!!
WHAT? HOW COME I NEED A BABY-SITTER?!
ガタ
BECAUSE YOU'RE THE ONLY ONE WITHOUT A CELL PHONE, RIGHT?

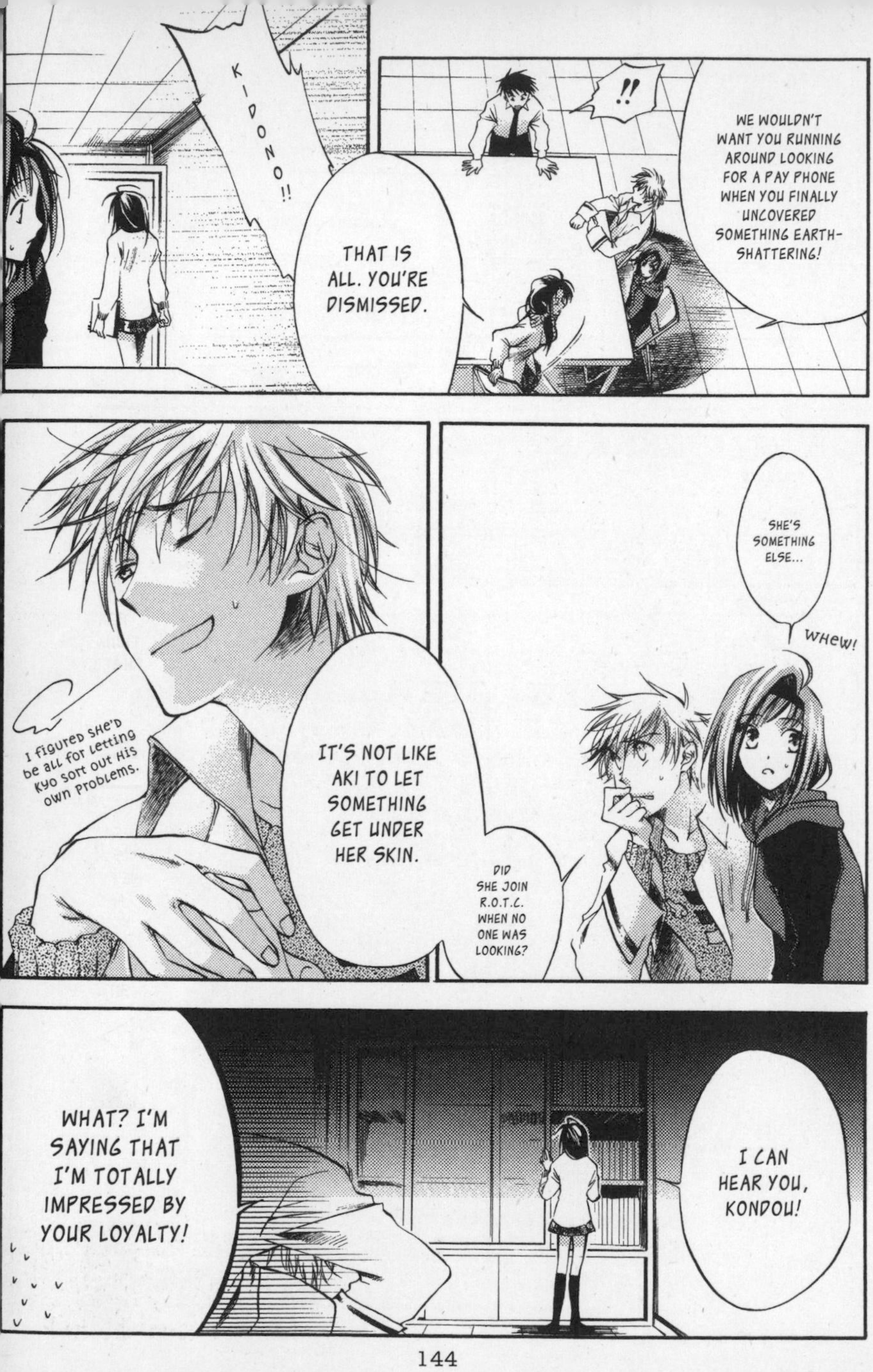
!!
WE WOULDN'T WANT YOU RUNNING AROUND LOOKING FOR A PAY PHONE WHEN YOU FINALLY UNCOVERED SOMETHING EARTH-SHATTERING!
THAT IS ALL. YOU'RE DISMISSED.
KIDONO!!
SHE'S SOMETHING ELSE...
WHEW!
DID SHE JOIN R.O.T.C. WHEN NO ONE WAS LOOKING?
IT'S NOT LIKE AKI TO LET SOMETHING GET UNDER HER SKIN.
I figured she'd be all for letting Kyo sort out his own problems.
I CAN HEAR YOU, KONDOU!
WHAT? I'M SAYING THAT I'M TOTALLY IMPRESSED BY YOUR LOYALTY!

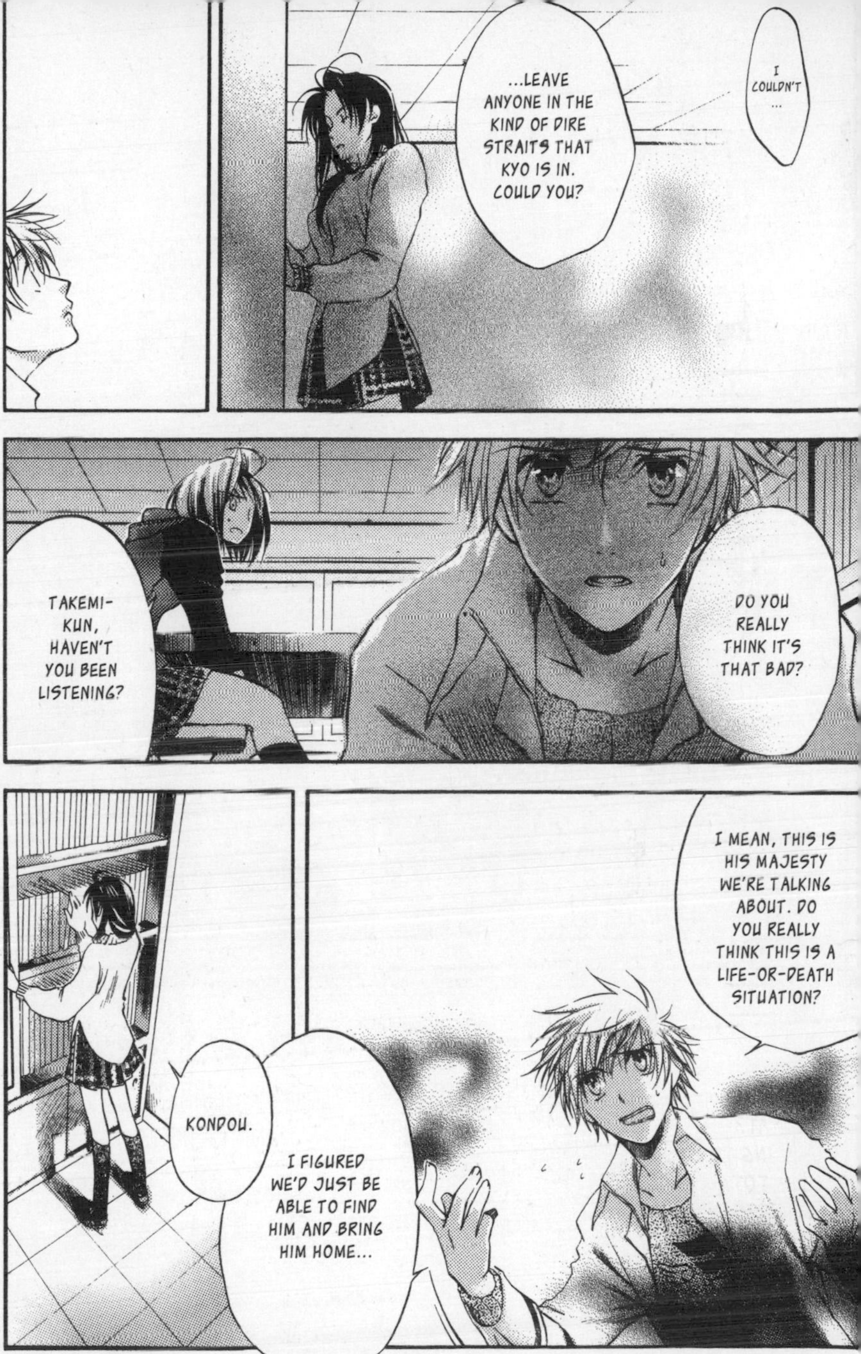
I couldn't ...
...leave anyone in the kind of dire straits that Kyo is in. Could you?
Do you really think it's that bad?
Takemi-kun, haven't you been listening?
I mean, this is his majesty we're talking about. Do you really think this is a life-or-death situation?
Kondou.
I figured we'd just be able to find him and bring him home...

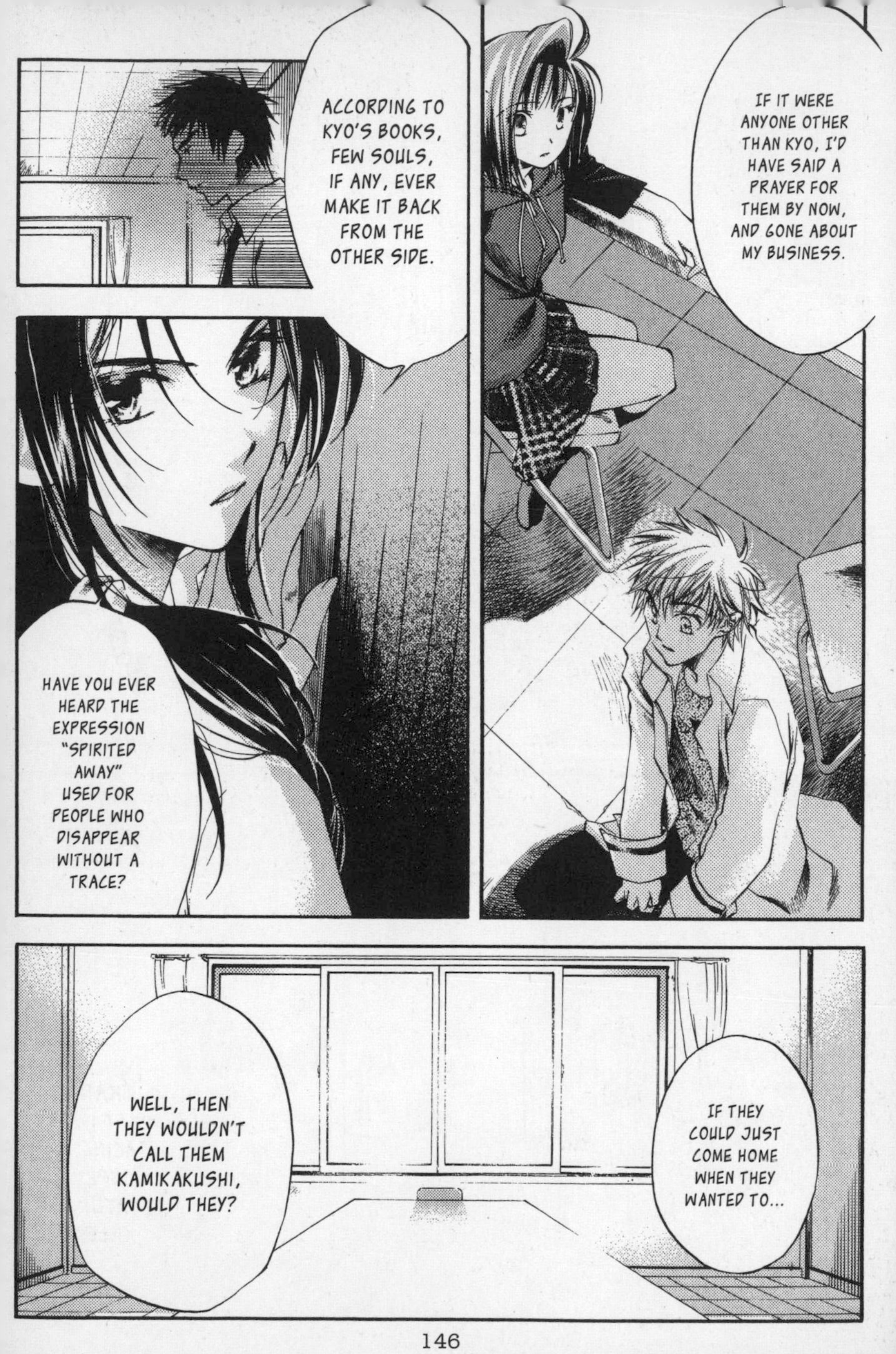
IF IT WERE ANYONE OTHER THAN KYO, I'D HAVE SAID A PRAYER FOR THEM BY NOW, AND GONE ABOUT MY BUSINESS.
ACCORDING TO KYO'S BOOKS, FEW SOULS, IF ANY, EVER MAKE IT BACK FROM THE OTHER SIDE.
HAVE YOU EVER HEARD THE EXPRESSION "SPIRITED AWAY" USED FOR PEOPLE WHO DISAPPEAR WITHOUT A TRACE?
IF THEY COULD JUST COME HOME WHEN THEY WANTED TO...
WELL, THEN THEY WOULDN'T CALL THEM KAMIKAKUSHI, WOULD THEY?

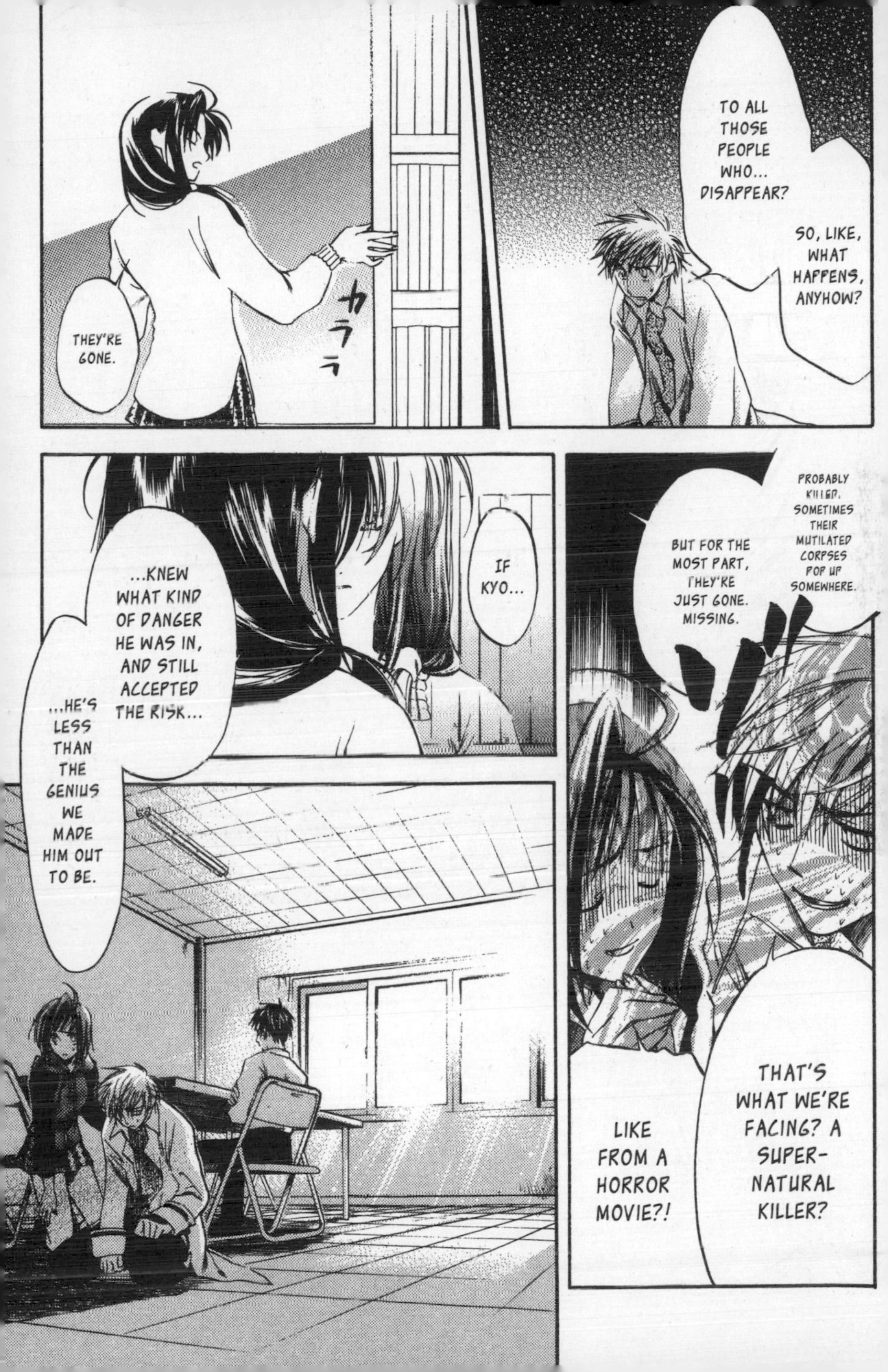
TO ALL THOSE PEOPLE WHO... DISAPPEAR?
SO, LIKE, WHAT HAPPENS, ANYHOW?
THEY'RE GONE.
カララ
PROBABLY KILLED. SOMETIMES THEIR MUTILATED CORPSES POP UP SOMEWHERE.
BUT FOR THE MOST PART, THEY'RE JUST GONE. MISSING.
THAT'S WHAT WE'RE FACING? A SUPER-NATURAL KILLER?
LIKE FROM A HORROR MOVIE?!
IF KYO...
...KNEW WHAT KIND OF DANGER HE WAS IN, AND STILL ACCEPTED THE RISK...
...HE'S LESS THAN THE GENIUS WE MADE HIM OUT TO BE.

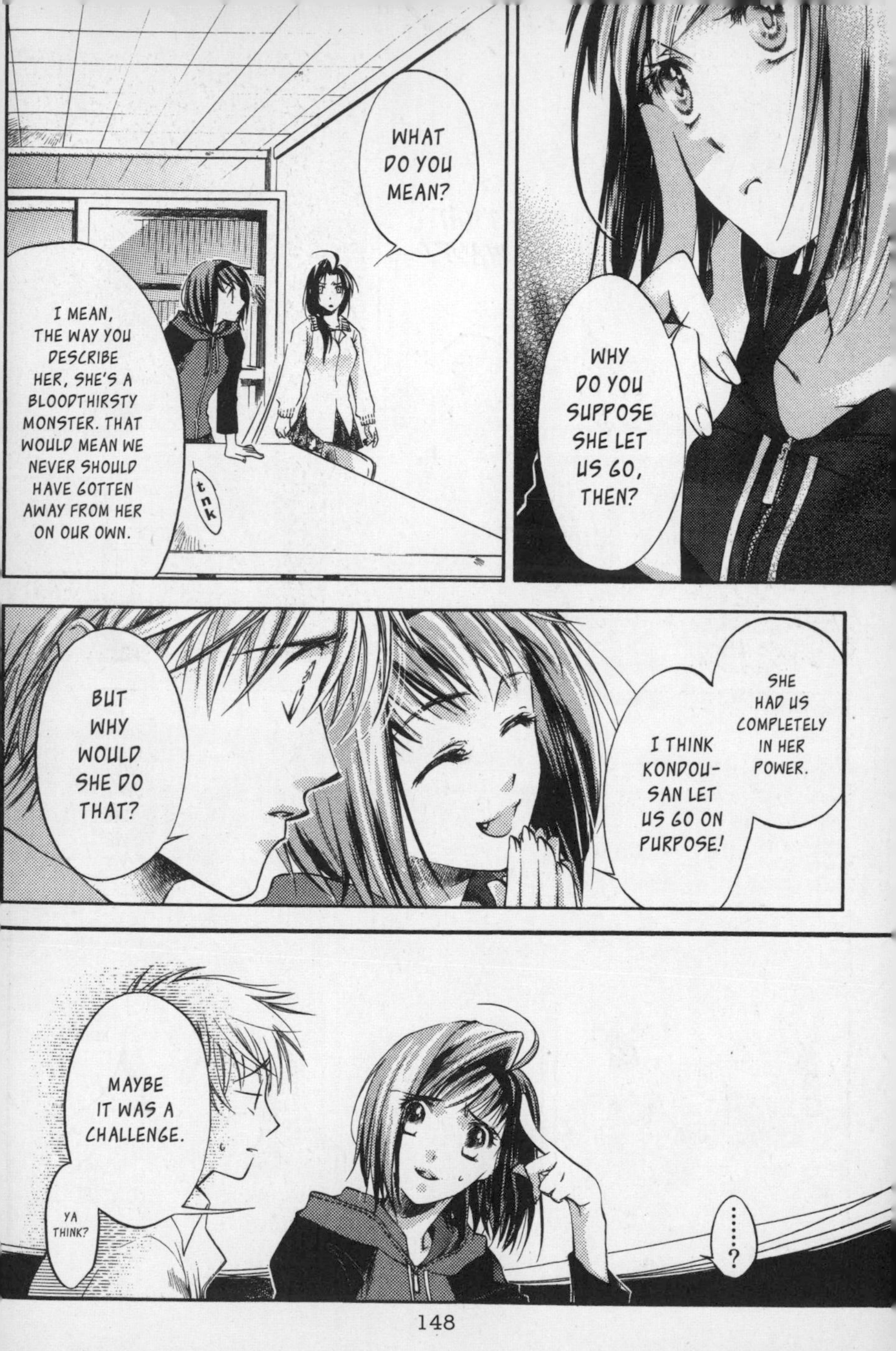
WHY DO YOU SUPPOSE SHE LET US GO, THEN?
WHAT DO YOU MEAN?
I MEAN, THE WAY YOU DESCRIBE HER, SHE'S A BLOODTHIRSTY MONSTER. THAT WOULD MEAN WE NEVER SHOULD HAVE GOTTEN AWAY FROM HER ON OUR OWN.
tnk
SHE HAD US COMPLETELY IN HER POWER.
I THINK KONDOU-SAN LET US GO ON PURPOSE!
BUT WHY WOULD SHE DO THAT?
......?
MAYBE IT WAS A CHALLENGE.
YA THINK?

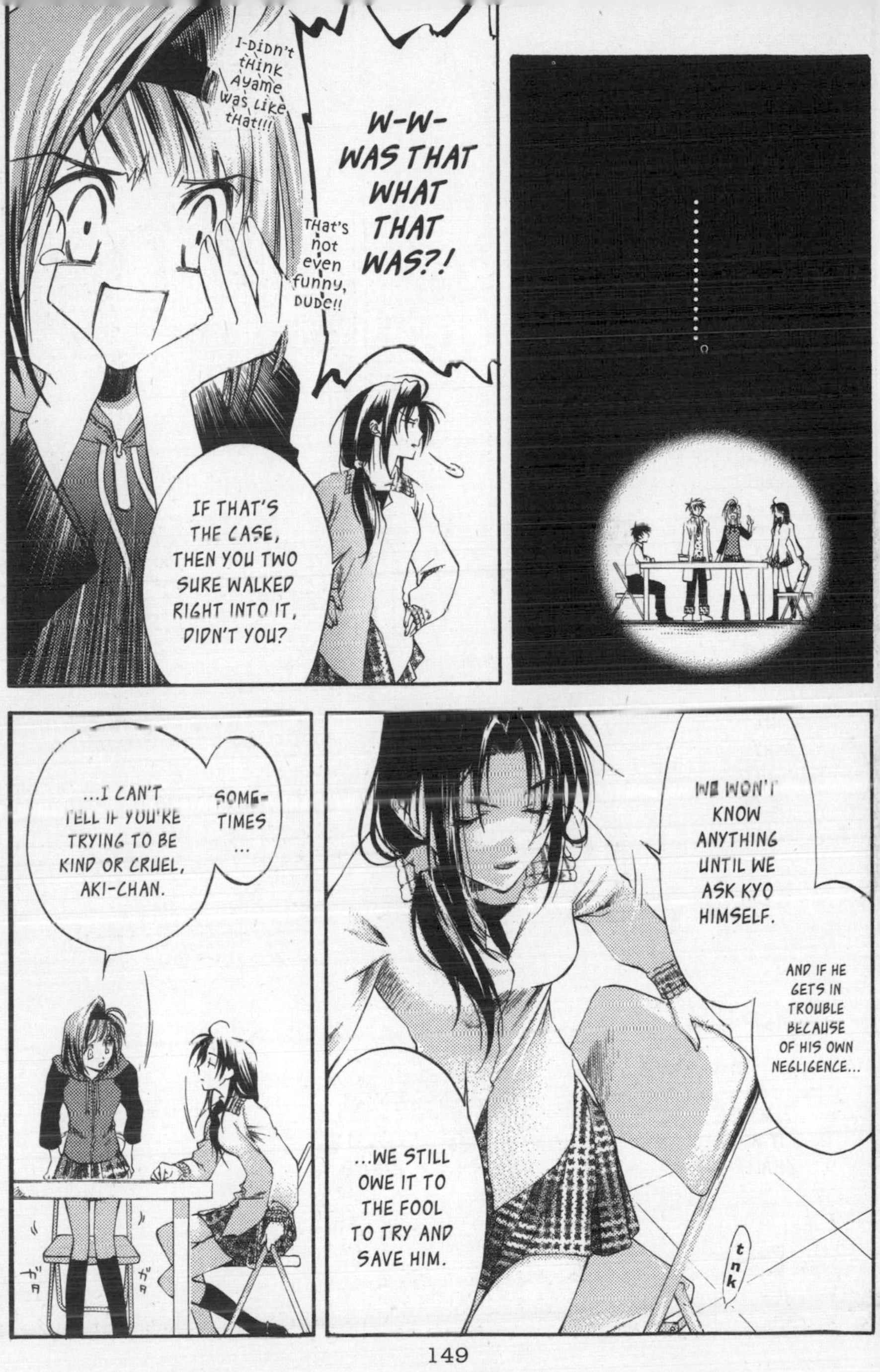
......
W-W-WAS THAT WHAT THAT WAS?!
I-Didn't think Ayame was like that!!!
That's not even funny, DUDE!!
IF THAT'S THE CASE, THEN YOU TWO SURE WALKED RIGHT INTO IT, DIDN'T YOU?
WE WON'T KNOW ANYTHING UNTIL WE ASK KYO HIMSELF.
AND IF HE GETS IN TROUBLE BECAUSE OF HIS OWN NEGLIGENCE...
...WE STILL OWE IT TO THE FOOL TO TRY AND SAVE HIM.
tnk
SOME-TIMES...
...I CAN'T TELL IF YOU'RE TRYING TO BE KIND OR CRUEL, AKI-CHAN.
ガタ
ガタ

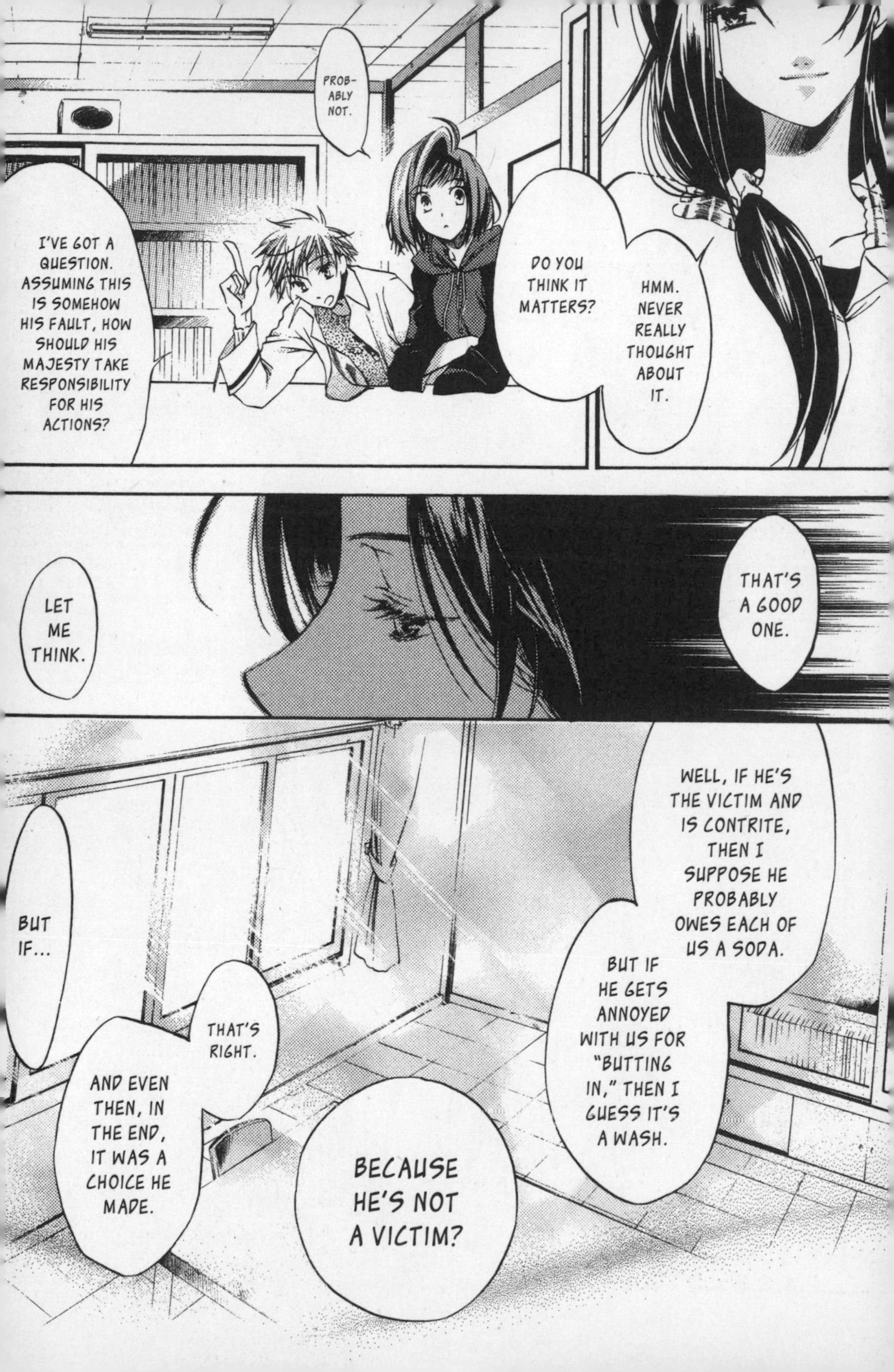
HMM. NEVER REALLY THOUGHT ABOUT IT.
DO YOU THINK IT MATTERS?
PROB-ABLY NOT.
I'VE GOT A QUESTION. ASSUMING THIS IS SOMEHOW HIS FAULT, HOW SHOULD HIS MAJESTY TAKE RESPONSIBILITY FOR HIS ACTIONS?
THAT'S A GOOD ONE.
LET ME THINK.
WELL, IF HE'S THE VICTIM AND IS CONTRITE, THEN I SUPPOSE HE PROBABLY OWES EACH OF US A SODA.
BUT IF HE GETS ANNOYED WITH US FOR "BUTTING IN," THEN I GUESS IT'S A WASH.
BECAUSE HE'S NOT A VICTIM?
THAT'S RIGHT.
AND EVEN THEN, IN THE END, IT WAS A CHOICE HE MADE.
BUT IF...

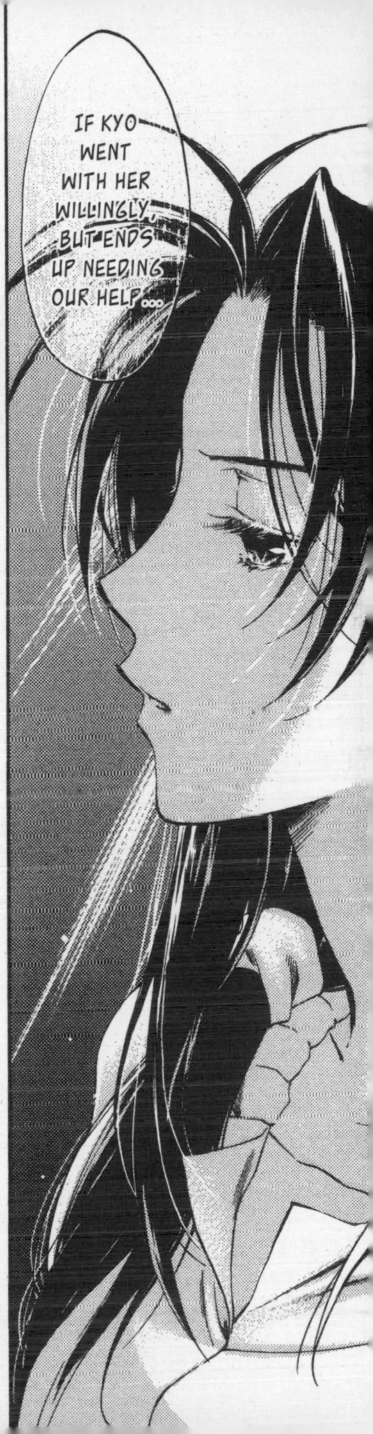
IF KYO WENT WITH HER WILLINGLY, BUT ENDS UP NEEDING OUR HELP...

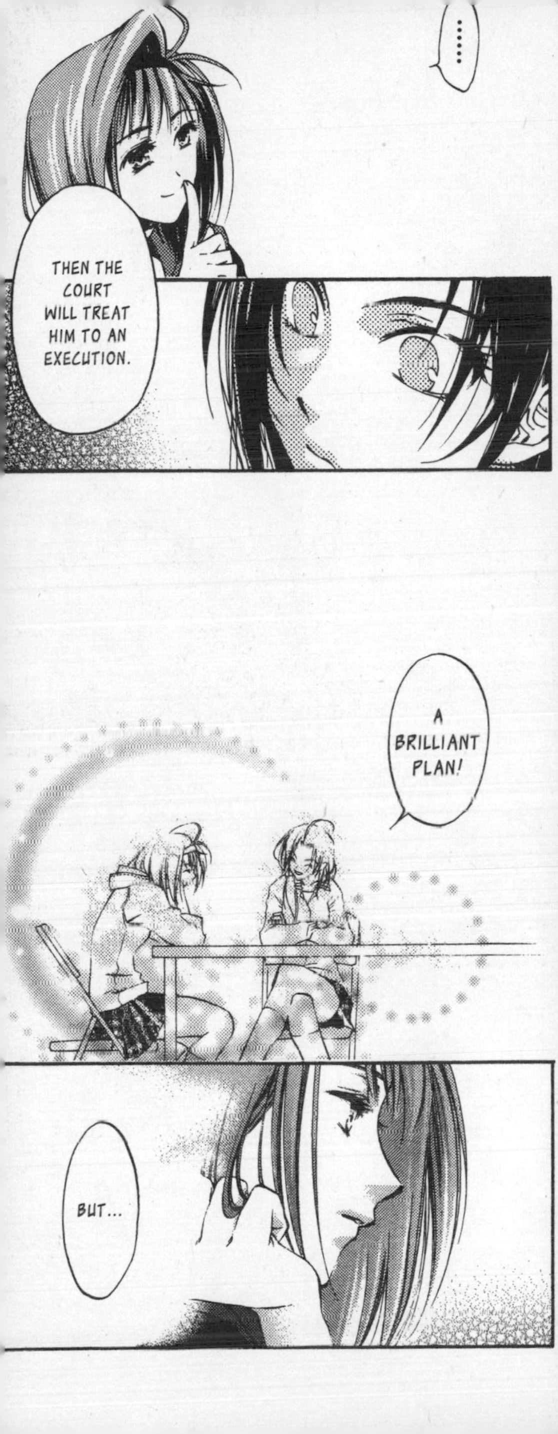
......
THEN THE COURT WILL TREAT HIM TO AN EXECUTION.
A BRILLIANT PLAN!
BUT...

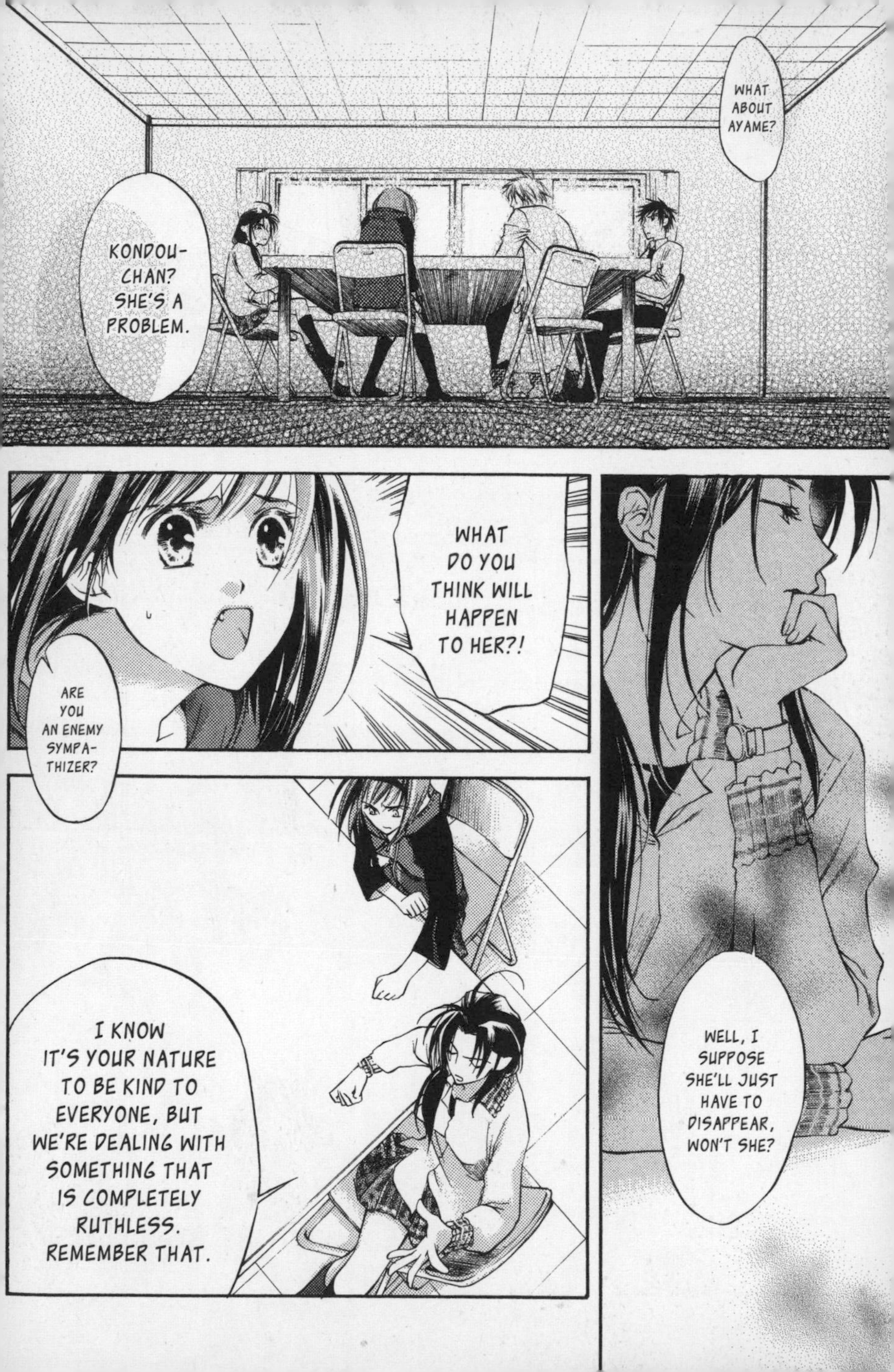
WHAT ABOUT AYAME?
KONDOU-CHAN? SHE'S A PROBLEM.
WELL, I SUPPOSE SHE'LL JUST HAVE TO DISAPPEAR, WON'T SHE?
WHAT DO YOU THINK WILL HAPPEN TO HER?!
ARE YOU AN ENEMY SYMPA-THIZER?
I KNOW IT'S YOUR NATURE TO BE KIND TO EVERYONE, BUT WE'RE DEALING WITH SOMETHING THAT IS COMPLETELY RUTHLESS. REMEMBER THAT.

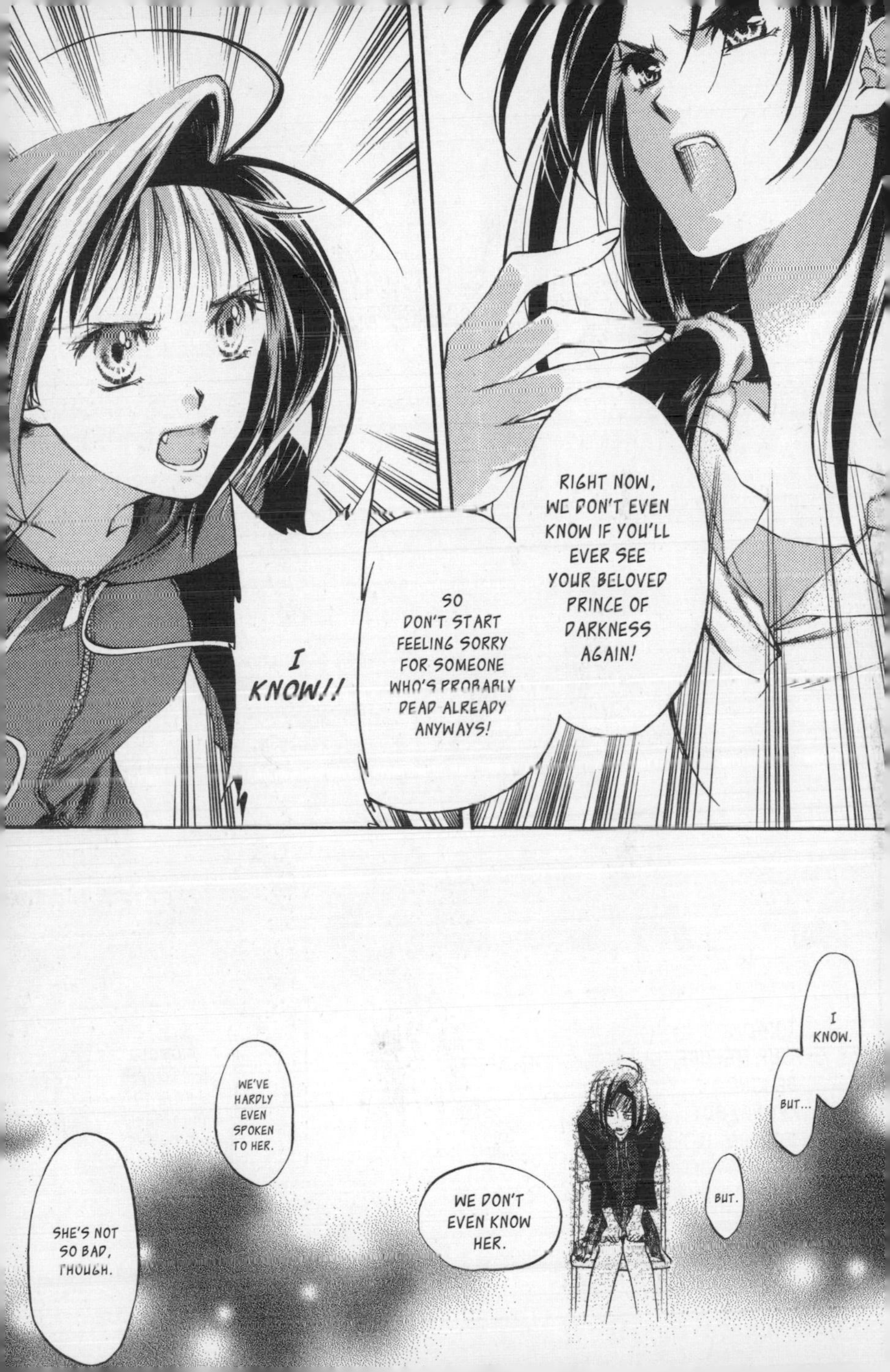
RIGHT NOW, WE DON'T EVEN KNOW IF YOU'LL EVER SEE YOUR BELOVED PRINCE OF DARKNESS AGAIN!
SO DON'T START FEELING SORRY FOR SOMEONE WHO'S PROBABLY DEAD ALREADY ANYWAYS!
I KNOW!!
I KNOW.
BUT...
BUT.
WE DON'T EVEN KNOW HER.
WE'VE HARDLY EVEN SPOKEN TO HER.
SHE'S NOT SO BAD, THOUGH.

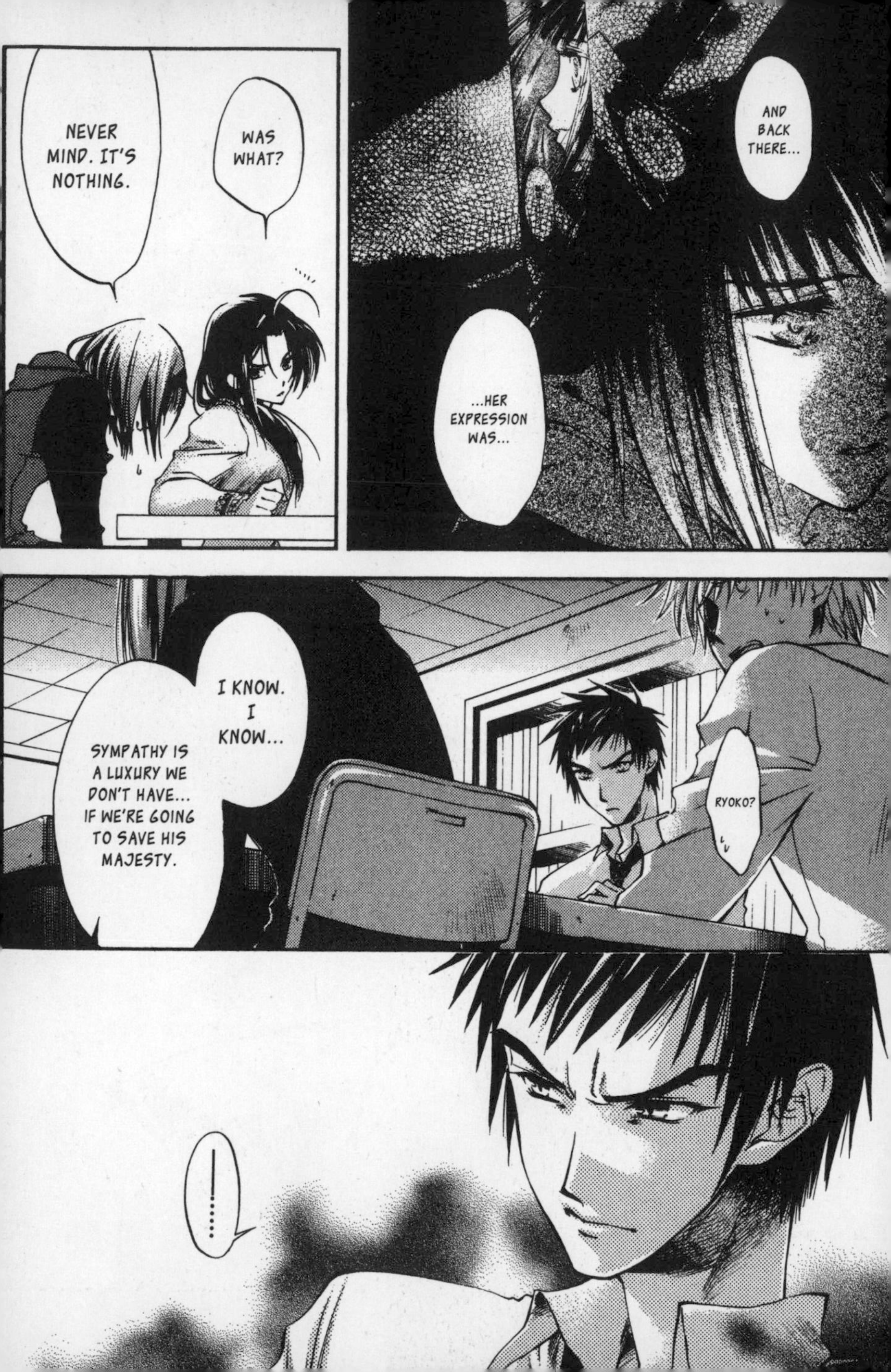
AND BACK THERE...
...HER EXPRESSION WAS...
WAS WHAT?
NEVER MIND. IT'S NOTHING.
RYOKO?
I KNOW. I KNOW...
SYMPATHY IS A LUXURY WE DON'T HAVE... IF WE'RE GOING TO SAVE HIS MAJESTY.
......!

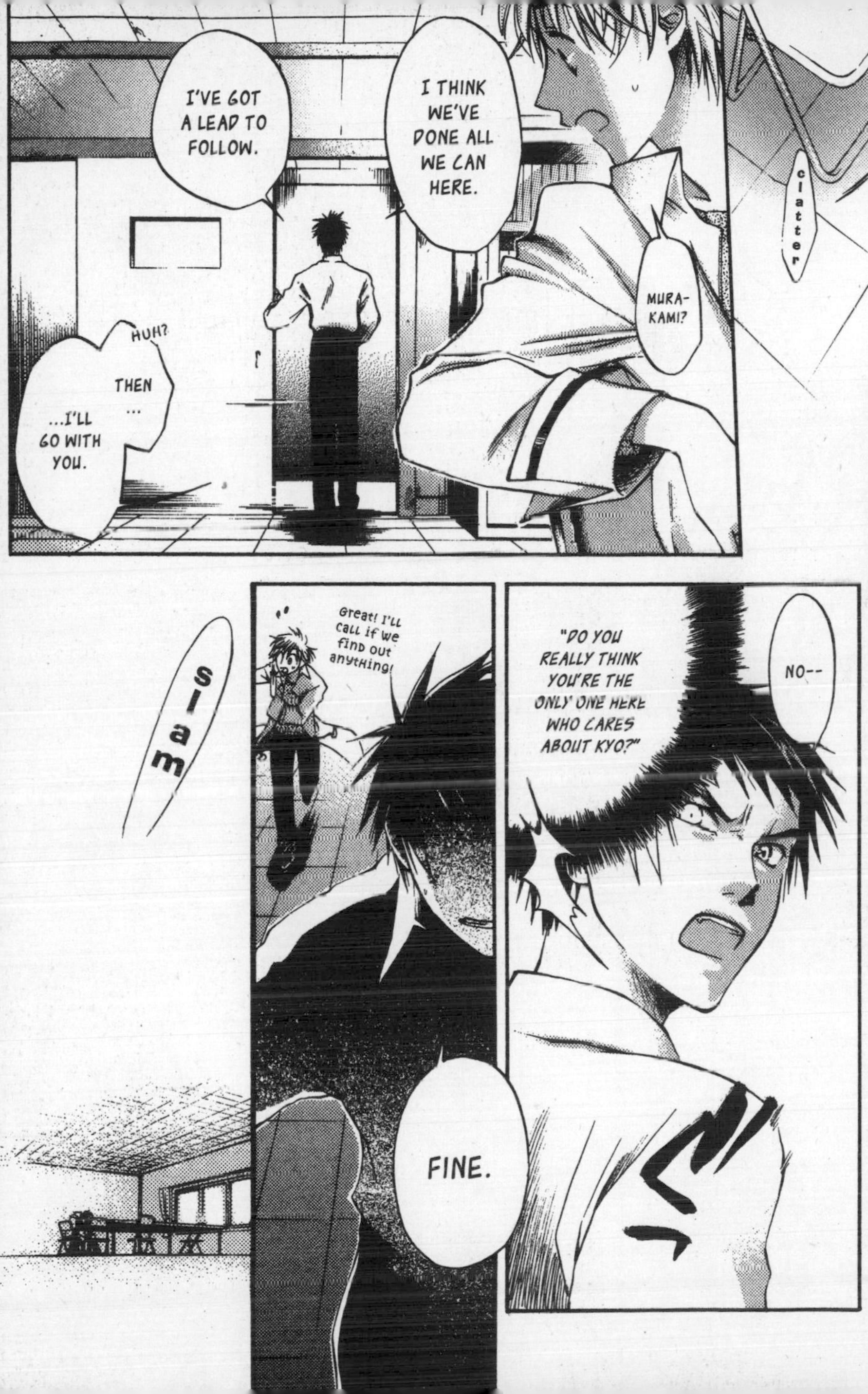
clatter
MURA-KAMI?
I THINK WE'VE DONE ALL WE CAN HERE.
I'VE GOT A LEAD TO FOLLOW.
HUH?
THEN ...
...I'LL GO WITH YOU.
NO--
"DO YOU REALLY THINK YOU'RE THE ONLY ONE HERE WHO CARES ABOUT KYO?"
Great! I'll call if we find out anything!
FINE.
slam

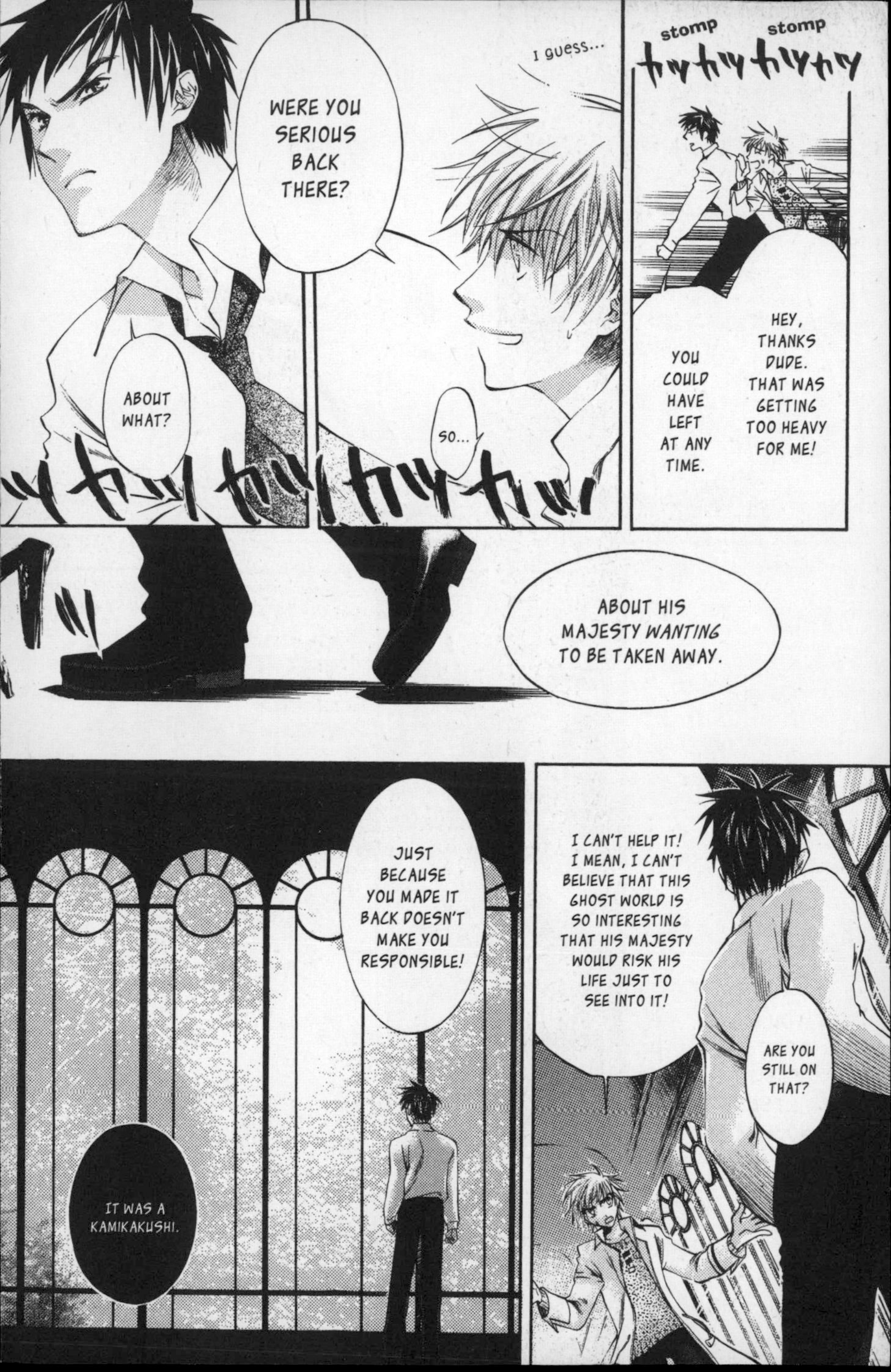
stomp stomp
HEY, THANKS DUDE. THAT WAS GETTING TOO HEAVY FOR ME!
YOU COULD HAVE LEFT AT ANY TIME.
I GUESS...
SO...
WERE YOU SERIOUS BACK THERE?
ABOUT WHAT?
ABOUT HIS MAJESTY *WANTING* TO BE TAKEN AWAY.
ARE YOU STILL ON THAT?
I CAN'T HELP IT! I MEAN, I CAN'T BELIEVE THAT THIS GHOST WORLD IS SO INTERESTING THAT HIS MAJESTY WOULD RISK HIS LIFE JUST TO SEE INTO IT!
JUST BECAUSE YOU MADE IT BACK DOESN'T MAKE YOU RESPONSIBLE!
IT WAS A KAMIKAKUSHI.

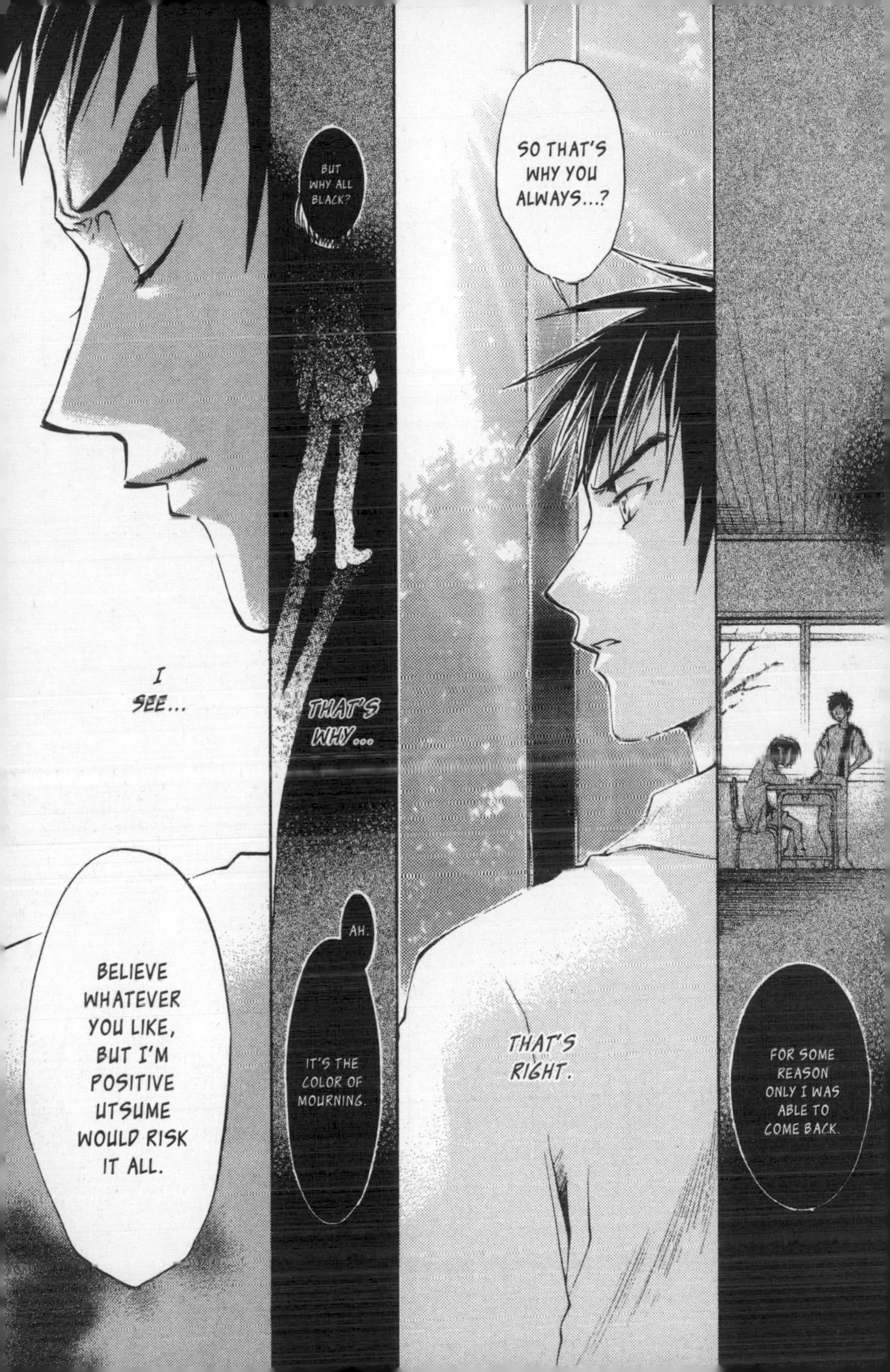
FOR SOME REASON ONLY I WAS ABLE TO COME BACK.
SO THAT'S WHY YOU ALWAYS...?
THAT'S RIGHT.
BUT WHY ALL BLACK?
THAT'S WHY...
AH.
IT'S THE COLOR OF MOURNING.
I SEE...
BELIEVE WHATEVER YOU LIKE, BUT I'M POSITIVE UTSUME WOULD RISK IT ALL.

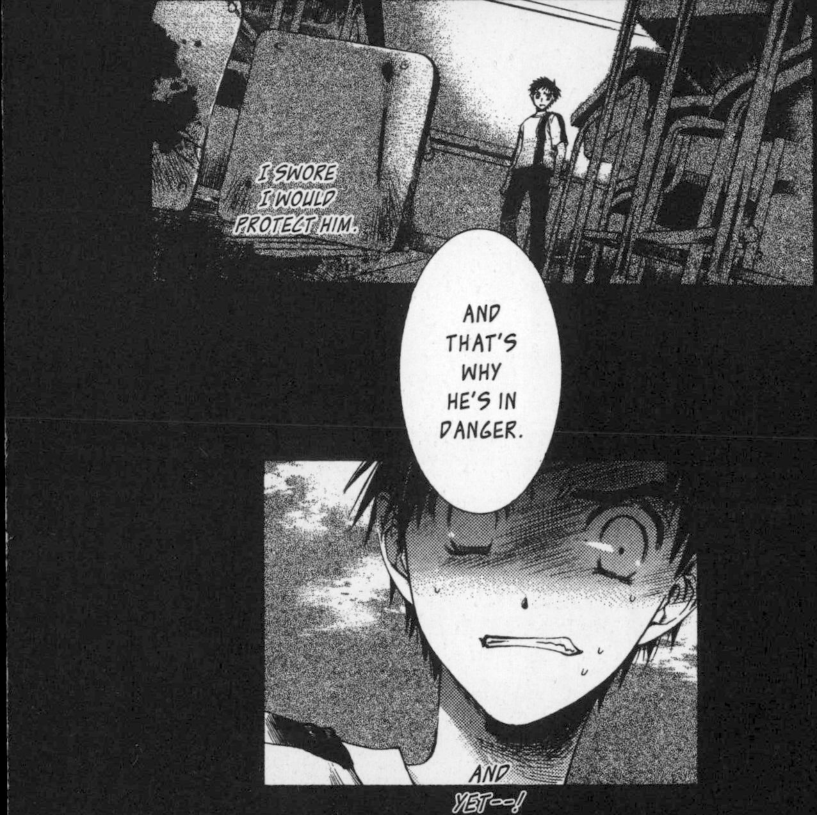
I SWORE I WOULD PROTECT HIM.
AND THAT'S WHY HE'S IN DANGER.
AND YET--!

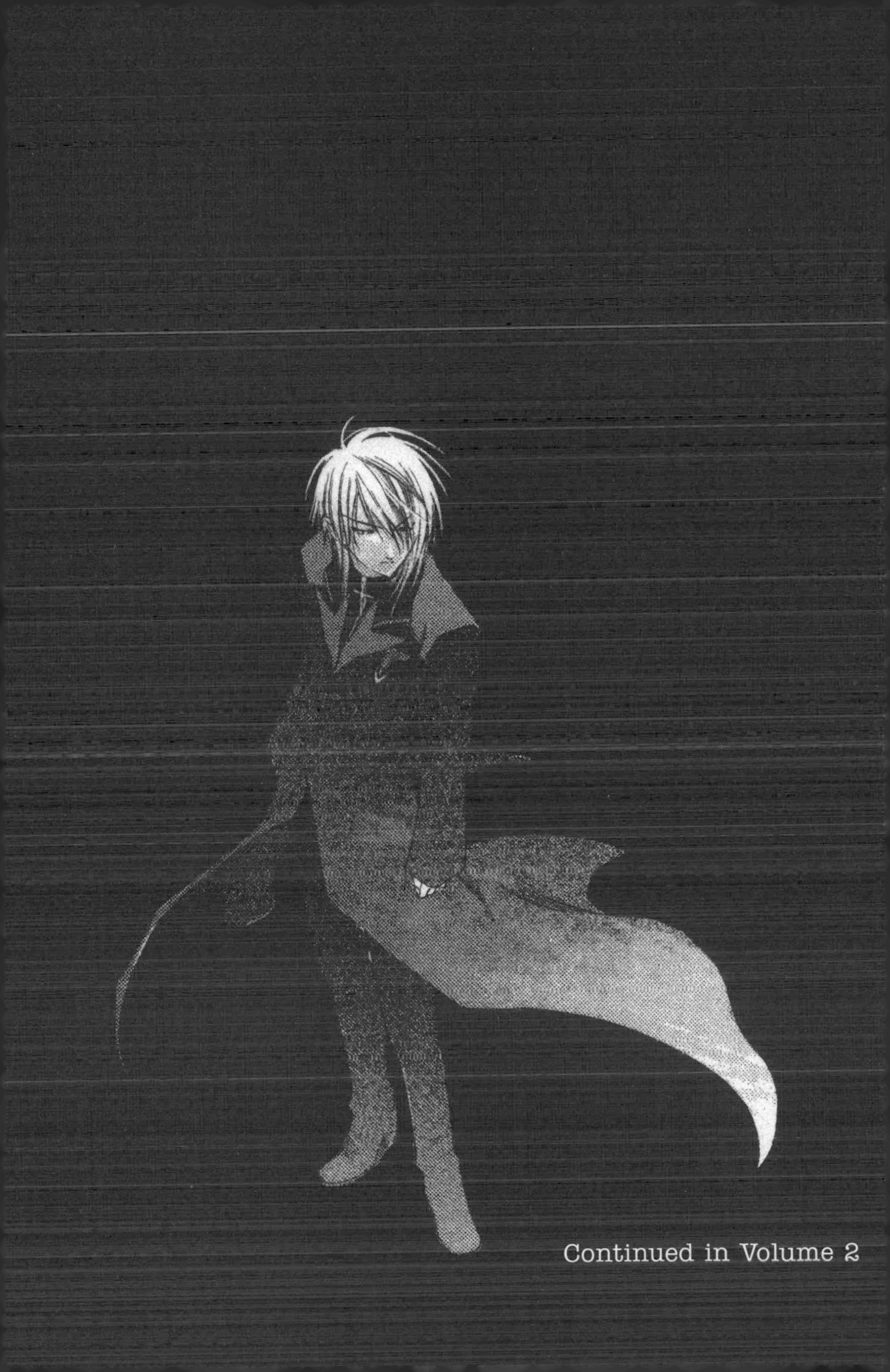

Continued in Volume 2

Afterword

...Wow. It's being released. It's finally being released.

Wow, this is great. But I really can't believe it. What if I'm actually just on some hidden camera show? What if it's all just some April Fool's joke...?

Whenever I go to a meeting with my editor, I can't help thinking things like that. Once I started on the cover illustration though, I could finally begin to accept that this was really happening.

Quite a bit happened between then and now, but I'm just so happy that it's finally coming out safe and sound. Please allow me to be the first to thank you, the fans of the *Missing* series. Coda-san, the author who not only so pleasantly welcomed the manga version, but was also very helpful and attentive in so many ways, my editor Mine-san, who banged on the great gates of Media Works and picked me up, to everyone that I inconvenienced so many times during the course of the comic creation process, Wada-san, an editor as well, all the designers and sales people, everyone at the printers and everyone that took such great care of me—thank you. I am so very sorry for all the delays in production I may have caused with my dawdling manner...

Forgive me for this late introduction. My name is Rei Mutsuki, and I am in charge of the manga version of *Missing*.

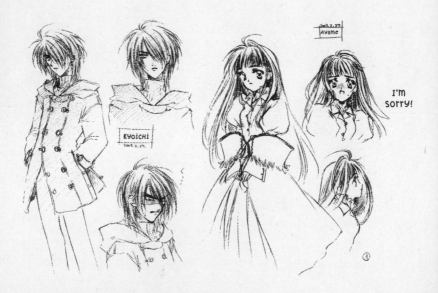

I'm sorry!

This is the same Mutsuki that submitted a rough character design showing Ryoko with canines, and was warned by my boss, "You can't just add fangs wherever you please!"

Then again, you're talking about the same Mutsuki who started out as an illustrator, stormed the gates at Dengeki Paperbacks on an illustration sales pitch, ended up with a manga deal and is now releasing a comic book. Wait, what just happened?

I'm also the one who was given a copy of the *Missing* novel by my big brother. Obviously, fate was at work here. Perhaps even our fates—mine and those belonging to you who are buying this manga—are intertwined somehow as well. And if you're just borrowing this comic from a friend, please go out and pick up a copy for yourself. (I'm begging, on my knees.)

And remember, if you put all the comic books together side-by-side, the covers connect and create one large, landscaped image. So please, buy them all at once. Please (once again on my knees)!!

I am truly hoping to be able to release the next volume soon...maybe. Yup, soon. Also, I'd love to hear what you think of my work, so please drop me a line. And on that note, after an insanely rambling afterword with absolutely no punch line, "I hope to see you again in Volume 2... I mean, see you again in Volume 2!"

Humbly,
Rei Mutsuki

※ Her eyes are
sort of
whitish.

②

Regarding the Comic Version

Hello everyone, my name is Gakuto Coda, and I am the writer of the original novel version of *Missing* upon which this comic is based.

First off, please allow me to thank everyone who picked up this book.

And to those who had a hand in making this comic book version possible–in particular one Rei Mutsuki who not only serialized the original comic, but also worked so hard in the publishing process for this book–my many, many heartfelt thanks.

My kindest regards to those of you who were familiar with the novel and tried out the comic, and also to those of you who were unfamiliar with the novel but purchased the comic anyway. And to all of you that love the Horror Fantasy genre, I hereby dedicate this book (without Mutsuki-san's permission) to you all.

Now then.

This work is the comic version of my debut novel, *Missing: Kamikakushi no Monogatari (Missing: A Kamikakushi Tale)*, published by Dengeki Paperbacks. When I was first approached for my thoughts on the manga, I simply said, "Novels and comics are done differently, so please, draw it however you wish," but Mutsuki-san worked so hard and was so intent on keeping the "feel" of the novels that I can safely say that the comic is highly faithful to the original work. That's right, wholly faithful.

So much so, in fact, that I actually wince with a tinge of embarrassment when I see–when I can actually bear to see–my "debut" in comic form, and am forced to reminisce how green, how inexperienced and how young I was back then!

But because of that faithfulness, I believe–if I may take that liberty–that the fans of the original work will be quite satisfied with the comic. And for those who are not familiar with the original novel, I believe that they will be drawn to it.

Even though the tale itself is a complete reflection of my interest in the Horror Fantasy genre, and is more a hobby to me than work, I am truly thankful and blessed that it became popular enough to have evolved into an entire series.

By the time this comic book comes out, the original series should have been concluded in the thirteenth novel.

If any of the following keywords—magic, curses, legends, folklore, ghost stories, urban legends, schools, witches or madness—"stir" a little something in you, then please do try out the original novel version of *Missing* as well. And perhaps then you might gain a little insight into this world of mine—a beautiful, beloved nightmare.

> "Let me spin you a tale,
> As melancholy as a nightmare,
> As crazed as the cherry blossoms,
> As precise as a clock."

I wonder if perhaps these words from the first volume of my novels – if this goal which I sought to fulfill – was achieved far better than I ever would or could in this comic...

And with that, allow me to once again extend my deepest thanks to those reading this. I hope and pray that we will one day meet again, but until then, please continue to support this comic.

Gakuto Coda. May 5th, 2005.

In the Next

MISSING
KAMIKAKUSHI NO MONOGATARI

In the next volume of *Missing: Kamikakushi no Monogatari*, Takemi Kondou and Toshiya Murakami's investigation into the disappearance of their beloved Kyoichi leads them deeper down the path into things beyond normal human experience. A fellow student directs them to a soul-chilling magician, who provides a valuable clue to the nature of mysterious Ayame and a useful charm for finding her. Meanwhile, Ryoko Kusakabe and Aki Kidono seek their own answers, starting with an exorcist.

The following is a preview of the novel series.
Please flip ahead six pages, and be sure to read
left-to-right.

MISSING

Coming to stores November 2007

scent of withered grass from her hair. The scent fascinated him, intoxicated him.

Her eyes were open now, and she gazed up at his face in bewilderment.

"I was waiting for you," he murmured.

She lowered her eyes. "I'm sorry," she said, her voice tearful. "I'm sorry . . ." It was not rejection. It was an apology.

Utsume said nothing. The wind swept around them. It whipped the girl's hair roughly, spreading the unseasonable scent of autumn. The long tendrils lashed at Utsume's face, and then caressed it in turns. Around them, the world returned to normal. The students, momentarily dumfounded, tore their eyes from the couple that had intruded into their day and went on about their business. Perhaps they would speak about the oddness of it, perhaps not. No matter how mysterious or significant the event, there were classes to attend, a basketball game to play, life to live.

It was an inexplicable occurrence—nothing more.

"Please," she said. "Forget you saw me. I . . . I can't explain—"

"I know," Utsume said, interrupting her.

"What?"

"I know what you are."

She shook her head in obvious confusion.

He gazed directly into her eyes. "And knowing what you are, I ask . . . will you come with me?"

She gazed up at him, stunned. "Come with you?" she repeated.

"I accept your isolation, your nature, all influences you may have on me. I know very well what it means to walk with you." Utsume held out his hand to her. "Come with me."

"No," she said, backing away. "No, you *don't* know. You *couldn't* know what I am. You don't know what will happen to you." She shook her head. "I'm a monster . . ."

Utsume grasped her shoulders. "Even so . . . I want you."

She shuddered, then her body went limp. Utsume gathered her against him, holding her in a firm embrace.

The air around them seemed to shiver and the atmosphere in the plaza changed. The basketball bounced across the pavement, but no one tried to catch it. The boys had abandoned their game, staring at the spot where the girl in the red cape had appeared suddenly in Utsume's arms. A few others in the teeming crowd had seen as well. They too stopped to stare, astounded, or altered their course to cut a wide swathe around the couple.

Utsume felt the shift—felt the two of them glide back into synch with the normal world. It was like waking from a dream, but he had brought a piece of the dream back with him, pressed against his heart.

Supporting the girl's listless frame, Utsume caught the

her by are equally illusory. Perhaps they would not have collided—she and the boy—but simply passed through one another.

A gust of wind blew past, bringing the girl's scent to Utsume. He caught it, faintly, but surely: the scent of unnatural autumn—he was sure of it—withered grass, and dry rust . . . the smell that had drawn him here.

In that instant, Utsume understood. He knew where the girl had come from, who she was, her true nature—in that instant, he understood everything about her. Understood it and accepted it.

He walked directly over to her, and stood in front of her.

She stopped dancing, her face registering a surprise far deeper than that of a girl suddenly approached by a strange boy. She *saw* him, looked up at him. Her expression went from surprise to puzzlement. "You can . . . *see* me?"

"Yes."

"Oh . . ." She put her hands to her mouth, her eyes going wide.

Utsume was aware of students continuing to pass them by, all unaware. Classes had changed and the little plaza was filling with ever more rushing bodies. But no one paused to eavesdrop on the strange conversation. No one even looked at them.

They stared at each other for some time, then Utsume took a step closer to the girl.

She raised her hand. "Don't," she whispered.

"Why not?"

"Don't come near me. If you are with me, you'll become like me. You won't be able to return," she said feebly. Her smile was unutterably sad and weary. Far too weary for a girl who looked only about fourteen or fifteen.

Utsume remained motionless.

while the wind wrapped itself about her, tossing her hair, rippling her long skirts and her red cape. She would have made an impossibly beautiful painting.

Her song felt very old to Utsume. It was more than a song; it was a chant; it was a spell. A song of the soul, expressing everything this girl felt.

Utsume noted irrelevantly that the song lacked a certain polish. The girl was improvising the words and rhythm. Her voice had resonance, yet it was strangely fragile, melting into the air like candied floss on the tongue. The wind danced around her, as if called by the loneliness in her song. It carried her scent, strewed flowers at her feet, and cleared a stage for her, setting her at its center as if everything else existed for her benefit. The stage was hers alone as she stood and sang her haunting melody.

Utsume's eyes narrowed in puzzlement. The plaza between the club building and the new school building across from it was, as usual, filled with students, coming and going. The bulletin board in front of the new building, the several benches placed around it, the pleasant presence of the cherry trees, were enough to make it a popular spot to hang out. At a glance, there were at least ten people using the benches—reading, talking, or just sitting. A basketball hoop had been affixed to the eaves of the club building. Beneath it a group of boys played a game of half court.

Not one of these people was looking at the girl. It was as if she wasn't there, or as if none of them could see her. Nor was she paying any attention to them. Even when one of the ball players brushed right past her to chase a loose ball, she ignored him, as he ignored her. They were mere inches from collision, but neither one seemed to be aware of the other.

If she is an illusion, Utsume thought, *then the students passing*

Anyone who experienced something like that knew the feeling. It happened all the time: just going about daily life one caught a familiar scent and paused, wrapped in a sudden, vivid memory and wondering what had triggered it.

That was it exactly. But this remembered scent created a mood far more gloomy than even Utsume's childhood memories.

The scent beckoned to him, tugged at him. He turned his nose to the wind. The source was upwind, and the dry aroma was so mixed with the perfume of the cherry blossoms that they almost overwhelmed it.

Utsume stood up, turning his slim, black-clad frame into the wind.

He began to follow the scent, bent to it like a hound. He followed it through a grove of cherry trees; a paved clearing spread out before him—a small plaza between buildings. And there, in the center of the plaza behind the club building . . .

There stood a girl.

Now the petals scatter,
Let us play between the breeze.
See a girl's dream in the flowers,
Slip between the wind.
A creature dances, dressed in the wind,
Which carries the scent of people.
It sings, wearing shackles that no human can touch.
Playing in the scent of flowers,
Longing for the scent of humans,
The wind maiden sings,
Of sadness beyond human understanding.

She sang these words, her voice clear and translucent,

Prologue:
Beneath the Cherry Grove in Full Bloom

Was their meeting coincidence or fate?

Is there really that much difference between the two?

A faint scent drifted on the breeze, carried through the school grounds past the swaying branches of sentinel trees. When he caught that scent, it brought such a strong sense of deja vu that Kyoichi Utsume, who had been lying on a shaded bench, sat up abruptly.

It was a scent from long ago, wildly out of place amid the cherry blossoms dancing on the spring breeze. If it wasn't his imagination, then it was a memory. And it did not belong in this school or in this season.

Utsume knew that the sense of smell was far more important than most people realized. The scent of moist earth and vegetation after a rain brought back memories of the garden at his grandfather's house where he played as a toddler.

MISSING

Gakuto Coda

STORY	Gakuto Coda	
TRANSLATION	Andrew Cunningham	
ENGLISH ADAPTATION	Maya Kaathryn Bohnhoff	
EDITOR	Kara Allison Stambach	
LAYOUT ARTIST	Courtney H. Geter	
COVER DESIGN	Joe Macasocol, Jr.	
ART DIRECTOR	Anne Marie Horne	
DIGITAL IMAGING MANAGER	Chris Buford	
PRODUCTION MANAGER	Elisabeth Brizzi	
MANAGING EDITOR	Vy Nguyen	
EDITOR-IN-CHIEF	Rob Tokar	
VP OF PRODUCTION	Ron Klamert	
PUBLISHER	Mike Kiley	
PRESIDENT AND C.O.O.	John Parker	
C.E.O. & CHIEF CREATIVE OFFICER	Stuart Levy	

First TOKYOPOP printing: November 2007
10 9 8 7 6 5 4 3 2 1
Printed in the USA

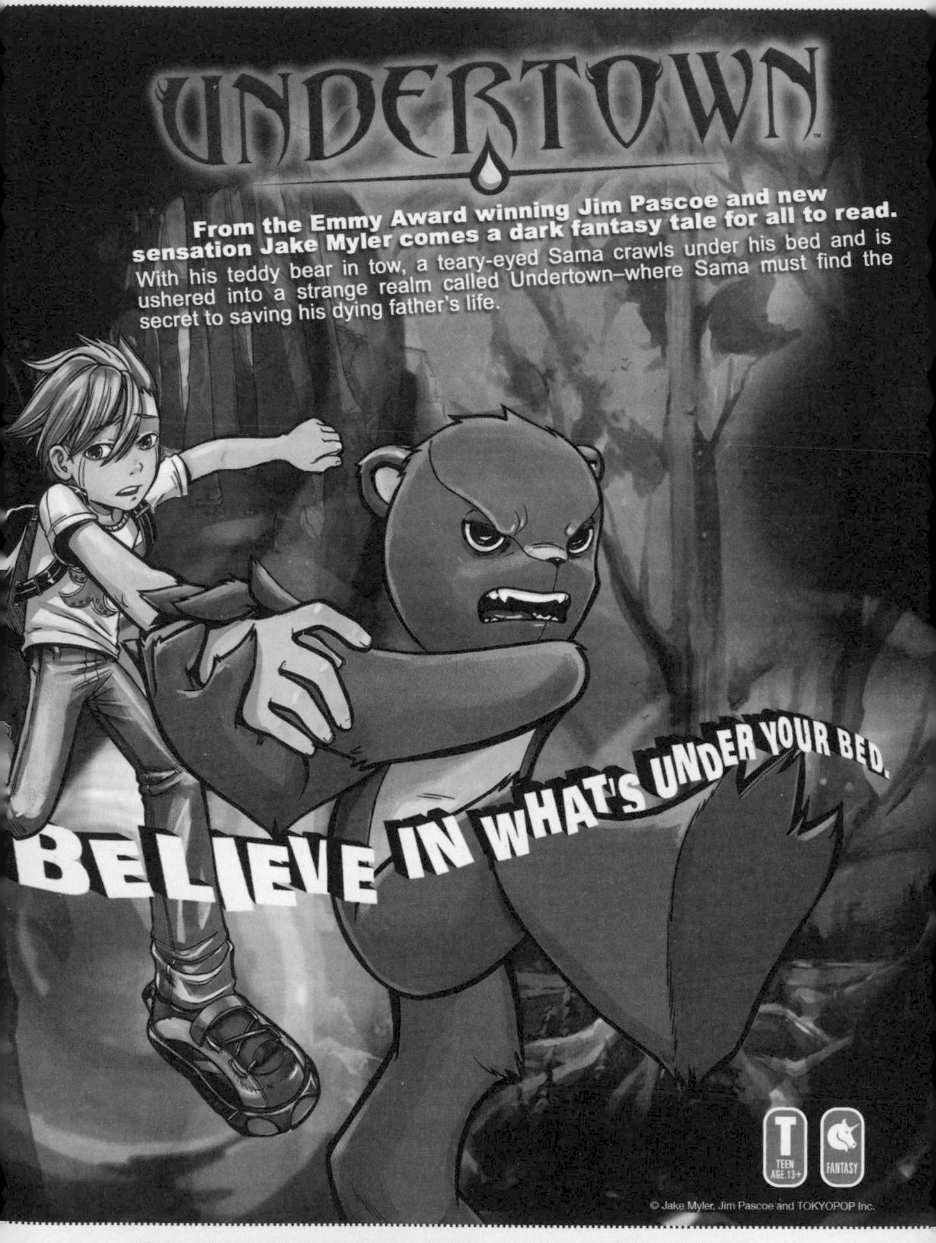
UNDERTOWN
From the Emmy Award winning Jim Pascoe and new sensation Jake Myler comes a dark fantasy tale for all to read.
With his teddy bear in tow, a teary-eyed Sama crawls under his bed and is ushered into a strange realm called Undertown–where Sama must find the secret to saving his dying father's life.
BELIEVE IN WHAT'S UNDER YOUR BED.
T TEEN AGE 13+
FANTASY
© Jake Myler, Jim Pascoe and TOKYOPOP Inc.

STOP!

This is the back of the book.
You wouldn't want to spoil a great ending!

This book is printed "manga-style," in the authentic Japanese right-to-left format. Since none of the artwork has been flipped or altered, readers get to experience the story just as the creator intended. You've been asking for it, so TOKYOPOP® delivered: authentic, hot-off-the-press, and far more fun!

DIRECTIONS

If this is your first time reading manga-style, here's a quick guide to help you understand how it works.

It's easy... just start in the top right panel and follow the numbers. Have fun, and look for more 100% authentic manga from TOKYOPOP®!